げんしけん

hiken

COND SEASON

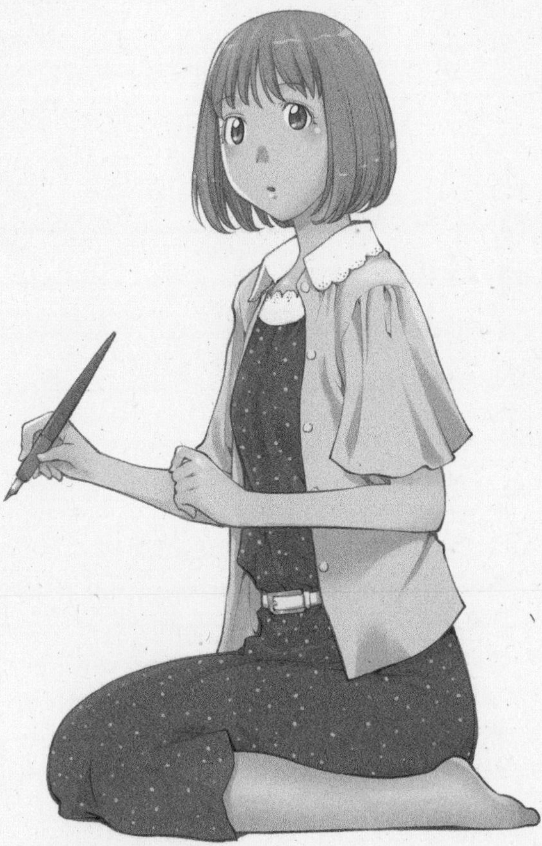

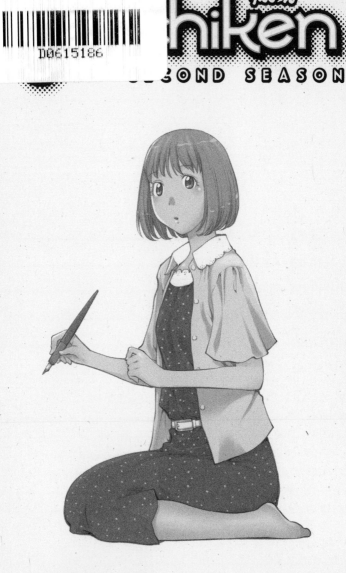

SHIMOKU KIO

genshiken
SECOND SEASON
Vol.11
CONTENTS

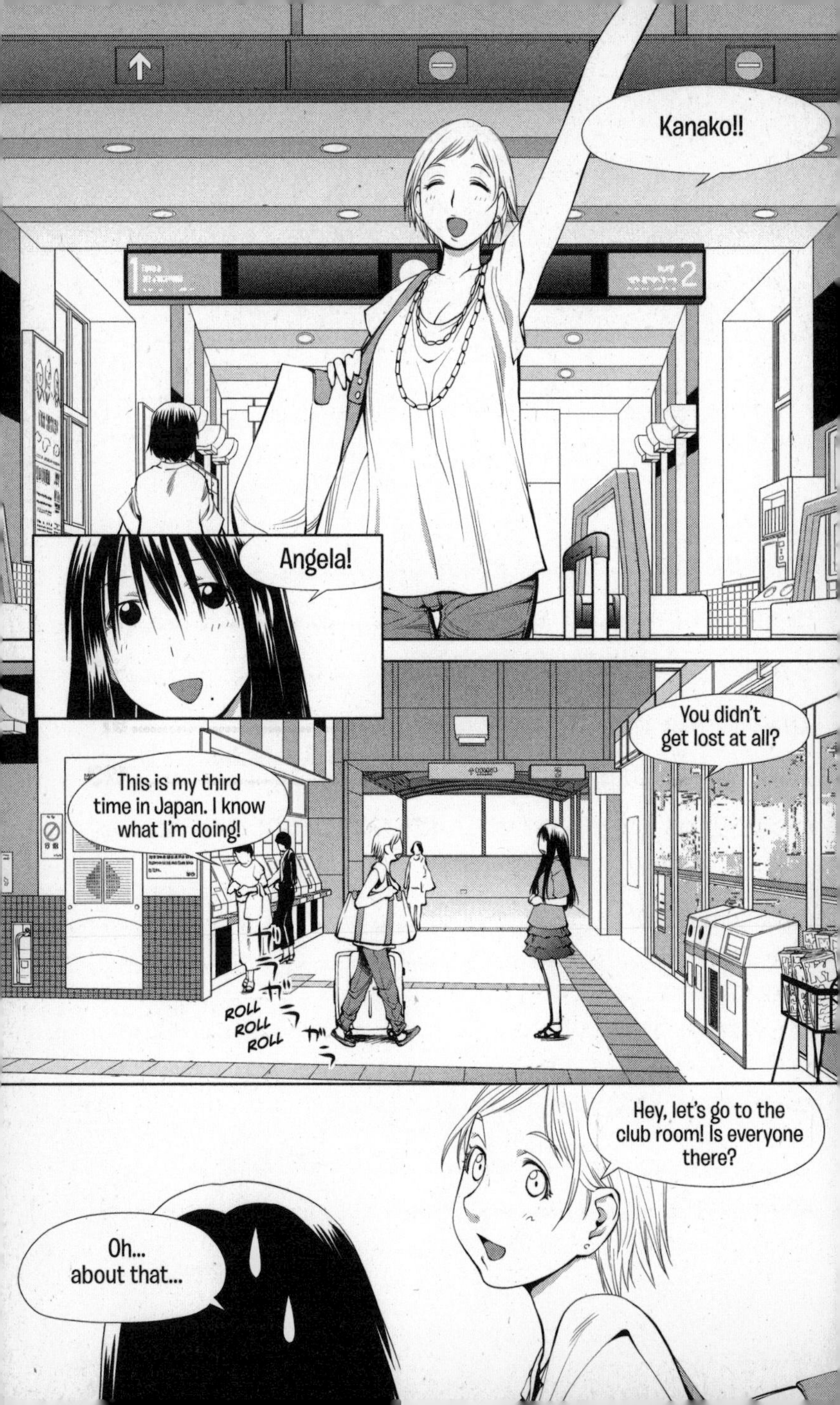
Kanako!!
Angela!
You didn't get lost at all?
This is my third time in Japan. I know what I'm doing!
ROLL ROLL ROLL
Hey, let's go to the club room! Is everyone there?
Oh... about that...

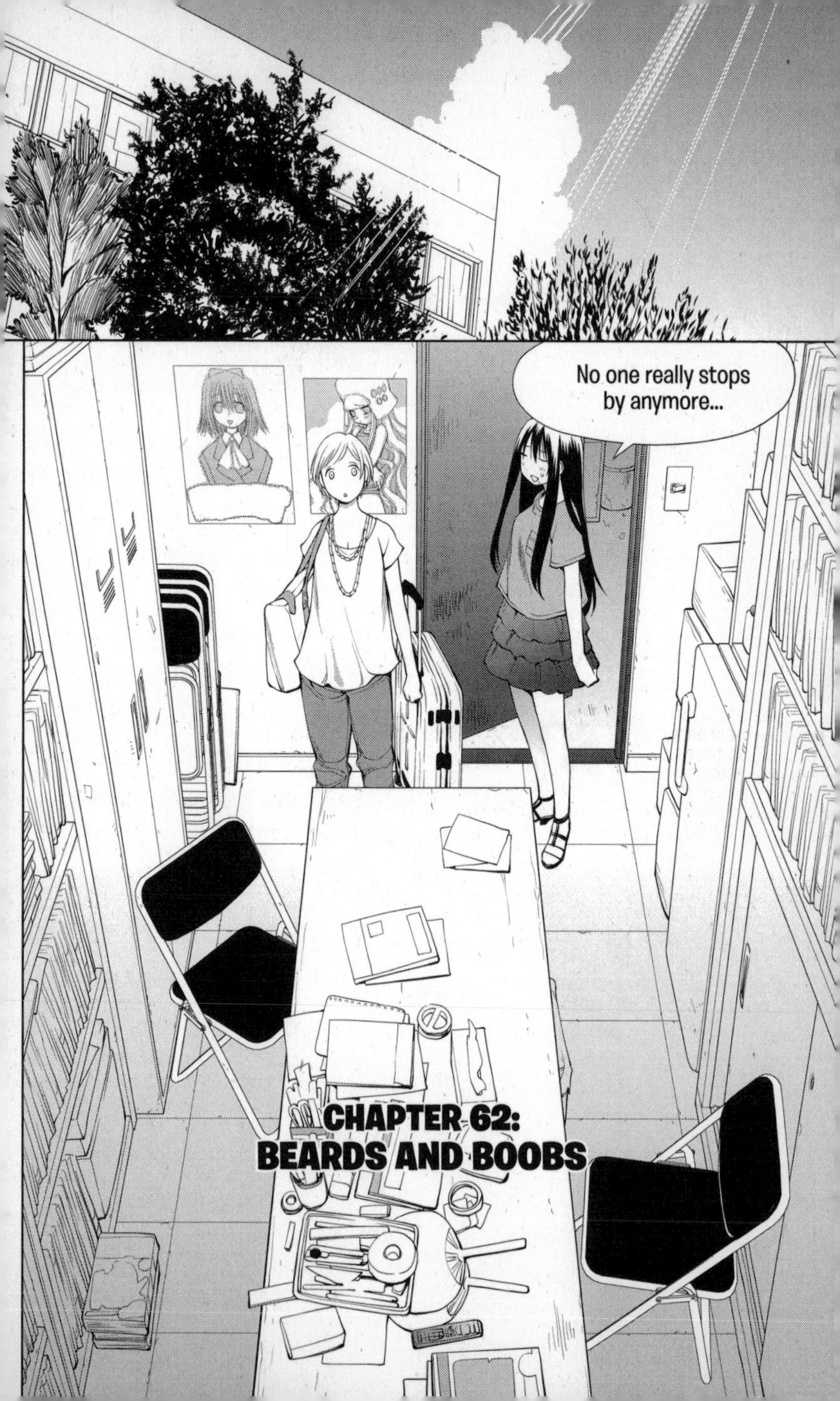
No one really stops by anymore...
CHAPTER 62:
BEARDS AND BOOBS

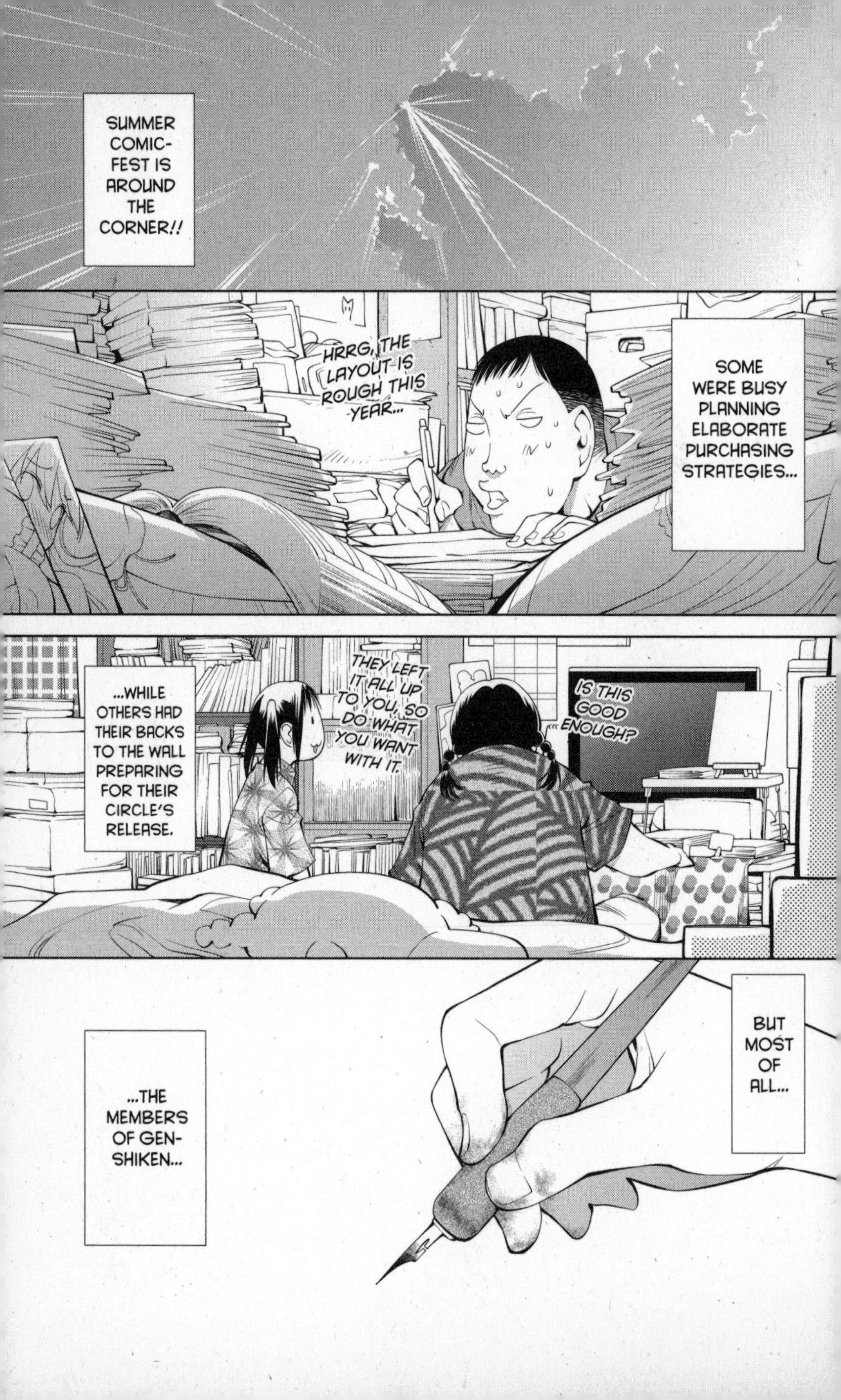
SUMMER COMIC-FEST IS AROUND THE CORNER!!
SOME WERE BUSY PLANNING ELABORATE PURCHASING STRATEGIES...
HRRG, THE LAYOUT IS ROUGH THIS YEAR...
IS THIS GOOD ENOUGH?
THEY LEFT IT ALL UP TO YOU, SO DO WHAT YOU WANT WITH IT.
...WHILE OTHERS HAD THEIR BACKS TO THE WALL PREPARING FOR THEIR CIRCLE'S RELEASE.
BUT MOST OF ALL...
...THE MEMBERS OF GEN-SHIKEN...

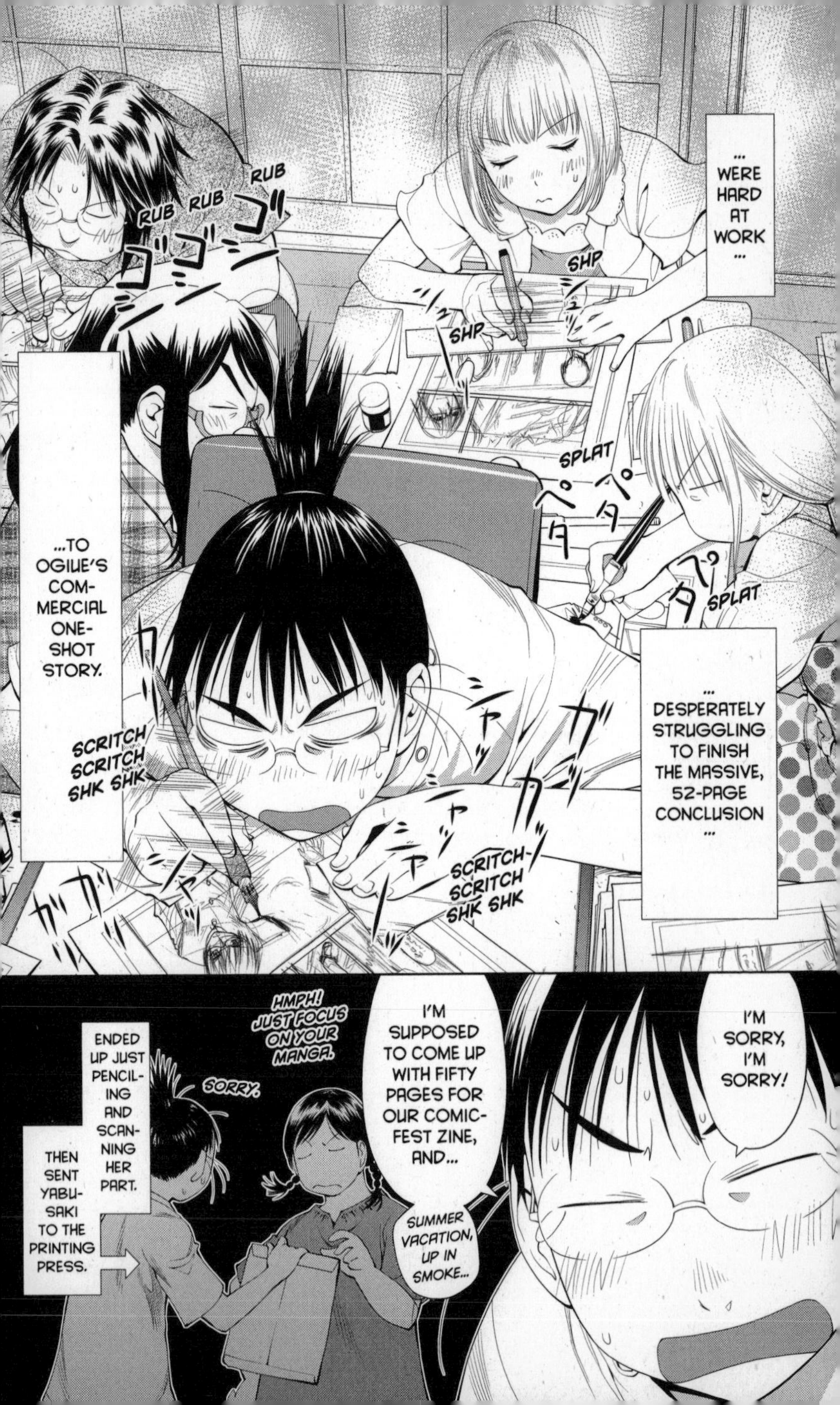
... WERE HARD AT WORK ...
SHP
SHP
RUB RUB RUB
SPLAT
SPLAT
... DESPERATELY STRUGGLING TO FINISH THE MASSIVE, 52-PAGE CONCLUSION ...
...TO OGIUE'S COMMERCIAL ONE-SHOT STORY.
SCRITCH-SCRITCH SHK SHK
SCRITCH SCRITCH SHK SHK
I'M SORRY, I'M SORRY!
I'M SUPPOSED TO COME UP WITH FIFTY PAGES FOR OUR COMIC-FEST ZINE, AND...
SUMMER VACATION, UP IN SMOKE...
HMPH! JUST FOCUS ON YOUR MANGA.
SORRY.
ENDED UP JUST PENCIL-ING AND SCAN-NING HER PART.
THEN SENT YABU-SAKI TO THE PRINTING PRESS.

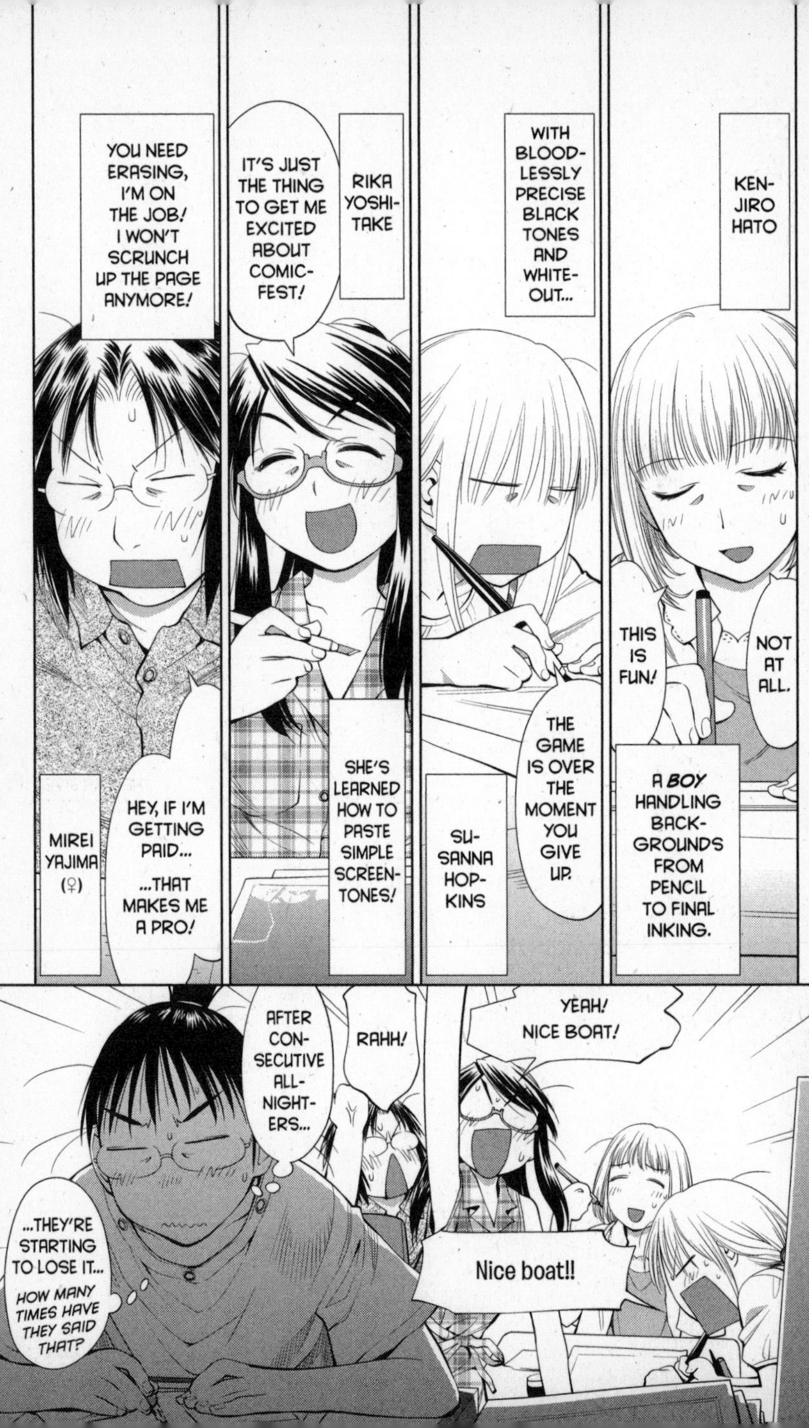
KENJIRO HATO
NOT AT ALL.
THIS IS FUN!
A *BOY* HANDLING BACKGROUNDS FROM PENCIL TO FINAL INKING.
WITH BLOODLESSLY PRECISE BLACK TONES AND WHITE-OUT...
THE GAME IS OVER THE MOMENT YOU GIVE UP.
SUSANNA HOPKINS
RIKA YOSHITAKE
IT'S JUST THE THING TO GET ME EXCITED ABOUT COMIC-FEST!
SHE'S LEARNED HOW TO PASTE SIMPLE SCREENTONES!
YOU NEED ERASING, I'M ON THE JOB! I WON'T SCRUNCH UP THE PAGE ANYMORE!
HEY, IF I'M GETTING PAID... ...THAT MAKES ME A PRO!
MIREI YAJIMA (♀)
YEAH! NICE BOAT!
RAHH!
AFTER CONSECUTIVE ALL-NIGHTERS...
Nice boat!!
...THEY'RE STARTING TO LOSE IT... *HOW MANY TIMES HAVE THEY SAID THAT?*

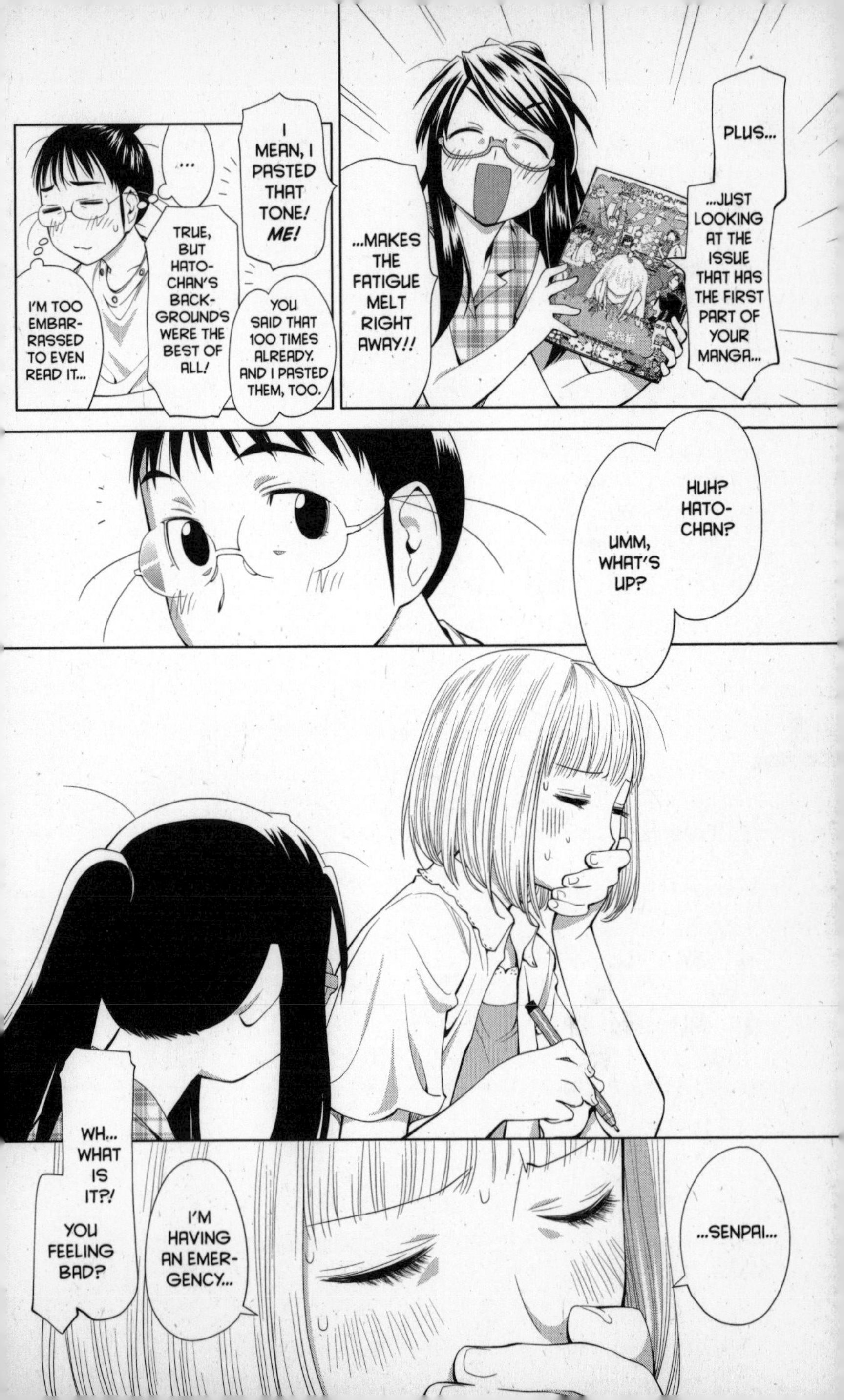
PLUS...
...JUST LOOKING AT THE ISSUE THAT HAS THE FIRST PART OF YOUR MANGA...
...MAKES THE FATIGUE MELT RIGHT AWAY!!
I MEAN, I PASTED THAT TONE! *ME!*
....
TRUE, BUT HATO-CHAN'S BACKGROUNDS WERE THE BEST OF ALL!
YOU SAID THAT 100 TIMES ALREADY. AND I PASTED THEM, TOO.
I'M TOO EMBARRASSED TO EVEN READ IT...
HUH? HATO-CHAN?
UMM, WHAT'S UP?
...SENPAI...
I'M HAVING AN EMERGENCY...
WH... WHAT IS IT?!
YOU FEELING BAD?

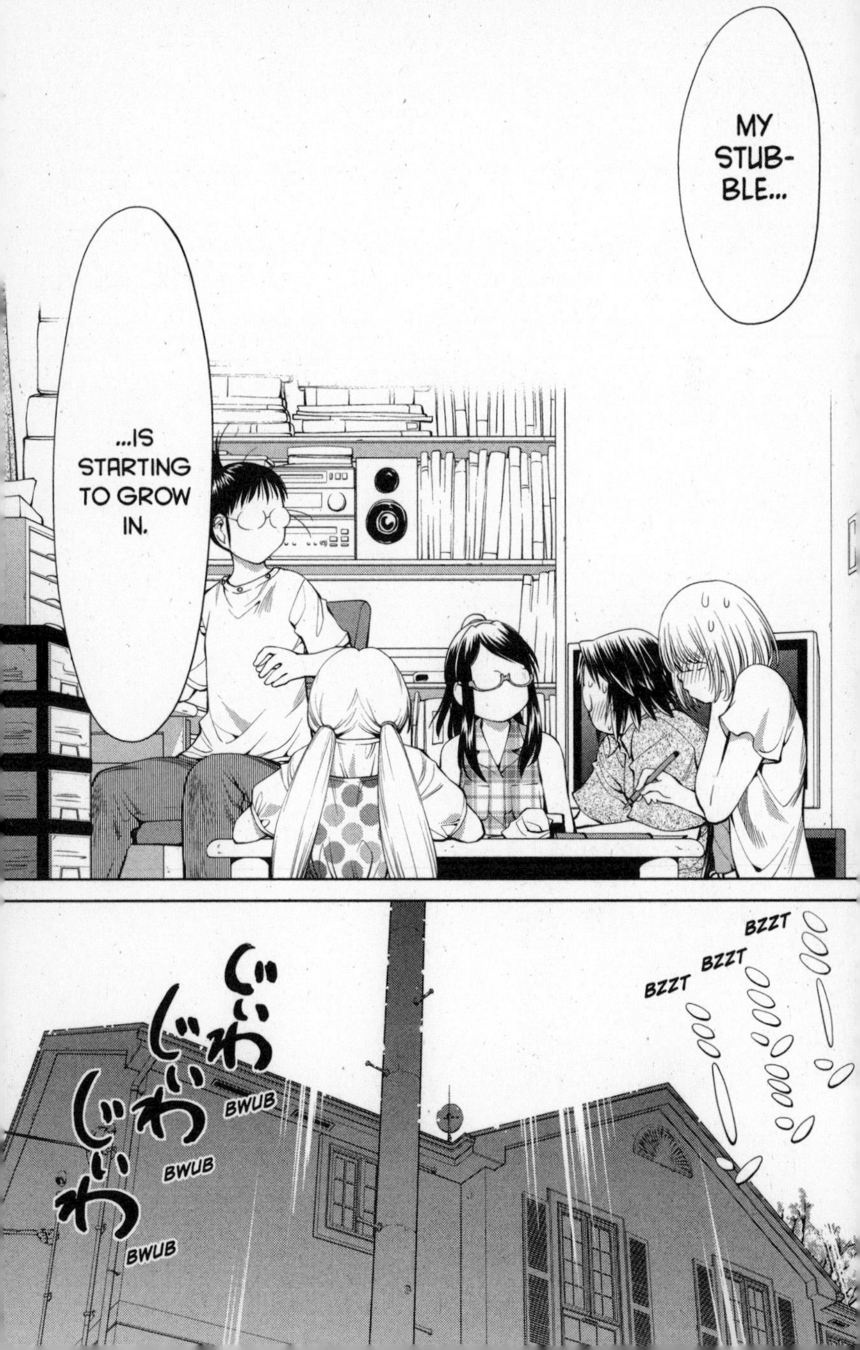
MY STUB-
BLE...
...IS STARTING TO GROW IN.
BZZT
BZZT
BZZT
じぃわ
BWUB
じぃわ
BWUB
じぃわ
BWUB

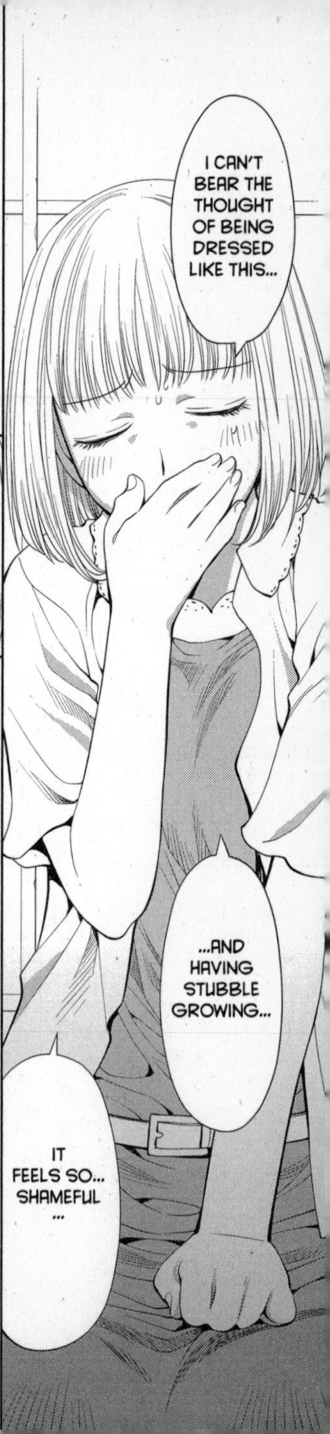
I CAN'T BEAR THE THOUGHT OF BEING DRESSED LIKE THIS...
...AND HAVING STUBBLE GROWING...
IT FEELS SO... SHAMEFUL ...

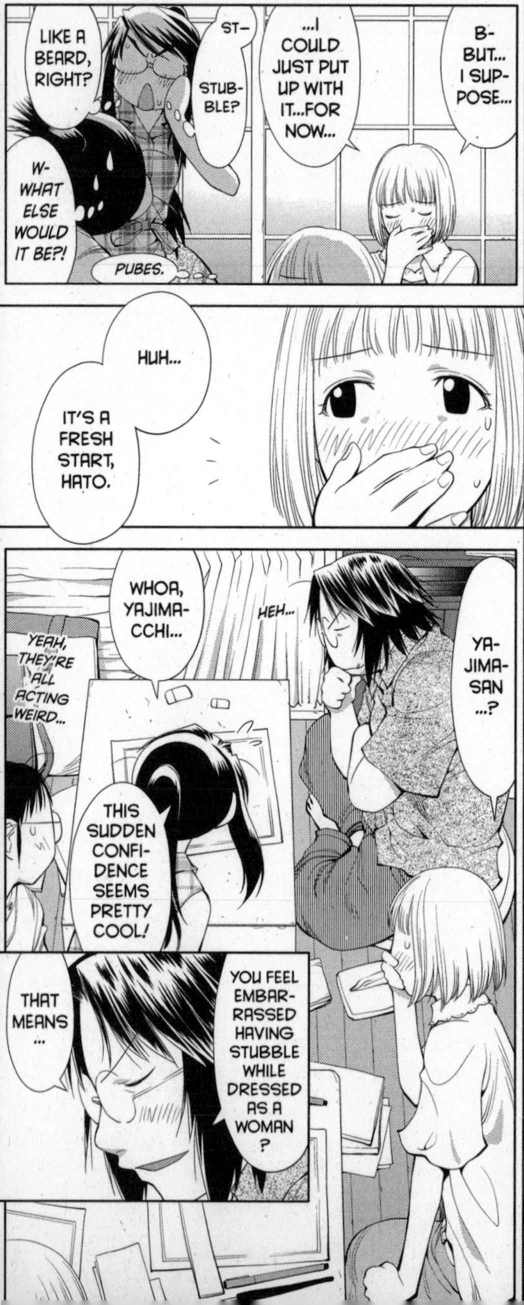
B-BUT... I SUP-POSE...
...I COULD JUST PUT UP WITH IT...FOR NOW...
ST— STUB-BLE?
LIKE A BEARD, RIGHT?
W-WHAT ELSE WOULD IT BE?!
PUBES.
HUH...
IT'S A FRESH START, HATO.
YA-JIMA-SAN ...?
HEH...
WHOA, YAJIMA-CCHI...
YEAH, THEY'RE ALL ACTING WEIRD...
THIS SUDDEN CONFI-DENCE SEEMS PRETTY COOL!
YOU FEEL EMBAR-RASSED HAVING STUBBLE WHILE DRESSED AS A WOMAN ?
THAT MEANS ...

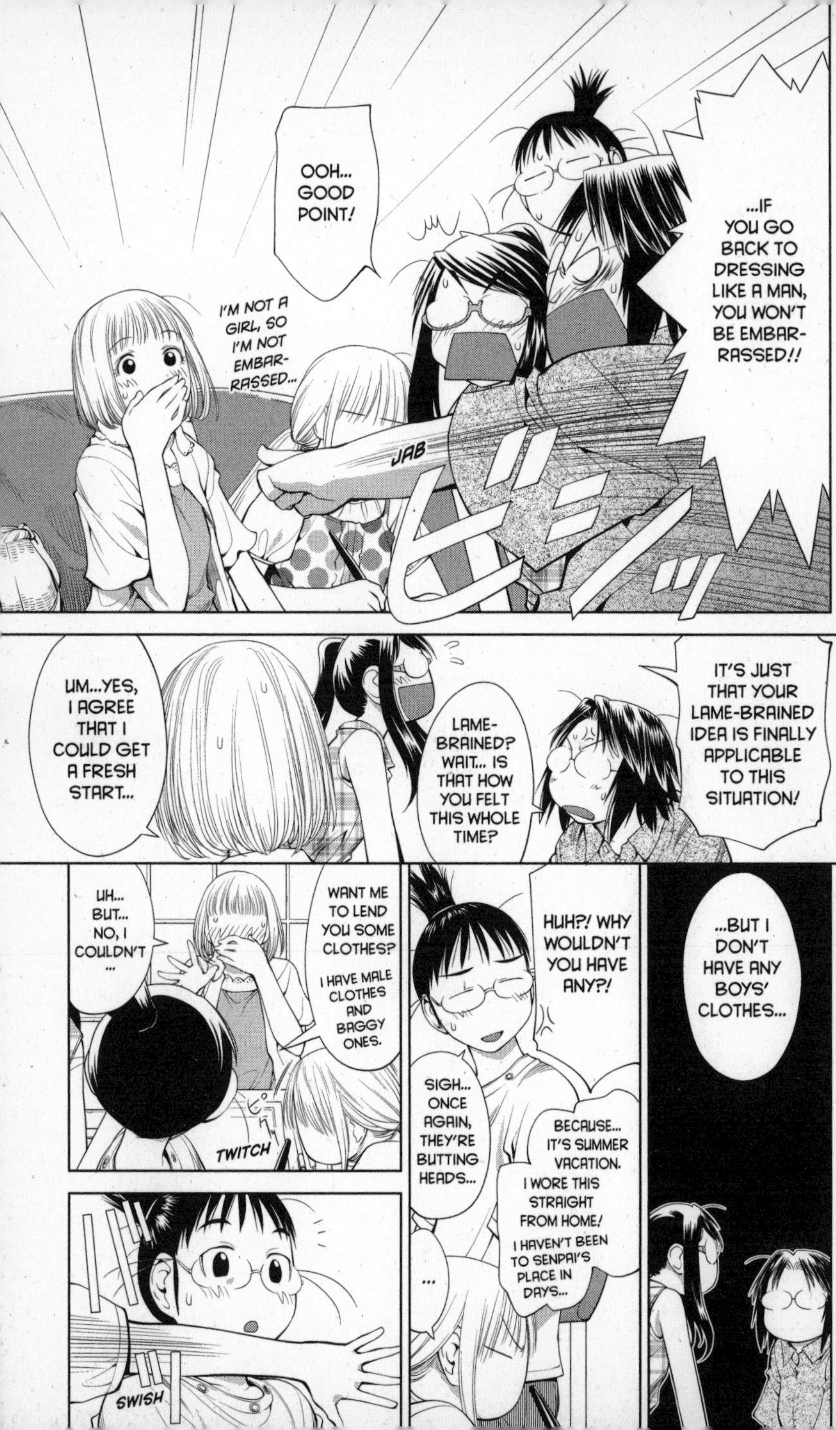
...IF YOU GO BACK TO DRESSING LIKE A MAN, YOU WON'T BE EMBARRASSED!!
JAB
OOH... GOOD POINT!
I'M NOT A GIRL, SO I'M NOT EMBARRASSED...
IT'S JUST THAT YOUR LAME-BRAINED IDEA IS FINALLY APPLICABLE TO THIS SITUATION!
LAME-BRAINED? WAIT... IS THAT HOW YOU FELT THIS WHOLE TIME?
UM...YES, I AGREE THAT I COULD GET A FRESH START...
...BUT I DON'T HAVE ANY BOYS' CLOTHES...
HUH?! WHY WOULDN'T YOU HAVE ANY?!
BECAUSE... IT'S SUMMER VACATION.
I WORE THIS STRAIGHT FROM HOME!
I HAVEN'T BEEN TO SENPAI'S PLACE IN DAYS...
SIGH... ONCE AGAIN, THEY'RE BUTTING HEADS...
...
WANT ME TO LEND YOU SOME CLOTHES?
I HAVE MALE CLOTHES AND BAGGY ONES.
UH... BUT... NO, I COULDN'T ...
TWITCH
SWISH

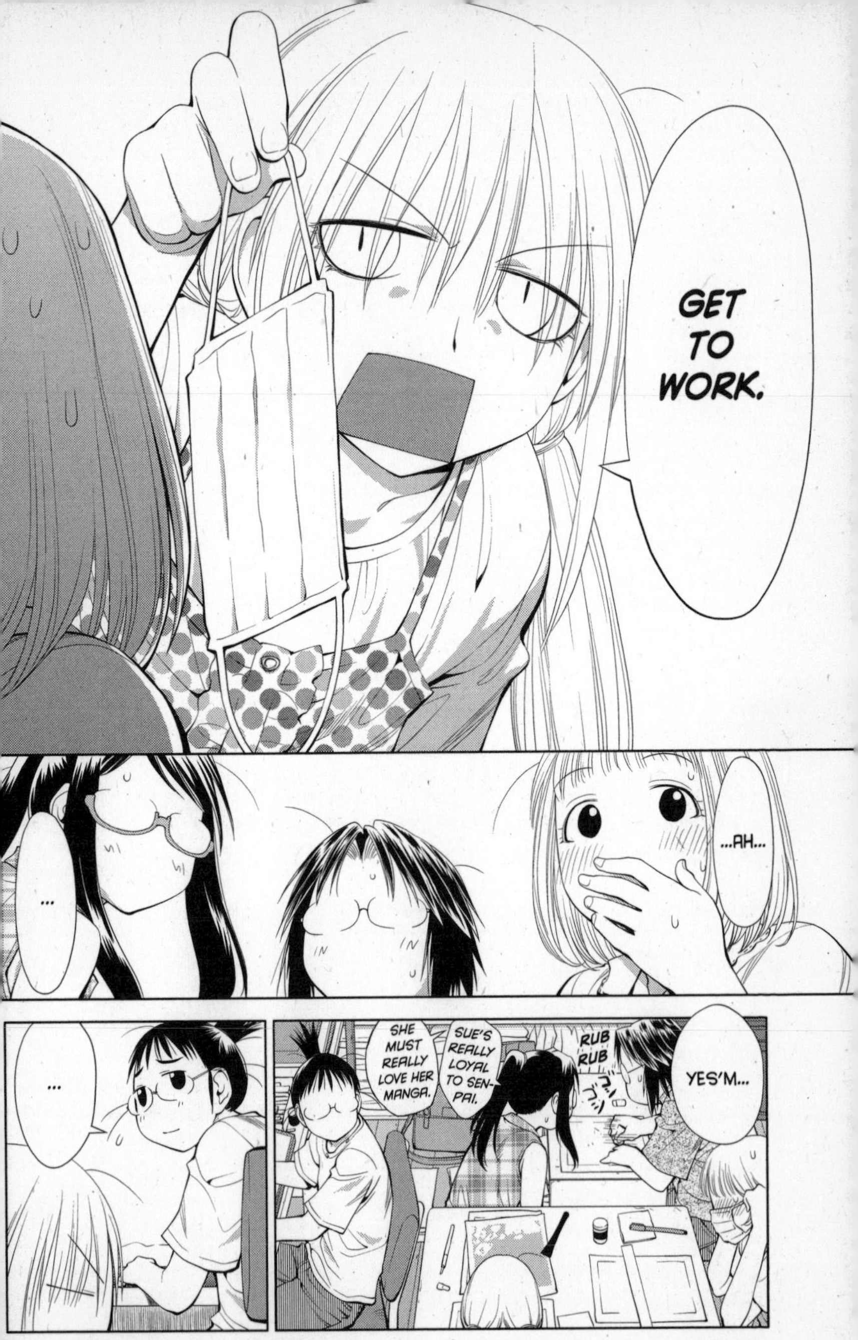
GET TO WORK.
...AH...
...
YES'M...
RUB RUB
SUE'S REALLY LOYAL TO SEN-PAI.
SHE MUST REALLY LOVE HER MANGA.
...

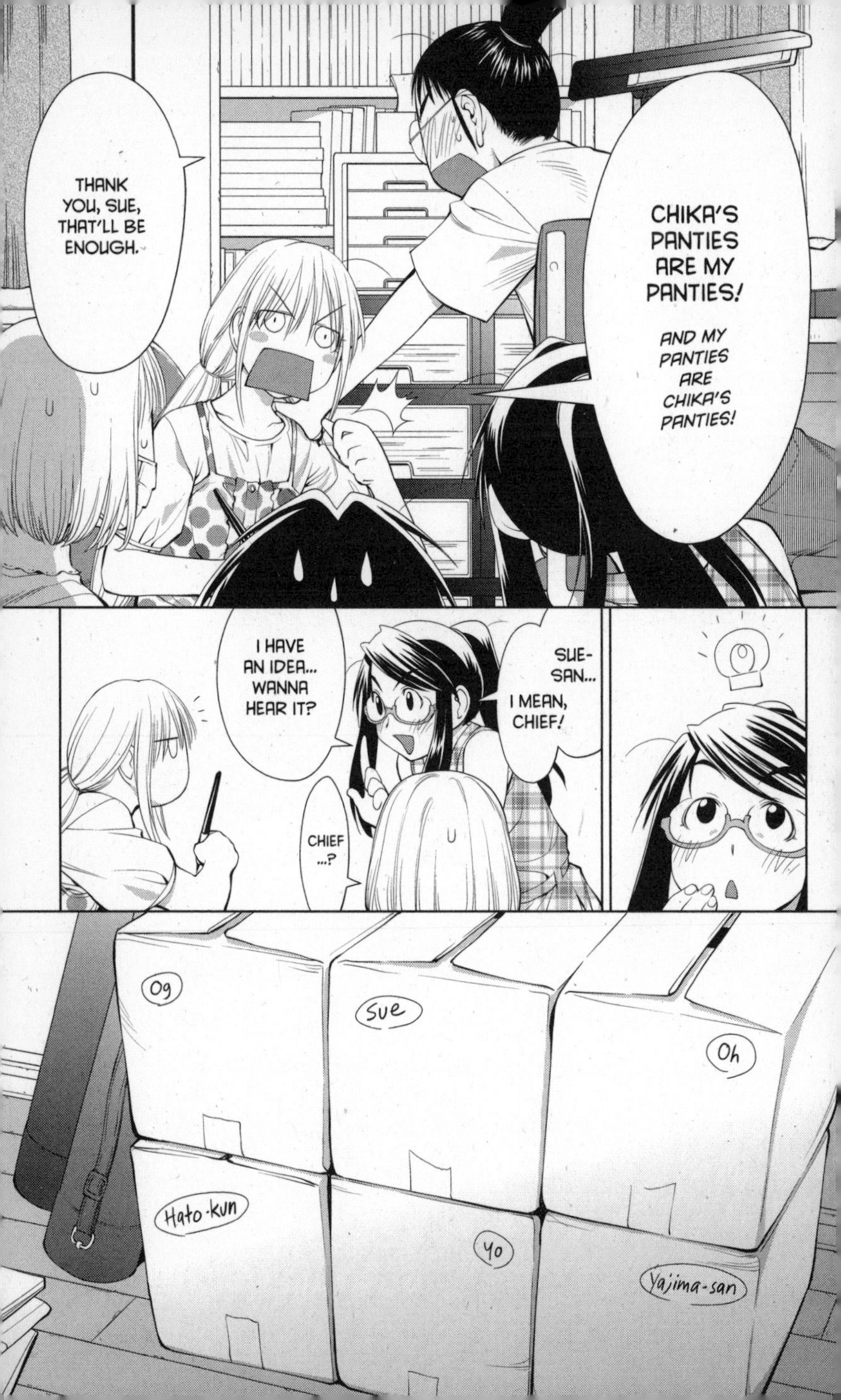
CHIKA'S PANTIES ARE MY PANTIES!
AND MY PANTIES ARE CHIKA'S PANTIES!
THANK YOU, SUE, THAT'LL BE ENOUGH.
SUE-SAN... I MEAN, CHIEF!
I HAVE AN IDEA... WANNA HEAR IT?
CHIEF ...?
Oh
Sue
Og
Yajima-san
Yo
Hato-kun

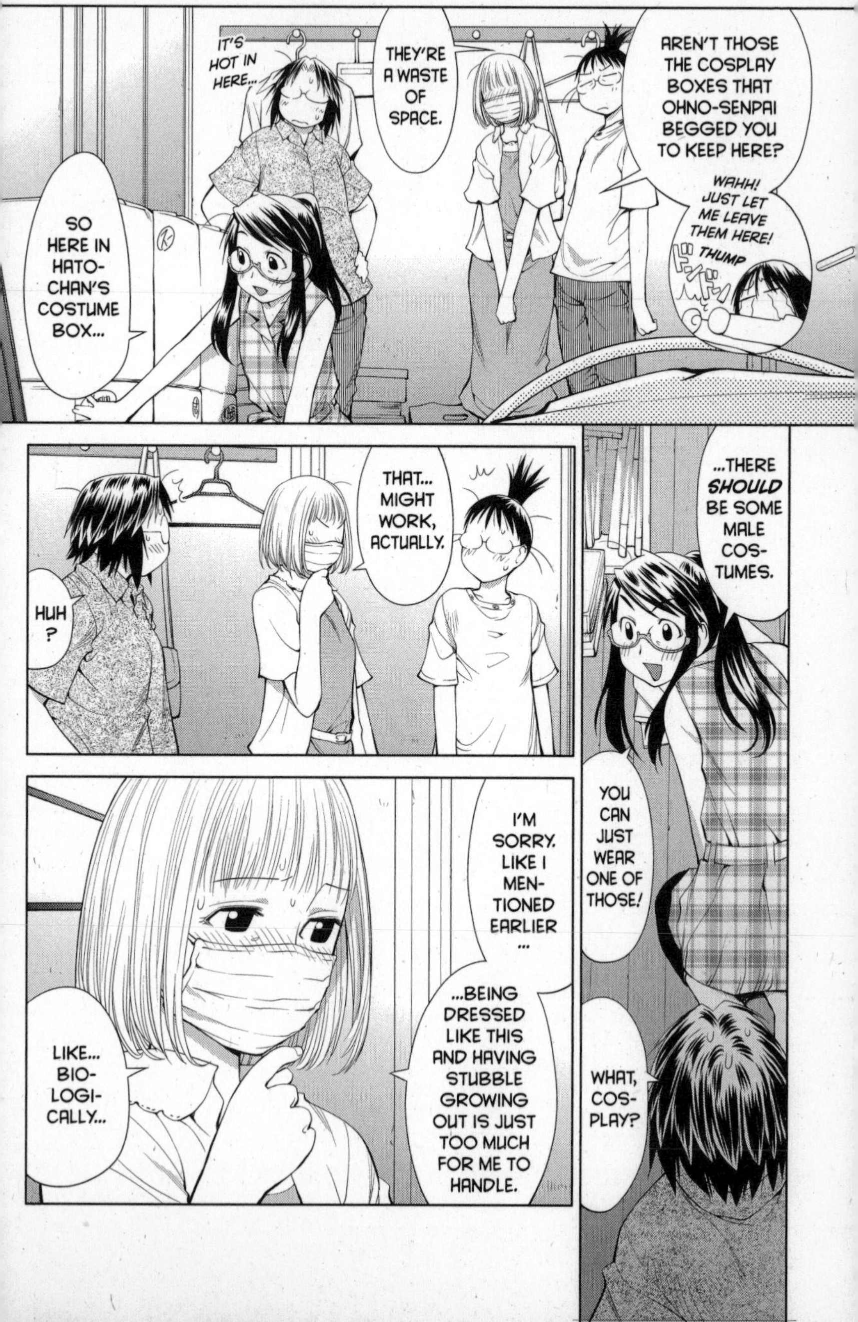
AREN'T THOSE THE COSPLAY BOXES THAT OHNO-SENPAI BEGGED YOU TO KEEP HERE?
WAHH! JUST LET ME LEAVE THEM HERE!
THUMP
THEY'RE A WASTE OF SPACE.
IT'S HOT IN HERE...
SO HERE IN HATO-CHAN'S COSTUME BOX...
...THERE *SHOULD* BE SOME MALE COS-TUMES.
YOU CAN JUST WEAR ONE OF THOSE!
WHAT, COS-PLAY?
THAT... MIGHT WORK, ACTUALLY.
HUH ?
I'M SORRY. LIKE I MEN-TIONED EARLIER ...
...BEING DRESSED LIKE THIS AND HAVING STUBBLE GROWING OUT IS JUST TOO MUCH FOR ME TO HANDLE.
LIKE... BIO-LOGI-CALLY...

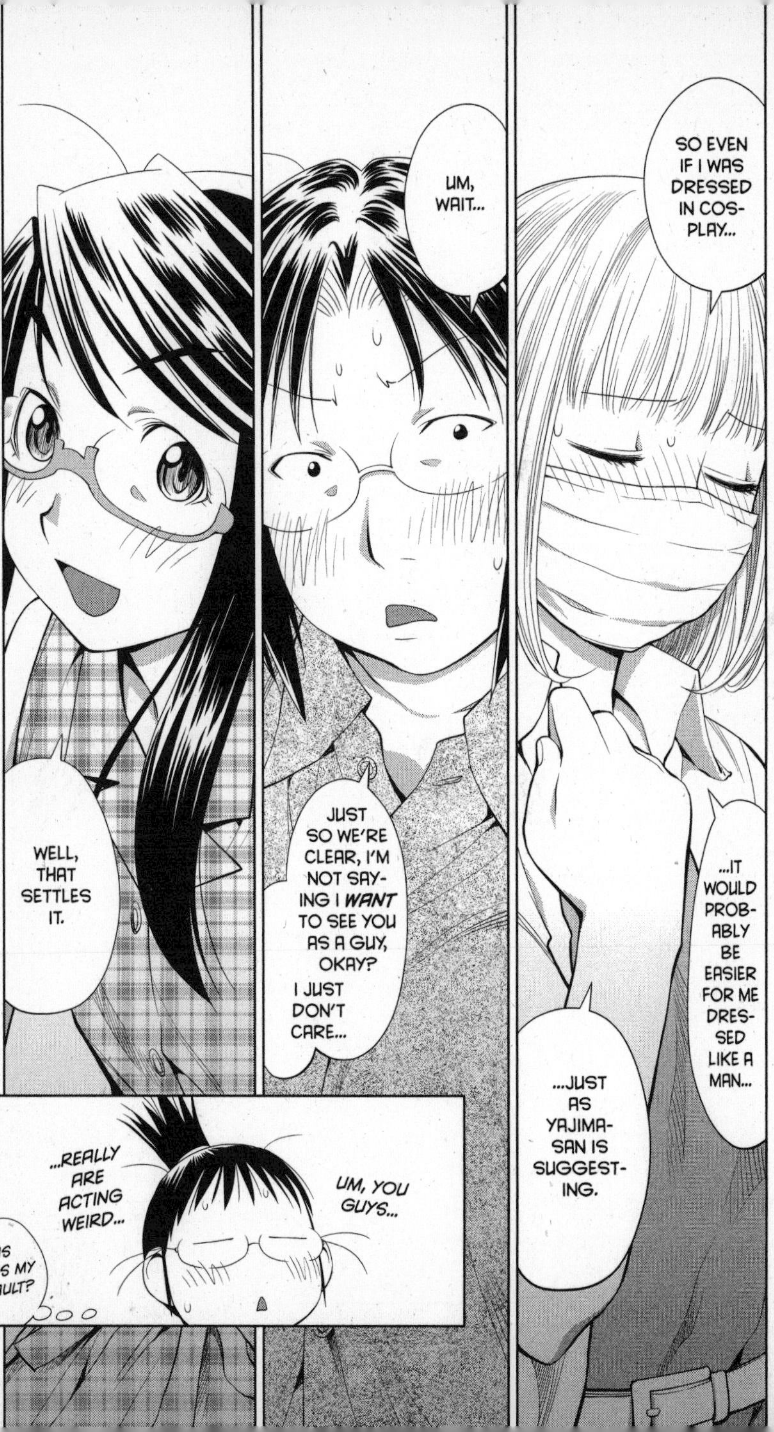
SO EVEN IF I WAS DRESSED IN COS-PLAY...
...IT WOULD PROBABLY BE EASIER FOR ME DRESSED LIKE A MAN...
...JUST AS YAJIMA-SAN IS SUGGESTING.
UM, WAIT...
JUST SO WE'RE CLEAR, I'M NOT SAYING I *WANT* TO SEE YOU AS A GUY, OKAY?
I JUST DON'T CARE...
WELL, THAT SETTLES IT.
UM, YOU GUYS...
...REALLY ARE ACTING WEIRD...
IS THIS MY FAULT?

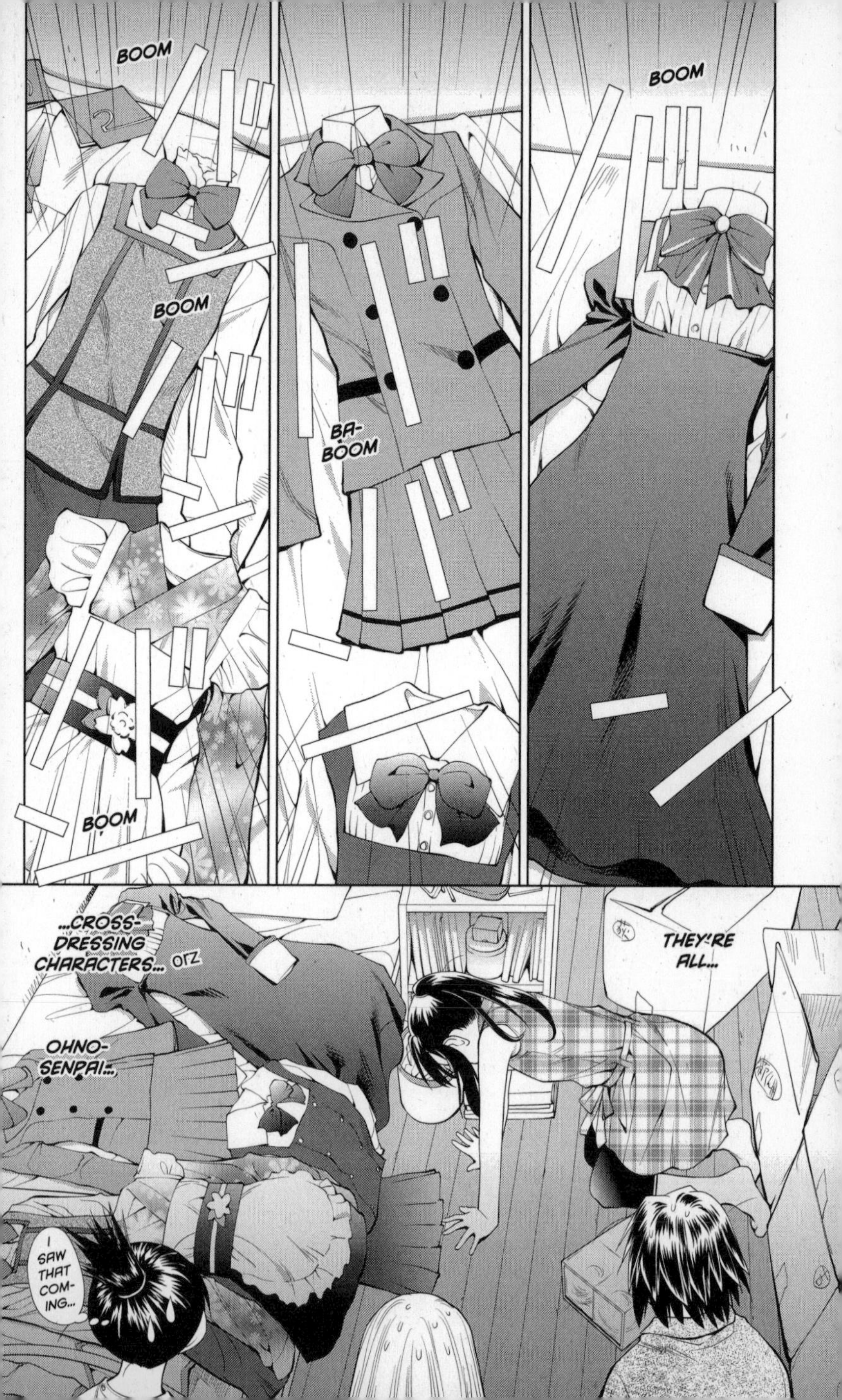
BOOM
BA-BOOM
BOOM
BOOM
BOOM
THEY'RE ALL...
...CROSS-DRESSING CHARACTERS... orz
OHNO-SENPAI...
I SAW THAT COMING...

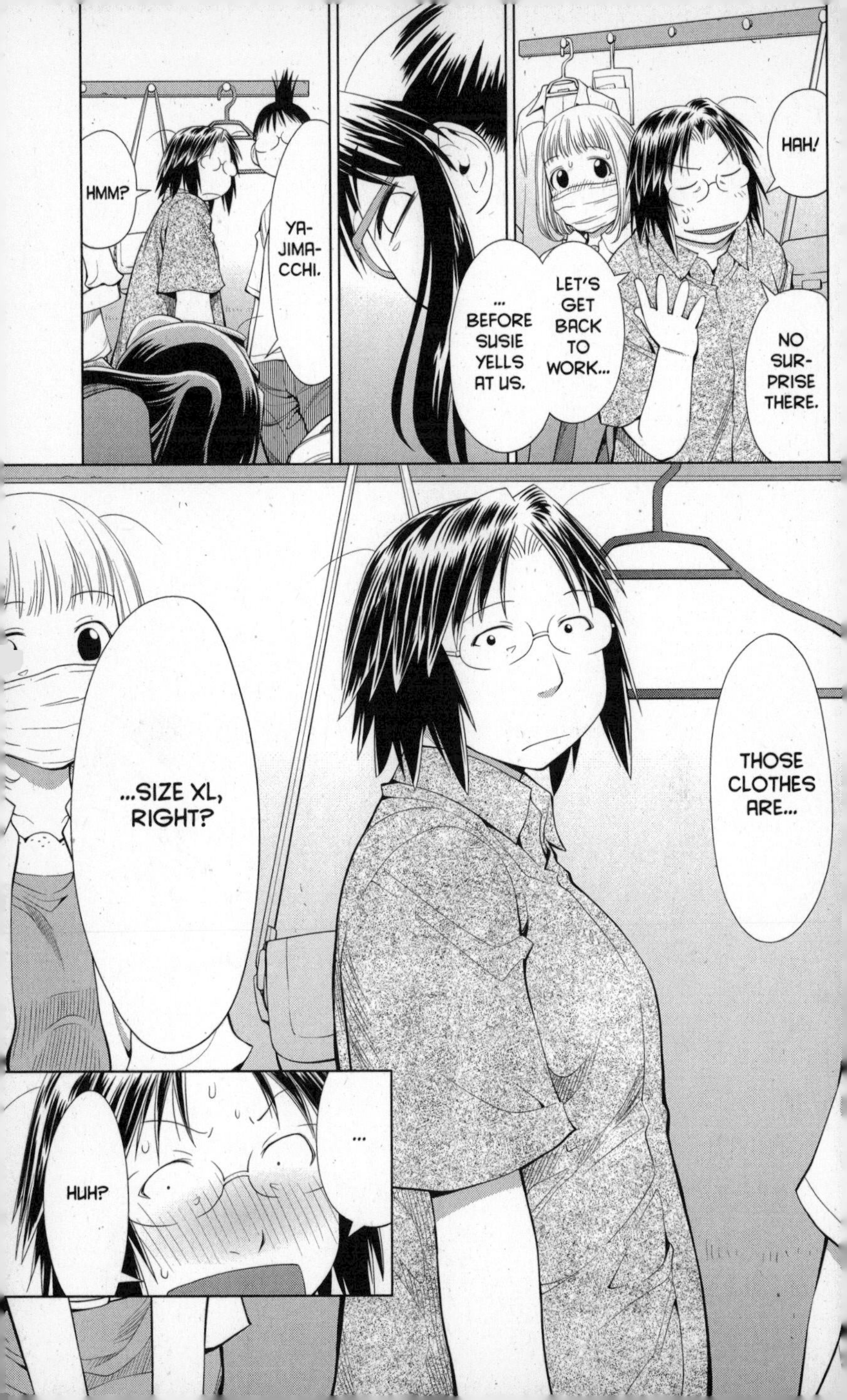
HAH!
NO SUR-PRISE THERE.
LET'S GET BACK TO WORK...
... BEFORE SUSIE YELLS AT US.
YA-JIMA-CCHI.
HMM?
THOSE CLOTHES ARE...
...SIZE XL, RIGHT?
...
HUH?

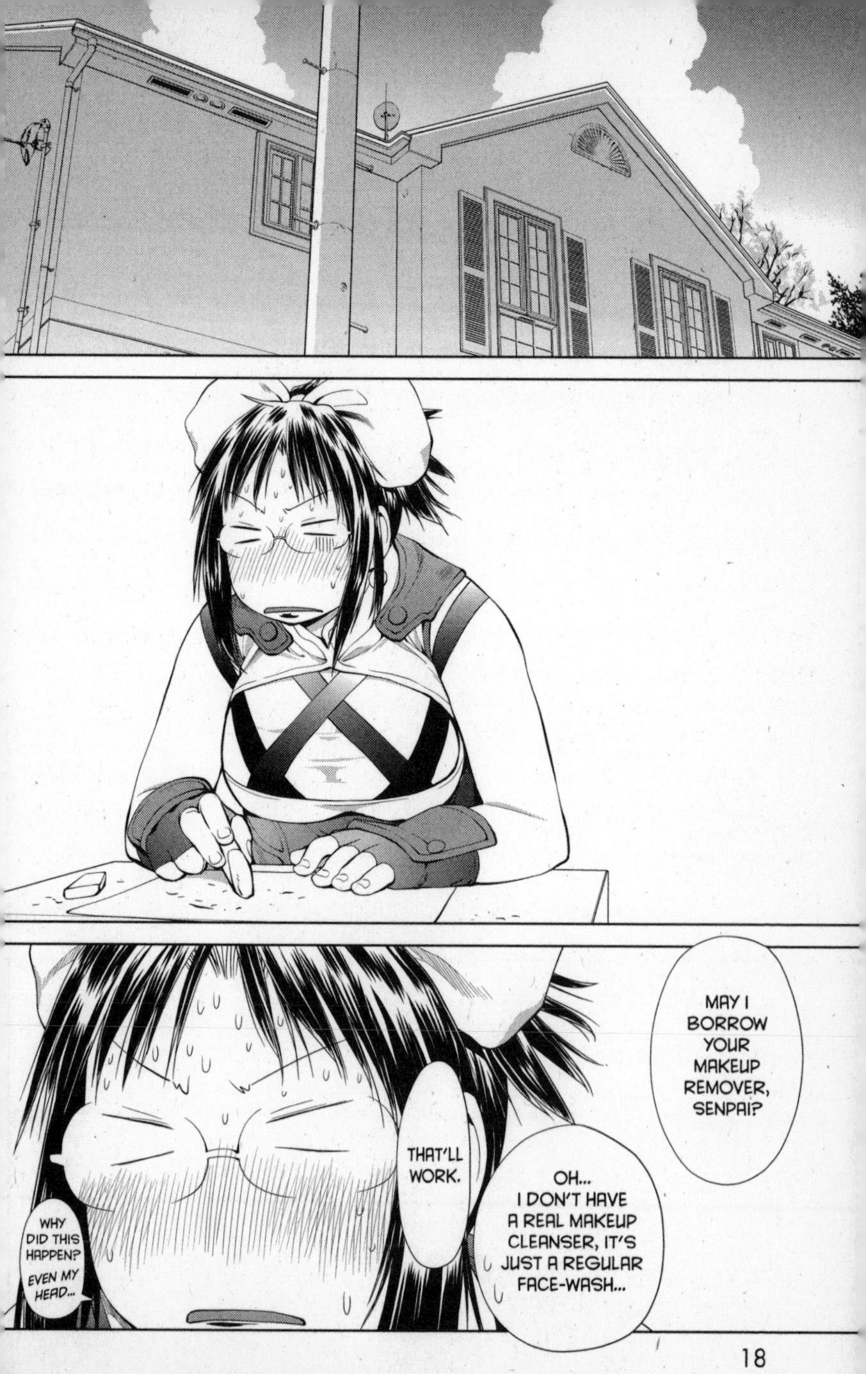
MAY I BORROW YOUR MAKEUP REMOVER, SENPAI?
OH... I DON'T HAVE A REAL MAKEUP CLEANSER, IT'S JUST A REGULAR FACE-WASH...
THAT'LL WORK.
WHY DID THIS HAPPEN? EVEN MY HEAD...

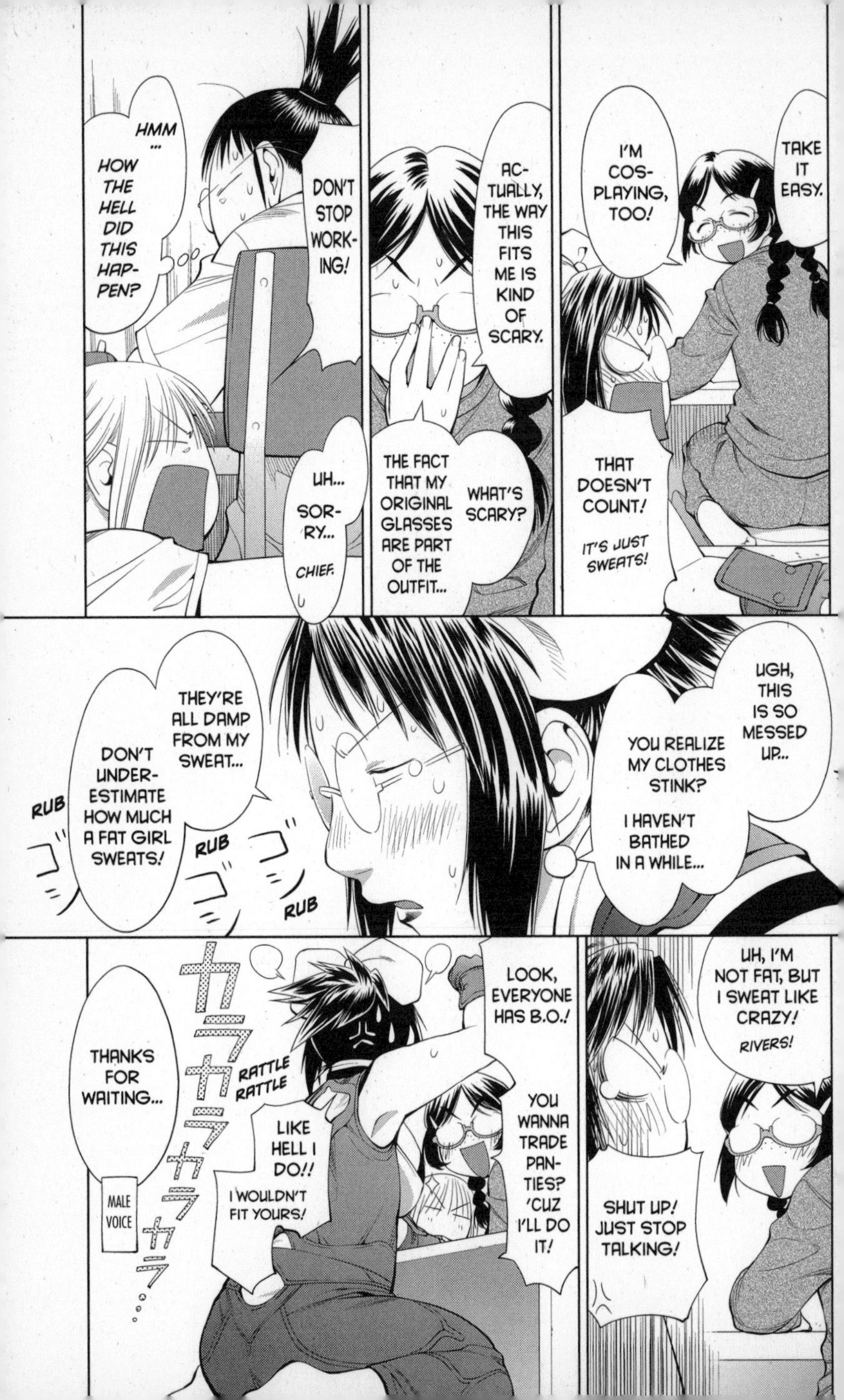
TAKE IT EASY.
I'M COS-PLAYING, TOO!
THAT DOESN'T COUNT!
IT'S JUST SWEATS!
AC-TUALLY, THE WAY THIS FITS ME IS KIND OF SCARY.
WHAT'S SCARY?
THE FACT THAT MY ORIGINAL GLASSES ARE PART OF THE OUTFIT...
DON'T STOP WORKING!
HMM... HOW THE HELL DID THIS HAP-PEN?
UH... SOR-RY...
CHIEF.
UGH, THIS IS SO MESSED UP...
YOU REALIZE MY CLOTHES STINK?
I HAVEN'T BATHED IN A WHILE...
THEY'RE ALL DAMP FROM MY SWEAT...
DON'T UNDER-ESTIMATE HOW MUCH A FAT GIRL SWEATS!
RUB
RUB
RUB
UH, I'M NOT FAT, BUT I SWEAT LIKE CRAZY!
RIVERS!
SHUT UP! JUST STOP TALKING!
LOOK, EVERYONE HAS B.O.!
YOU WANNA TRADE PAN-TIES? 'CUZ I'LL DO IT!
LIKE HELL I DO!!
I WOULDN'T FIT YOURS!
カラカラカラ
RATTLE RATTLE
THANKS FOR WAITING...
MALE VOICE

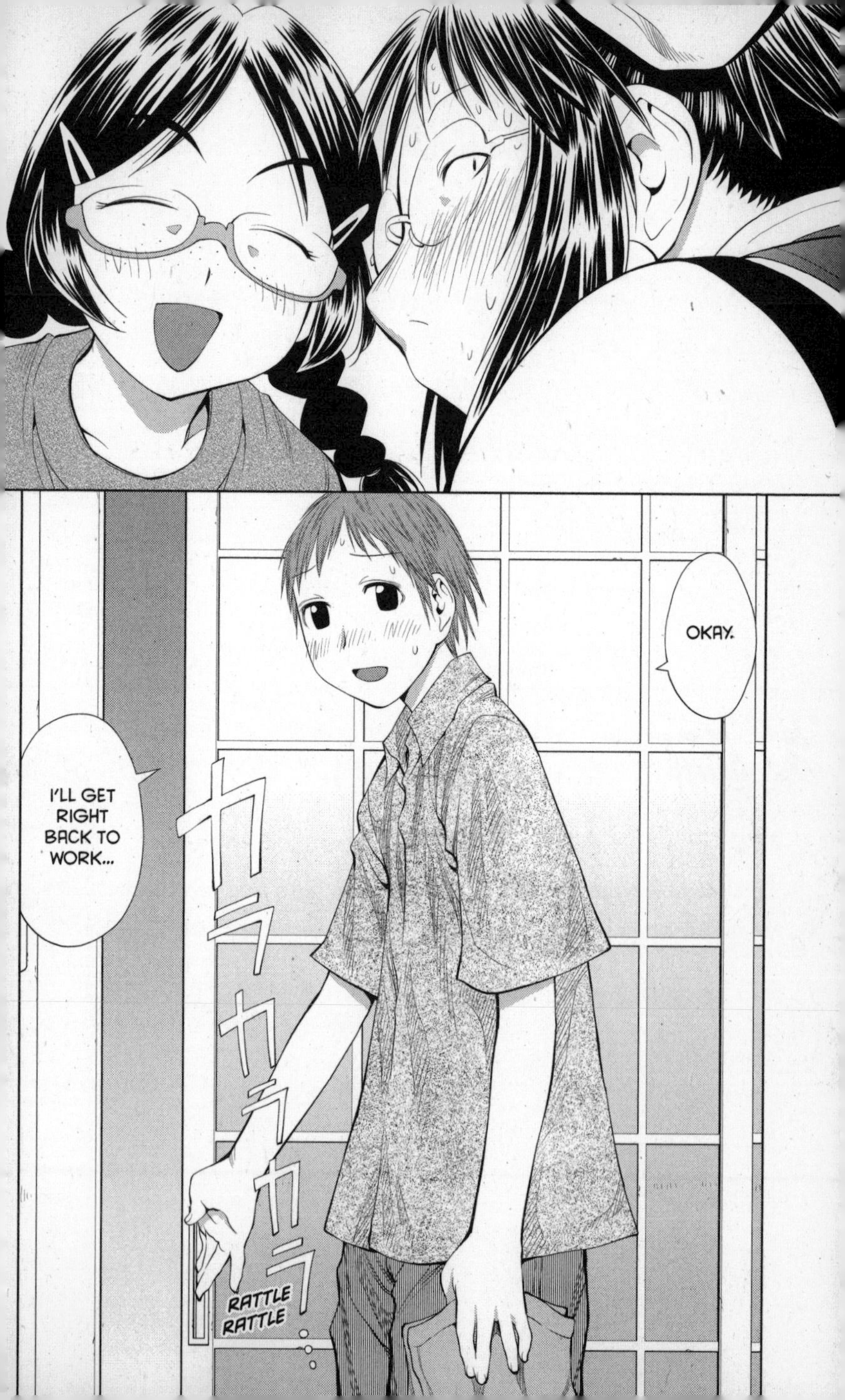
OKAY.
I'LL GET RIGHT BACK TO WORK...
カラカラカラ
RATTLE RATTLE

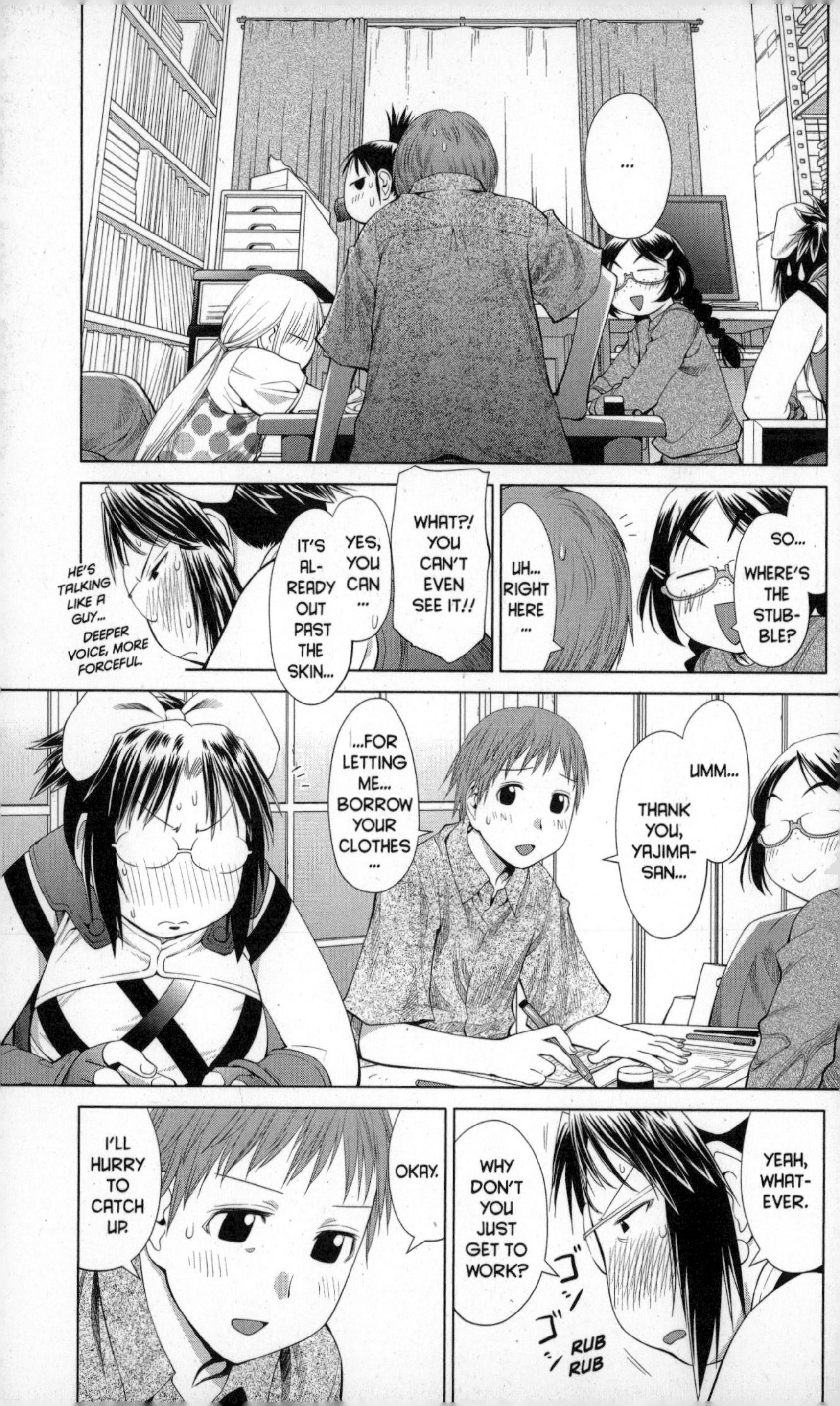
...
SO... WHERE'S THE STUBBLE?
UH... RIGHT HERE...
WHAT?! YOU CAN'T EVEN SEE IT!!
YES, YOU CAN...
IT'S ALREADY OUT PAST THE SKIN...
HE'S TALKING LIKE A GUY... DEEPER VOICE, MORE FORCEFUL.
UMM... THANK YOU, YAJIMA-SAN...
...FOR LETTING ME... BORROW YOUR CLOTHES...
YEAH, WHATEVER.
WHY DON'T YOU JUST GET TO WORK?
RUB RUB
OKAY.
I'LL HURRY TO CATCH UP.

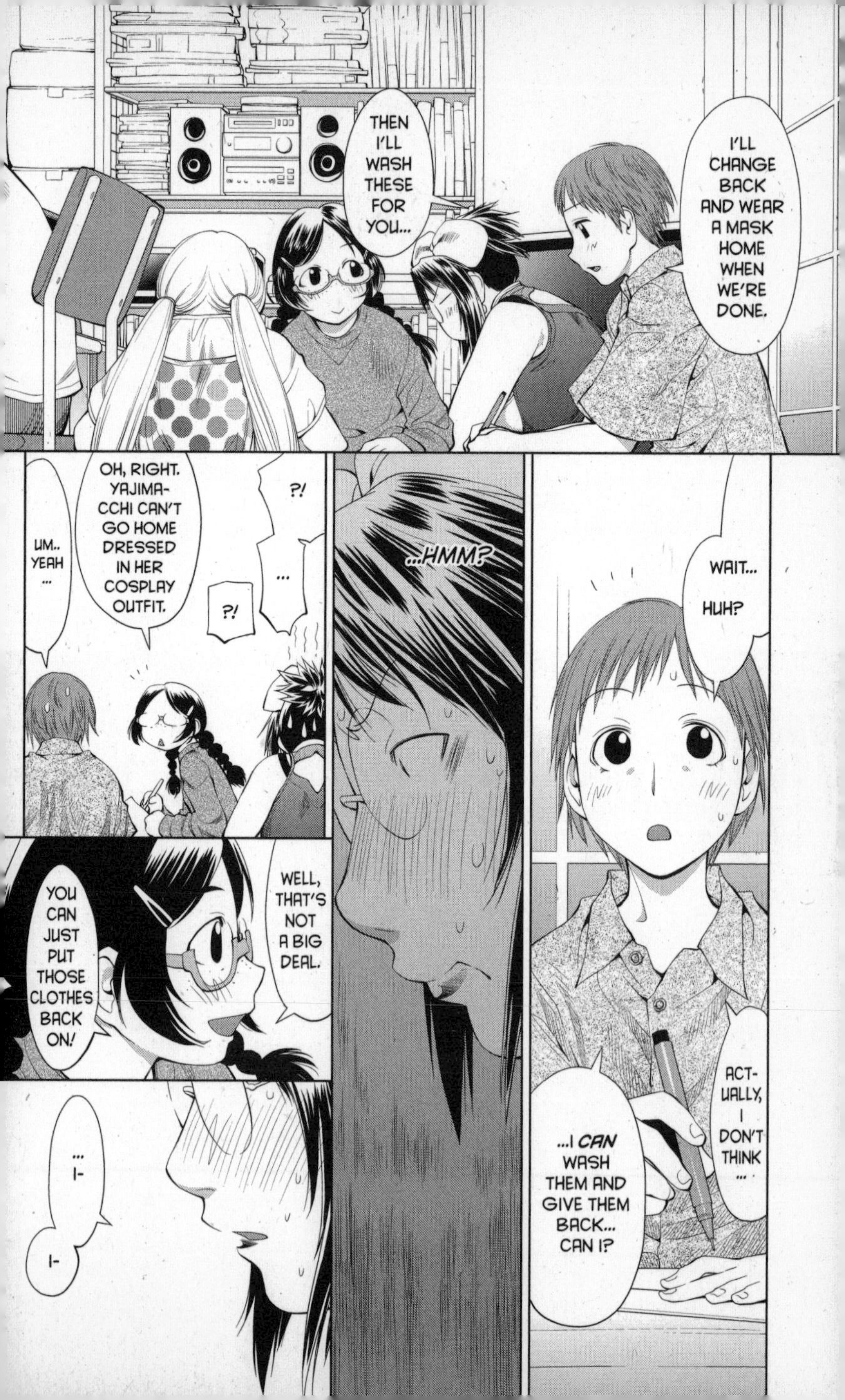
I'LL CHANGE BACK AND WEAR A MASK HOME WHEN WE'RE DONE.
THEN I'LL WASH THESE FOR YOU...
WAIT...
HUH?
ACT-UALLY, I DON'T THINK ...
...I *CAN* WASH THEM AND GIVE THEM BACK... CAN I?
...HMM?
?!
...
OH, RIGHT. YAJIMA-CCHI CAN'T GO HOME DRESSED IN HER COSPLAY OUTFIT.
?!
UM.. YEAH ...
WELL, THAT'S NOT A BIG DEAL.
YOU CAN JUST PUT THOSE CLOTHES BACK ON!
... I-
I-

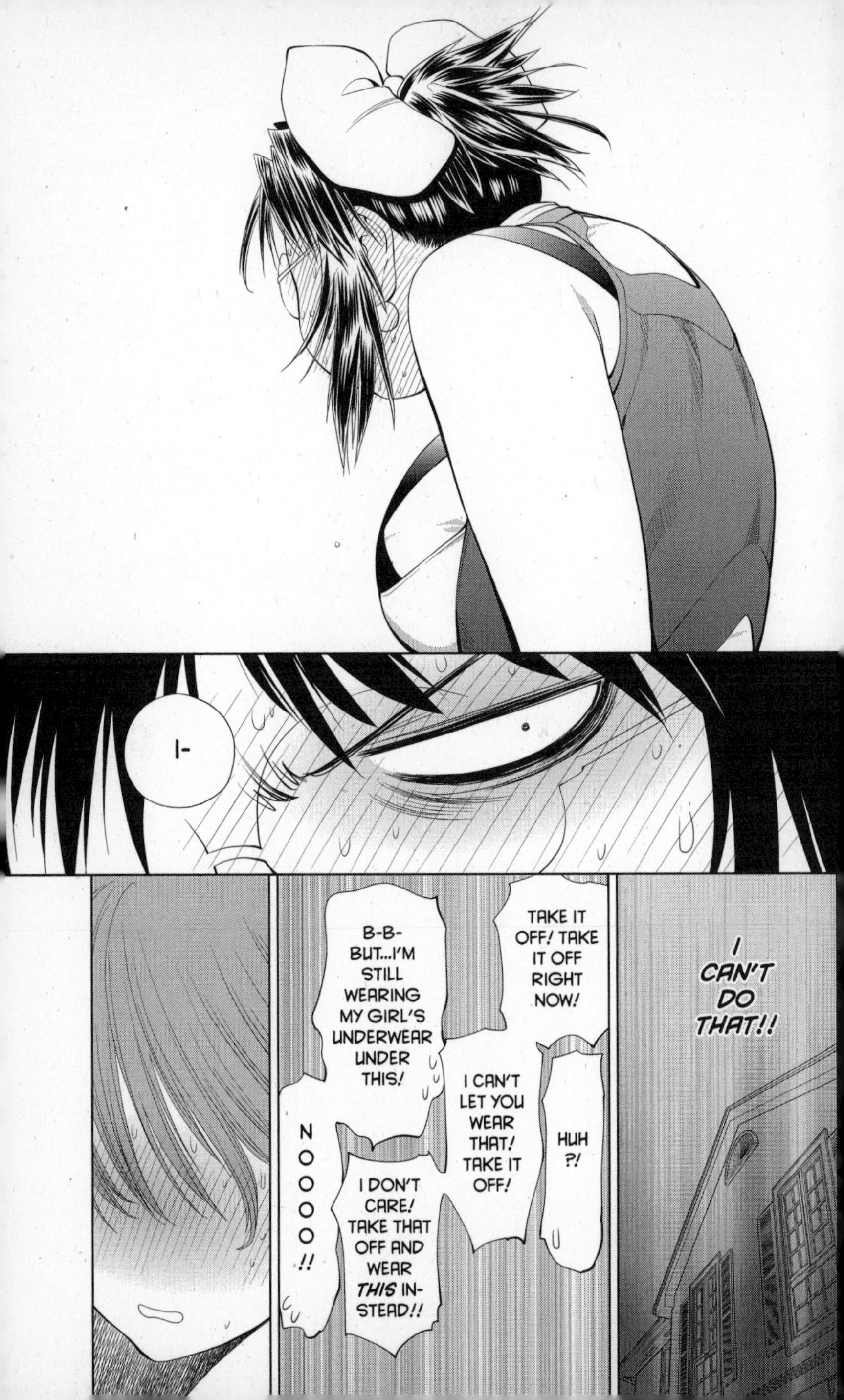
I-
I CAN'T DO THAT!!
TAKE IT OFF! TAKE IT OFF RIGHT NOW!
B-B-BUT...I'M STILL WEARING MY GIRL'S UNDERWEAR UNDER THIS!
HUH?!
I CAN'T LET YOU WEAR THAT! TAKE IT OFF!
I DON'T CARE! TAKE THAT OFF AND WEAR THIS IN-STEAD!!
NOOOOO!!

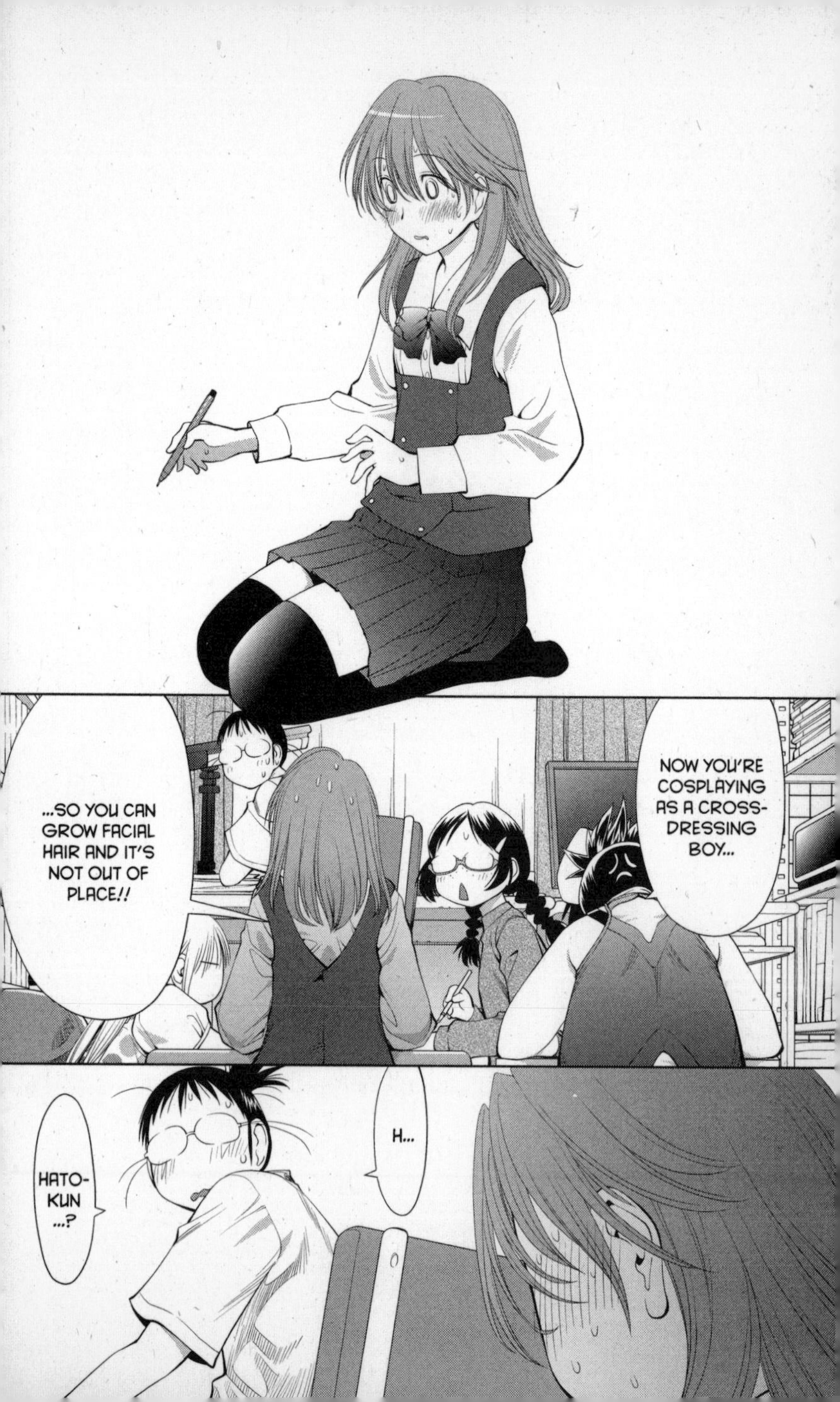
NOW YOU'RE COSPLAYING AS A CROSS-DRESSING BOY...
...SO YOU CAN GROW FACIAL HAIR AND IT'S NOT OUT OF PLACE!!
H...
HATO-KUN ...?

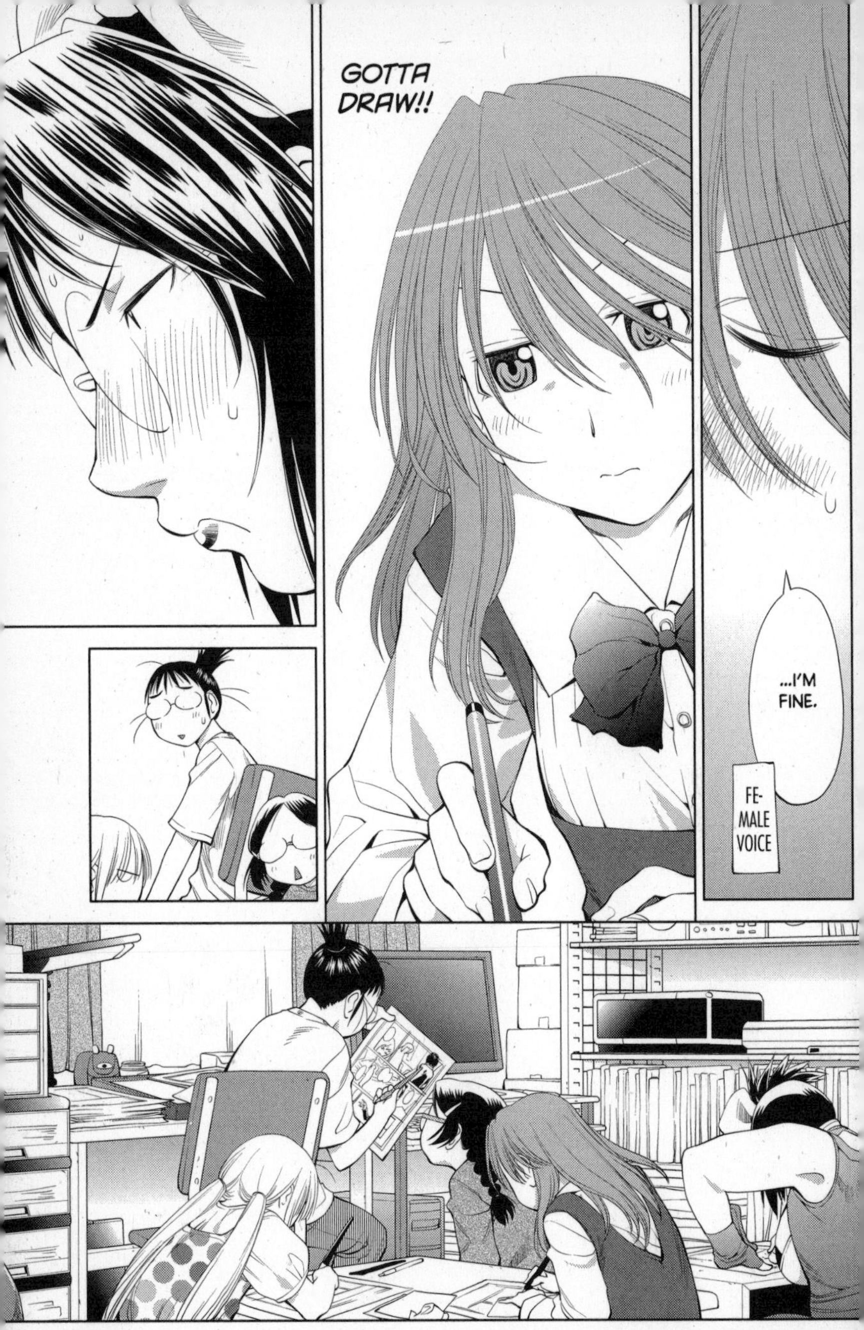
...I'M FINE.
FE-MALE VOICE
GOTTA DRAW!!

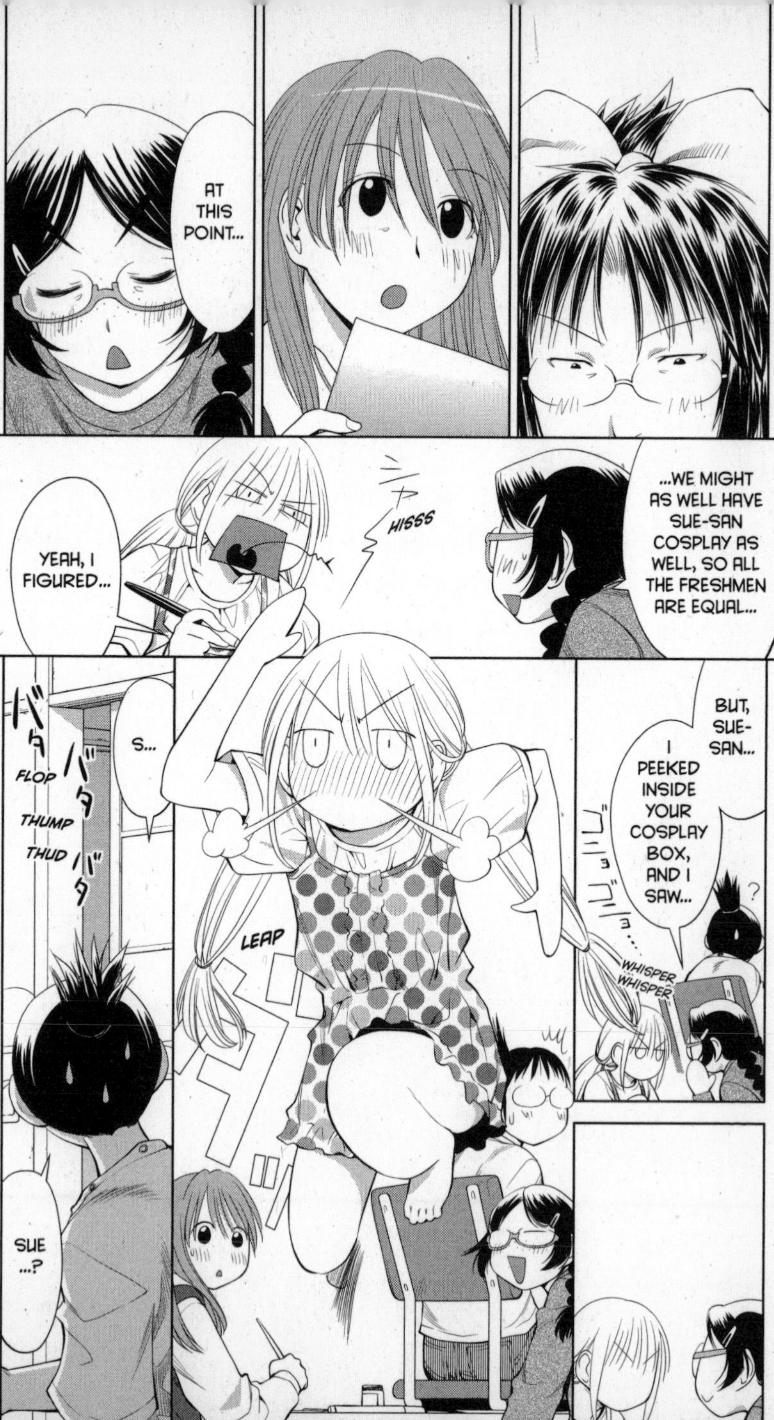
AT THIS POINT...
...WE MIGHT AS WELL HAVE SUE-SAN COSPLAY AS WELL, SO ALL THE FRESHMEN ARE EQUAL...
HISSS
YEAH, I FIGURED...
BUT, SUE-SAN...
I PEEKED INSIDE YOUR COSPLAY BOX, AND I SAW...
WHISPER WHISPER
?
LEAP
S...
FLOP
THUMP
THUD
SUE ...?

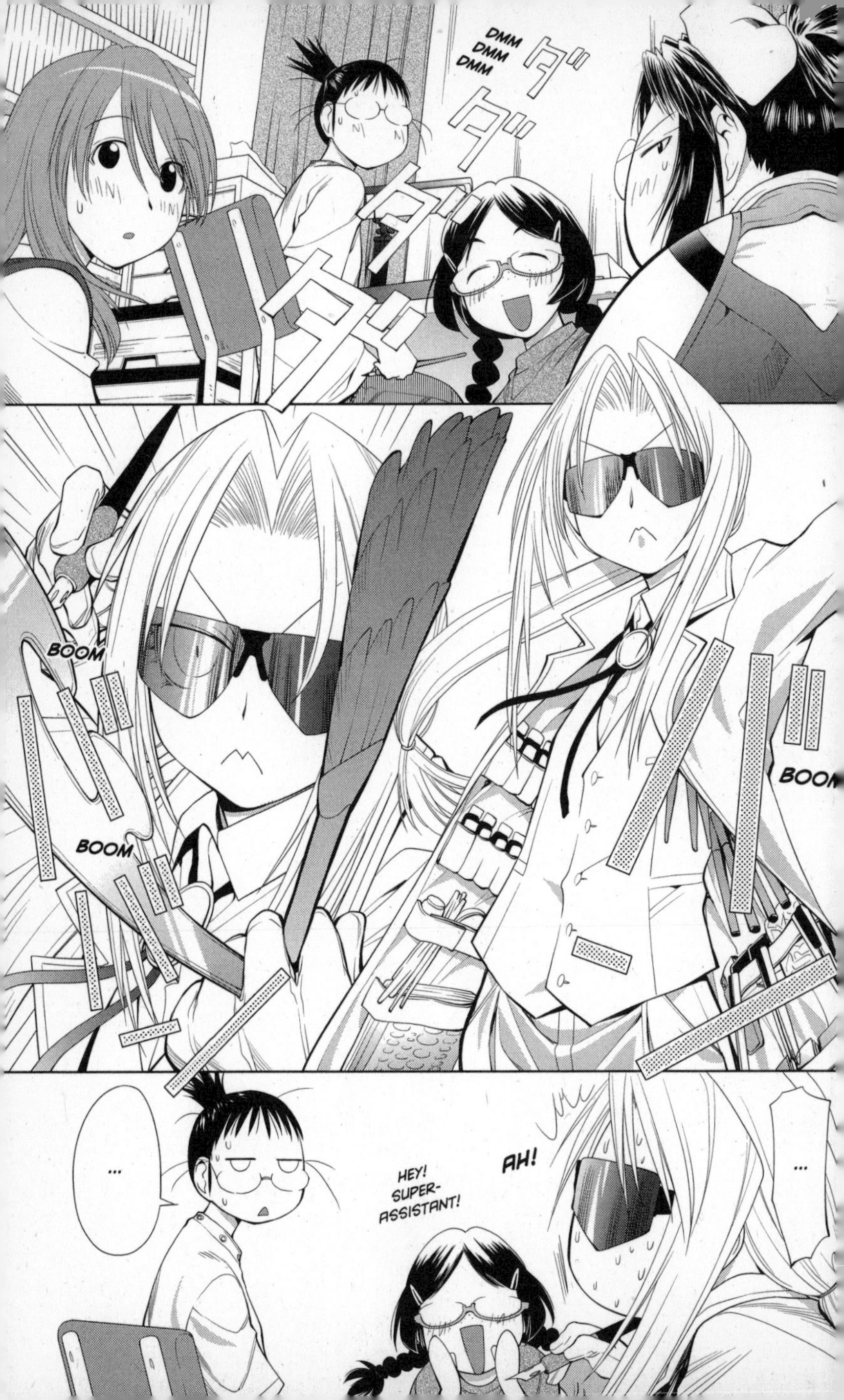
DMM
DMM
DMM
BOO
BOOM
BOOM
...
AH!
HEY! SUPER-ASSISTANT!
...

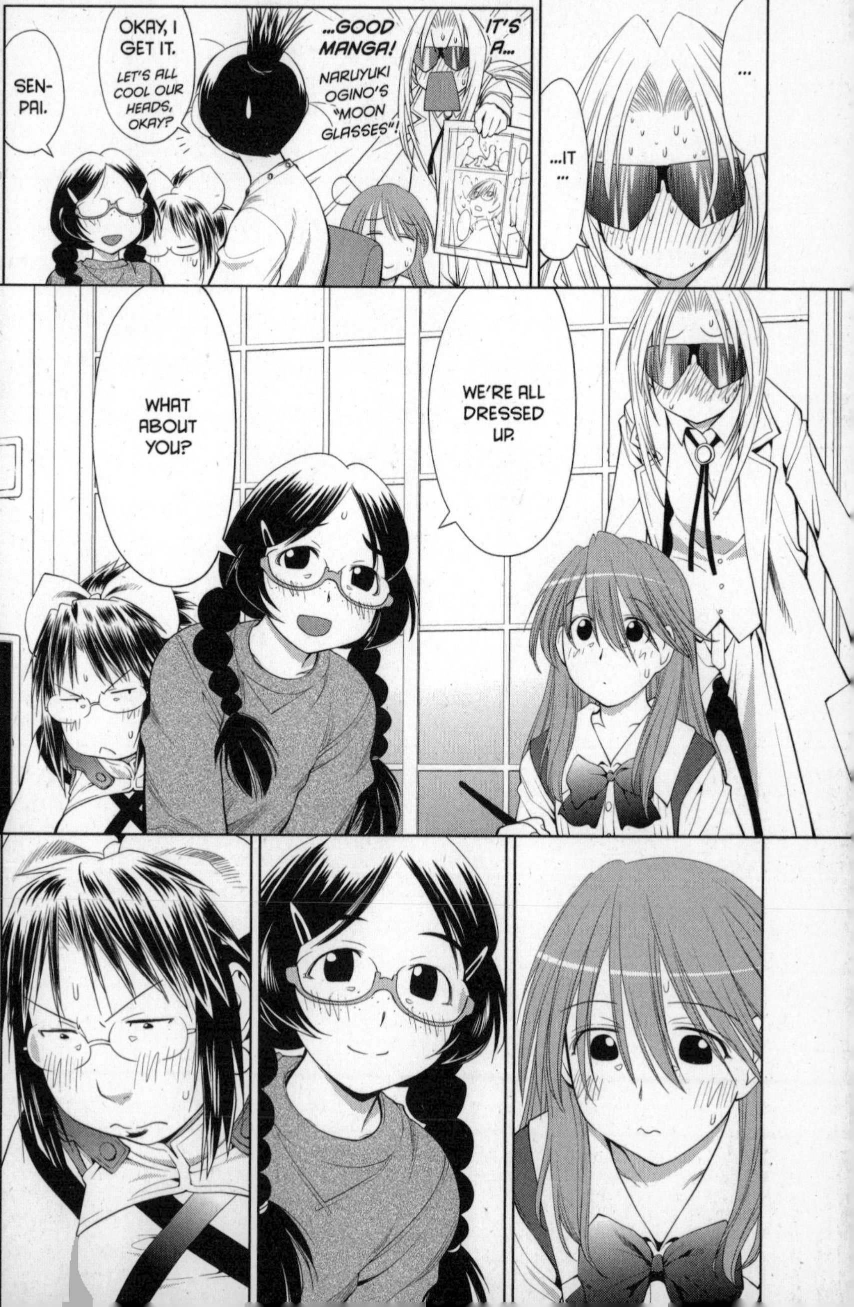
...
...IT ...
IT'S A...
...GOOD MANGA!
NARUYUKI OGINO'S "MOON GLASSES"!
OKAY, I GET IT.
LET'S ALL COOL OUR HEADS, OKAY?
SEN-PAI.
WE'RE ALL DRESSED UP.
WHAT ABOUT YOU?

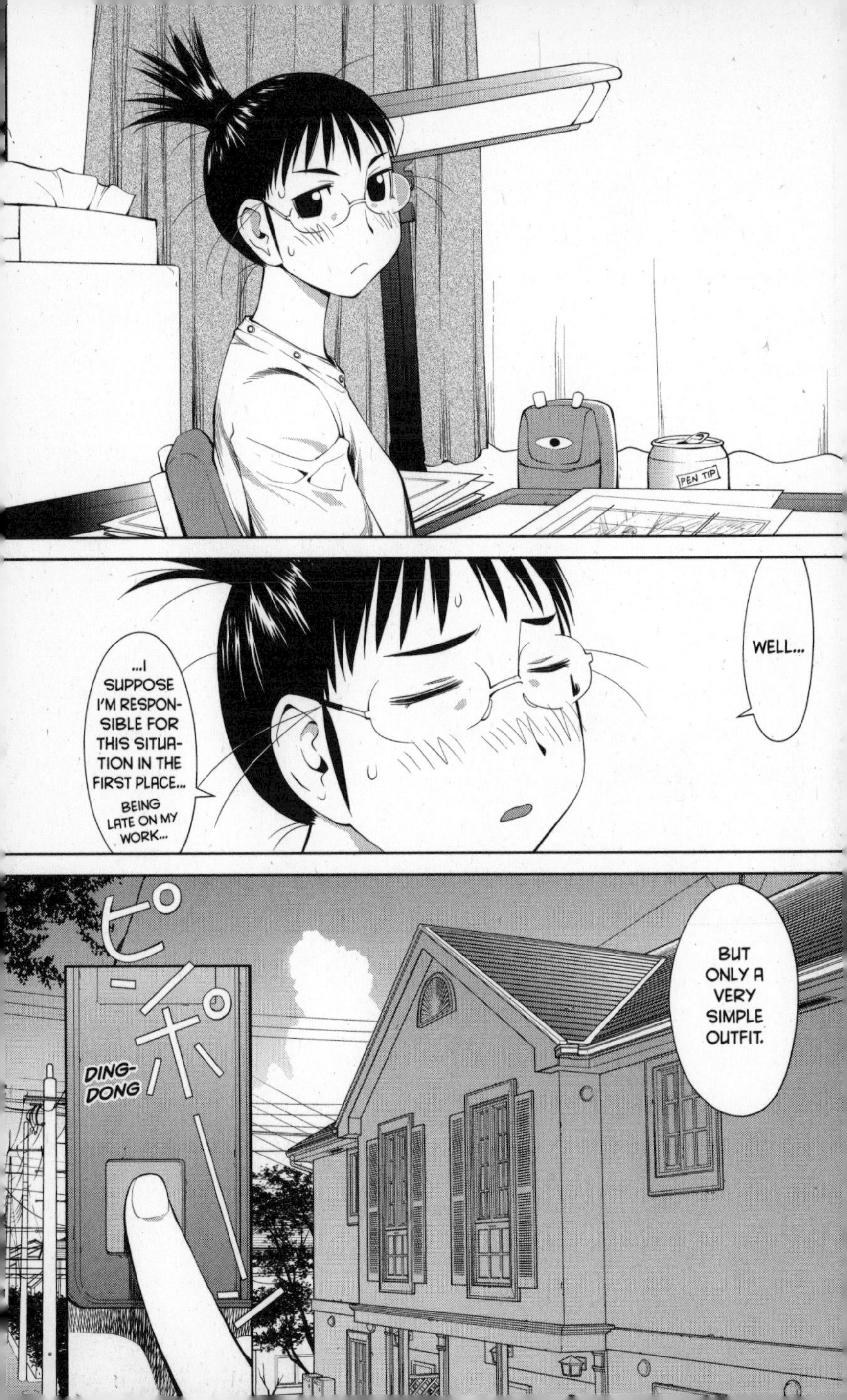
PEN TIP
WELL...
...I SUPPOSE I'M RESPONSIBLE FOR THIS SITUATION IN THE FIRST PLACE... BEING LATE ON MY WORK...
BUT ONLY A VERY SIMPLE OUTFIT.
ピーンポーン
DING-DONG

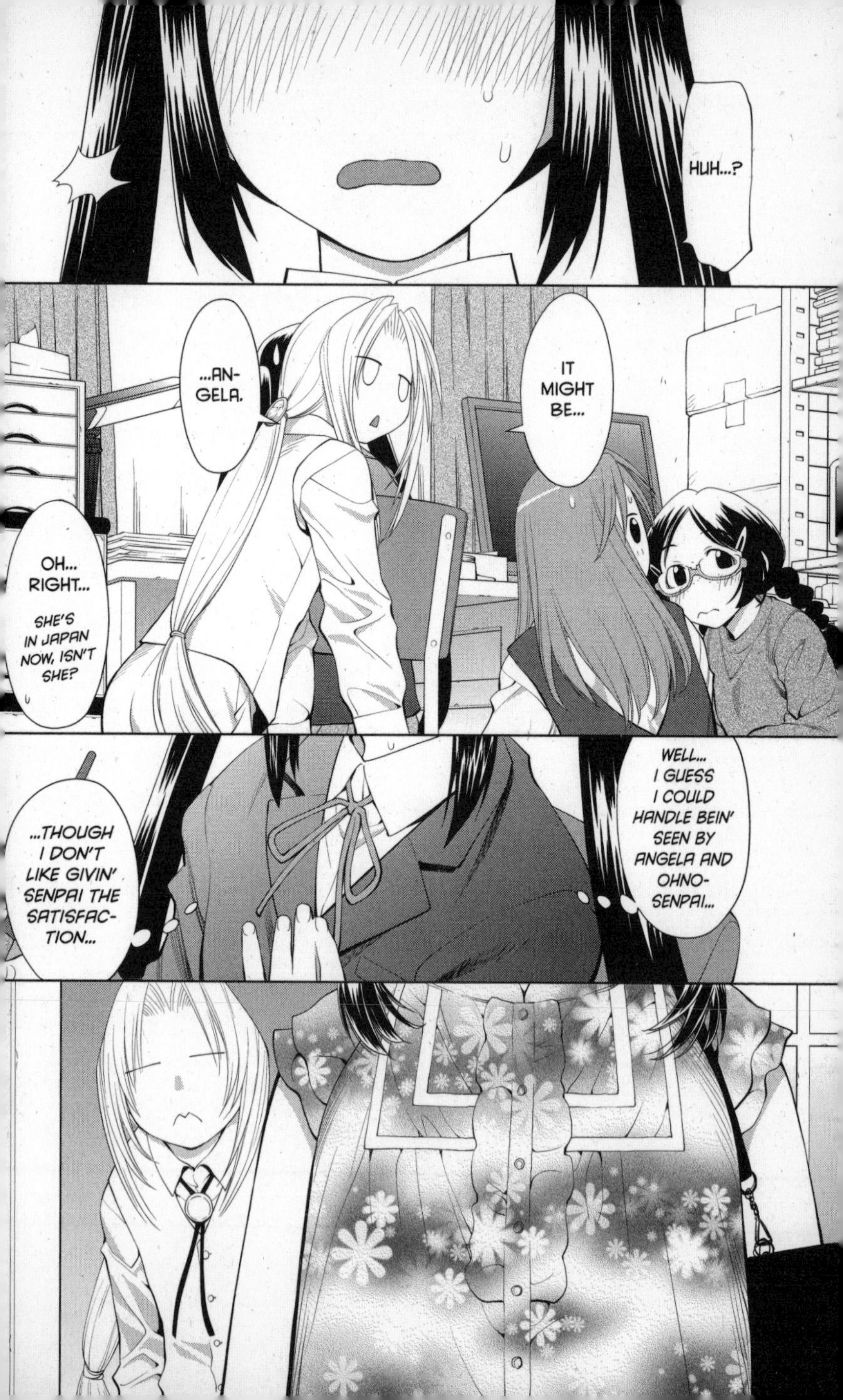
HUH...?
IT MIGHT BE...
...AN-GELA.
OH... RIGHT...
SHE'S IN JAPAN NOW, ISN'T SHE?
WELL... I GUESS I COULD HANDLE BEIN' SEEN BY ANGELA AND OHNO-SENPAI...
...THOUGH I DON'T LIKE GIVIN' SENPAI THE SATISFACTION...

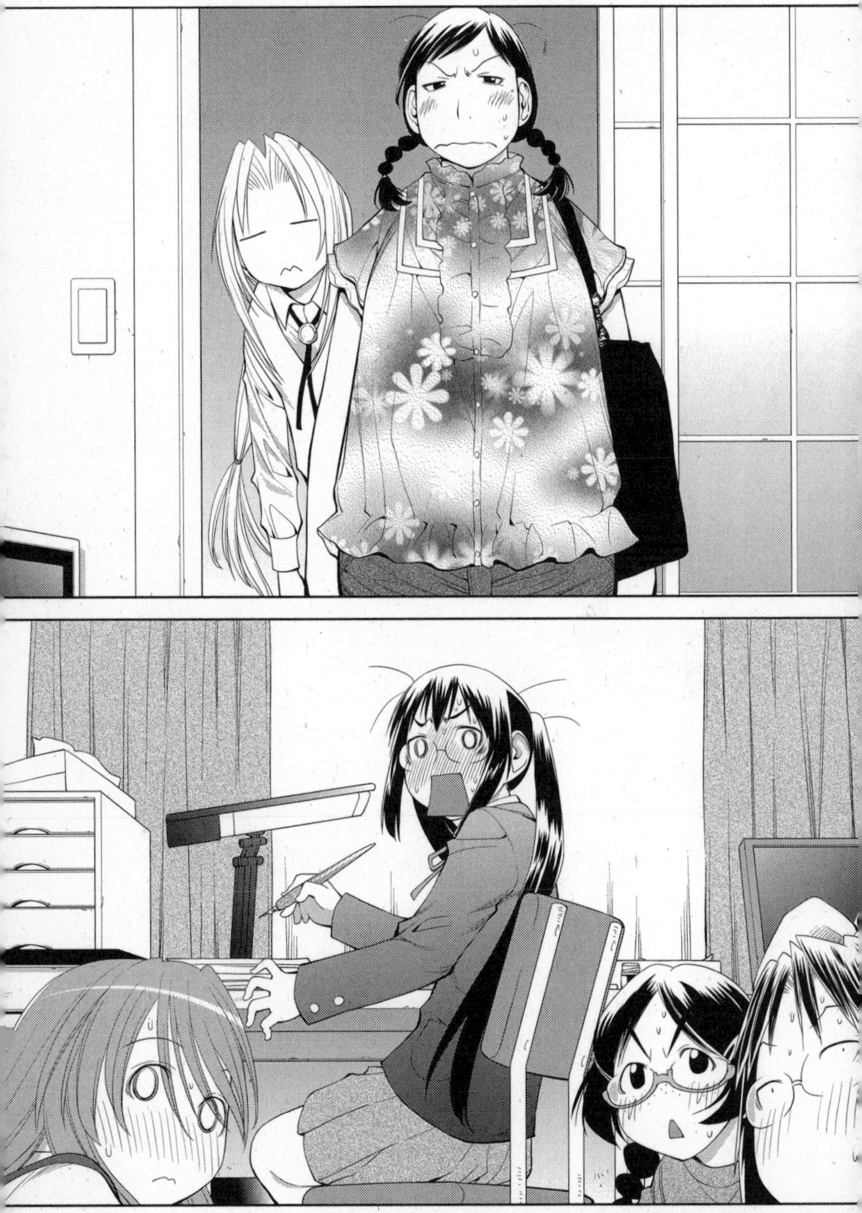

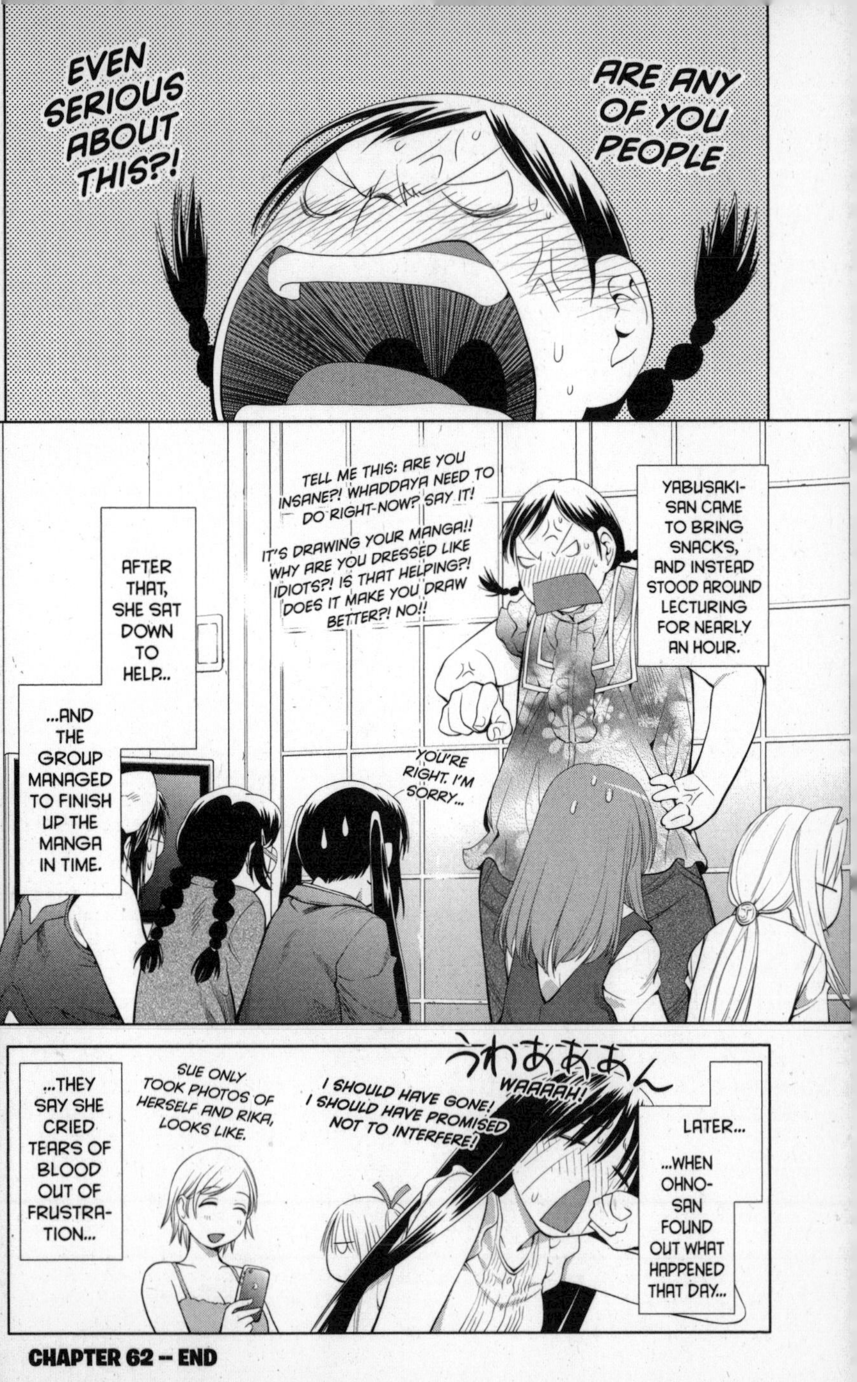
ARE ANY OF YOU PEOPLE
EVEN SERIOUS ABOUT THIS?!
YABUSAKI-SAN CAME TO BRING SNACKS, AND INSTEAD STOOD AROUND LECTURING FOR NEARLY AN HOUR.
TELL ME THIS: ARE YOU INSANE?! WHADDAYA NEED TO DO RIGHT-NOW? SAY IT!
IT'S DRAWING YOUR MANGA!! WHY ARE YOU DRESSED LIKE IDIOTS?! IS THAT HELPING?! DOES IT MAKE YOU DRAW BETTER?! NO!!
YOU'RE RIGHT. I'M SORRY...
AFTER THAT, SHE SAT DOWN TO HELP...
...AND THE GROUP MANAGED TO FINISH UP THE MANGA IN TIME.
LATER...
...WHEN OHNO-SAN FOUND OUT WHAT HAPPENED THAT DAY...
うわあああん
WAAAAAH!
I SHOULD HAVE GONE! I SHOULD HAVE PROMISED NOT TO INTERFERE!
SUE ONLY TOOK PHOTOS OF HERSELF AND RIKA, LOOKS LIKE.
...THEY SAY SHE CRIED TEARS OF BLOOD OUT OF FRUSTRA-TION...

CHAPTER 62 -- END

CHAPTER 62 - MOMENTS LATER

AT LEAST THEY'RE FULL-BODY TIGHTS

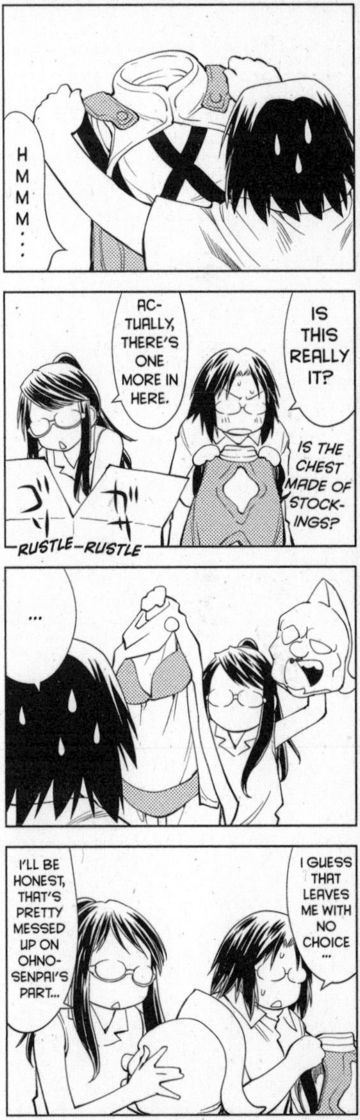
HMMM...
IS THIS REALLY IT?
IS THE CHEST MADE OF STOCKINGS?
ACTUALLY, THERE'S ONE MORE IN HERE.
RUSTLE—RUSTLE
...
I GUESS THAT LEAVES ME WITH NO CHOICE...
I'LL BE HONEST, THAT'S PRETTY MESSED UP ON OHNO-SENPAI'S PART...

FIRST TIME

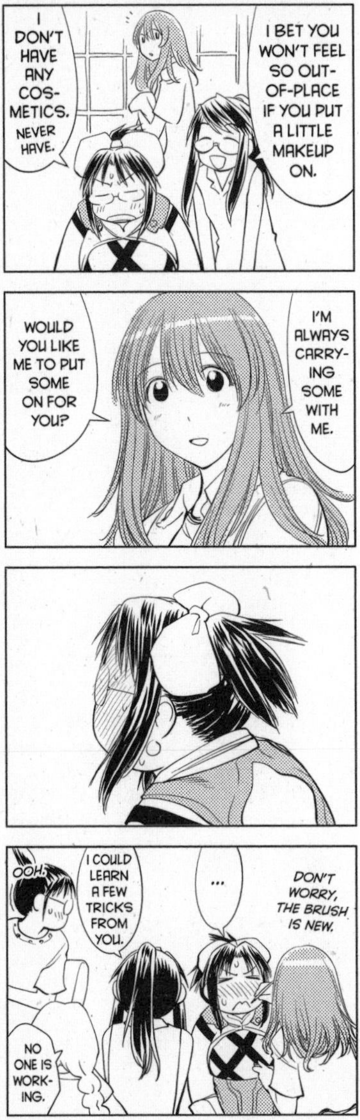
I BET YOU WON'T FEEL SO OUT-OF-PLACE IF YOU PUT A LITTLE MAKEUP ON.
I DON'T HAVE ANY COSMETICS.
NEVER HAVE.
I'M ALWAYS CARRYING SOME WITH ME.
WOULD YOU LIKE ME TO PUT SOME ON FOR YOU?
DON'T WORRY, THE BRUSH IS NEW.
...
I COULD LEARN A FEW TRICKS FROM YOU.
OOH.
NO ONE IS WORKING.

3-D

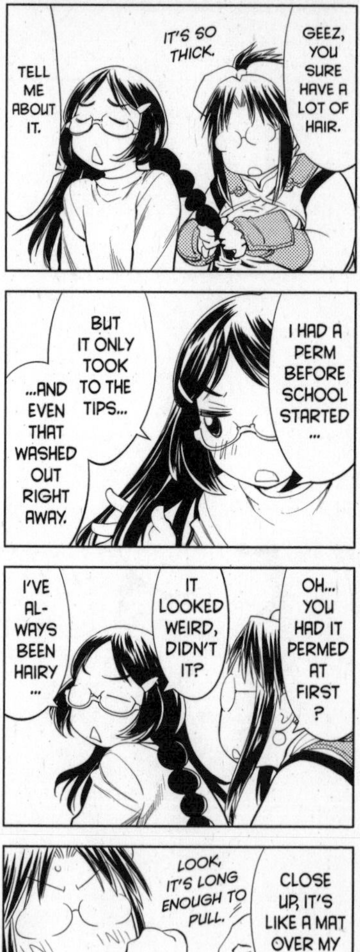
GEEZ, YOU SURE HAVE A LOT OF HAIR.
IT'S SO THICK.
TELL ME ABOUT IT.
I HAD A PERM BEFORE SCHOOL STARTED...
BUT IT ONLY TOOK TO THE TIPS...
...AND EVEN THAT WASHED OUT RIGHT AWAY.
OH... YOU HAD IT PERMED AT FIRST?
IT LOOKED WEIRD, DIDN'T IT?
I'VE ALWAYS BEEN HAIRY...
CLOSE UP, IT'S LIKE A MAT OVER MY SKIN.
LOOK, IT'S LONG ENOUGH TO PULL.
TUG TUG
I DIDN'T NEED TO SEE THAT.

HEIR TO THE LEGENDARY PROTAGONIST

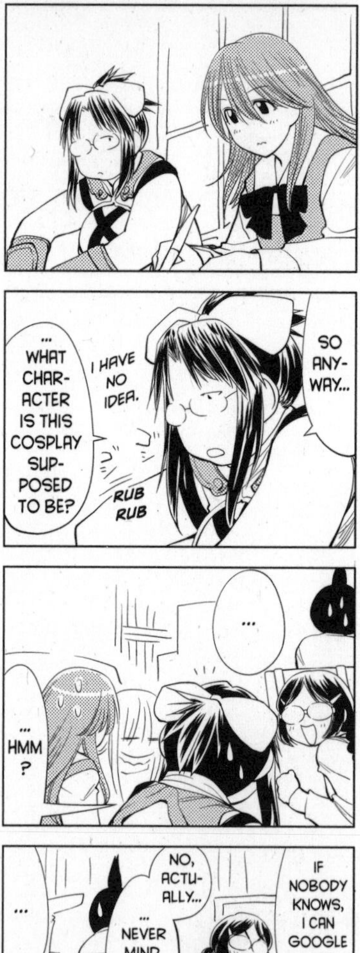
SO ANYWAY...
I HAVE NO IDEA.
...WHAT CHARACTER IS THIS COSPLAY SUPPOSED TO BE?
RUB RUB
...
...HMM?
IF NOBODY KNOWS, I CAN GOOGLE IT REAL QUICK...
NO, ACTUALLY... ...NEVER MIND. SORRY.
...
GET TO WORK.

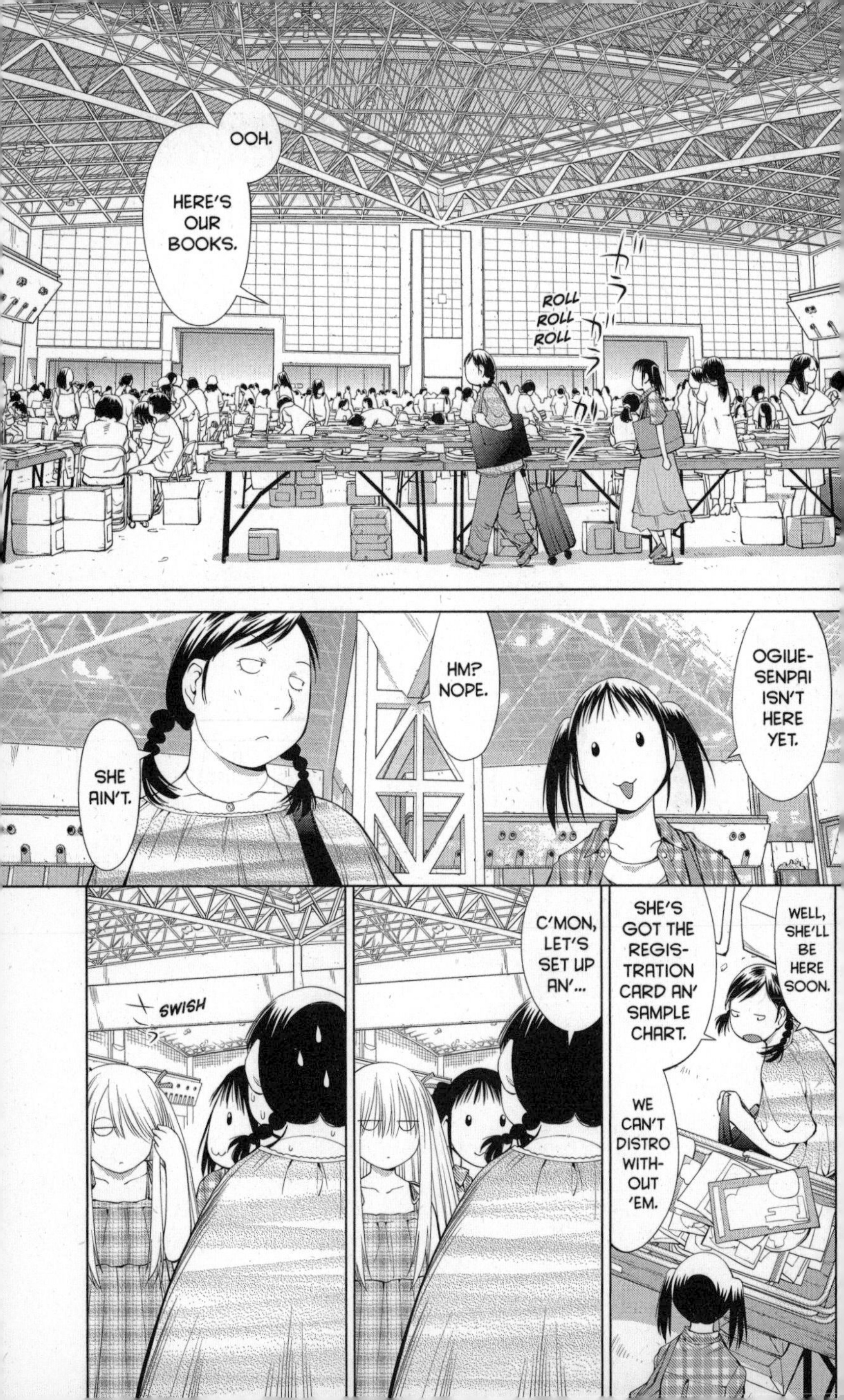
OOH.
HERE'S OUR BOOKS.
ROLL ROLL ROLL
OGIUE-SENPAI ISN'T HERE YET.
HM? NOPE.
SHE AIN'T.
WELL, SHE'LL BE HERE SOON.
SHE'S GOT THE REGIS-TRATION CARD AN' SAMPLE CHART.
WE CAN'T DISTRO WITH-OUT 'EM.
C'MON, LET'S SET UP AN'...
SWISH

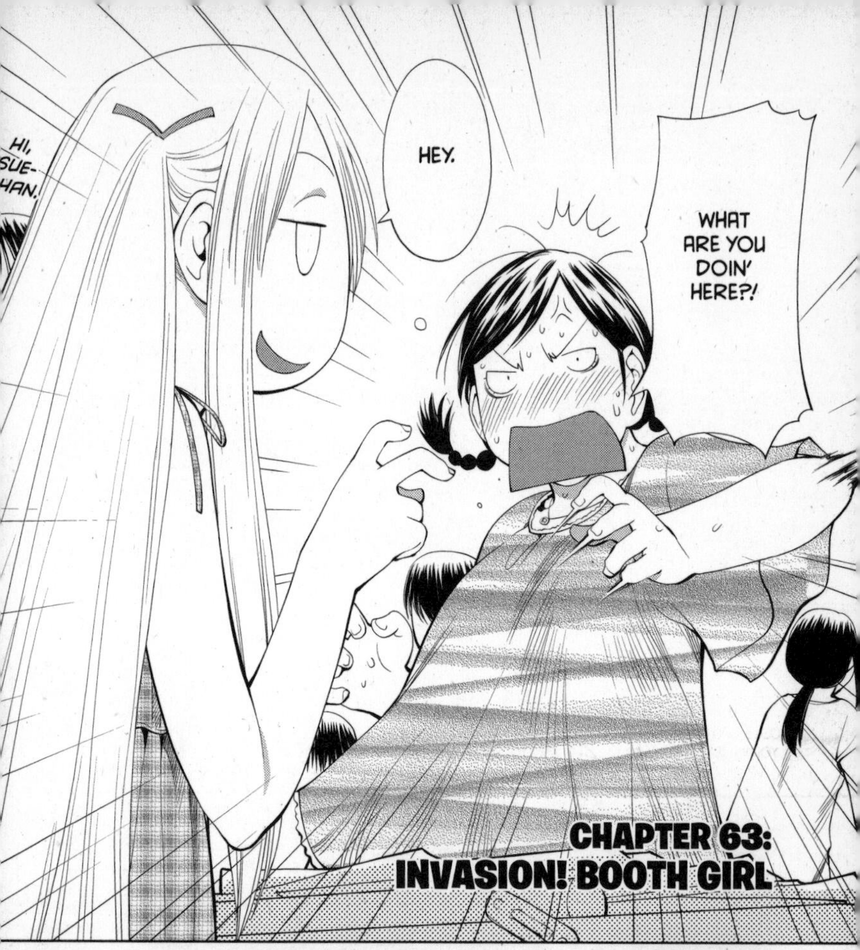
WHAT ARE YOU DOIN' HERE?!
HEY.
HI, SUE-HAN!
CHAPTER 63:
INVASION! BOOTH GIRL

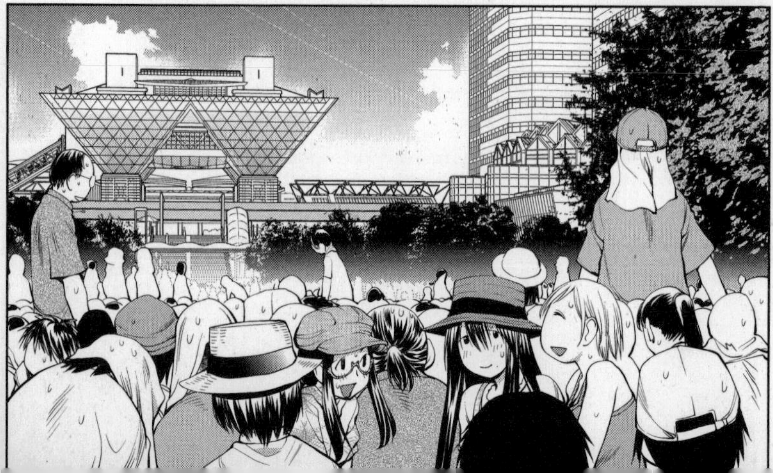

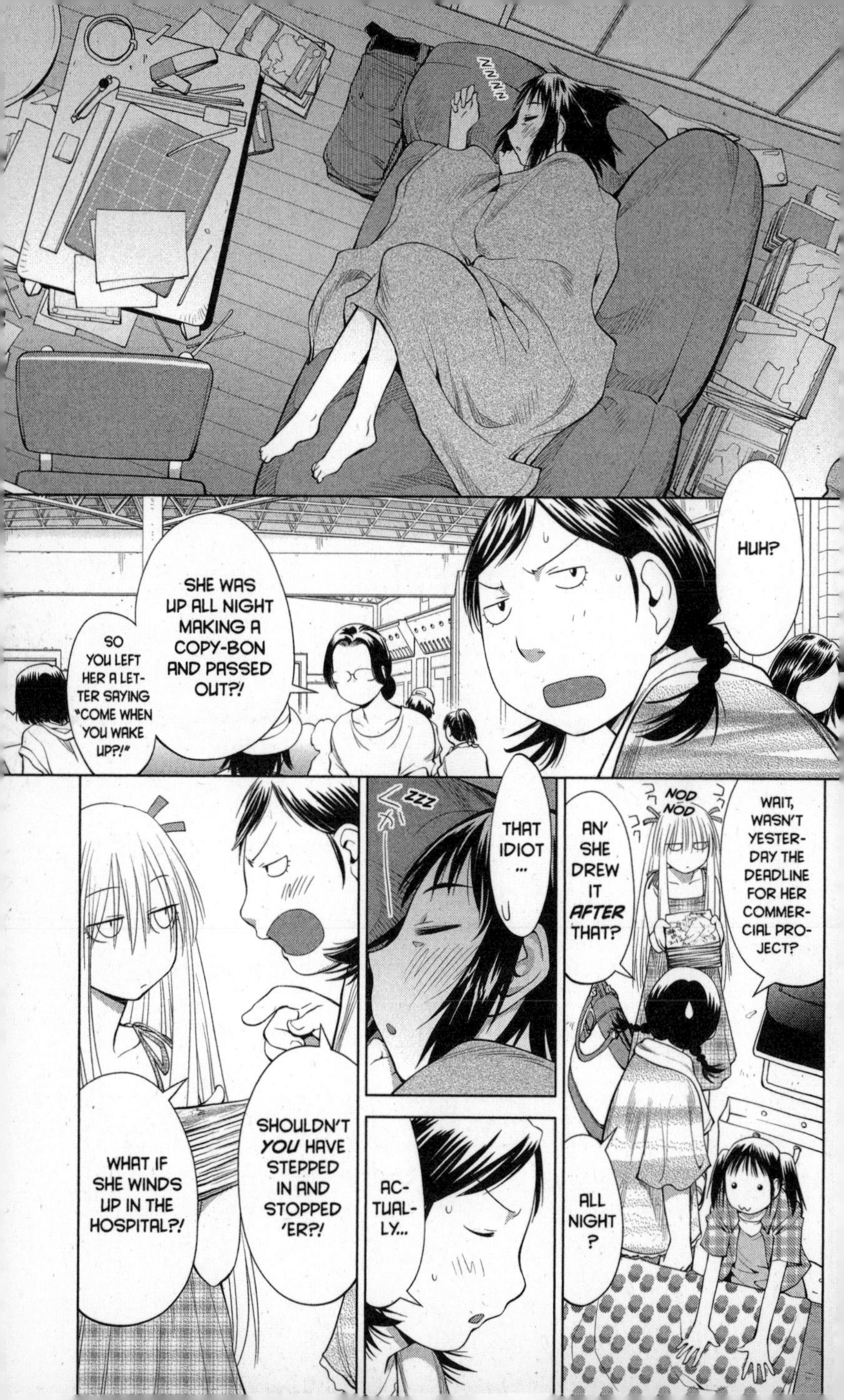
ZZZZ
HUH?
SHE WAS UP ALL NIGHT MAKING A COPY-BON AND PASSED OUT?!
SO YOU LEFT HER A LETTER SAYING "COME WHEN YOU WAKE UP?!"
WAIT, WASN'T YESTERDAY THE DEADLINE FOR HER COMMERCIAL PROJECT?
NOD NOD
AN' SHE DREW IT AFTER THAT?
ALL NIGHT?
THAT IDIOT...
ZZZ
ACTUALLY...
SHOULDN'T YOU HAVE STEPPED IN AND STOPPED 'ER?!
WHAT IF SHE WINDS UP IN THE HOSPITAL?!

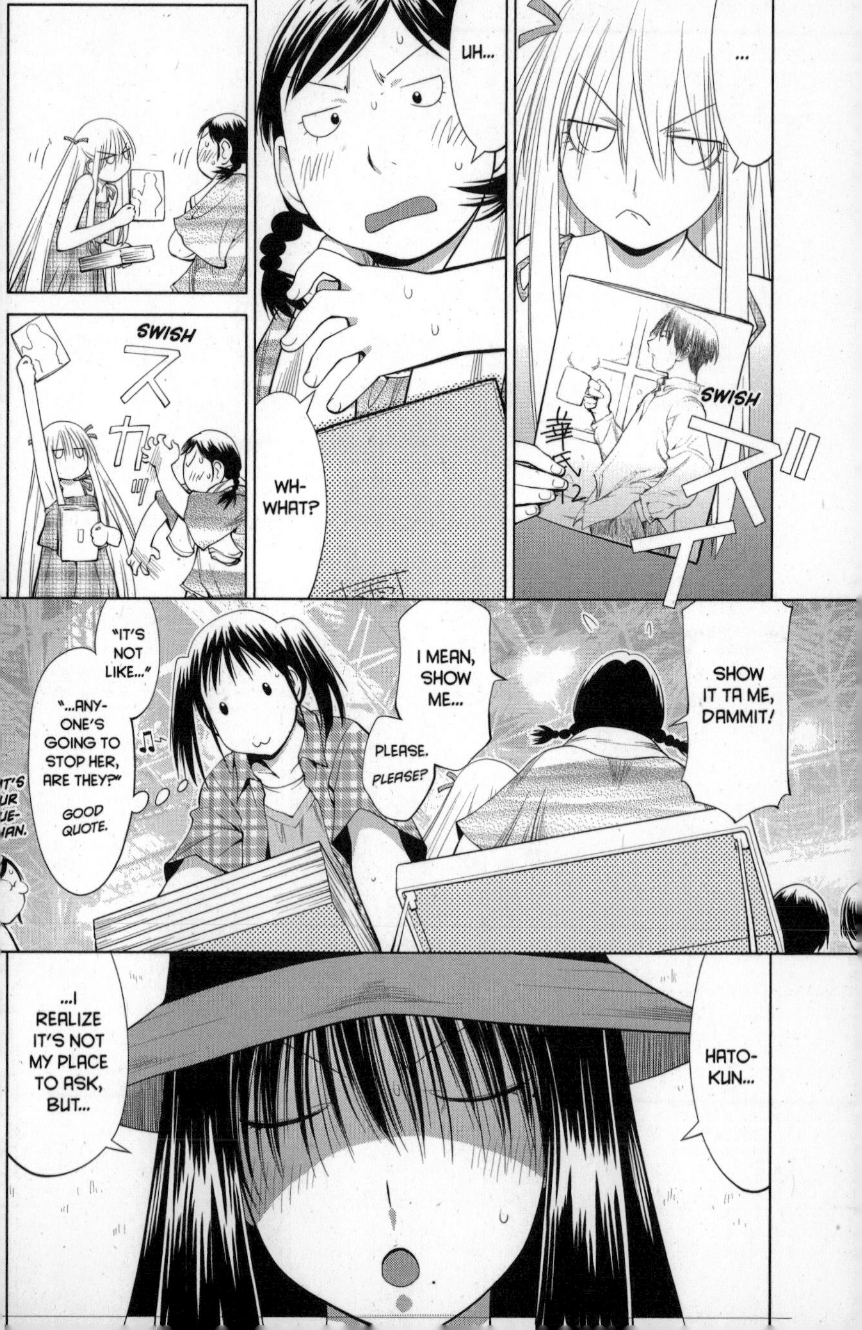
...
SWISH
UH...
WH- WHAT?
SWISH
スカッ
SHOW IT TA ME, DAMMIT!
I MEAN, SHOW ME...
PLEASE.
PLEASE?
"IT'S NOT LIKE..."
"...ANY-ONE'S GOING TO STOP HER, ARE THEY?"
GOOD QUOTE.
HATO-KUN...
...I REALIZE IT'S NOT MY PLACE TO ASK, BUT...

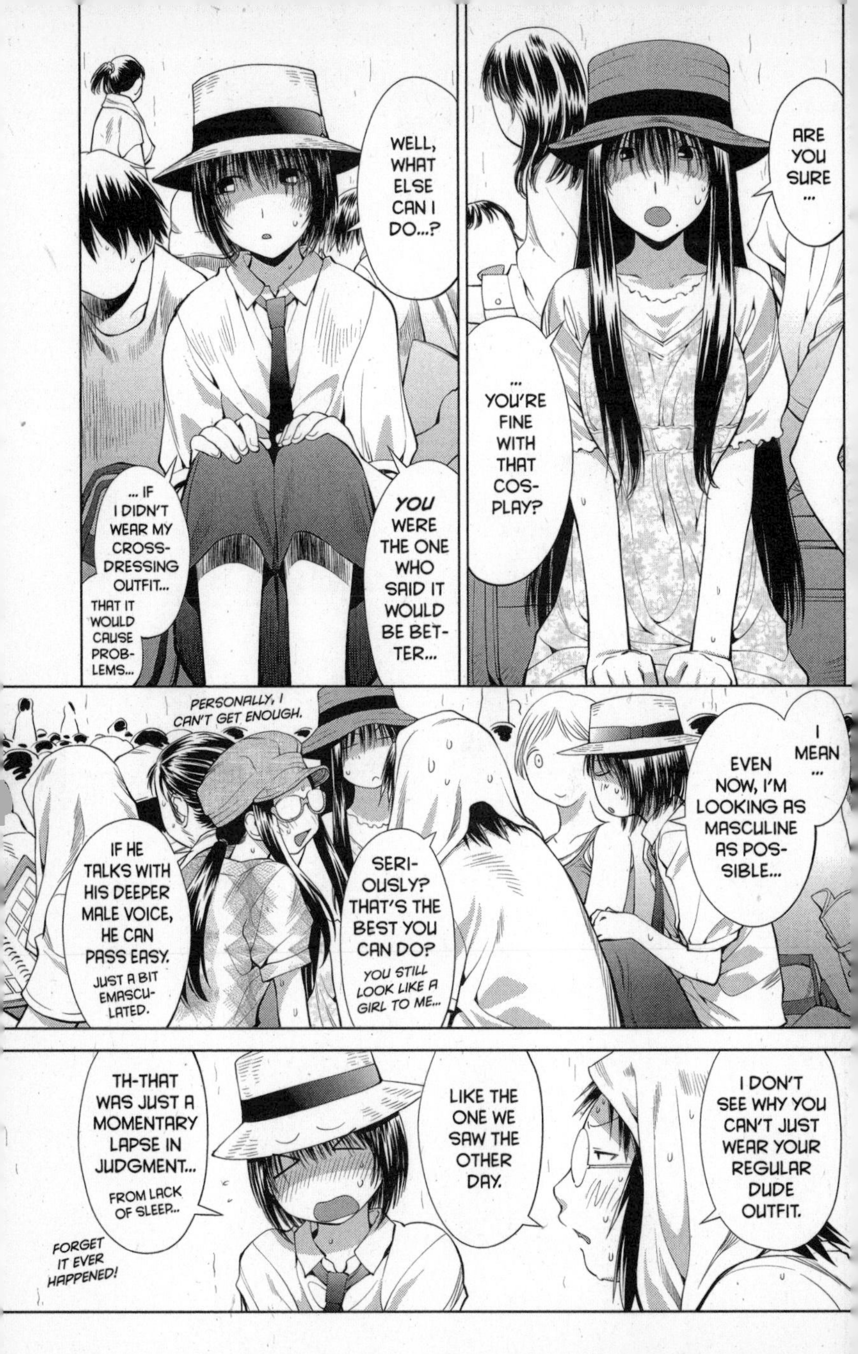
ARE YOU SURE ...
... YOU'RE FINE WITH THAT COS-PLAY?
WELL, WHAT ELSE CAN I DO...?
YOU WERE THE ONE WHO SAID IT WOULD BE BET-TER...
... IF I DIDN'T WEAR MY CROSS-DRESSING OUTFIT...
THAT IT WOULD CAUSE PROB-LEMS...
I MEAN ...
EVEN NOW, I'M LOOKING AS MASCULINE AS POS-SIBLE...
PERSONALLY, I CAN'T GET ENOUGH.
SERI-OUSLY? THAT'S THE BEST YOU CAN DO?
YOU STILL LOOK LIKE A GIRL TO ME...
IF HE TALKS WITH HIS DEEPER MALE VOICE, HE CAN PASS EASY.
JUST A BIT EMASCU-LATED.
I DON'T SEE WHY YOU CAN'T JUST WEAR YOUR REGULAR DUDE OUTFIT.
LIKE THE ONE WE SAW THE OTHER DAY.
TH-THAT WAS JUST A MOMENTARY LAPSE IN JUDGMENT...
FROM LACK OF SLEEP...
FORGET IT EVER HAPPENED!

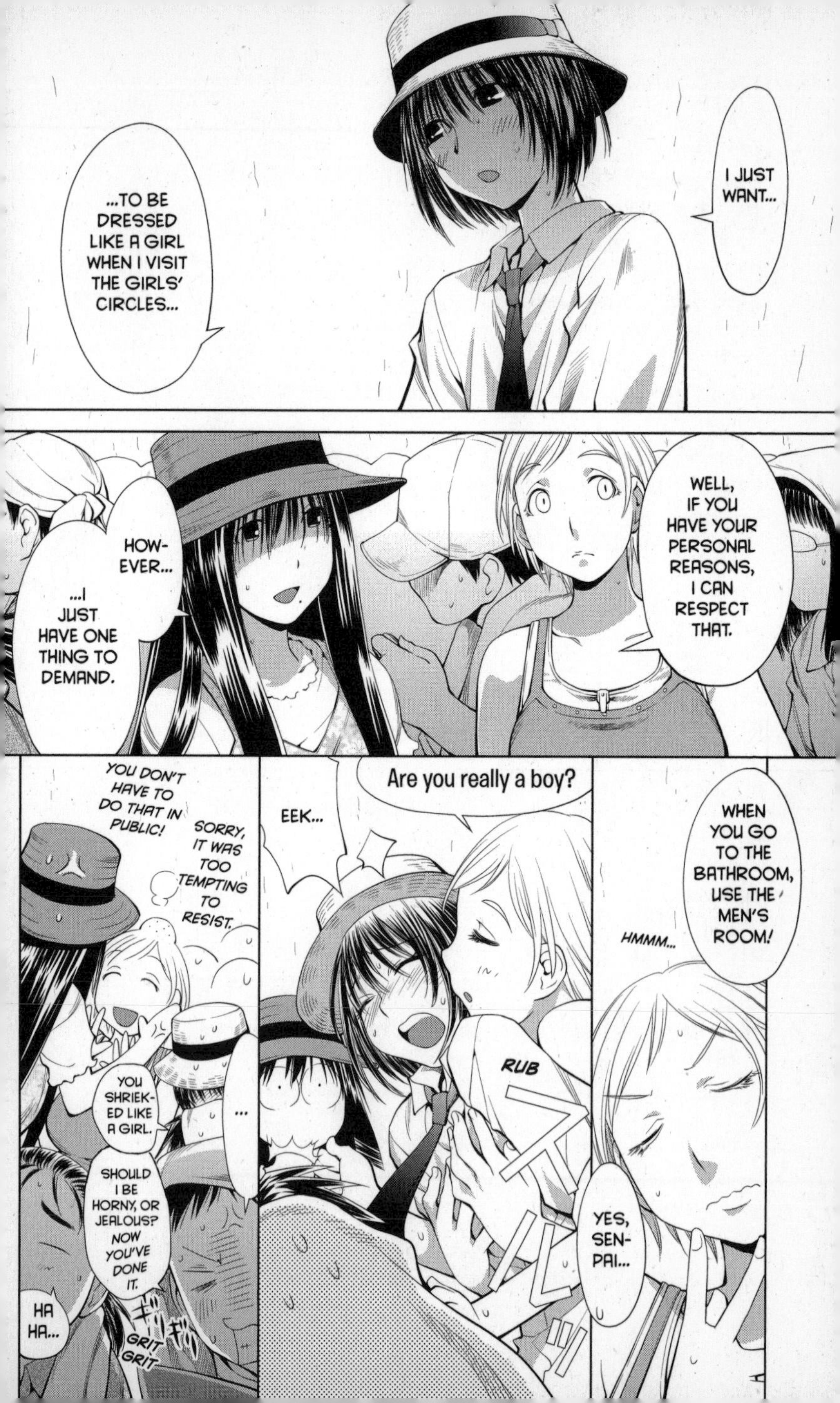
I JUST WANT...
...TO BE DRESSED LIKE A GIRL WHEN I VISIT THE GIRLS' CIRCLES...
WELL, IF YOU HAVE YOUR PERSONAL REASONS, I CAN RESPECT THAT.
HOW-EVER...
...I JUST HAVE ONE THING TO DEMAND.
WHEN YOU GO TO THE BATHROOM, USE THE MEN'S ROOM!
HMMM...
YES, SEN-PAI...
Are you really a boy?
EEK...
RUB
YOU DON'T HAVE TO DO THAT IN PUBLIC!
SORRY, IT WAS TOO TEMPTING TO RESIST.
YOU SHRIEKED LIKE A GIRL.
...
SHOULD I BE HORNY, OR JEALOUS? NOW YOU'VE DONE IT.
HA HA...
GRIT GRIT

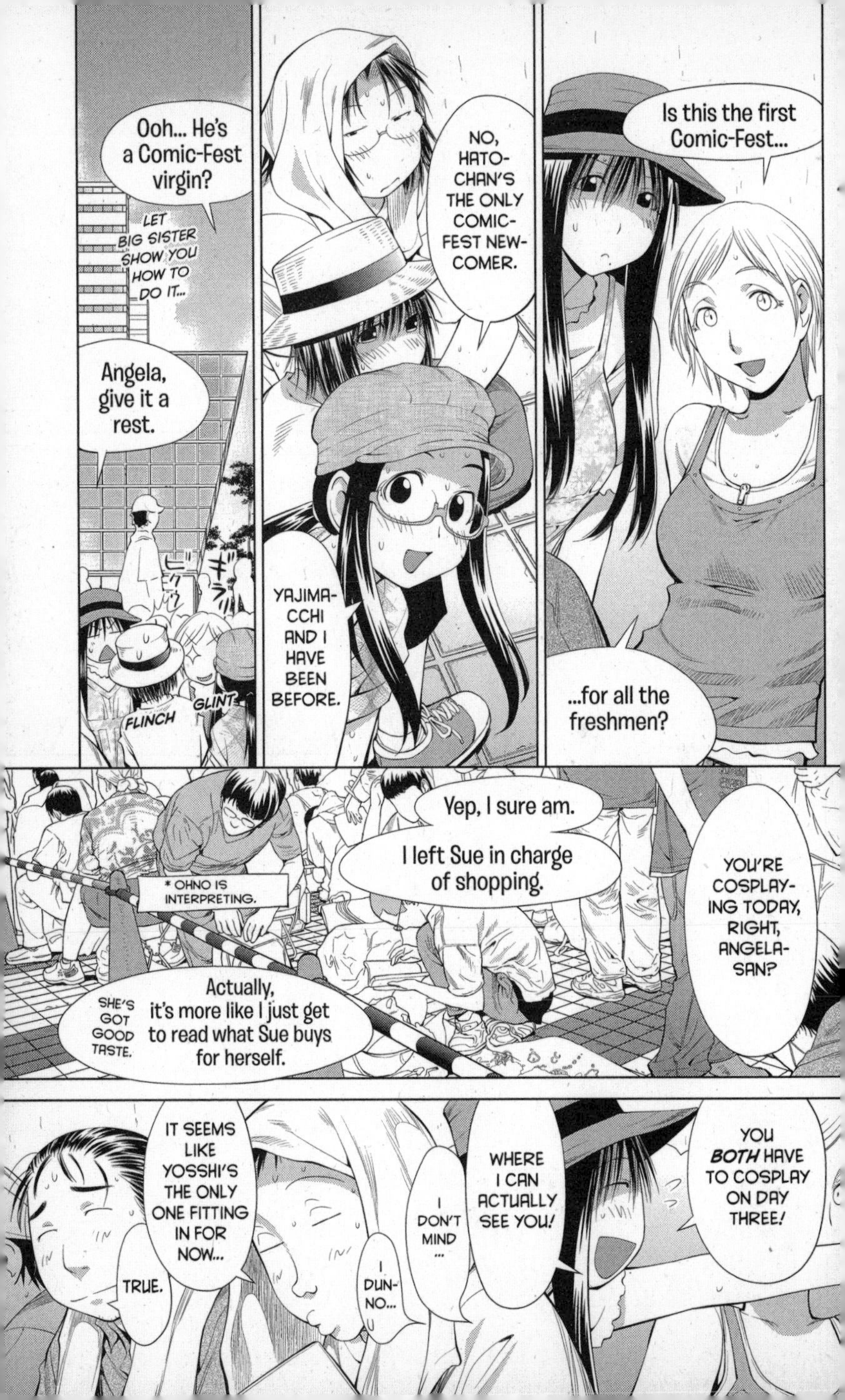

Is this the first Comic-Fest...
...for all the freshmen?
NO, HATO-CHAN'S THE ONLY COMIC-FEST NEWCOMER.
YAJIMACCHI AND I HAVE BEEN BEFORE.
Ooh... He's a Comic-Fest virgin?
LET BIG SISTER SHOW YOU HOW TO DO IT...
Angela, give it a rest.
GLINT
FLINCH
YOU'RE COSPLAYING TODAY, RIGHT, ANGELA-SAN?
Yep, I sure am.
I left Sue in charge of shopping.
* OHNO IS INTERPRETING.
Actually, it's more like I just get to read what Sue buys for herself.
SHE'S GOT GOOD TASTE.
YOU *BOTH* HAVE TO COSPLAY ON DAY THREE!
WHERE I CAN ACTUALLY SEE YOU!
I DON'T MIND...
I DUNNO...
IT SEEMS LIKE YOSSHI'S THE ONLY ONE FITTING IN FOR NOW...
TRUE.

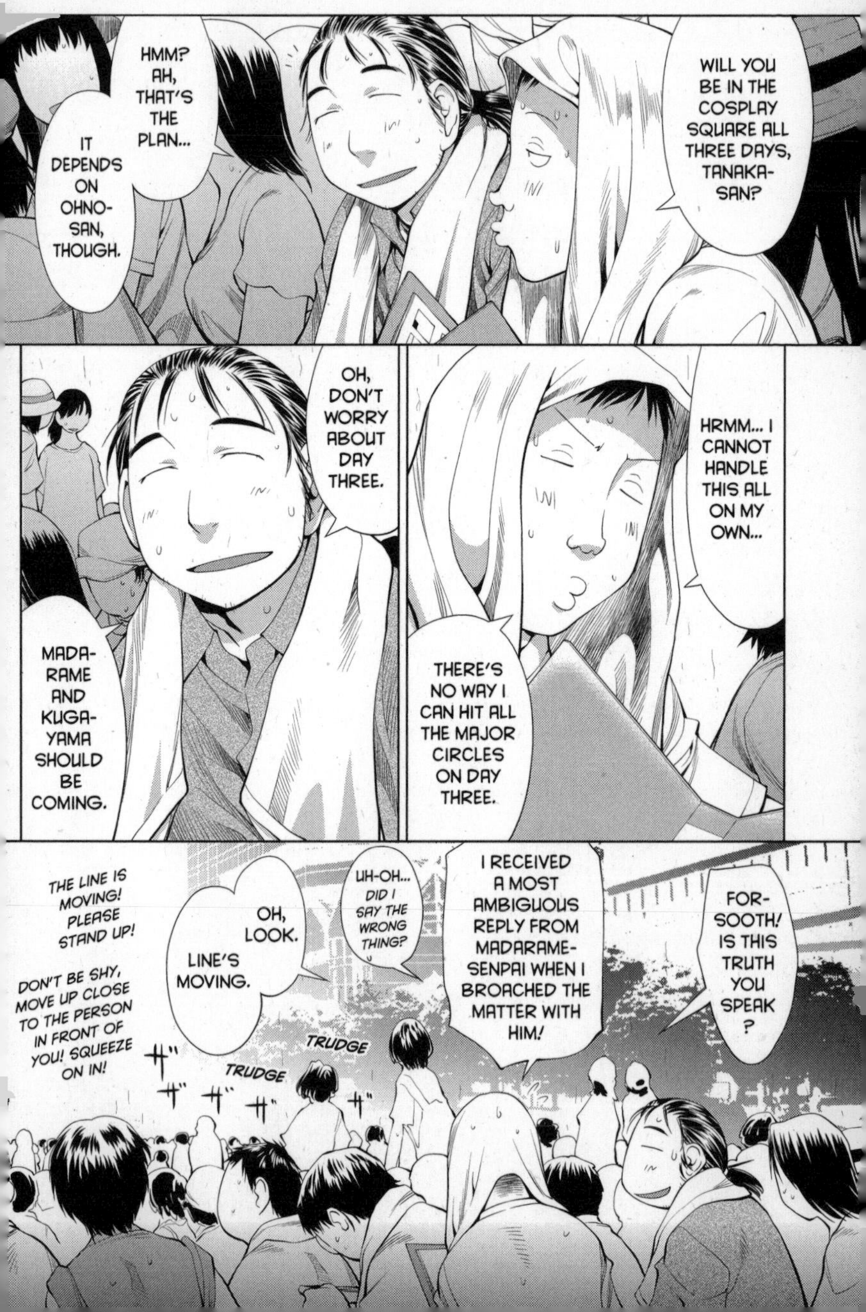
WILL YOU BE IN THE COSPLAY SQUARE ALL THREE DAYS, TANAKA-SAN?
HMM? AH, THAT'S THE PLAN...
IT DEPENDS ON OHNO-SAN, THOUGH.
HRMM... I CANNOT HANDLE THIS ALL ON MY OWN...
THERE'S NO WAY I CAN HIT ALL THE MAJOR CIRCLES ON DAY THREE.
OH, DON'T WORRY ABOUT DAY THREE.
MADARAME AND KUGAYAMA SHOULD BE COMING.
FORSOOTH! IS THIS TRUTH YOU SPEAK?
I RECEIVED A MOST AMBIGUOUS REPLY FROM MADARAME-SENPAI WHEN I BROACHED THE MATTER WITH HIM!
UH-OH... DID I SAY THE WRONG THING?
OH, LOOK. LINE'S MOVING.
TRUDGE
TRUDGE
THE LINE IS MOVING! PLEASE STAND UP!
DON'T BE SHY, MOVE UP CLOSE TO THE PERSON IN FRONT OF YOU! SQUEEZE ON IN!

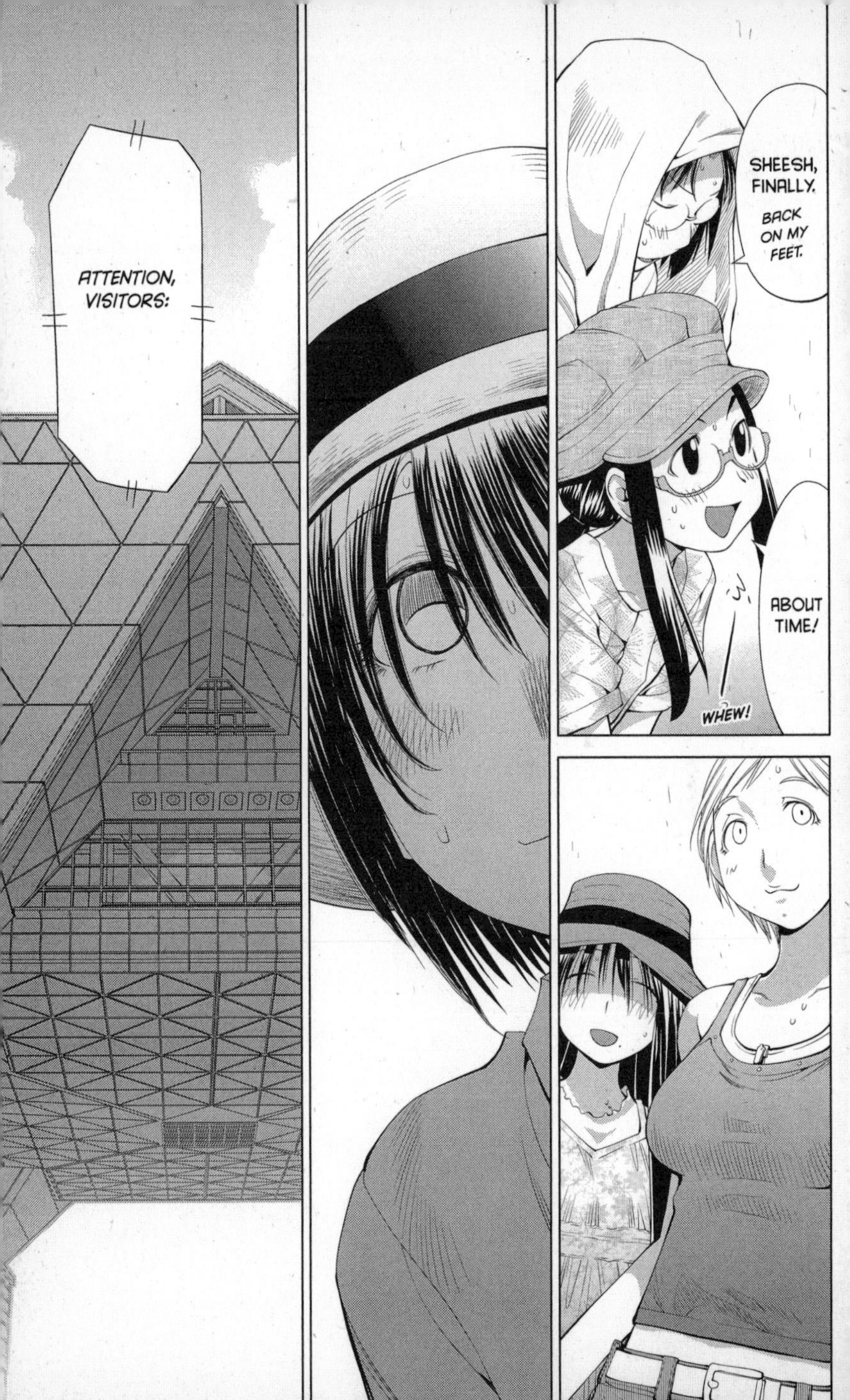
SHEESH, FINALLY.
BACK ON MY FEET.
ABOUT TIME!
WHEW!
ATTENTION, VISITORS:

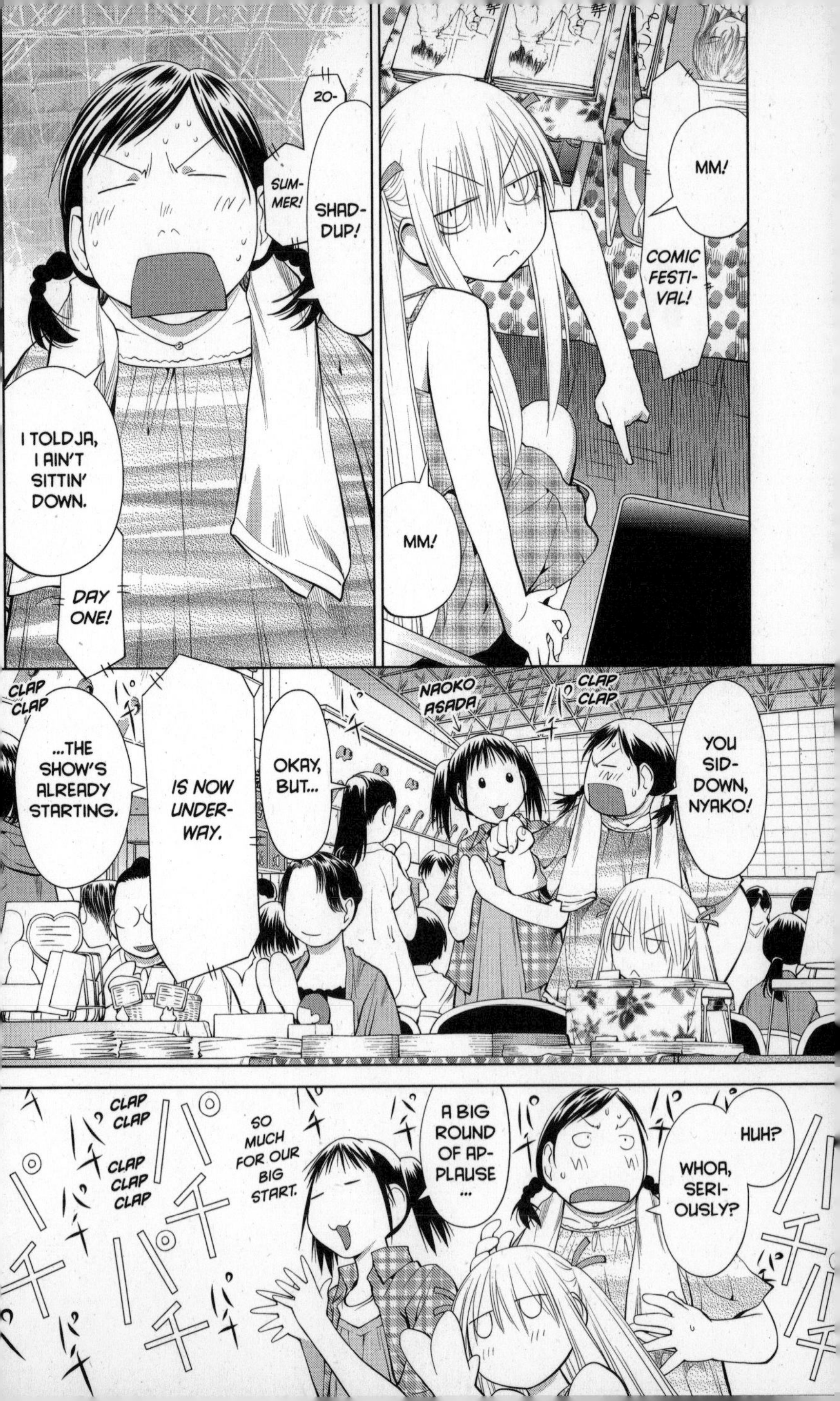
MM!
COMIC FESTIVAL!
MM!
SHADDUP!
ZO- SUMMER!
I TOLDJA, I AIN'T SITTIN' DOWN.
DAY ONE!
CLAP CLAP
NAOKO ASADA
YOU SIDDOWN, NYAKO!
OKAY, BUT...
IS NOW UNDERWAY.
...THE SHOW'S ALREADY STARTING.
CLAP CLAP
HUH?
WHOA, SERIOUSLY?
A BIG ROUND OF APPLAUSE...
SO MUCH FOR OUR BIG START.
CLAP CLAP
CLAP CLAP CLAP

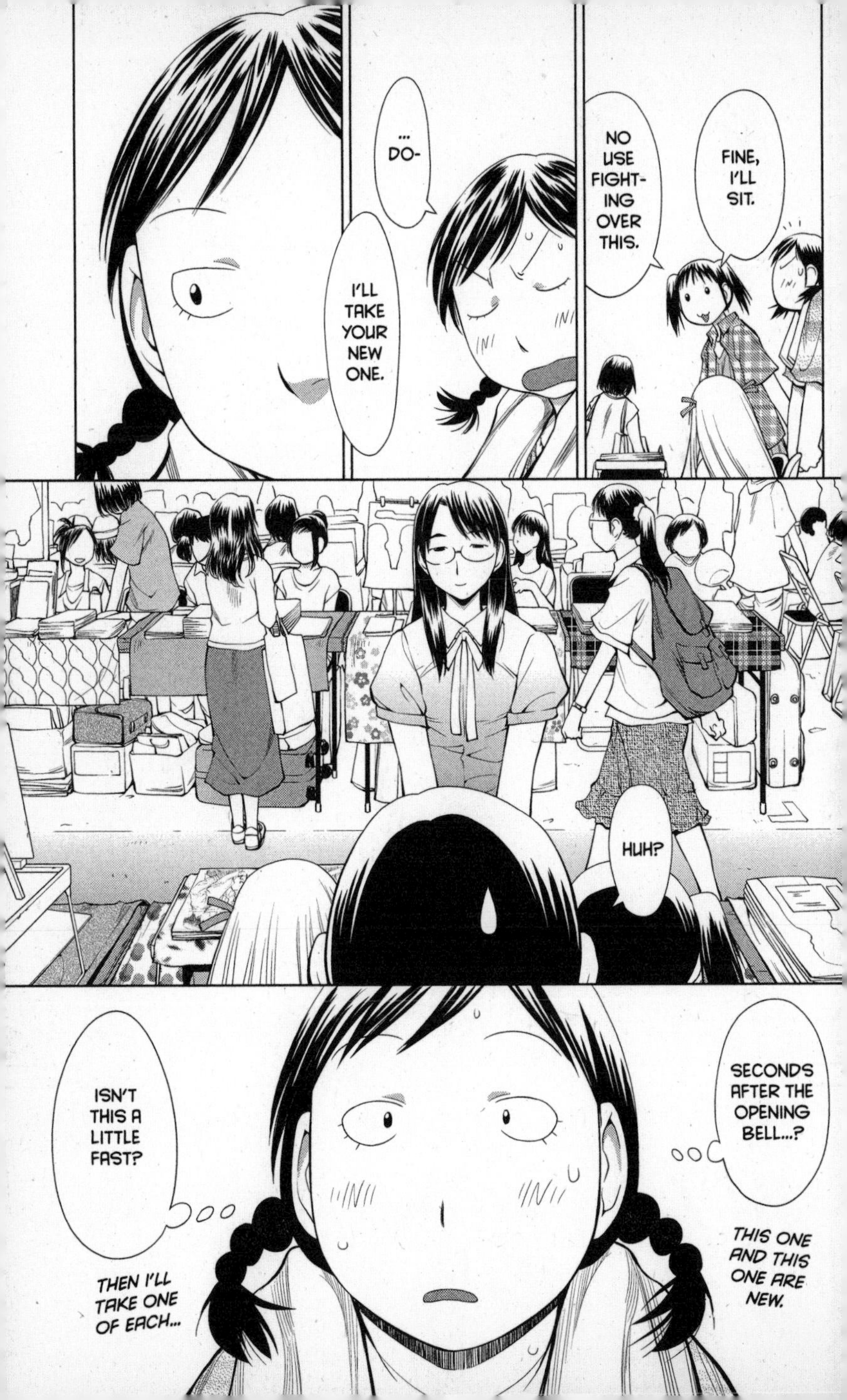
FINE, I'LL SIT.
NO USE FIGHTING OVER THIS.
... DO-
I'LL TAKE YOUR NEW ONE.
HUH?
SECONDS AFTER THE OPENING BELL...?
THIS ONE AND THIS ONE ARE NEW.
ISN'T THIS A LITTLE FAST?
THEN I'LL TAKE ONE OF EACH...

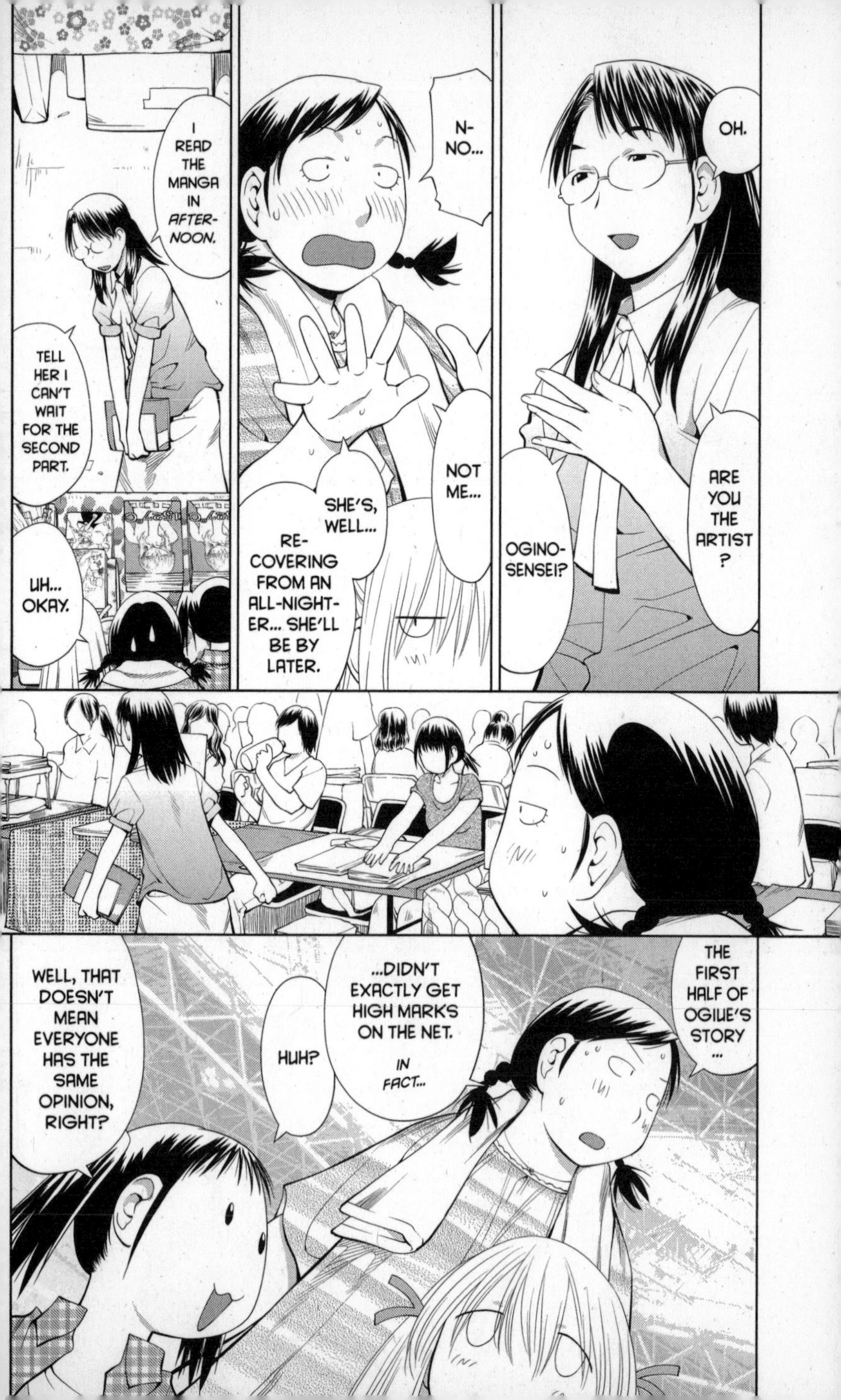
OH.
ARE YOU THE ARTIST?
OGINO-SENSEI?
N-NO...
NOT ME...
SHE'S, WELL...
RE-COVERING FROM AN ALL-NIGHTER... SHE'LL BE BY LATER.
I READ THE MANGA IN AFTERNOON.
TELL HER I CAN'T WAIT FOR THE SECOND PART.
UH... OKAY.
THE FIRST HALF OF OGIUE'S STORY...
...DIDN'T EXACTLY GET HIGH MARKS ON THE NET.
IN FACT...
HUH?
WELL, THAT DOESN'T MEAN EVERYONE HAS THE SAME OPINION, RIGHT?

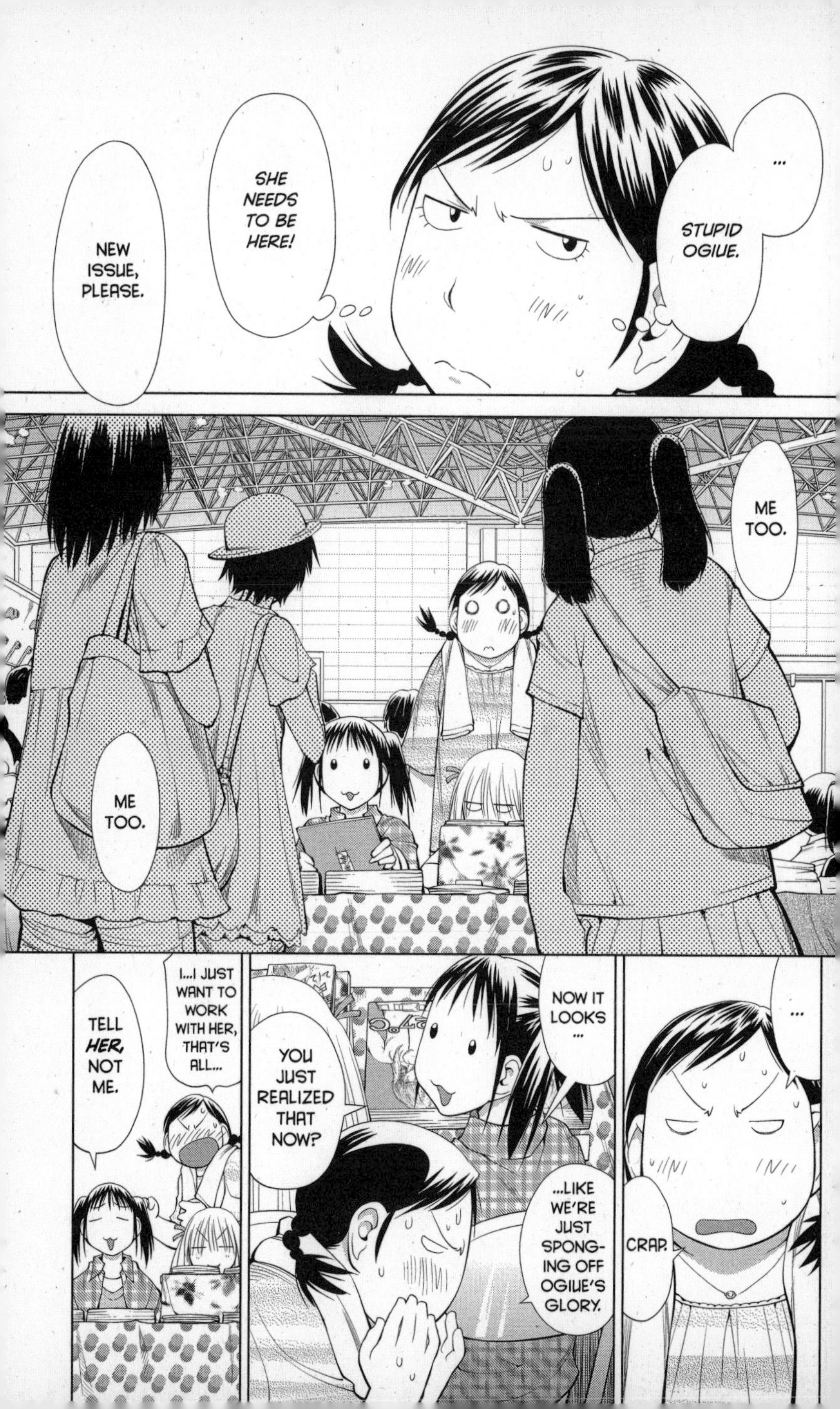
...
STUPID OGIUE.
SHE NEEDS TO BE HERE!
NEW ISSUE, PLEASE.
ME TOO.
ME TOO.
...
CRAP.
NOW IT LOOKS ...
...LIKE WE'RE JUST SPONG-ING OFF OGIUE'S GLORY.
YOU JUST REALIZED THAT NOW?
I...I JUST WANT TO WORK WITH HER, THAT'S ALL...
TELL *HER,* NOT ME.

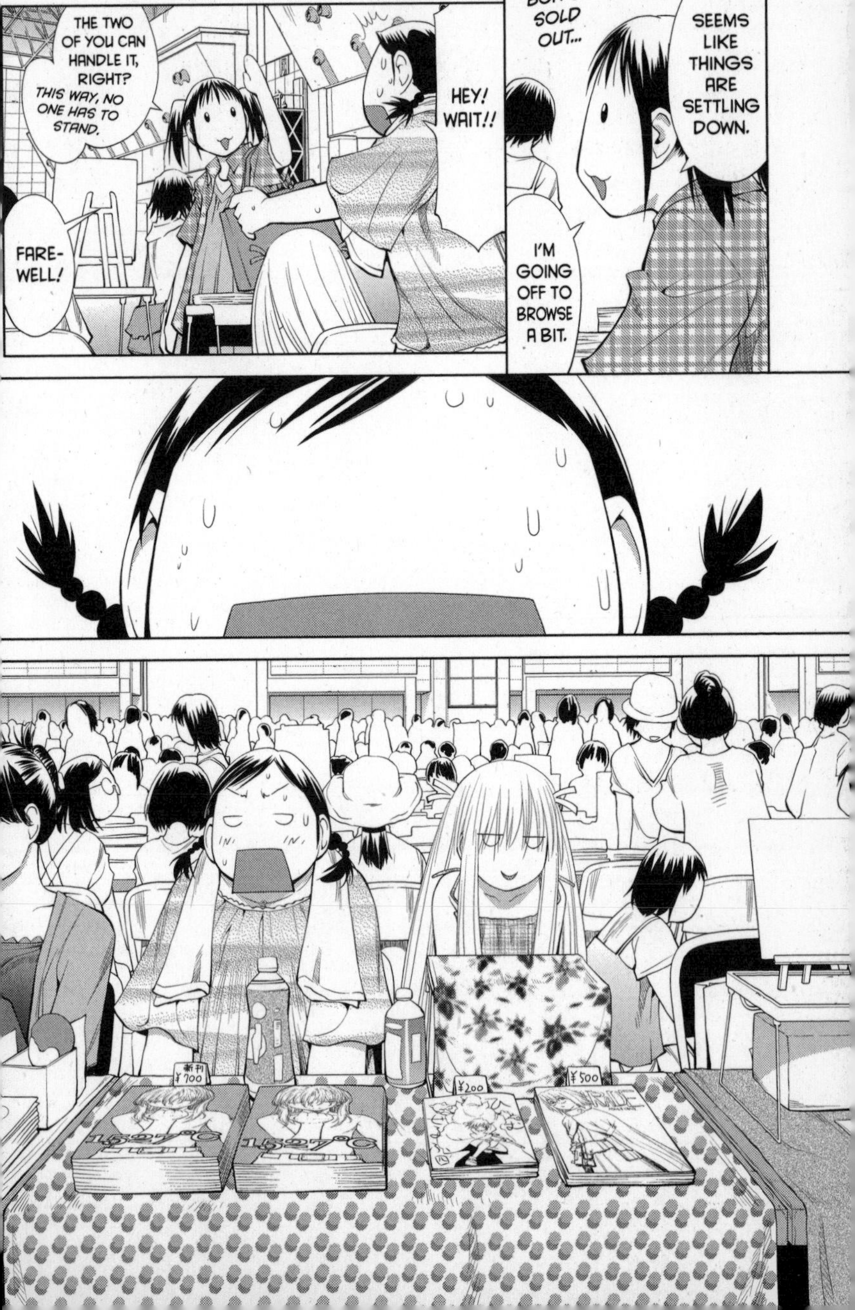

SEEMS LIKE THINGS ARE SETTLING DOWN.
COPY-BON'S SOLD OUT...
I'M GOING OFF TO BROWSE A BIT.
HEY! WAIT!!
THE TWO OF YOU CAN HANDLE IT, RIGHT?
THIS WAY, NO ONE HAS TO STAND.
FARE-WELL!
¥500
¥200
新刊 ¥700

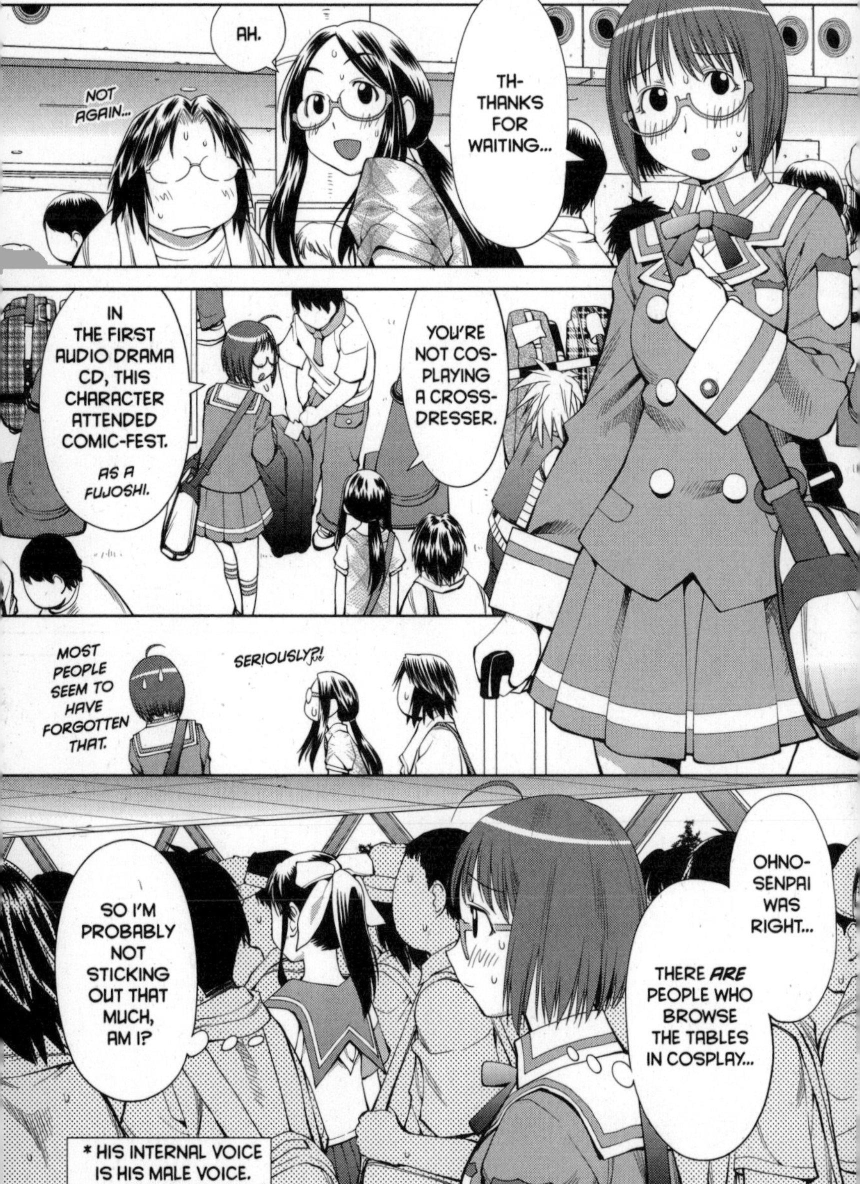
TH- THANKS FOR WAITING...
AH.
NOT AGAIN...
YOU'RE NOT COS-PLAYING A CROSS-DRESSER.
IN THE FIRST AUDIO DRAMA CD, THIS CHARACTER ATTENDED COMIC-FEST.
AS A FUJOSHI.
SERIOUSLY?!
MOST PEOPLE SEEM TO HAVE FORGOTTEN THAT.
OHNO-SENPAI WAS RIGHT...
THERE *ARE* PEOPLE WHO BROWSE THE TABLES IN COSPLAY...
SO I'M PROBABLY NOT STICKING OUT THAT MUCH, AM I?
* HIS INTERNAL VOICE IS HIS MALE VOICE.

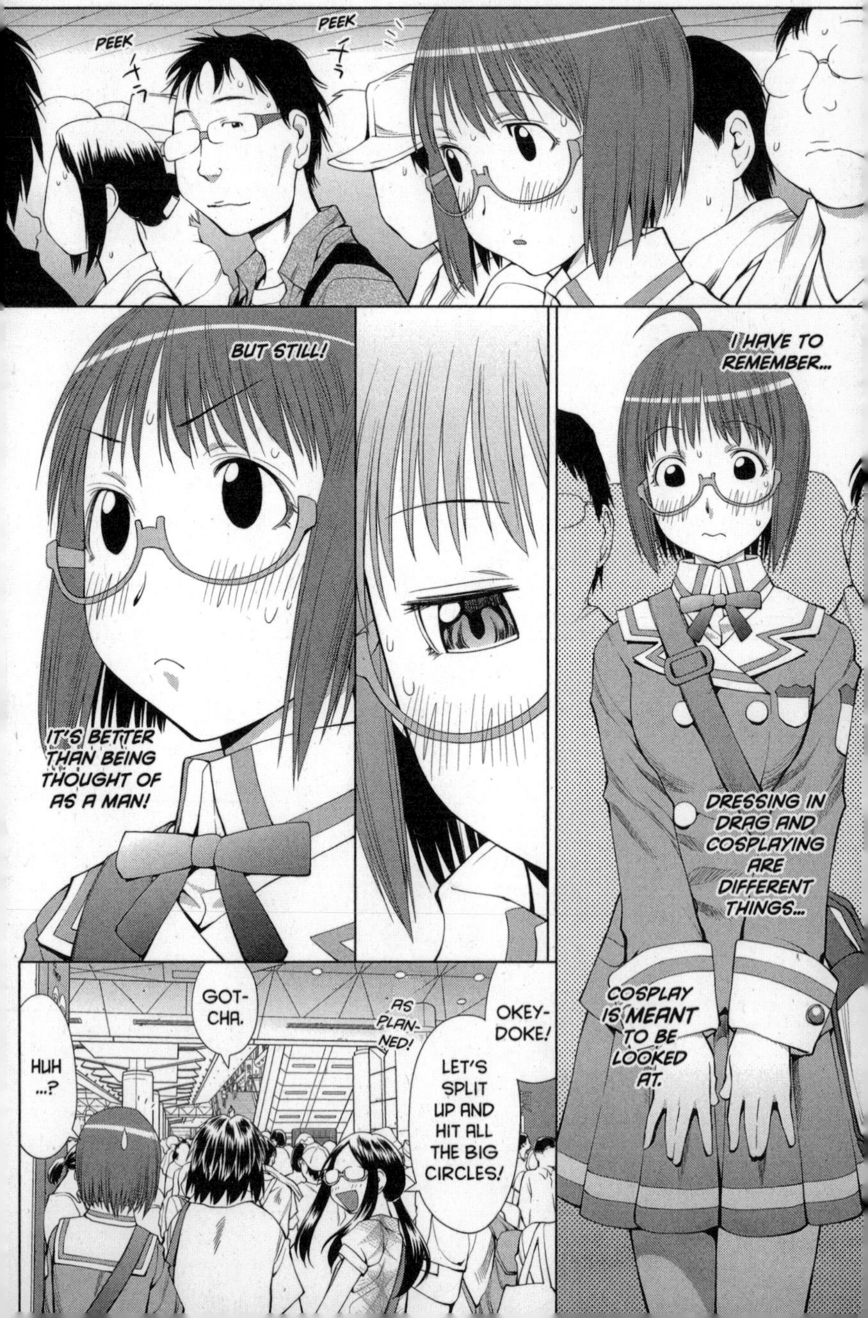
PEEK
PEEK
I HAVE TO REMEMBER...
DRESSING IN DRAG AND COSPLAYING ARE DIFFERENT THINGS...
COSPLAY IS MEANT TO BE LOOKED AT.
BUT STILL!
IT'S BETTER THAN BEING THOUGHT OF AS A MAN!
OKEY-DOKE!
LET'S SPLIT UP AND HIT ALL THE BIG CIRCLES!
AS PLANNED!
GOT-CHA.
HUH ...?

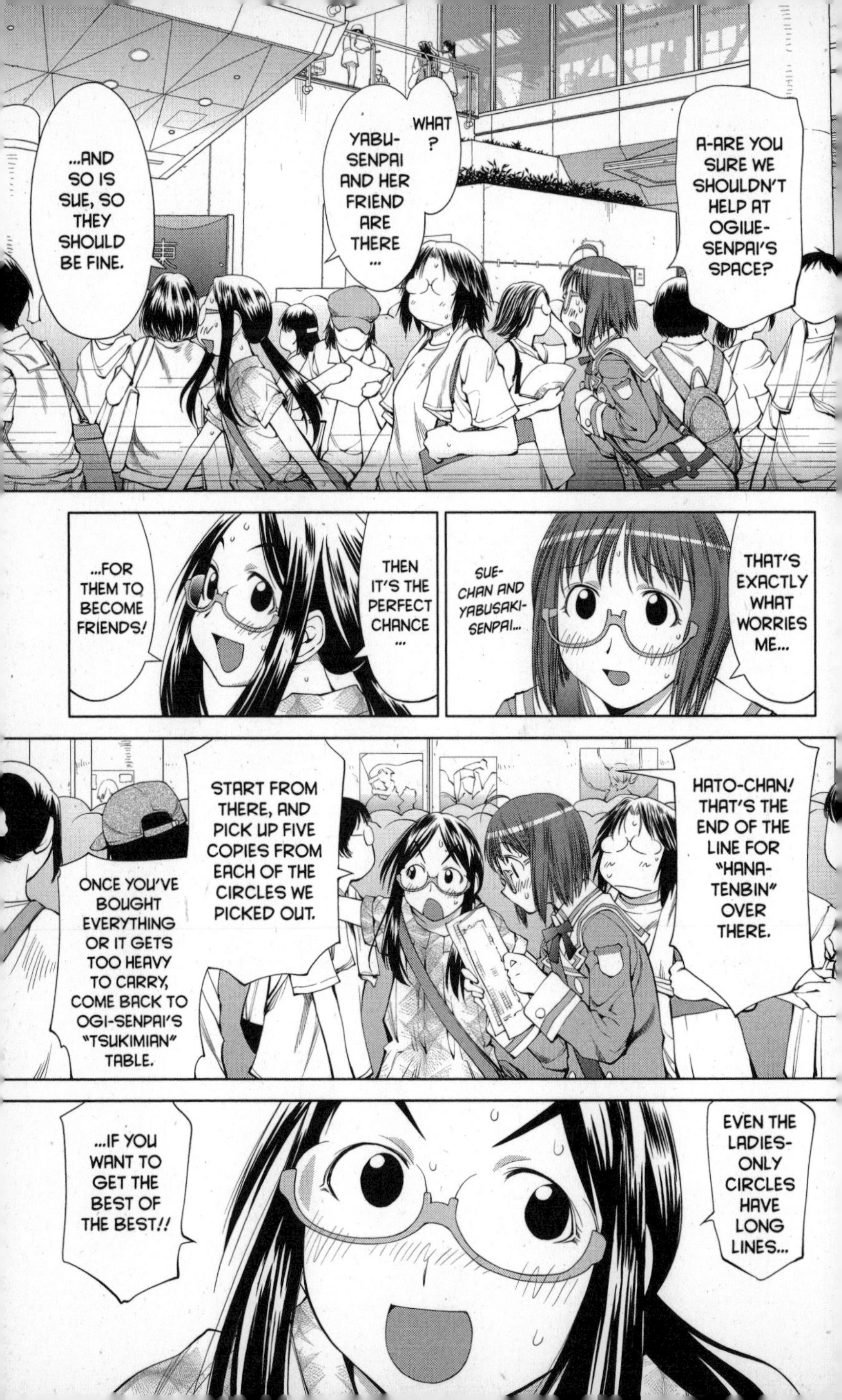
A-ARE YOU SURE WE SHOULDN'T HELP AT OGIUE-SENPAI'S SPACE?
WHAT?
YABU-SENPAI AND HER FRIEND ARE THERE...
...AND SO IS SUE, SO THEY SHOULD BE FINE.
THAT'S EXACTLY WHAT WORRIES ME...
SUE-CHAN AND YABUSAKI-SENPAI...
THEN IT'S THE PERFECT CHANCE...
...FOR THEM TO BECOME FRIENDS!
HATO-CHAN! THAT'S THE END OF THE LINE FOR "HANA-TENBIN" OVER THERE.
START FROM THERE, AND PICK UP FIVE COPIES FROM EACH OF THE CIRCLES WE PICKED OUT.
ONCE YOU'VE BOUGHT EVERYTHING OR IT GETS TOO HEAVY TO CARRY, COME BACK TO OGI-SENPAI'S "TSUKIMIAN" TABLE.
EVEN THE LADIES-ONLY CIRCLES HAVE LONG LINES...
...IF YOU WANT TO GET THE BEST OF THE BEST!!

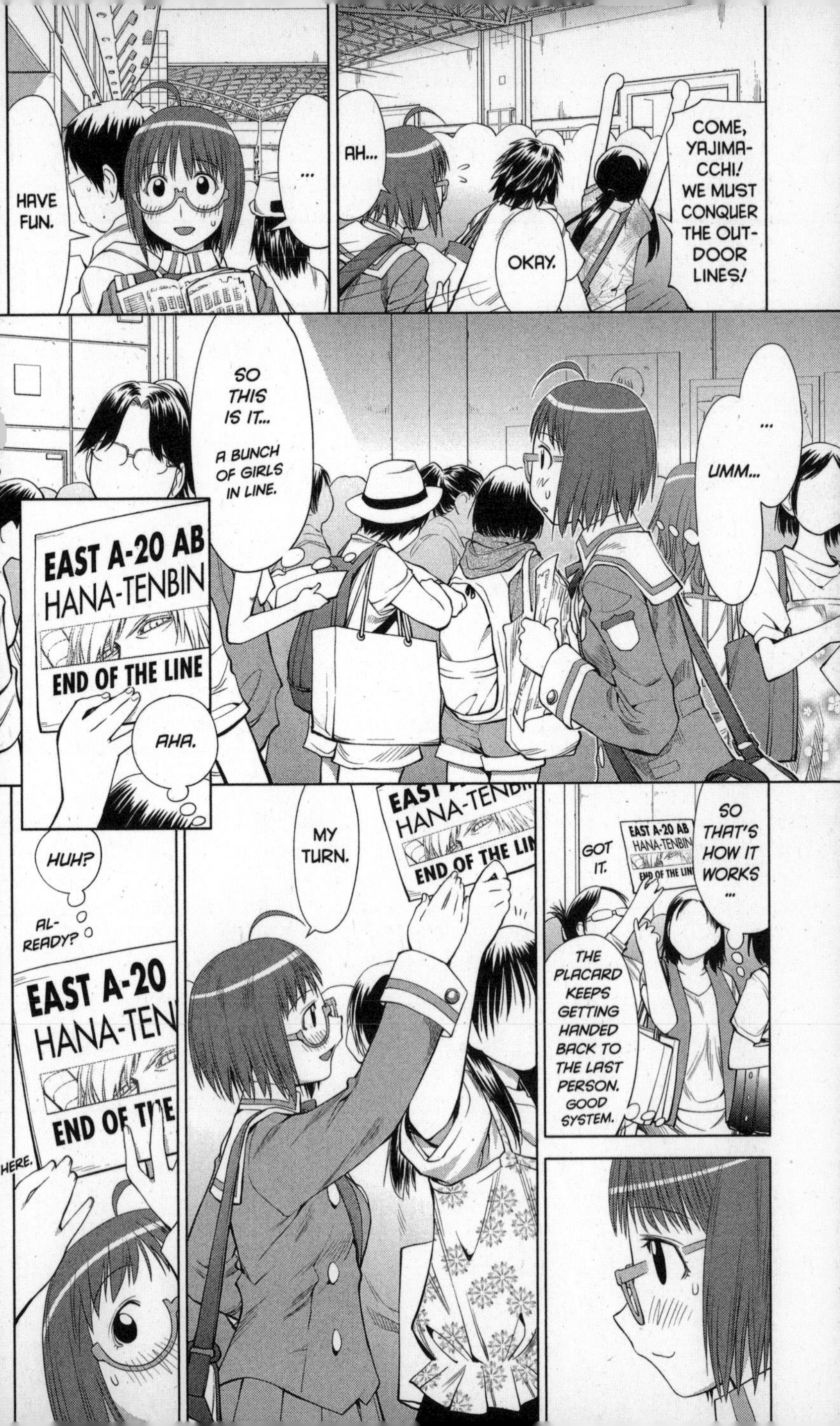
COME, YAJIMA-CCHI! WE MUST CONQUER THE OUT-DOOR LINES!
OKAY.
AH...
...
HAVE FUN.
...
UMM...
SO THIS IS IT...
A BUNCH OF GIRLS IN LINE.
EAST A-20 AB HANA-TENBIN END OF THE LINE
AHA.
SO THAT'S HOW IT WORKS ...
GOT IT.
EAST A-20 AB HANA-TENBIN END OF THE LIN
THE PLACARD KEEPS GETTING HANDED BACK TO THE LAST PERSON. GOOD SYSTEM.
MY TURN.
EAST A HANA-TENBI END OF THE LIN
HUH?
AL-READY?
EAST A-20 HANA-TEN END OF THE
HERE.

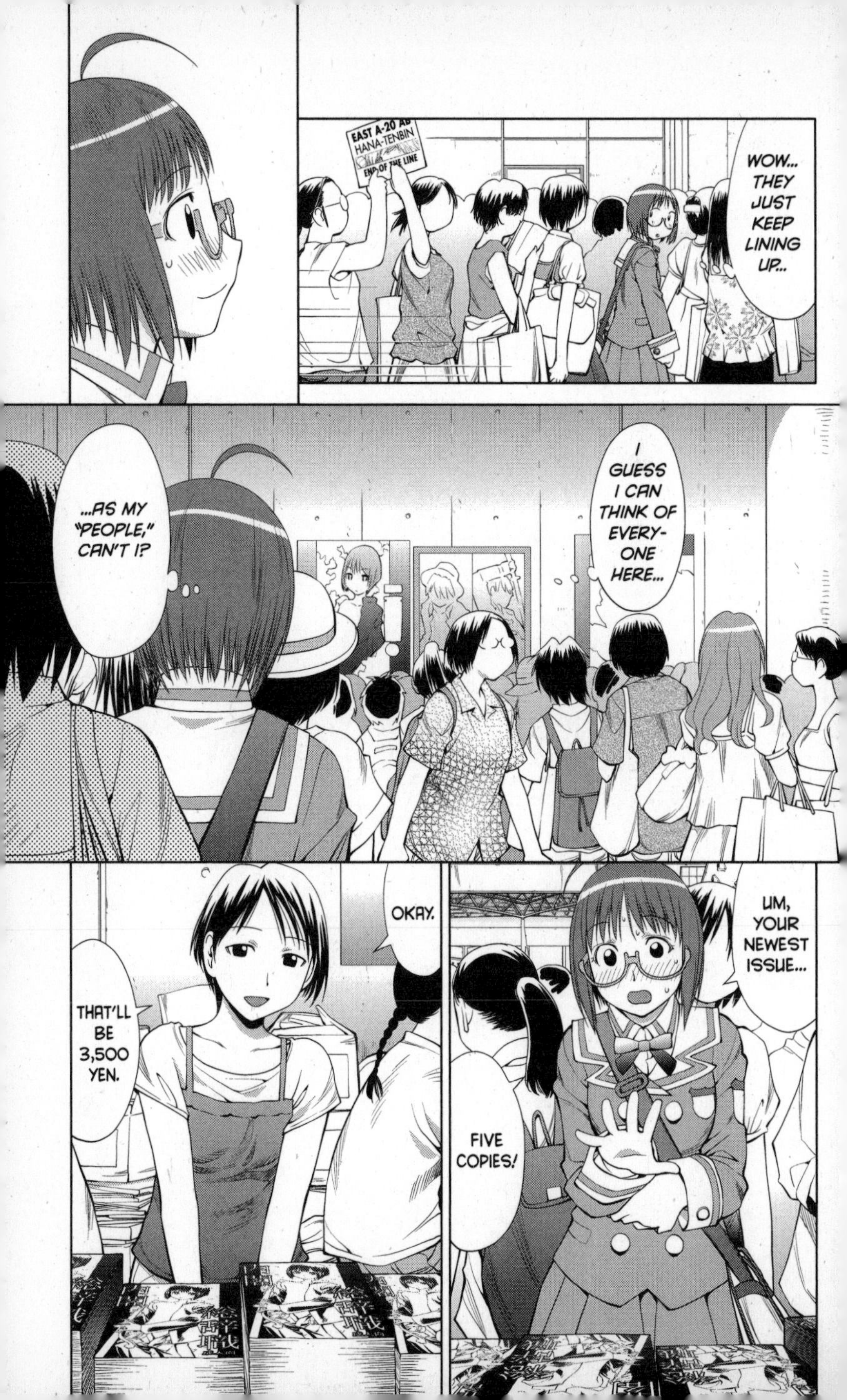
WOW... THEY JUST KEEP LINING UP...
EAST A-20 AB
HANA-TENBIN
END OF THE LINE
I GUESS I CAN THINK OF EVERY-ONE HERE...
...AS MY "PEOPLE," CAN'T I?
UM, YOUR NEWEST ISSUE...
FIVE COPIES!
OKAY.
THAT'LL BE 3,500 YEN.

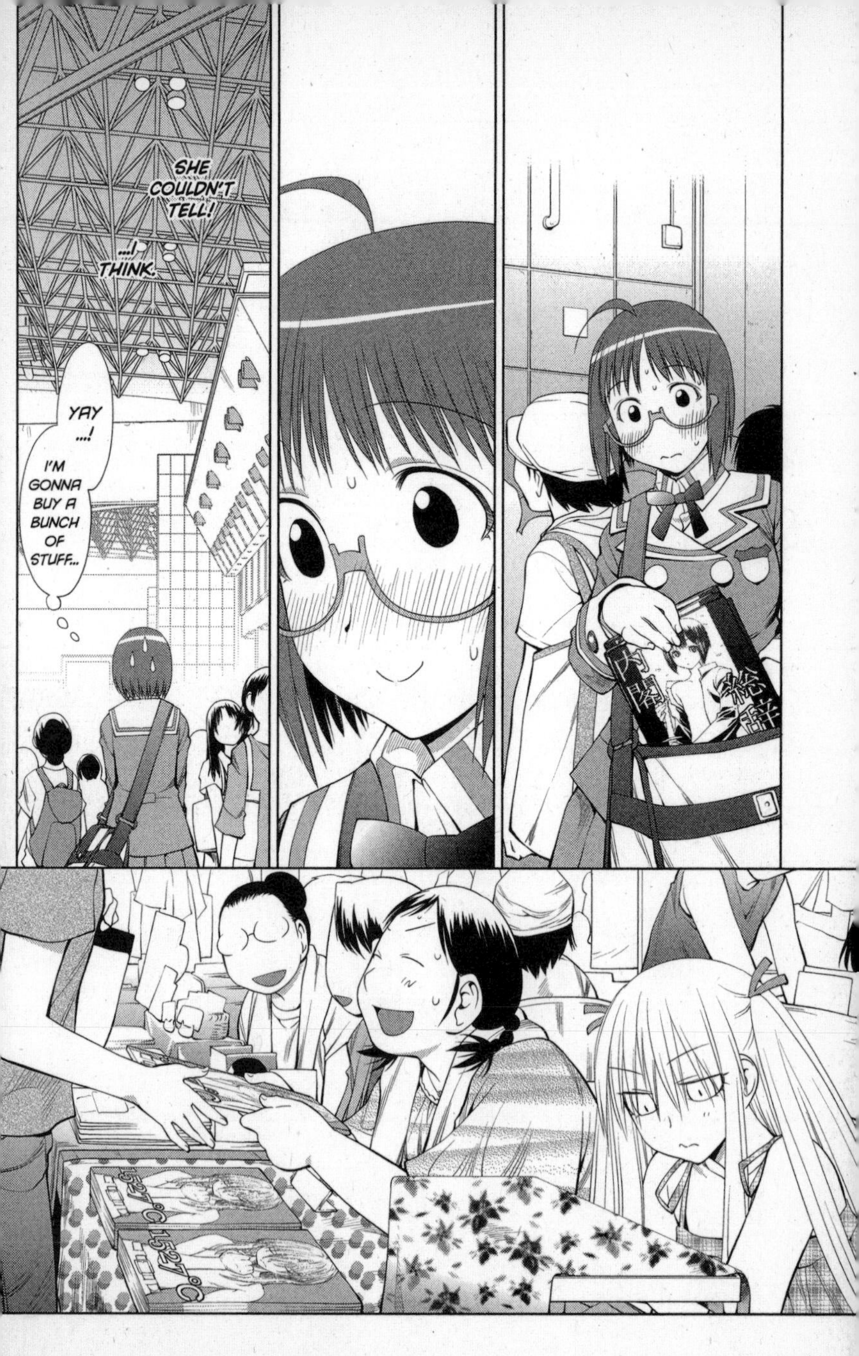
SHE COULDN'T TELL!
...I THINK.
YAY ...! I'M GONNA BUY A BUNCH OF STUFF...

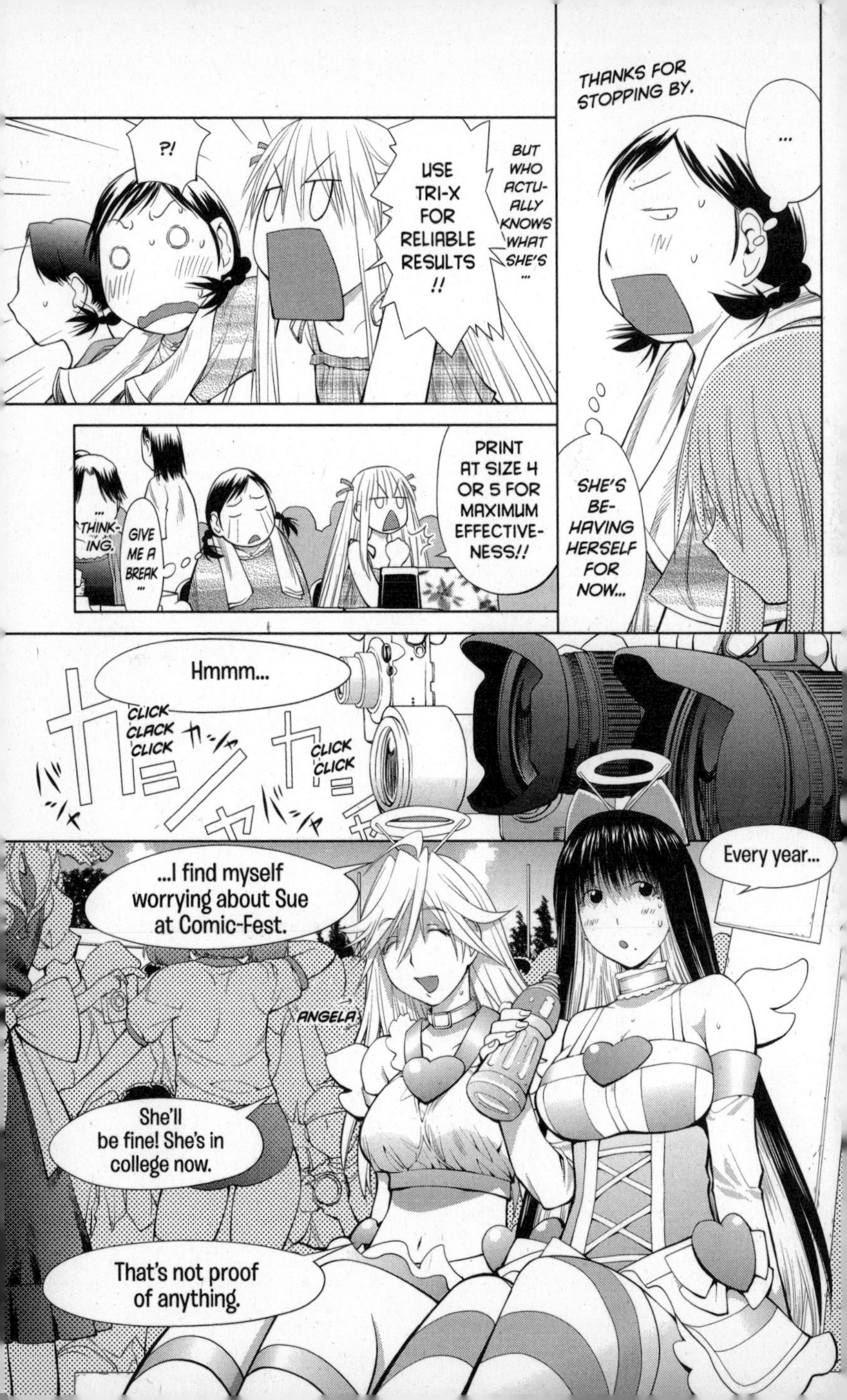
THANKS FOR STOPPING BY.
...
SHE'S BE-HAVING HERSELF FOR NOW...
BUT WHO ACTU-ALLY KNOWS WHAT SHE'S ...
USE TRI-X FOR RELIABLE RESULTS !!
?!
PRINT AT SIZE 4 OR 5 FOR MAXIMUM EFFECTIVE-NESS!!
GIVE ME A BREAK ...
... THINK-ING.
Hmmm...
CLICK CLICK
CLICK CLACK CLICK
Every year...
...I find myself worrying about Sue at Comic-Fest.
ANGELA
She'll be fine! She's in college now.
That's not proof of anything.

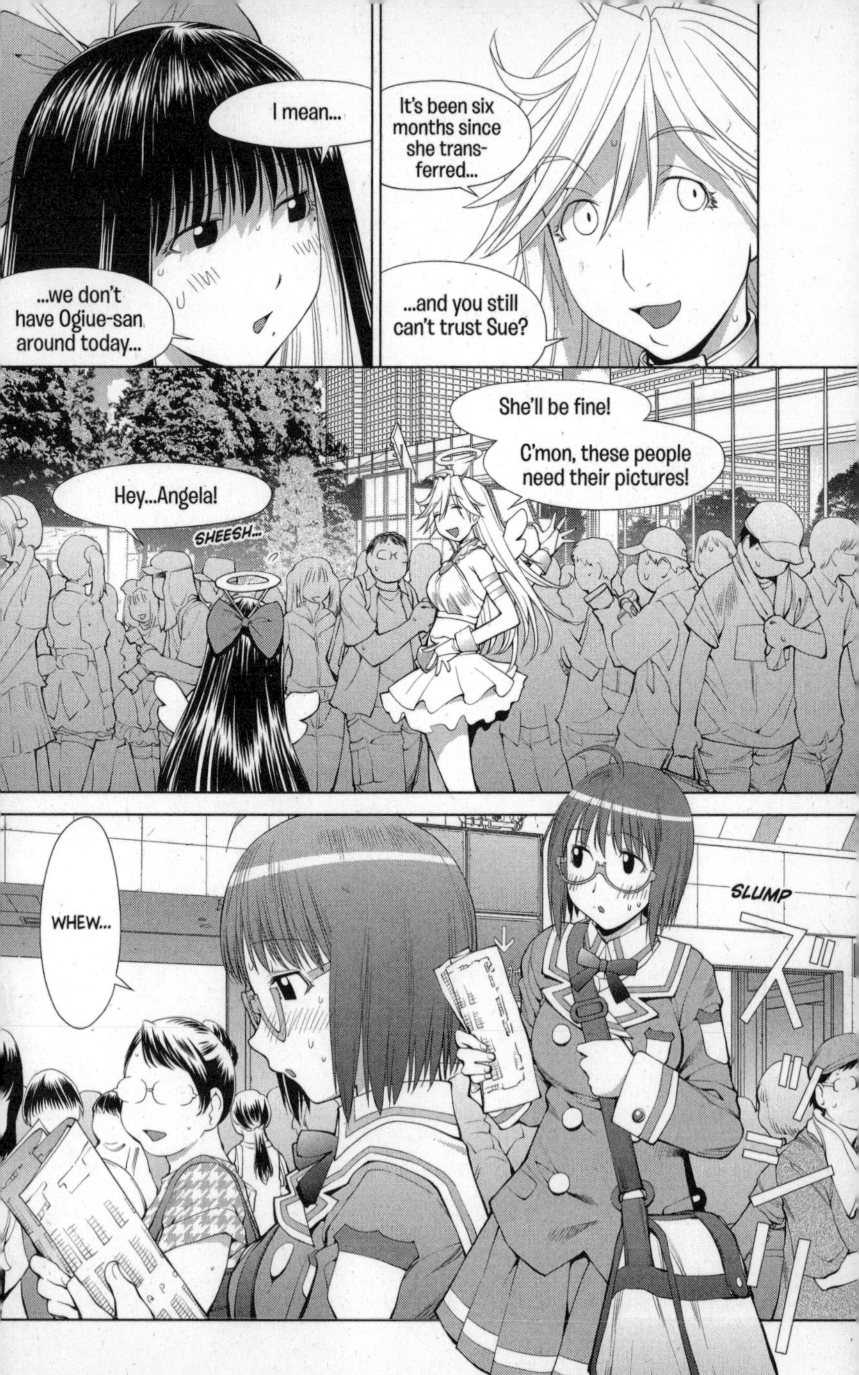
It's been six months since she trans-ferred...
...and you still can't trust Sue?
I mean...
...we don't have Ogiue-san around today...
She'll be fine!
C'mon, these people need their pictures!
Hey...Angela!
SHEESH...
SLUMP
WHEW...

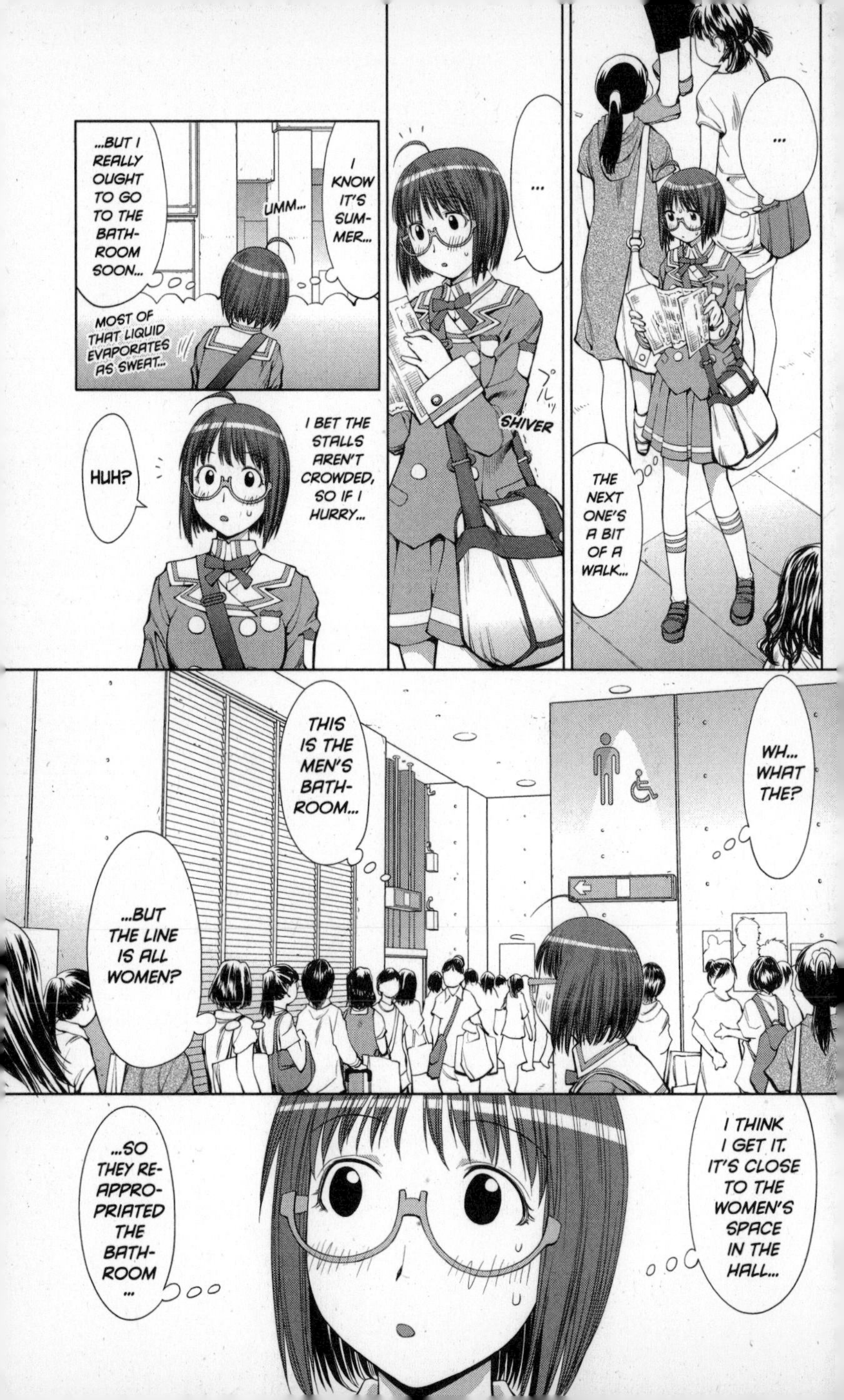
...
THE NEXT ONE'S A BIT OF A WALK...
...
プルッ
SHIVER
I KNOW IT'S SUMMER...
UMM...
...BUT I REALLY OUGHT TO GO TO THE BATHROOM SOON...
MOST OF THAT LIQUID EVAPORATES AS SWEAT...
I BET THE STALLS AREN'T CROWDED, SO IF I HURRY...
HUH?
WH... WHAT THE?
THIS IS THE MEN'S BATHROOM...
...BUT THE LINE IS ALL WOMEN?
I THINK I GET IT. IT'S CLOSE TO THE WOMEN'S SPACE IN THE HALL...
...SO THEY RE-APPROPRIATED THE BATHROOM...

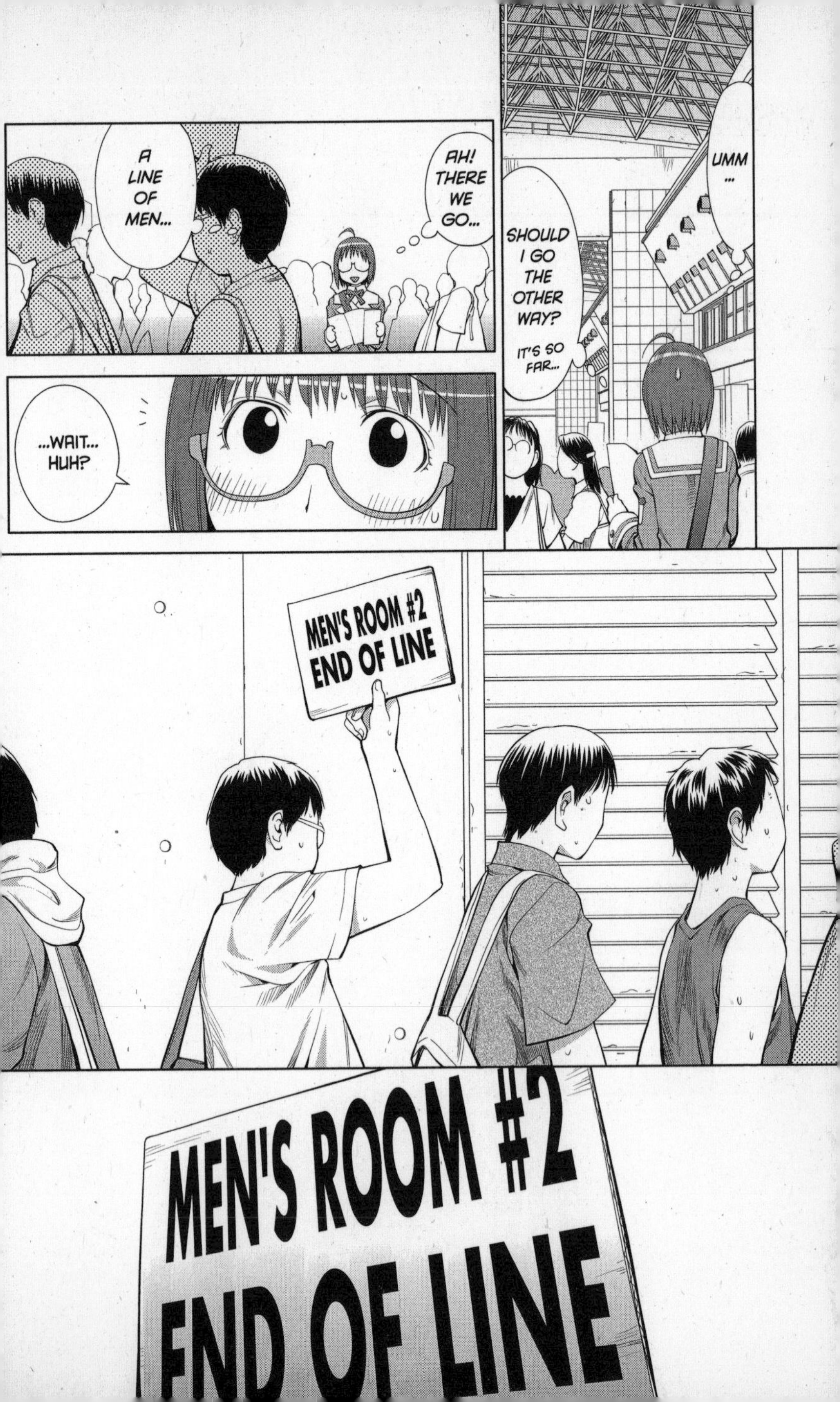
UMM ...
SHOULD I GO THE OTHER WAY?
IT'S SO FAR...
AH! THERE WE GO...
A LINE OF MEN...
...WAIT... HUH?
MEN'S ROOM #2 END OF LINE
MEN'S ROOM #2 END OF LINE

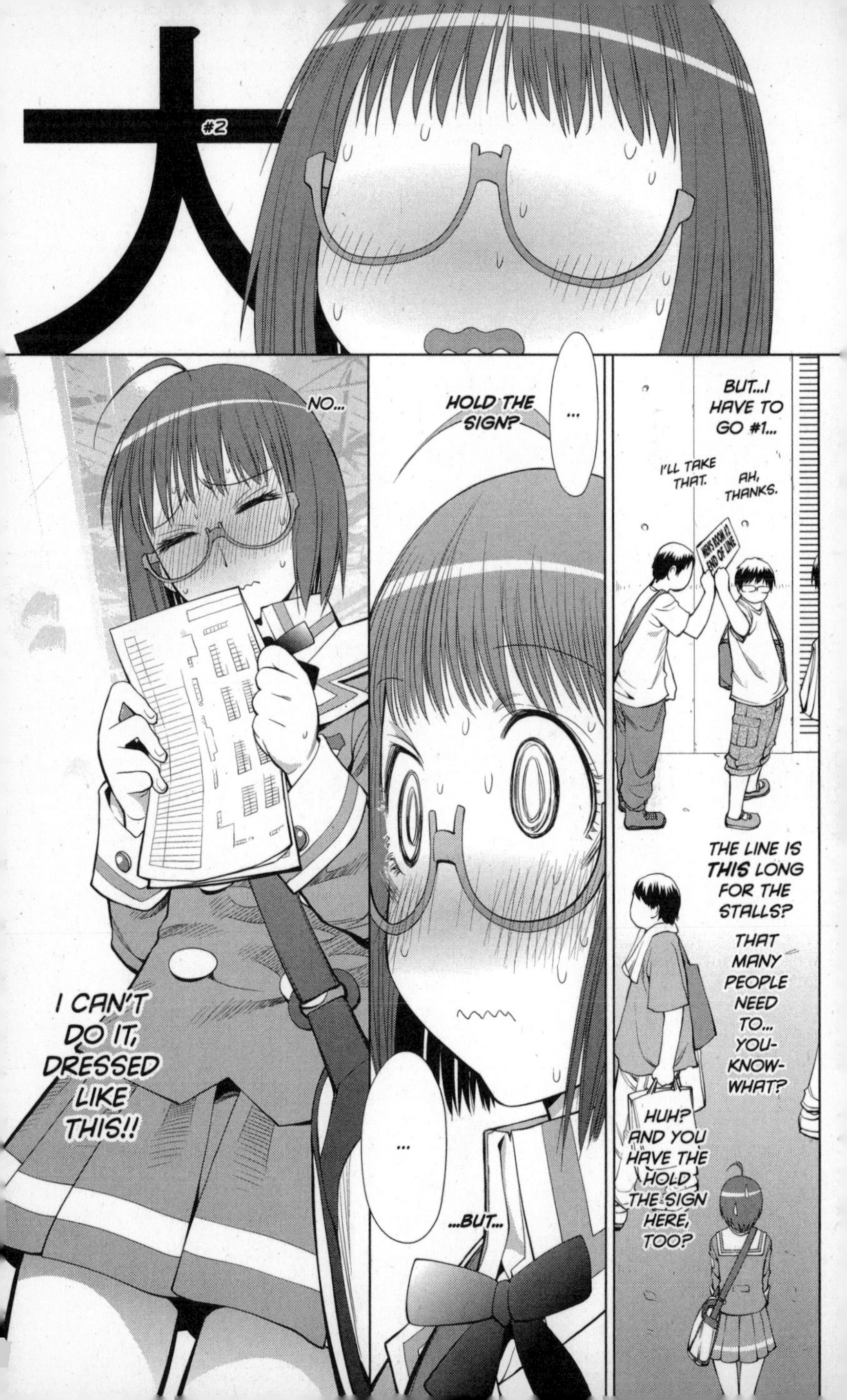
大
#2
BUT...I HAVE TO GO #1...
I'LL TAKE THAT.
AH, THANKS.
MEN'S ROOM #2 END OF LINE
THE LINE IS THIS LONG FOR THE STALLS?
THAT MANY PEOPLE NEED TO... YOU-KNOW-WHAT?
HUH? AND YOU HAVE THE HOLD THE SIGN HERE, TOO?
...
HOLD THE SIGN?
...
...BUT...
NO...
I CAN'T DO IT, DRESSED LIKE THIS!!

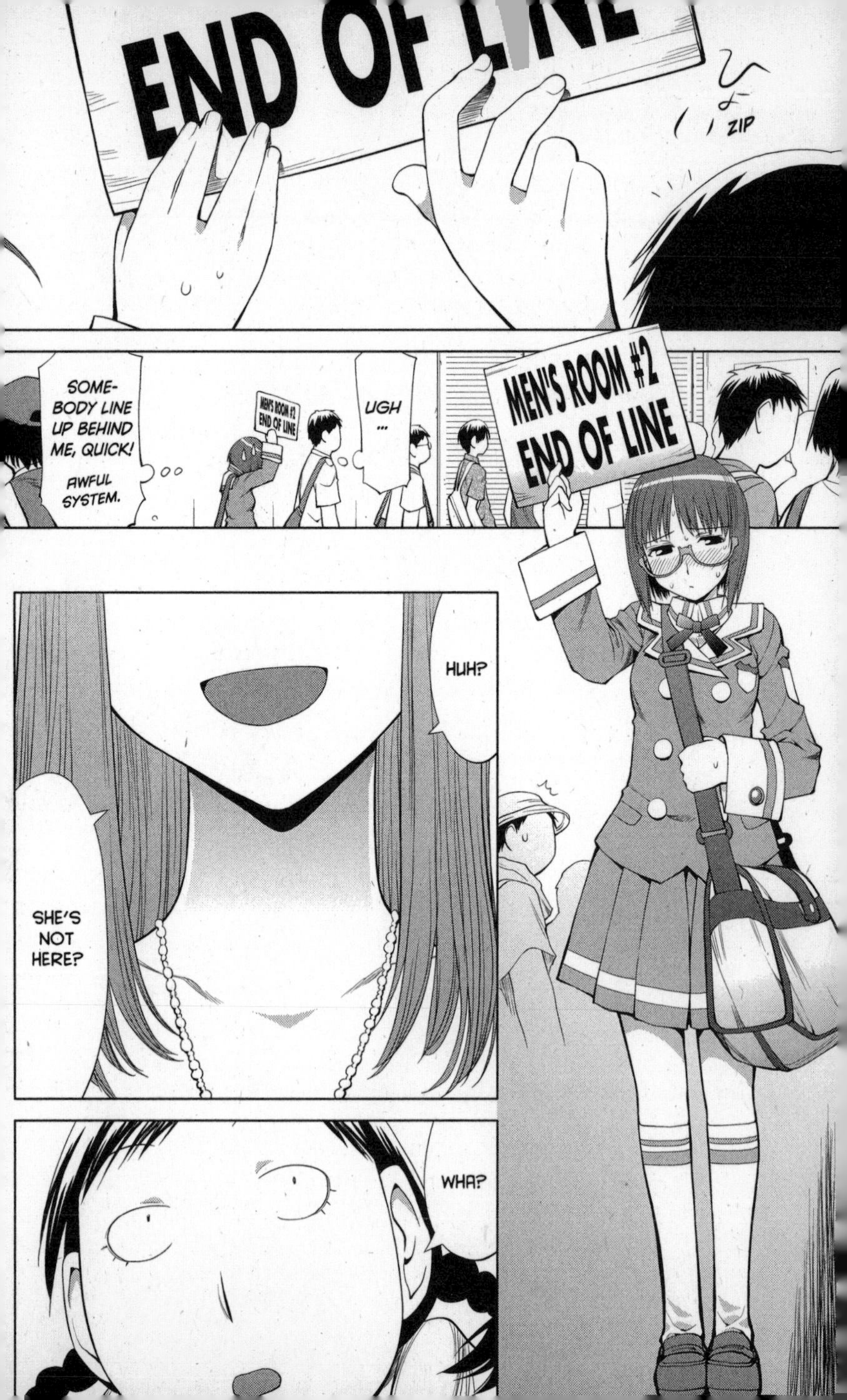
END OF LINE
ひょ
ZIP
MEN'S ROOM #2 END OF LINE
UGH ...
SOME-BODY LINE UP BEHIND ME, QUICK!
AWFUL SYSTEM.
MEN'S ROOM #2 END OF LINE
HUH?
SHE'S NOT HERE?
WHA?

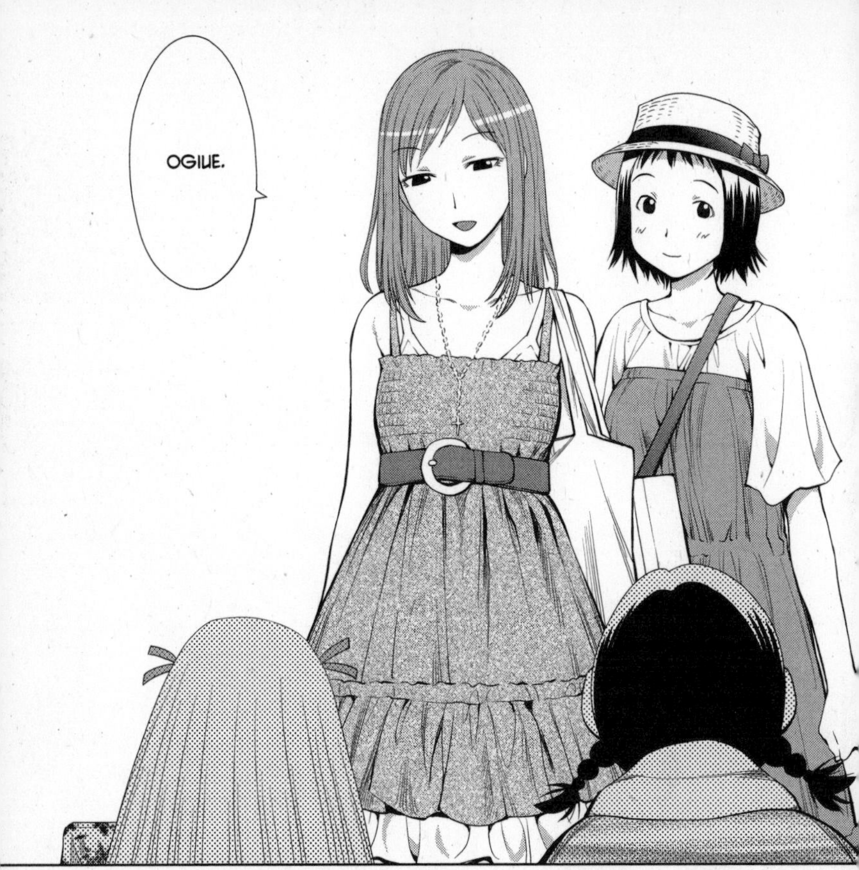
OGIUE.
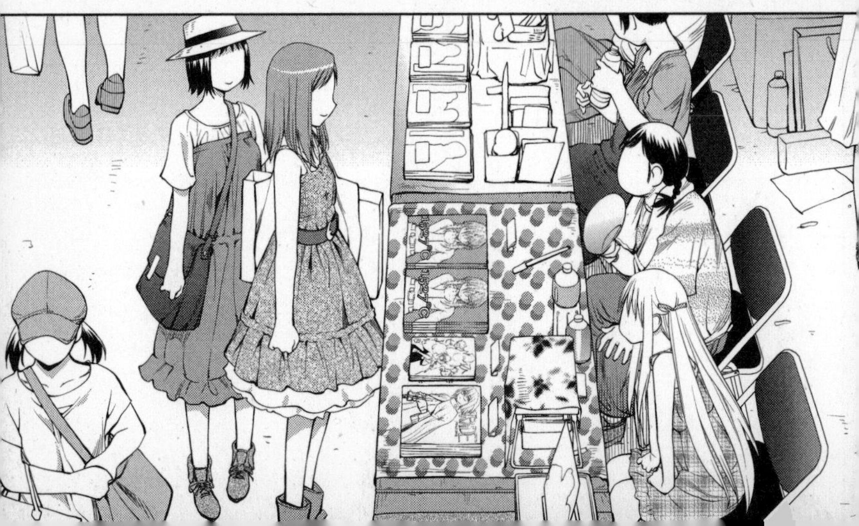

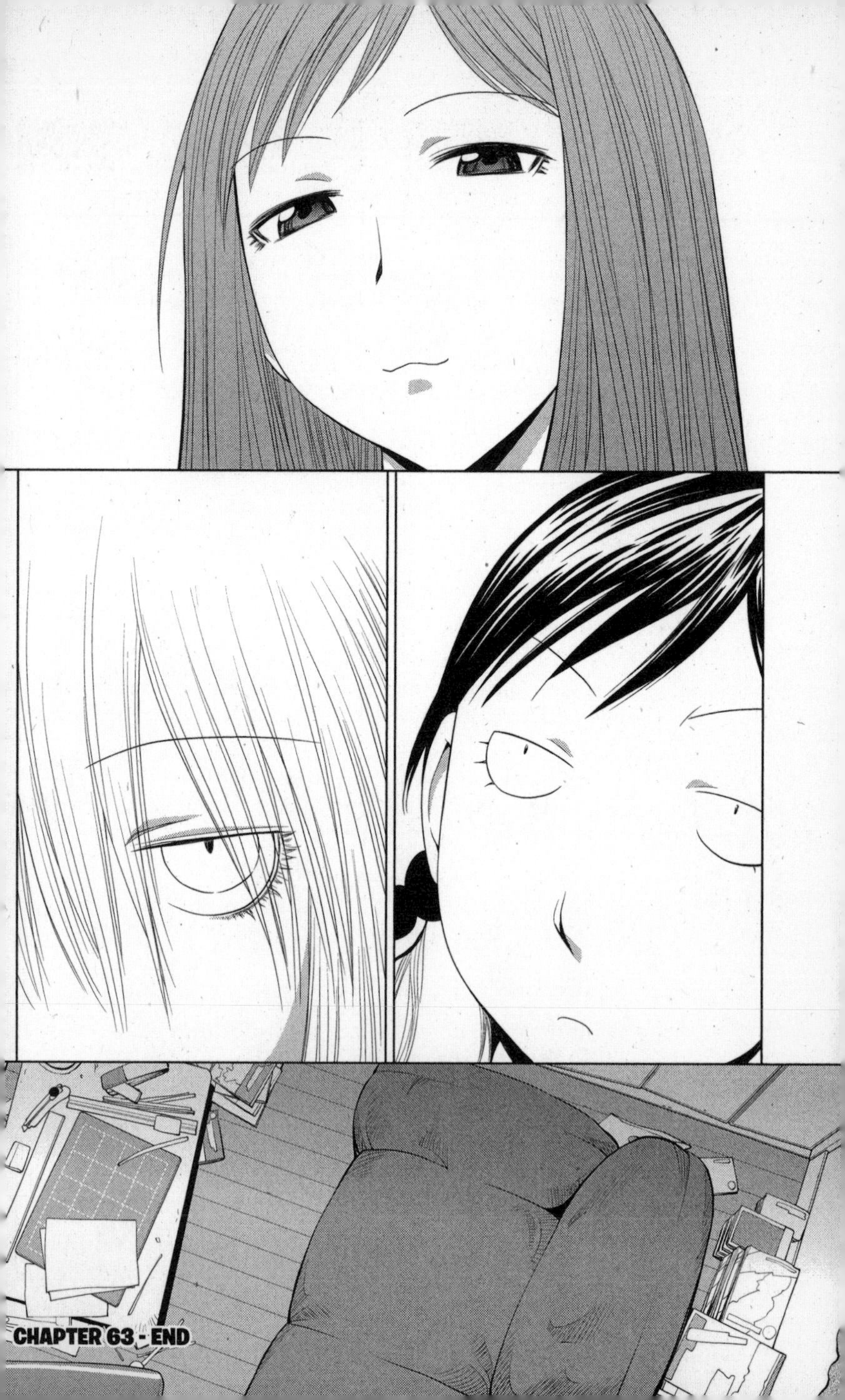
CHAPTER 63 - END

CHAPTER 63 - MOMENTS LATER

KEEPING ABREAST: *ANDANTE*

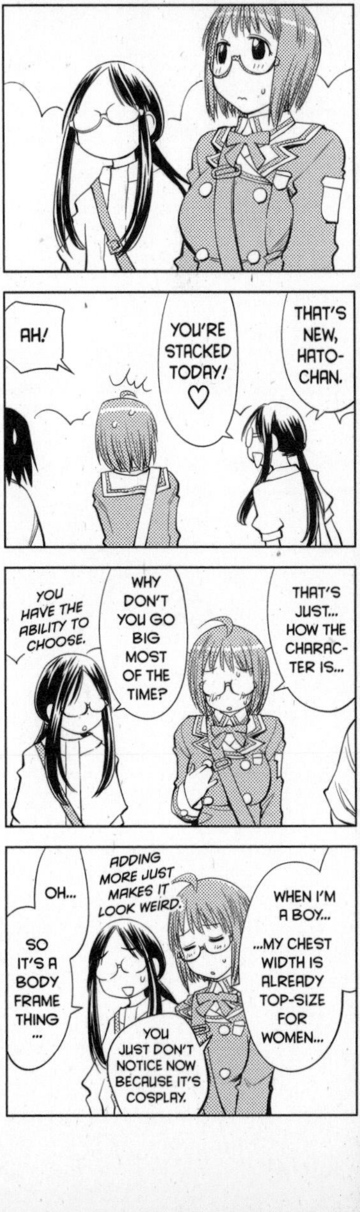
THAT'S NEW, HATO-CHAN.
YOU'RE STACKED TODAY! ♡
AH!
THAT'S JUST... HOW THE CHARACTER IS...
WHY DON'T YOU GO BIG MOST OF THE TIME?
YOU HAVE THE ABILITY TO CHOOSE.
WHEN I'M A BOY... ...MY CHEST WIDTH IS ALREADY TOP-SIZE FOR WOMEN...
ADDING MORE JUST MAKES IT LOOK WEIRD.
OH...
SO IT'S A BODY FRAME THING ...
YOU JUST DON'T NOTICE NOW BECAUSE IT'S COSPLAY.

KEEPING ABREAST: *ALLEGRO*

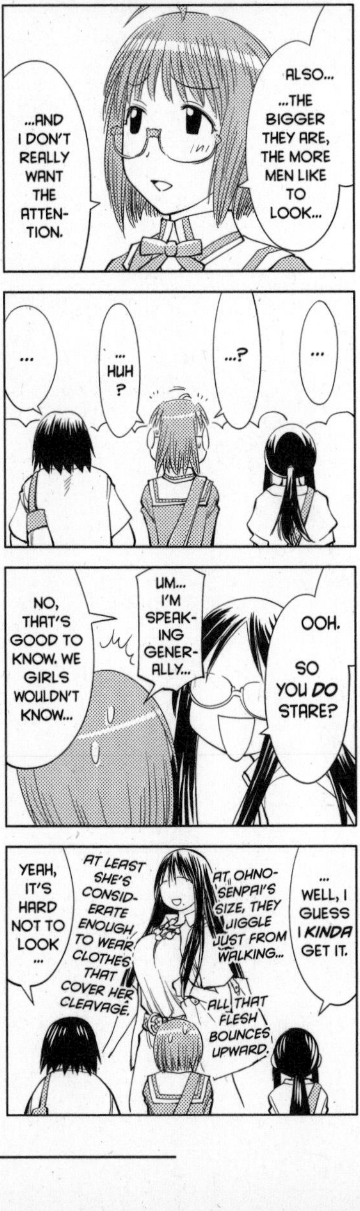
ALSO... ...THE BIGGER THEY ARE, THE MORE MEN LIKE TO LOOK...
...AND I DON'T REALLY WANT THE ATTEN-TION.
...
...?
... HUH ?
...
OOH. SO YOU *DO* STARE?
UM... I'M SPEAK-ING GENER-ALLY...
NO, THAT'S GOOD TO KNOW. WE GIRLS WOULDN'T KNOW...
... WELL, I GUESS I *KINDA* GET IT.
AT OHNO-SENPAI'S SIZE, THEY JIGGLE JUST FROM WALKING...
AT LEAST SHE'S CONSID-ERATE ENOUGH TO WEAR CLOTHES THAT COVER HER CLEAVAGE.
YEAH, IT'S HARD NOT TO LOOK ...
ALL THAT FLESH BOUNCES UPWARD.

KEEPING ABREAST: *VIVACE*

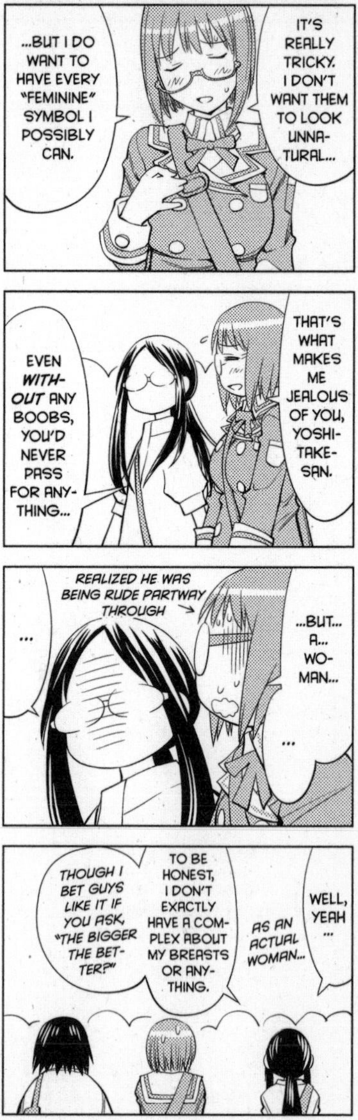
IT'S REALLY TRICKY. I DON'T WANT THEM TO LOOK UNNATURAL...
...BUT I DO WANT TO HAVE EVERY "FEMININE" SYMBOL I POSSIBLY CAN.
THAT'S WHAT MAKES ME JEALOUS OF YOU, YOSHITAKE-SAN.
EVEN *WITHOUT* ANY BOOBS, YOU'D NEVER PASS FOR ANYTHING...
...BUT... A... WOMAN...
REALIZED HE WAS BEING RUDE PARTWAY THROUGH
...
...
WELL, YEAH...
AS AN ACTUAL WOMAN...
TO BE HONEST, I DON'T EXACTLY HAVE A COMPLEX ABOUT MY BREASTS OR ANYTHING.
THOUGH I BET GUYS LIKE IT IF YOU ASK, "THE BIGGER THE BETTER?"

KEEPING ABREAST ?

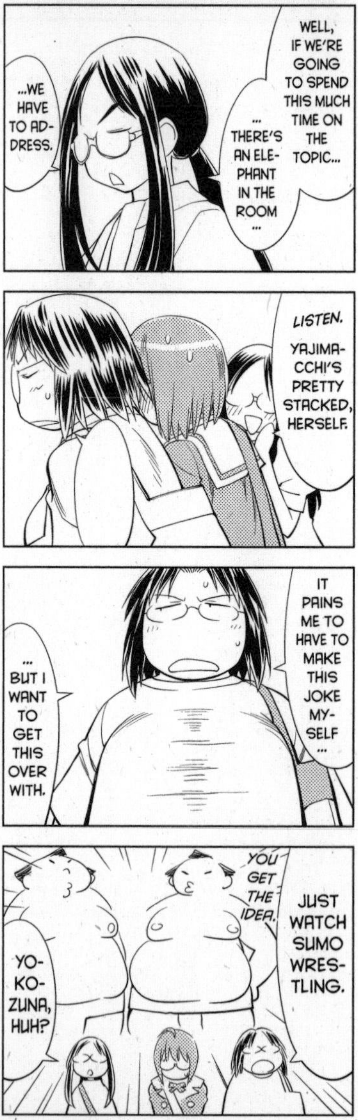
WELL, IF WE'RE GOING TO SPEND THIS MUCH TIME ON THE TOPIC...
...THERE'S AN ELEPHANT IN THE ROOM...
...WE HAVE TO ADDRESS.
LISTEN. YAJIMACCHI'S PRETTY STACKED, HERSELF.
IT PAINS ME TO HAVE TO MAKE THIS JOKE MYSELF...
...BUT I WANT TO GET THIS OVER WITH.
JUST WATCH SUMO WRESTLING.
YOU GET THE IDEA.
YOKOZUNA, HUH?

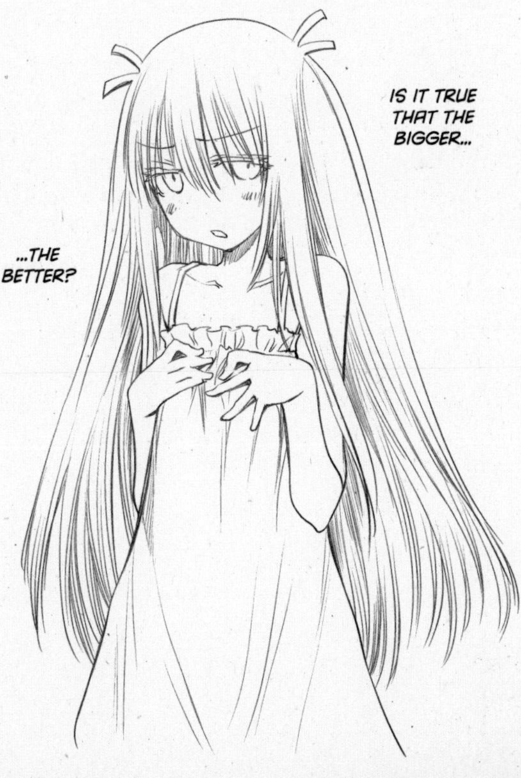
IS IT TRUE THAT THE BIGGER...
...THE BETTER?

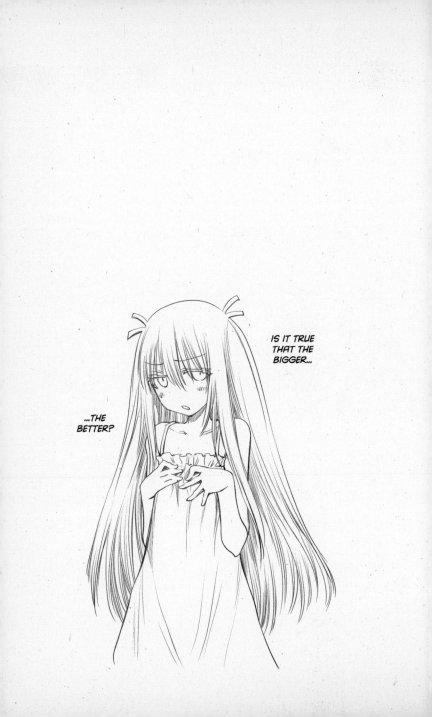

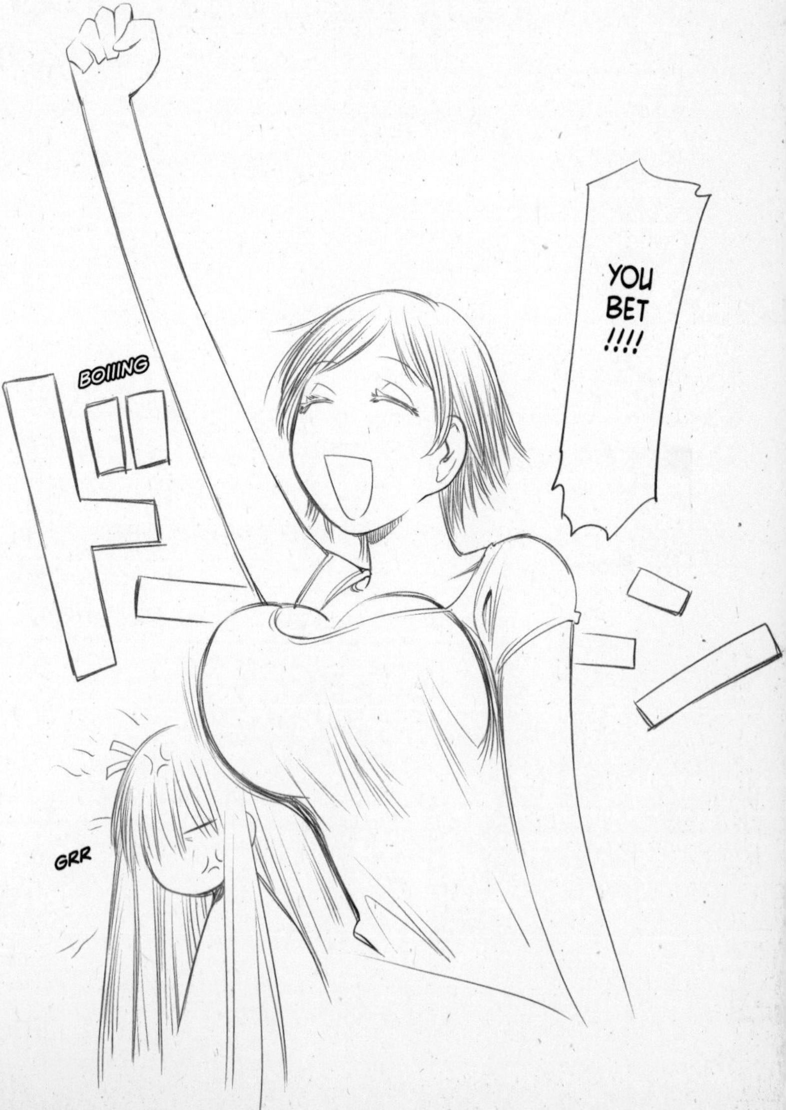
YOU BET !!!!
BOIIING
GRR

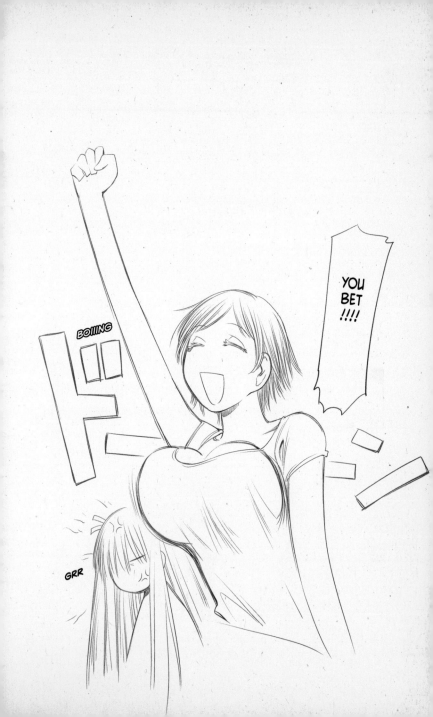

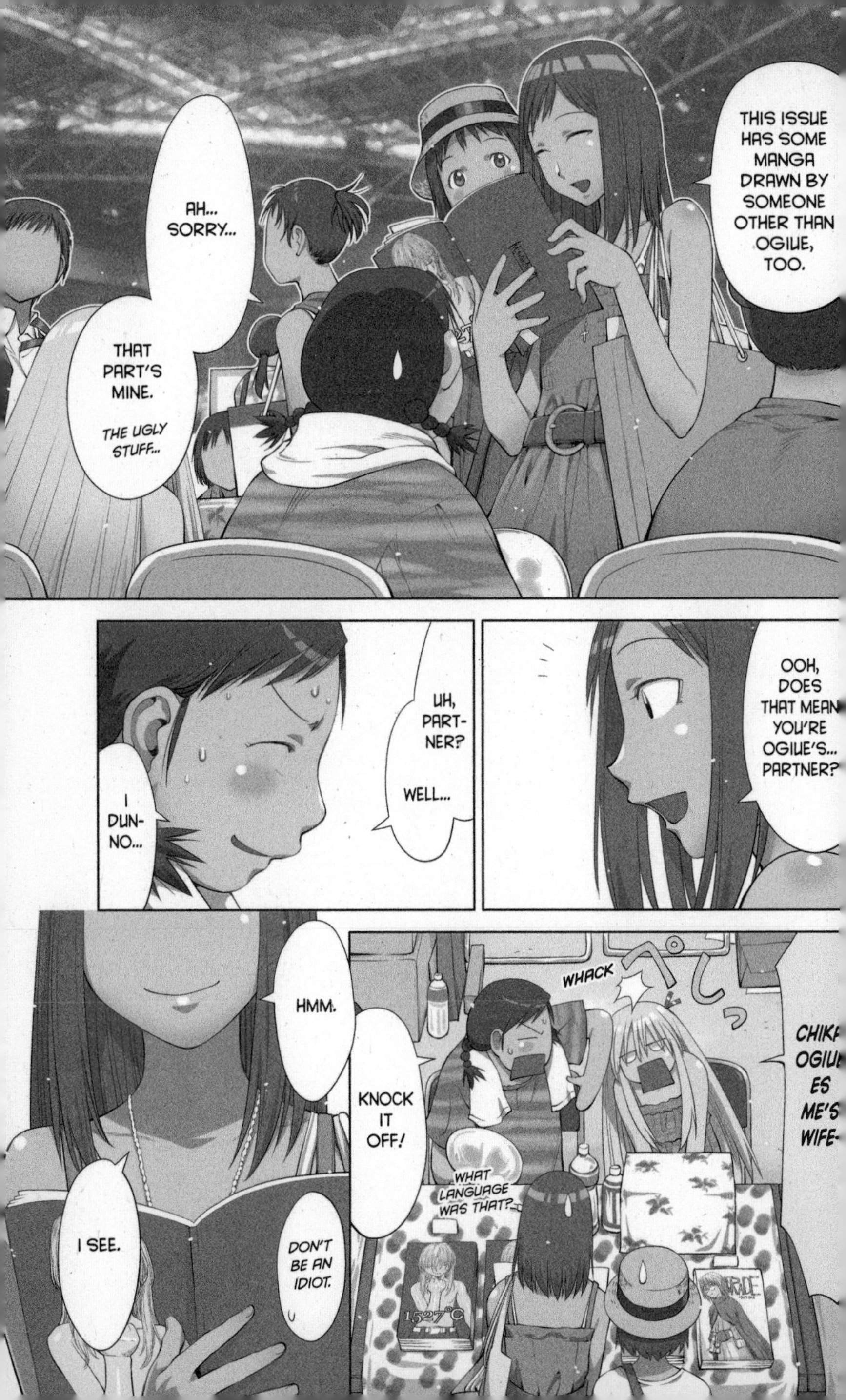
THIS ISSUE HAS SOME MANGA DRAWN BY SOMEONE OTHER THAN OGIUE, TOO.
AH... SORRY...
THAT PART'S MINE.
THE UGLY STUFF...
OOH, DOES THAT MEAN YOU'RE OGIUE'S... PARTNER?
UH, PART-NER?
WELL...
I DUN-NO...
CHIK OGIU ES ME'S WIFE-
WHACK
KNOCK IT OFF!
WHAT LANGUAGE WAS THAT?
HMM.
I SEE.
DON'T BE AN IDIOT.

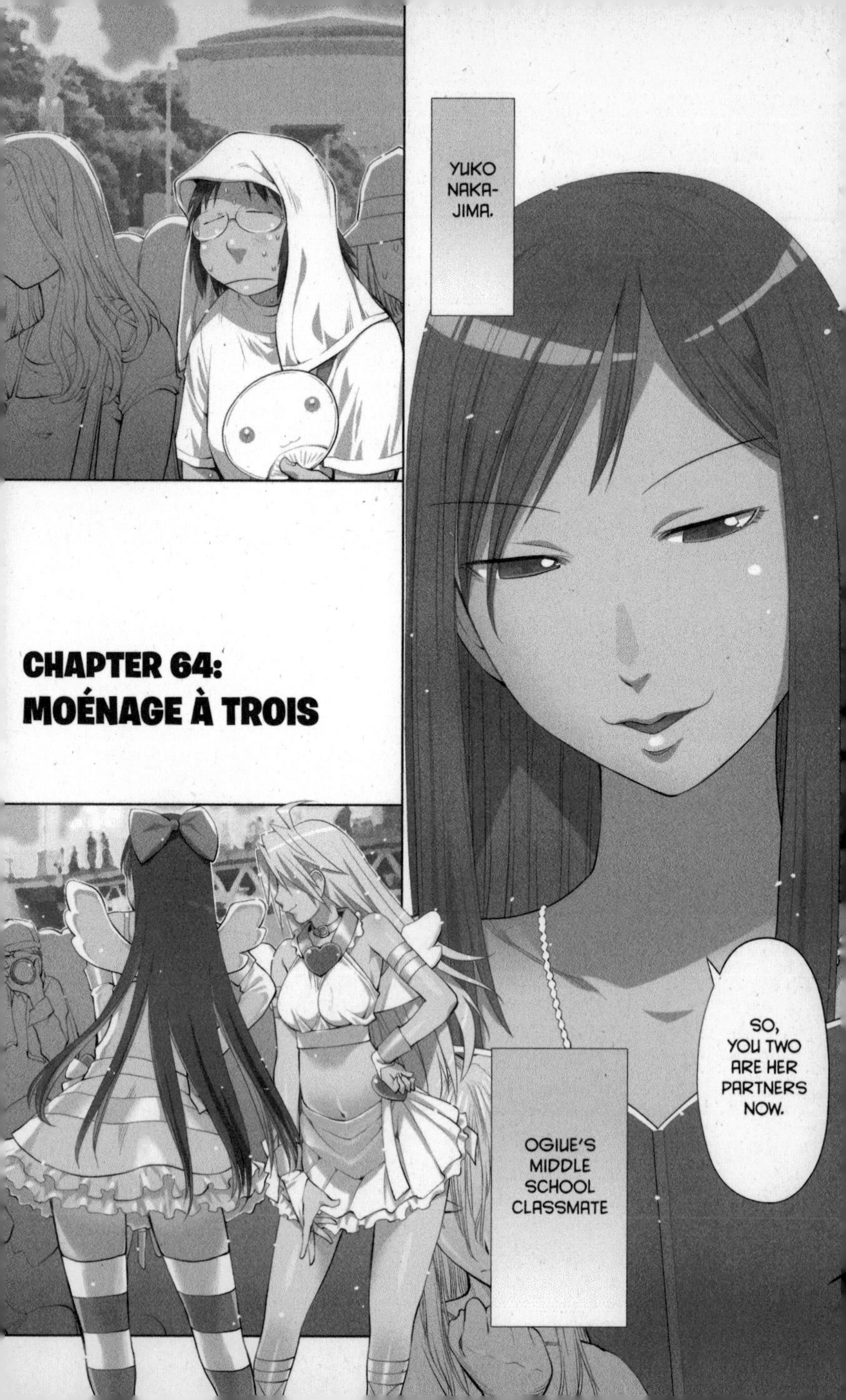
YUKO NAKA-JIMA.
SO, YOU TWO ARE HER PARTNERS NOW.
OGIUE'S MIDDLE SCHOOL CLASSMATE

CHAPTER 64: MOÉNAGE À TROIS

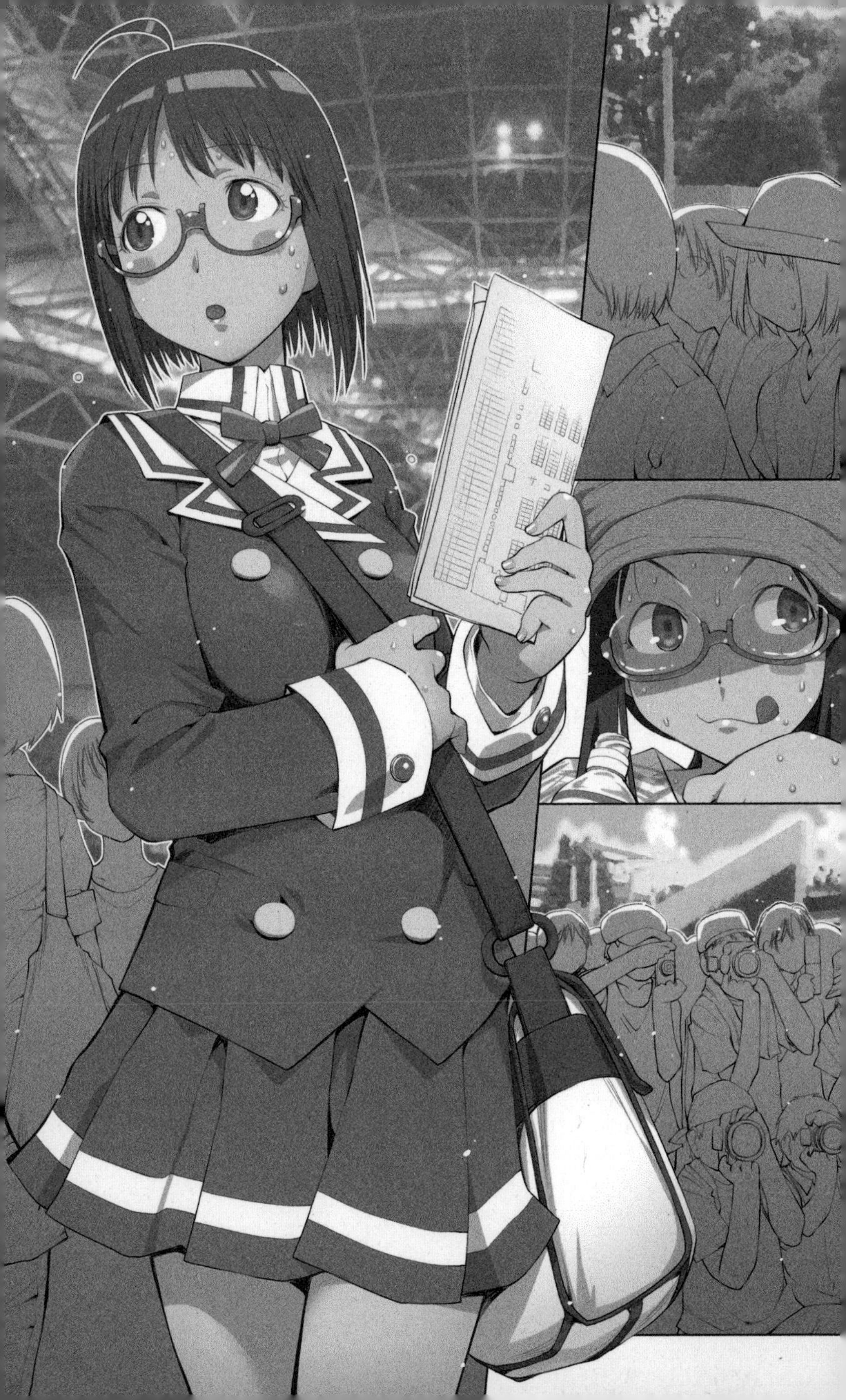

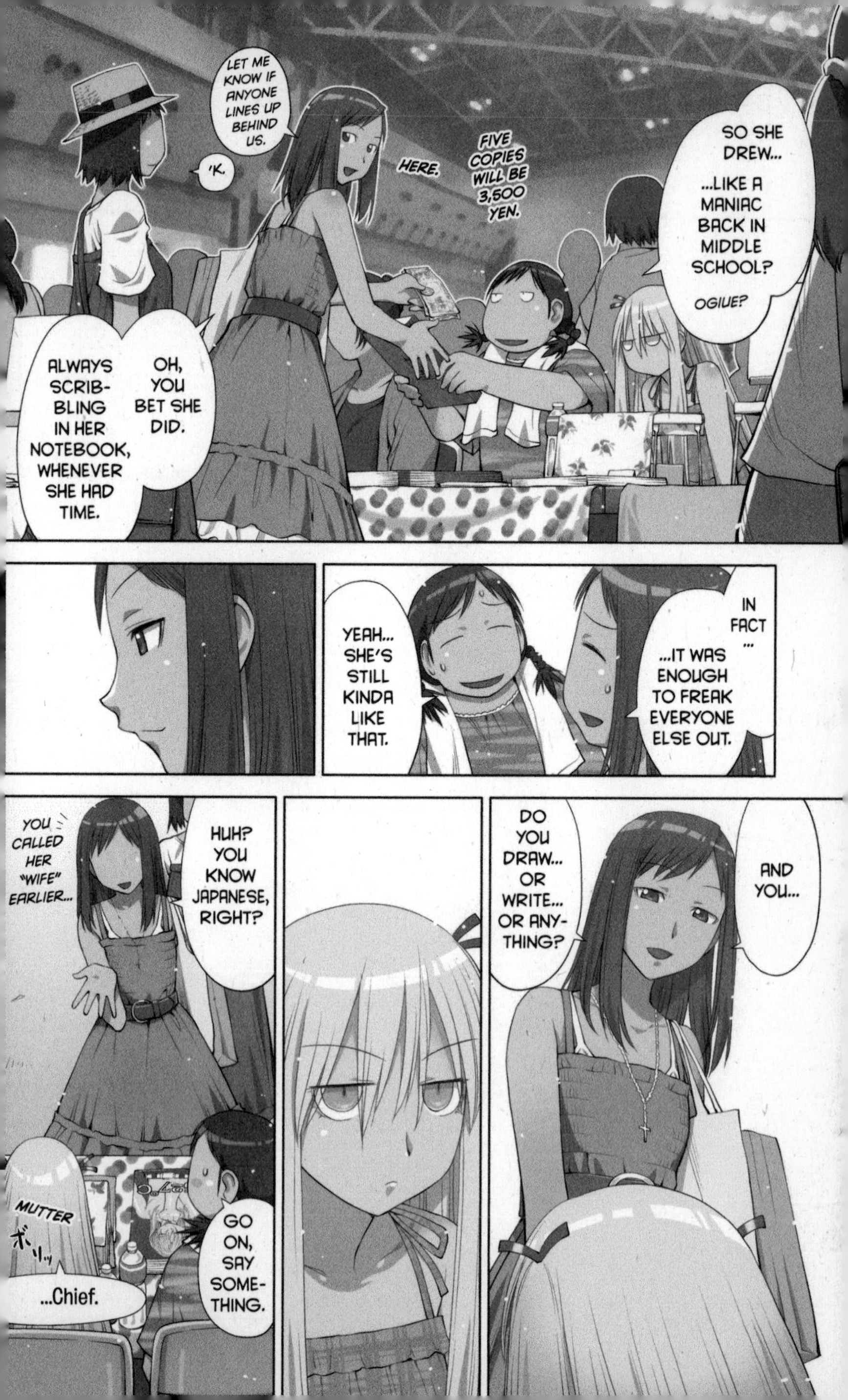
SO SHE DREW...
...LIKE A MANIAC BACK IN MIDDLE SCHOOL?
OGIUE?
FIVE COPIES WILL BE 3,500 YEN.
HERE.
LET ME KNOW IF ANYONE LINES UP BEHIND US.
'K.
OH, YOU BET SHE DID.
ALWAYS SCRIB-BLING IN HER NOTEBOOK, WHENEVER SHE HAD TIME.
IN FACT...
...IT WAS ENOUGH TO FREAK EVERYONE ELSE OUT.
YEAH... SHE'S STILL KINDA LIKE THAT.
AND YOU...
DO YOU DRAW... OR WRITE... OR ANY-THING?
HUH? YOU KNOW JAPANESE, RIGHT?
YOU CALLED HER "WIFE" EARLIER...
GO ON, SAY SOME-THING.
MUTTER
ボリッ
...Chief.

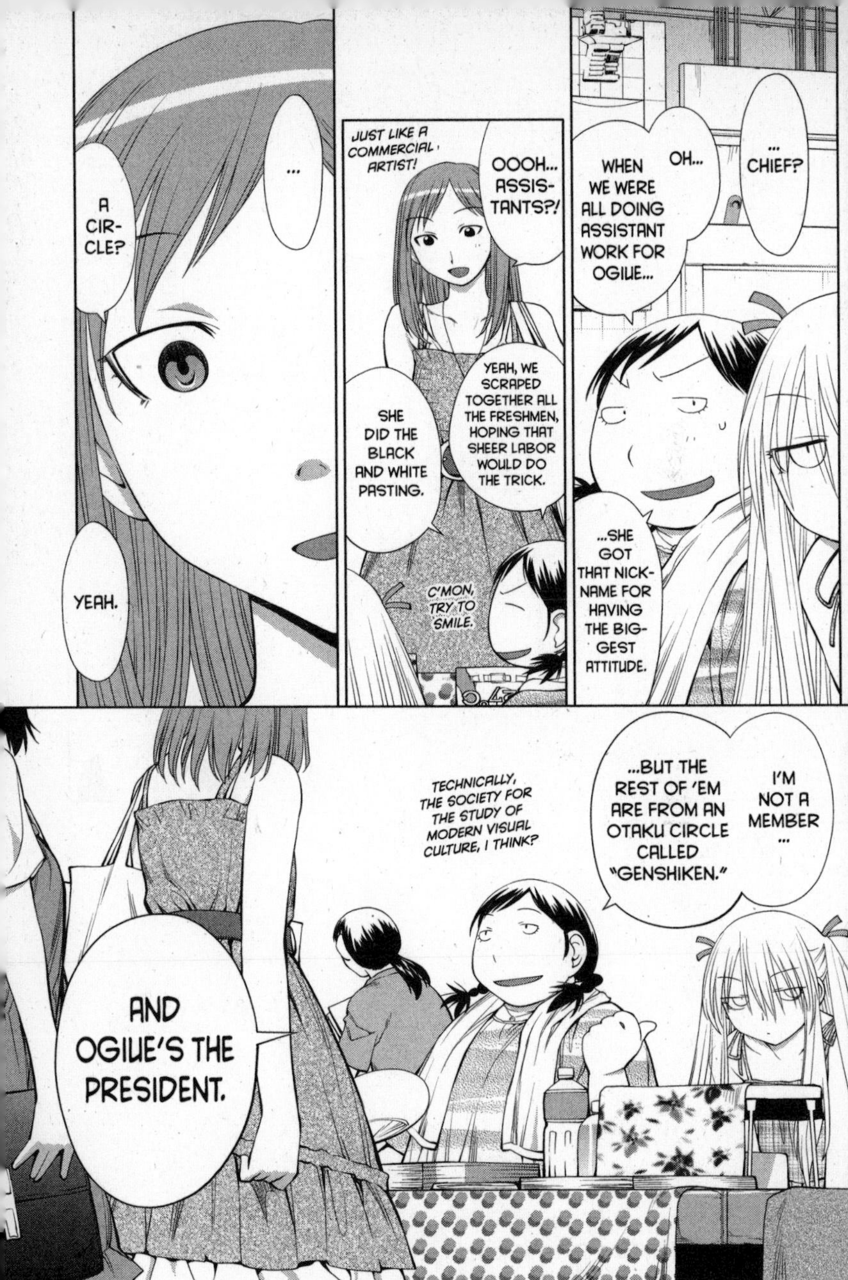
...CHIEF?
OH...
WHEN WE WERE ALL DOING ASSISTANT WORK FOR OGIUE...
...SHE GOT THAT NICKNAME FOR HAVING THE BIGGEST ATTITUDE.
OOOH... ASSISTANTS?!
JUST LIKE A COMMERCIAL ARTIST!
YEAH, WE SCRAPED TOGETHER ALL THE FRESHMEN, HOPING THAT SHEER LABOR WOULD DO THE TRICK.
SHE DID THE BLACK AND WHITE PASTING.
C'MON, TRY TO SMILE.
...
A CIRCLE?
YEAH.
I'M NOT A MEMBER ...
...BUT THE REST OF 'EM ARE FROM AN OTAKU CIRCLE CALLED "GENSHIKEN."
TECHNICALLY, THE SOCIETY FOR THE STUDY OF MODERN VISUAL CULTURE, I THINK?
AND OGIUE'S THE PRESIDENT.

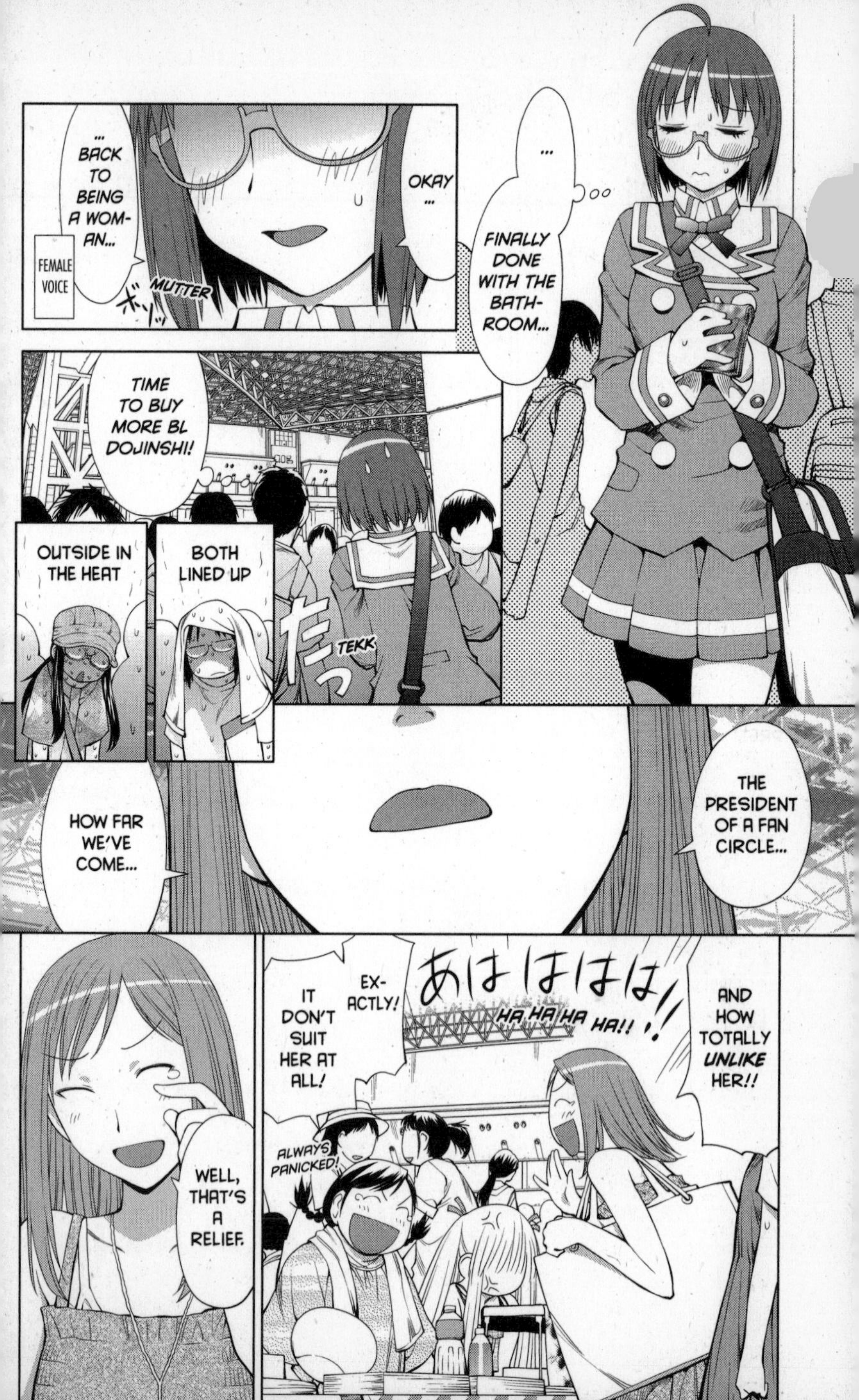

...
FINALLY DONE WITH THE BATH-ROOM...
OKAY ...
... BACK TO BEING A WOM-AN...
FEMALE VOICE
MUTTER
TIME TO BUY MORE BL DOJINSHI!
TEKK
BOTH LINED UP
OUTSIDE IN THE HEAT
THE PRESIDENT OF A FAN CIRCLE...
HOW FAR WE'VE COME...
AND HOW TOTALLY UNLIKE HER!!
あははははは
HA HA HA HA!!
EX-ACTLY!
IT DON'T SUIT HER AT ALL!
ALWAYS PANICKED!
WELL, THAT'S A RELIEF.

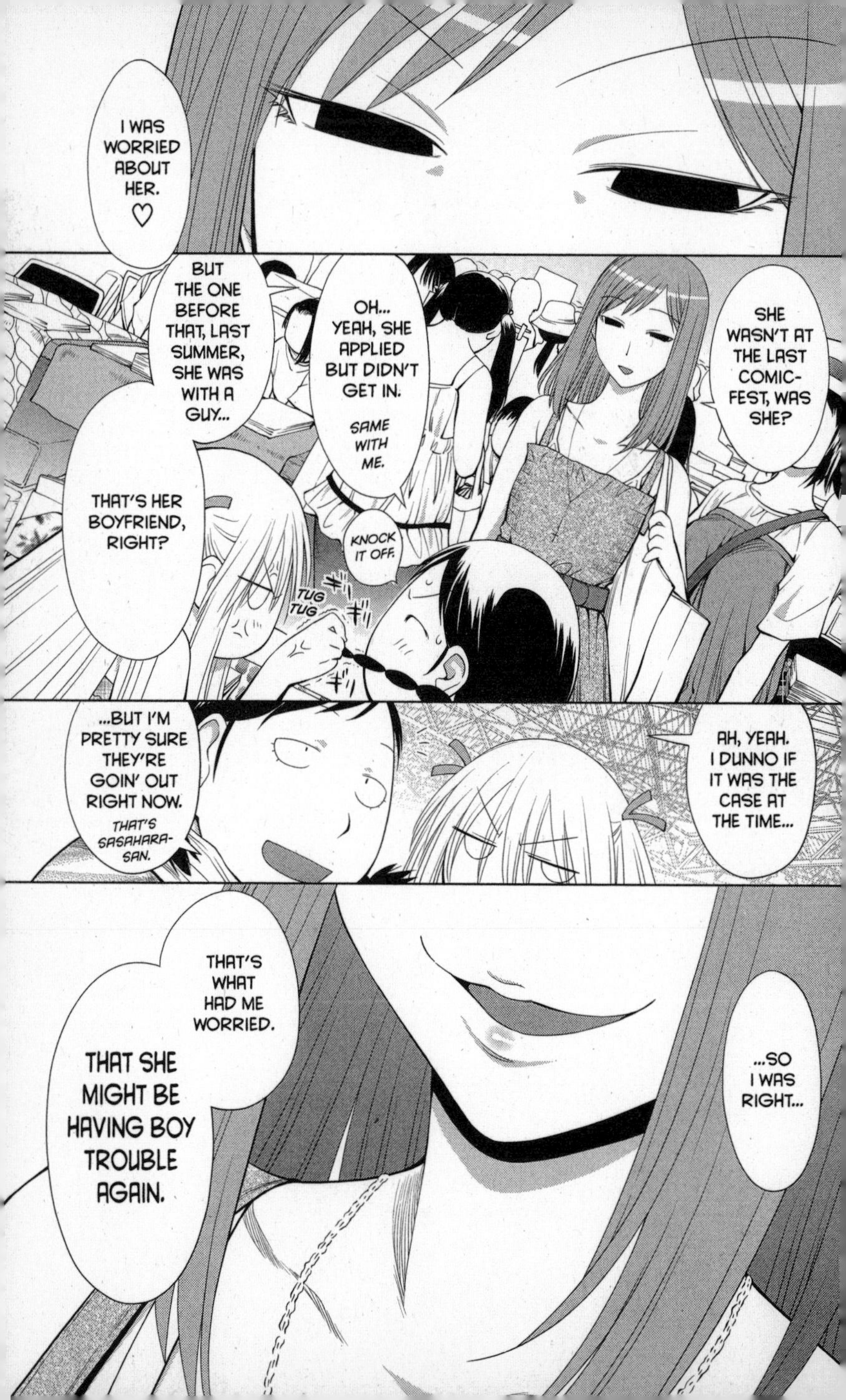
I WAS WORRIED ABOUT HER. ♡
SHE WASN'T AT THE LAST COMIC-FEST, WAS SHE?
OH... YEAH, SHE APPLIED BUT DIDN'T GET IN.
SAME WITH ME.
BUT THE ONE BEFORE THAT, LAST SUMMER, SHE WAS WITH A GUY...
KNOCK IT OFF.
THAT'S HER BOYFRIEND, RIGHT?
TUG TUG
AH, YEAH. I DUNNO IF IT WAS THE CASE AT THE TIME...
...BUT I'M PRETTY SURE THEY'RE GOIN' OUT RIGHT NOW.
THAT'S SASAHARA-SAN.
...SO I WAS RIGHT...
THAT'S WHAT HAD ME WORRIED.
THAT SHE MIGHT BE HAVING BOY TROUBLE AGAIN.

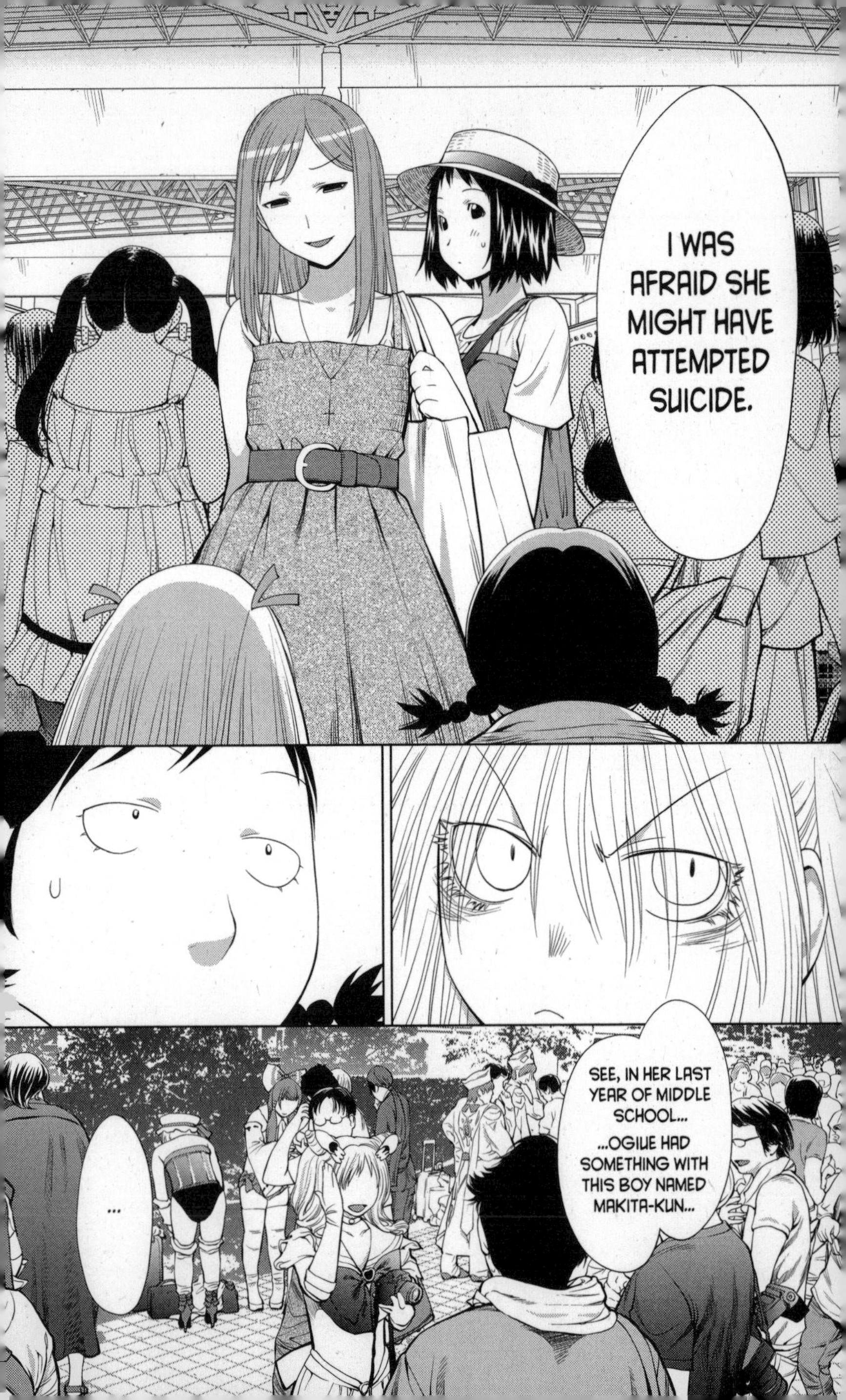
I WAS AFRAID SHE MIGHT HAVE ATTEMPTED SUICIDE.
SEE, IN HER LAST YEAR OF MIDDLE SCHOOL...
...OGIUE HAD SOMETHING WITH THIS BOY NAMED MAKITA-KUN...
...

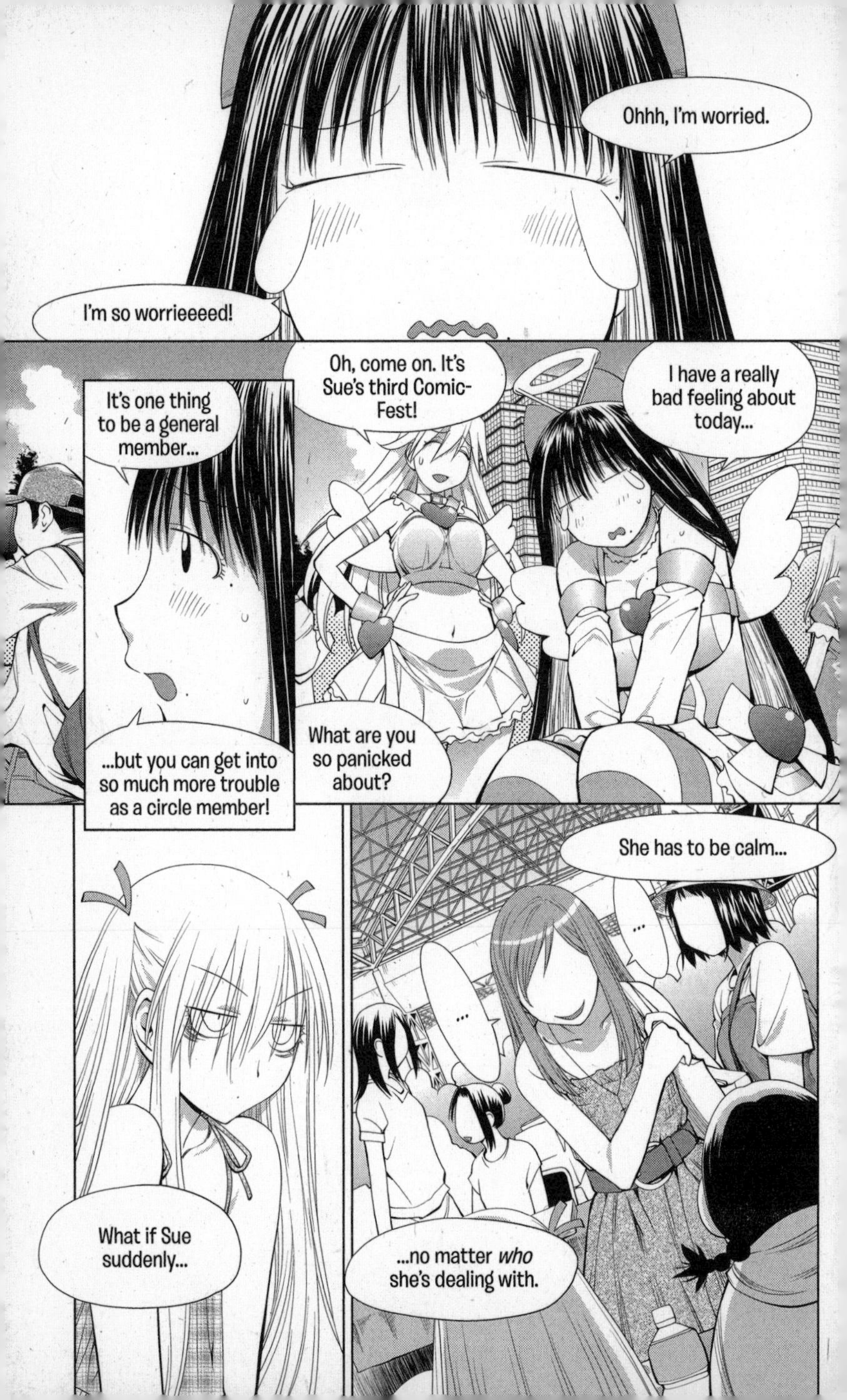
Ohhh, I'm worried.
I'm so worrieeeed!
I have a really bad feeling about today...
Oh, come on. It's Sue's third Comic-Fest!
What are you so panicked about?
It's one thing to be a general member...
...but you can get into so much more trouble as a circle member!
She has to be calm...
...
...
...no matter *who* she's dealing with.
What if Sue suddenly...

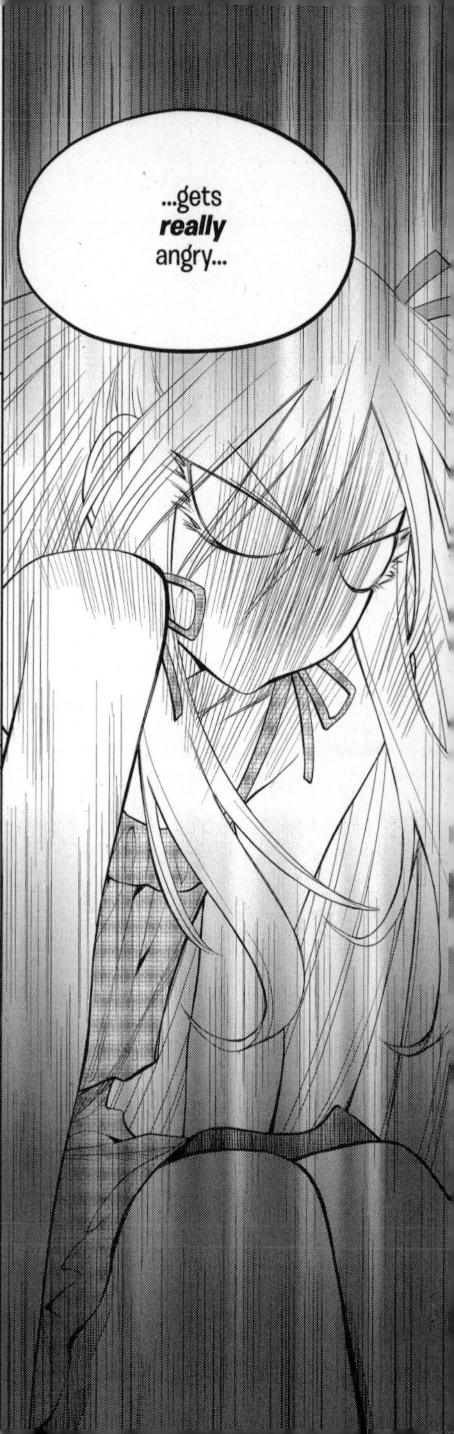
...gets **really** angry...

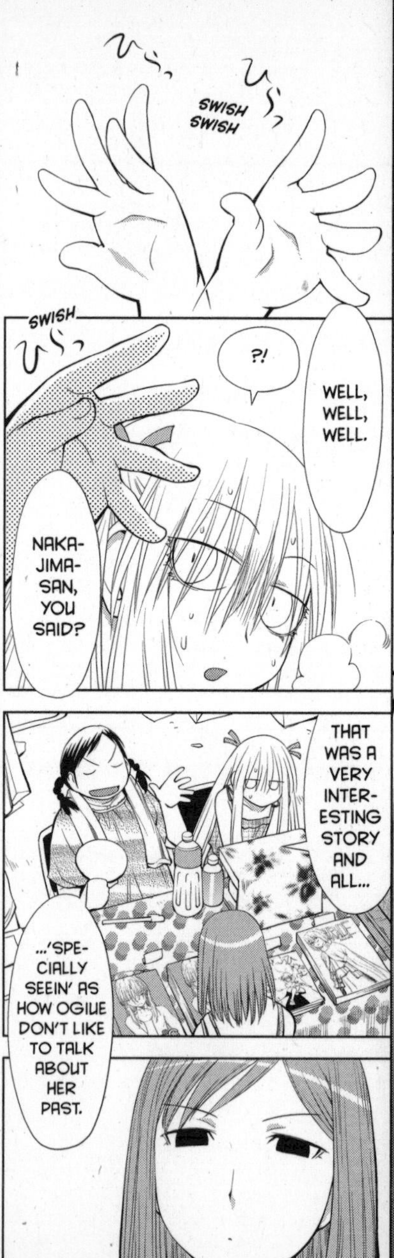
SWISH SWISH
?!
WELL, WELL, WELL.
SWISH
NAKAJIMA-SAN, YOU SAID?
THAT WAS A VERY INTERESTING STORY AND ALL...
...'SPECIALLY SEEIN' AS HOW OGIUE DON'T LIKE TO TALK ABOUT HER PAST.

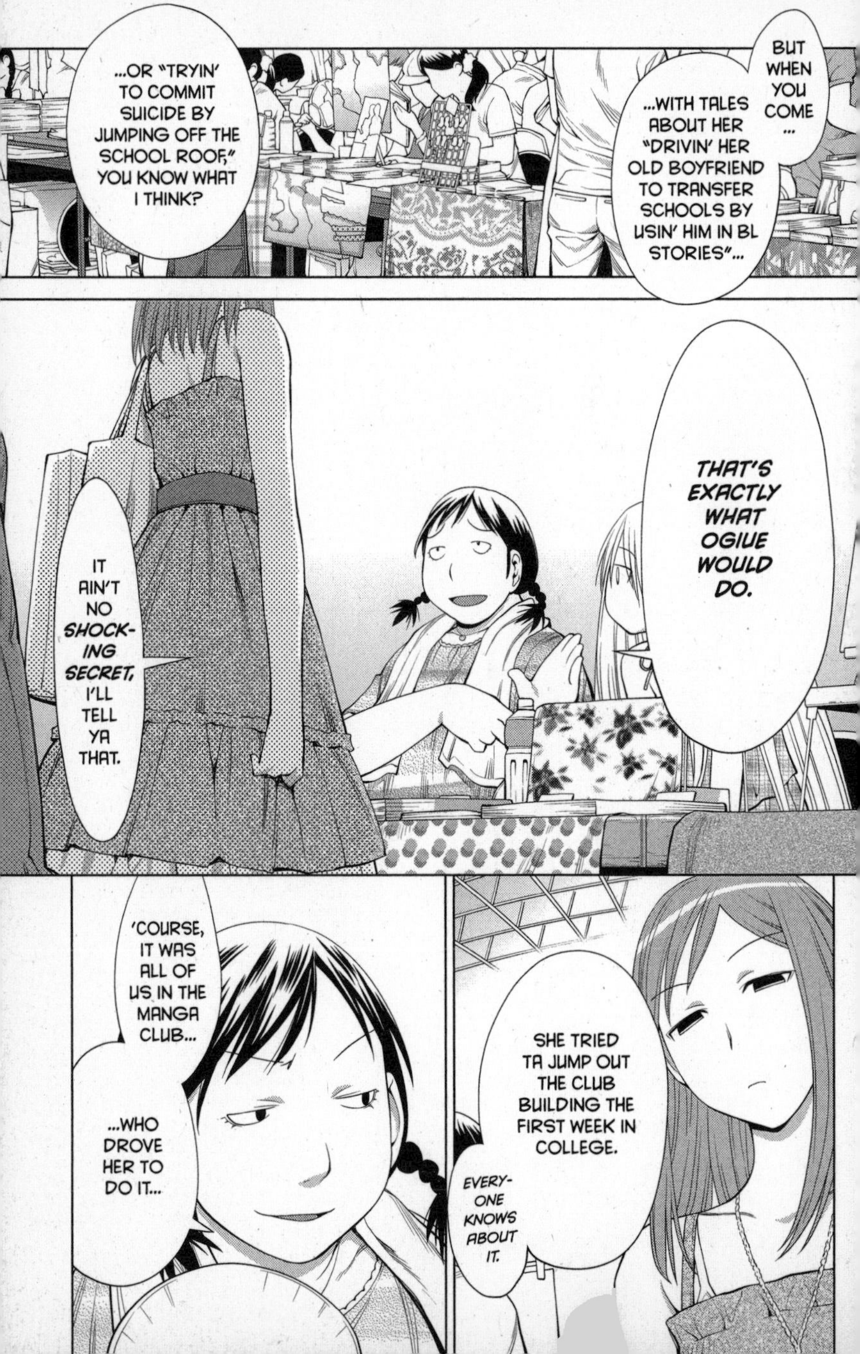
BUT WHEN YOU COME...
...WITH TALES ABOUT HER "DRIVIN' HER OLD BOYFRIEND TO TRANSFER SCHOOLS BY USIN' HIM IN BL STORIES"...
...OR "TRYIN' TO COMMIT SUICIDE BY JUMPING OFF THE SCHOOL ROOF," YOU KNOW WHAT I THINK?
THAT'S EXACTLY WHAT OGIUE WOULD DO.
IT AIN'T NO SHOCKING SECRET, I'LL TELL YA THAT.
SHE TRIED TA JUMP OUT THE CLUB BUILDING THE FIRST WEEK IN COLLEGE.
EVERYONE KNOWS ABOUT IT.
'COURSE, IT WAS ALL OF US IN THE MANGA CLUB...
...WHO DROVE HER TO DO IT...

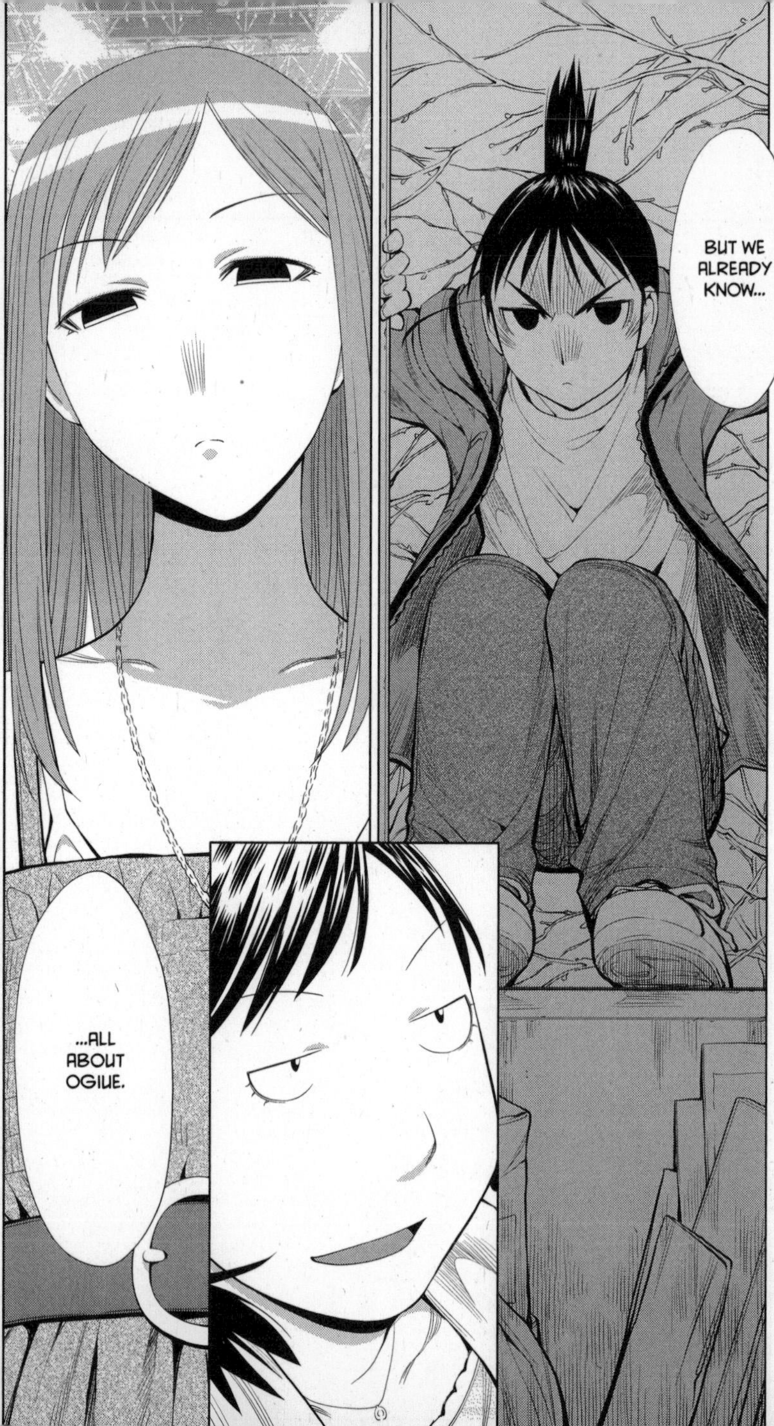
BUT WE ALREADY KNOW...
...ALL ABOUT OGIUE.

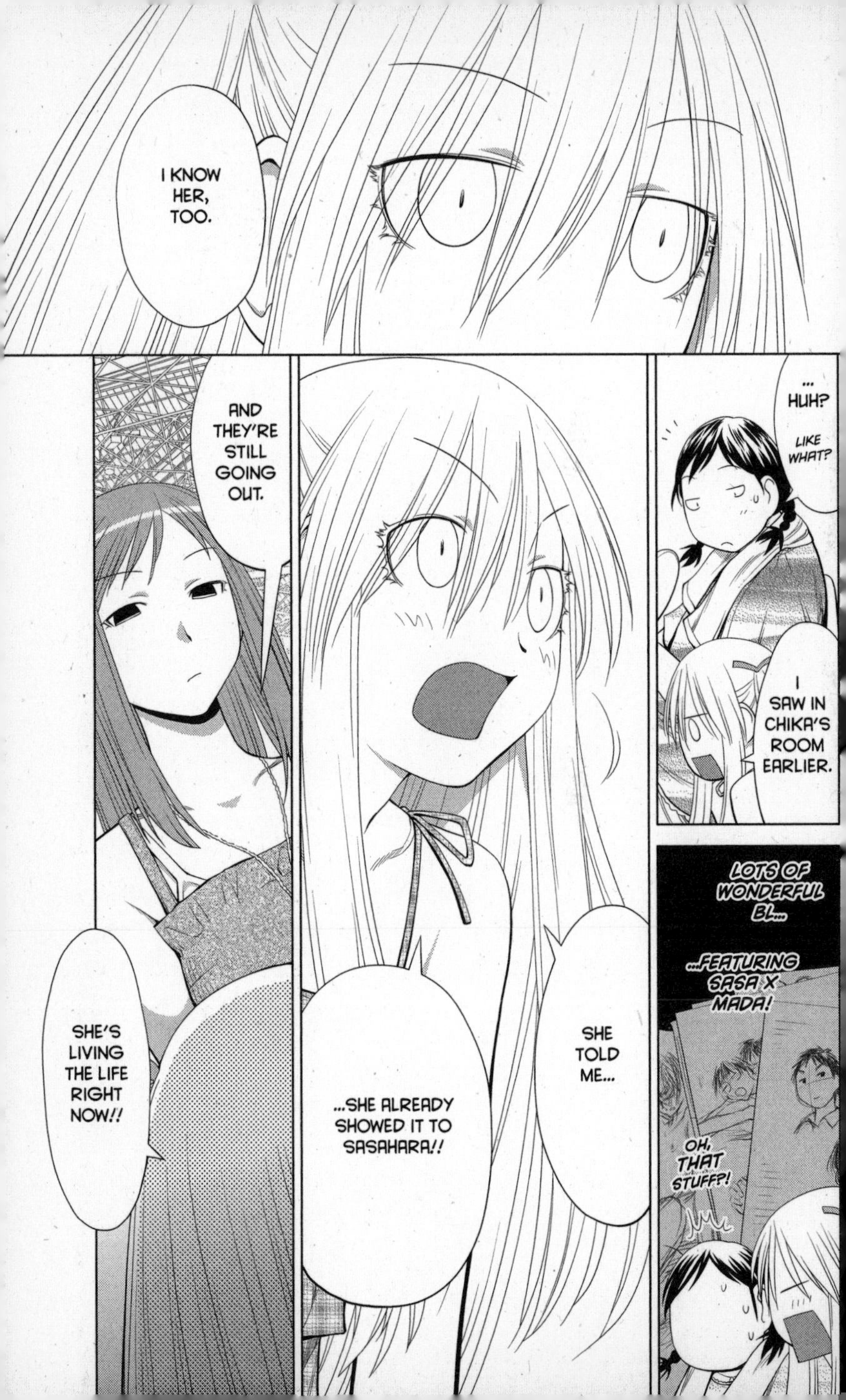
I KNOW HER, TOO.
... HUH?
LIKE WHAT?
I SAW IN CHIKA'S ROOM EARLIER.
LOTS OF WONDERFUL BL...
...FEATURING SASA X MADA!
OH, THAT STUFF?!
SHE TOLD ME...
...SHE ALREADY SHOWED IT TO SASAHARA!!
AND THEY'RE STILL GOING OUT.
SHE'S LIVING THE LIFE RIGHT NOW!!

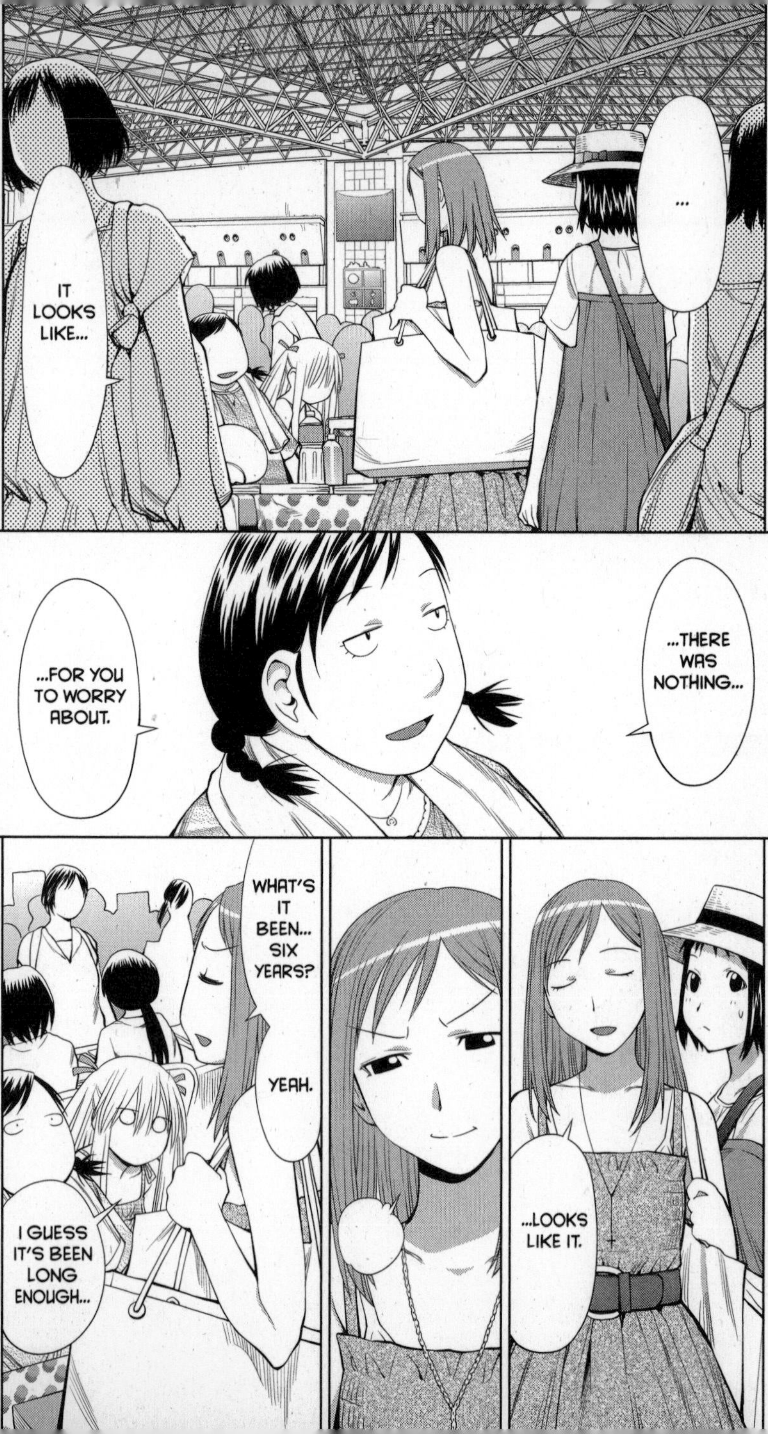
...
IT LOOKS LIKE...
...THERE WAS NOTHING...
...FOR YOU TO WORRY ABOUT.
...LOOKS LIKE IT.
WHAT'S IT BEEN... SIX YEARS?
YEAH.
I GUESS IT'S BEEN LONG ENOUGH...

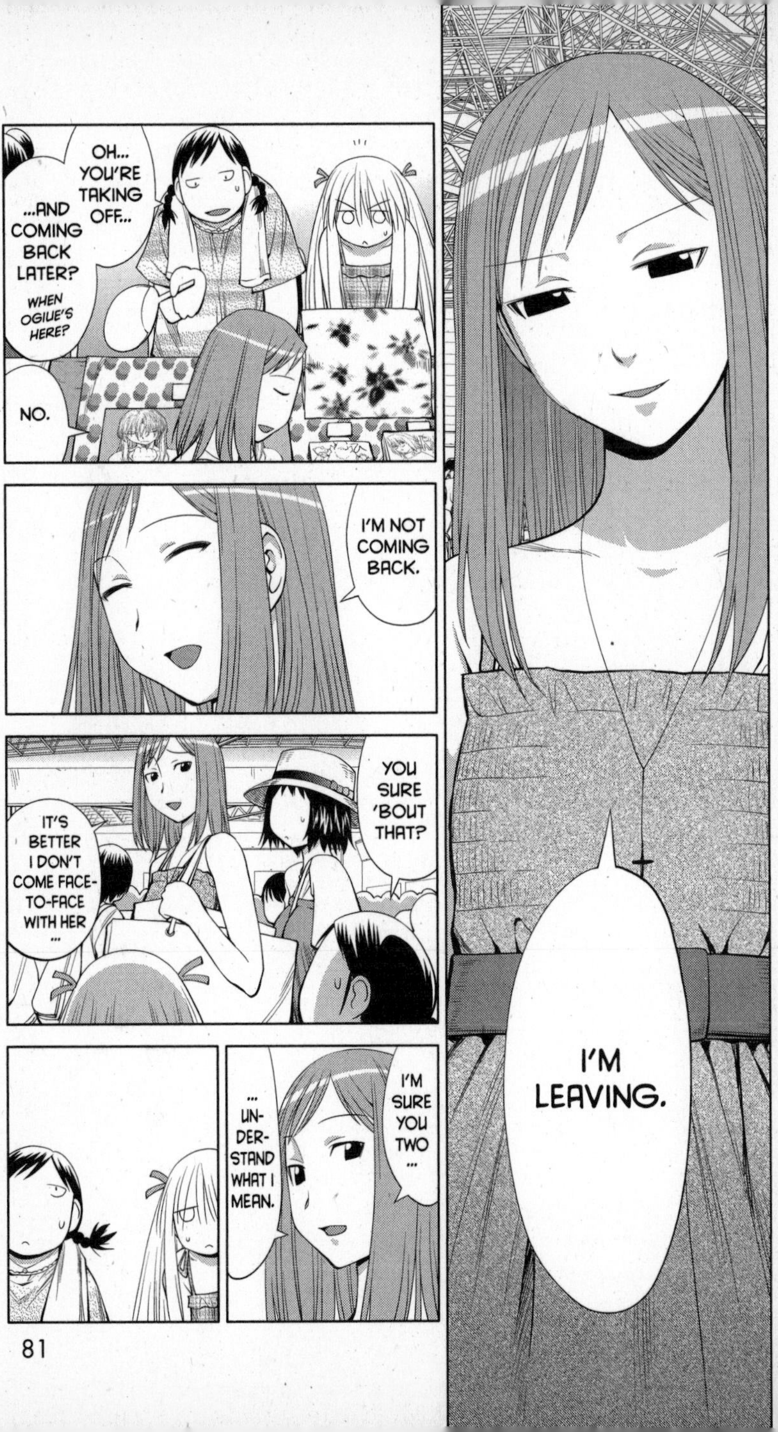
I'M LEAVING.
OH... YOU'RE TAKING OFF...
...AND COMING BACK LATER?
WHEN OGIUE'S HERE?
NO.
I'M NOT COMING BACK.
YOU SURE 'BOUT THAT?
IT'S BETTER I DON'T COME FACE-TO-FACE WITH HER ...
I'M SURE YOU TWO ...
... UNDERSTAND WHAT I MEAN.

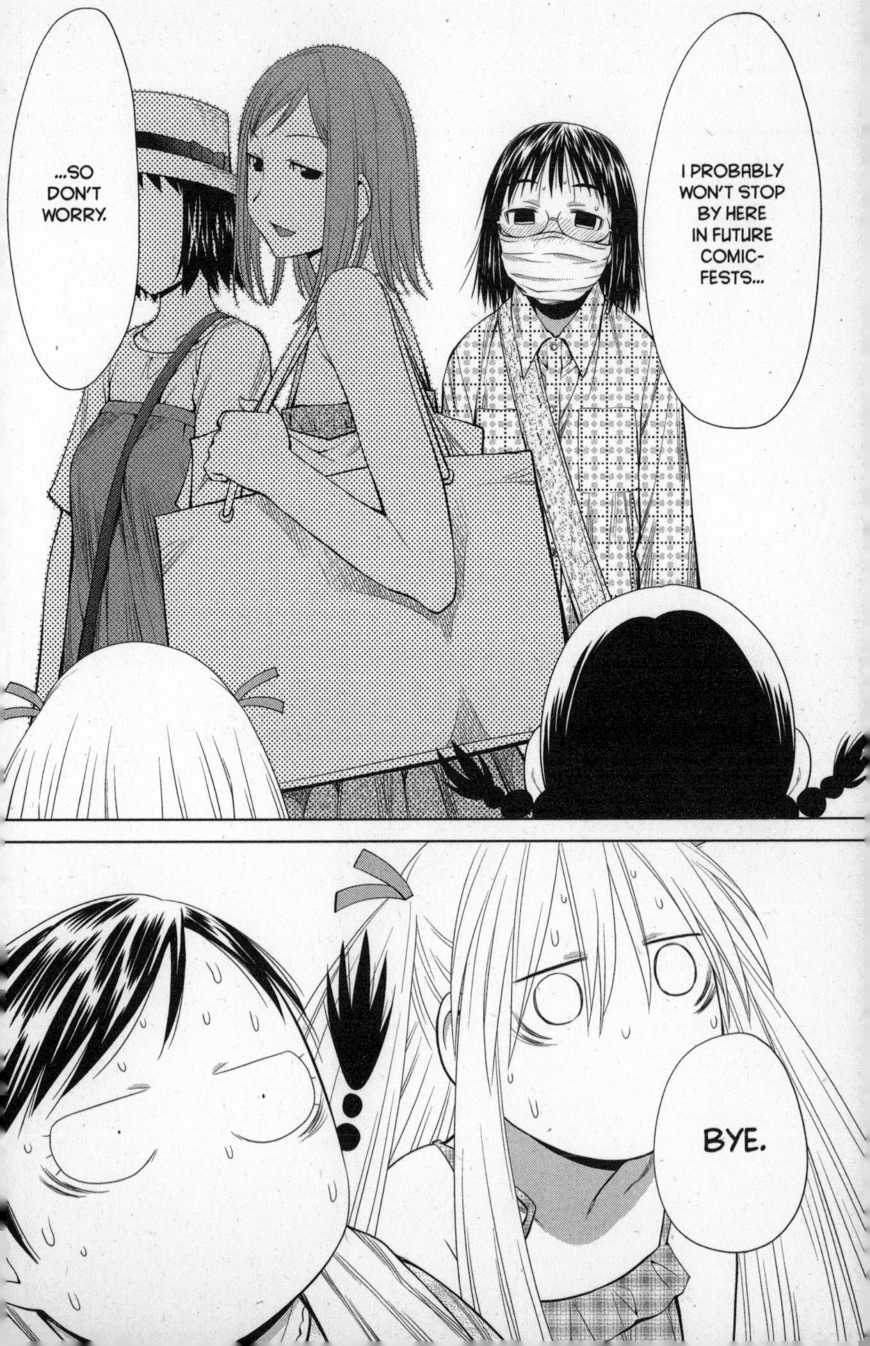
I PROBABLY WON'T STOP BY HERE IN FUTURE COMIC-FESTS...
...SO DON'T WORRY.
BYE.

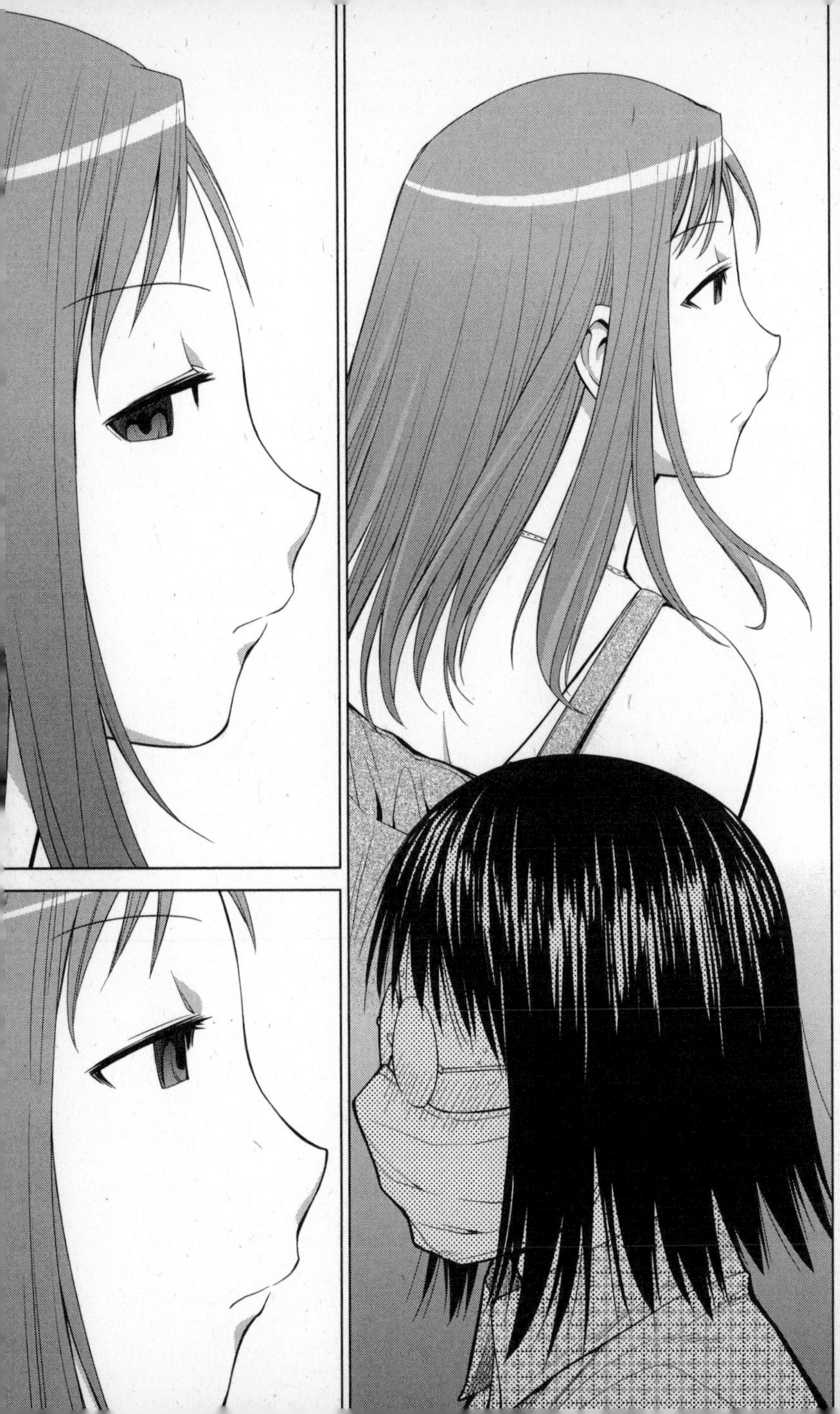

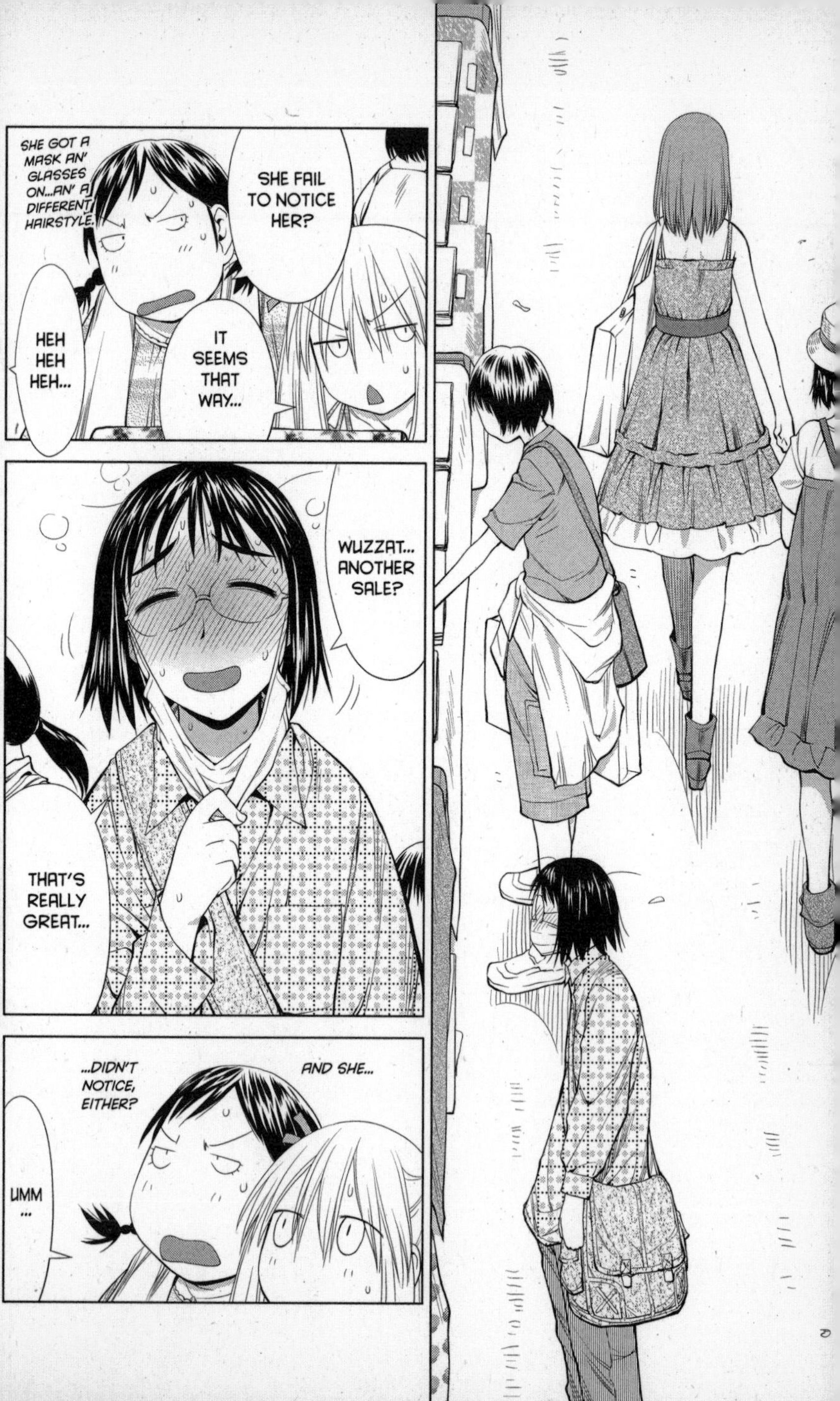
SHE FAIL TO NOTICE HER?
SHE GOT A MASK AN' GLASSES ON...AN' A DIFFERENT HAIRSTYLE.
IT SEEMS THAT WAY...
HEH HEH HEH...
WUZZAT... ANOTHER SALE?
THAT'S REALLY GREAT...
AND SHE...
...DIDN'T NOTICE, EITHER?
UMM ...

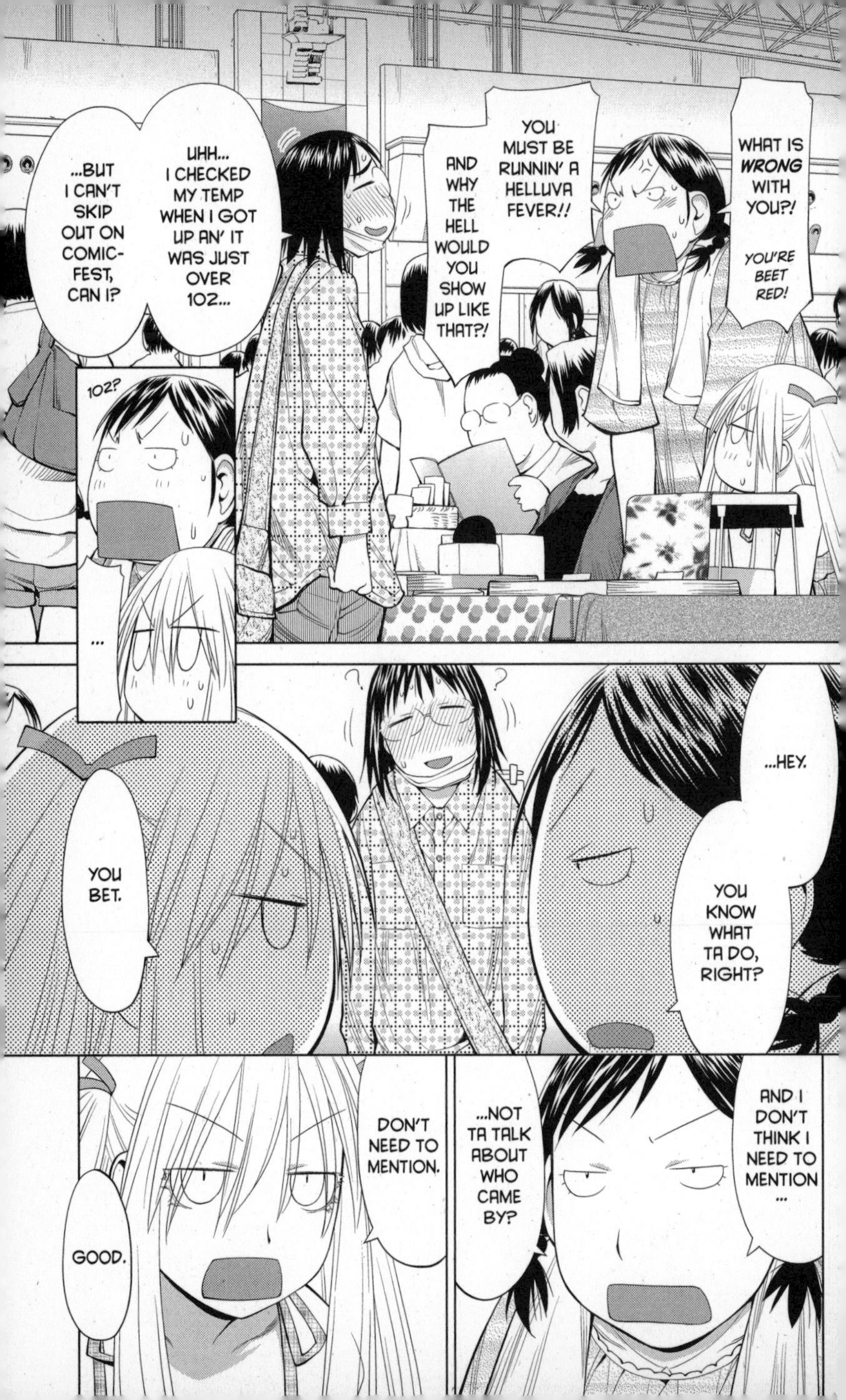
WHAT IS *WRONG* WITH YOU?!
YOU'RE BEET RED!
YOU MUST BE RUNNIN' A HELLUVA FEVER!!
AND WHY THE HELL WOULD YOU SHOW UP LIKE THAT?!
UHH... I CHECKED MY TEMP WHEN I GOT UP AN' IT WAS JUST OVER 102...
...BUT I CAN'T SKIP OUT ON COMIC-FEST, CAN I?
102?
...
...HEY.
YOU KNOW WHAT TA DO, RIGHT?
YOU BET.
AND I DON'T THINK I NEED TO MENTION ...
...NOT TA TALK ABOUT WHO CAME BY?
DON'T NEED TO MENTION.
GOOD.

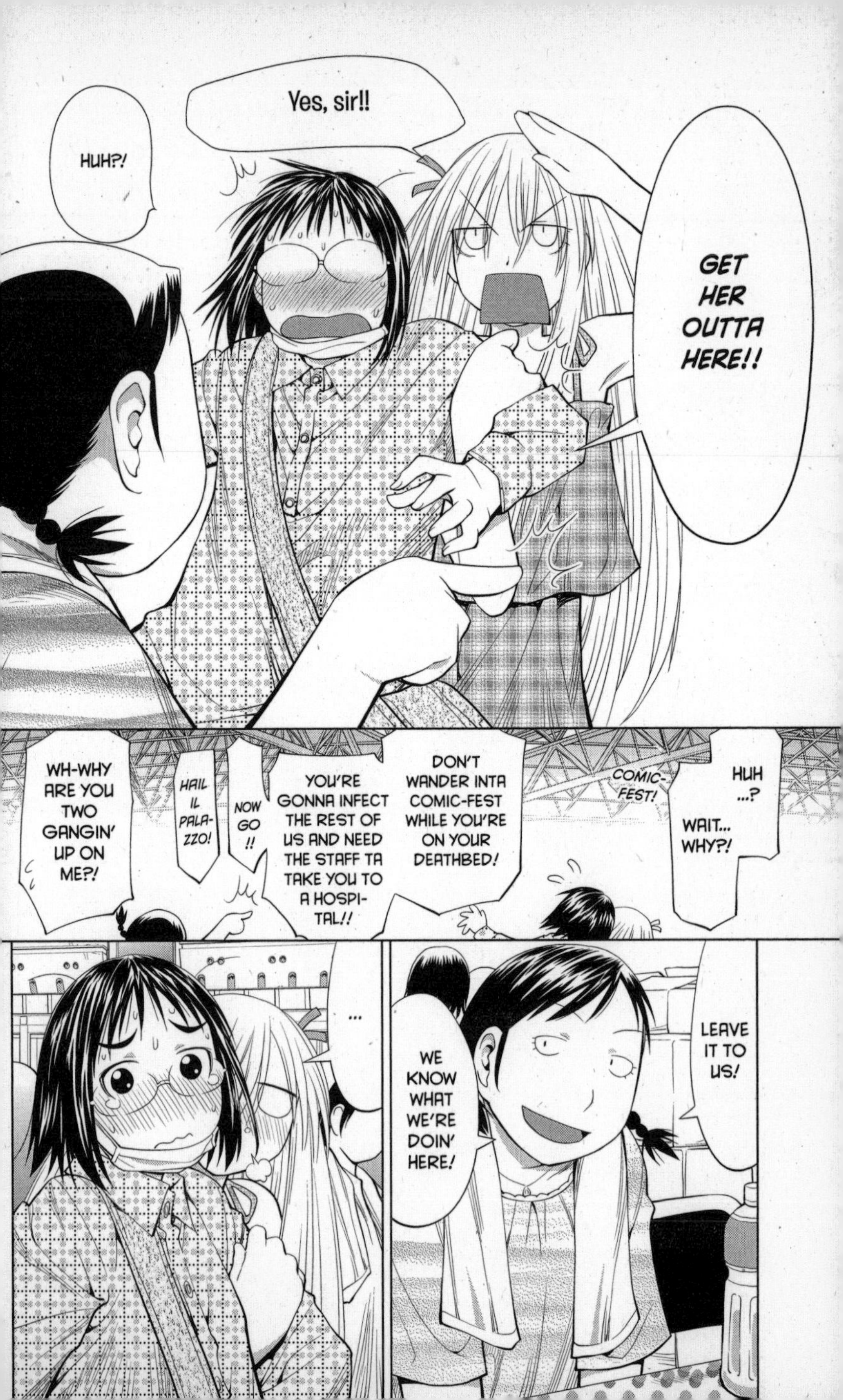

GET HER OUTTA HERE!!
Yes, sir!!
HUH?!
HUH ...? WAIT... WHY?!
COMIC-FEST!
DON'T WANDER INTA COMIC-FEST WHILE YOU'RE ON YOUR DEATHBED!
YOU'RE GONNA INFECT THE REST OF US AND NEED THE STAFF TA TAKE YOU TO A HOSPI-TAL!!
NOW GO !!
HAIL IL PALA-ZZO!
WH-WHY ARE YOU TWO GANGIN' UP ON ME?!
LEAVE IT TO US!
WE KNOW WHAT WE'RE DOIN' HERE!
...

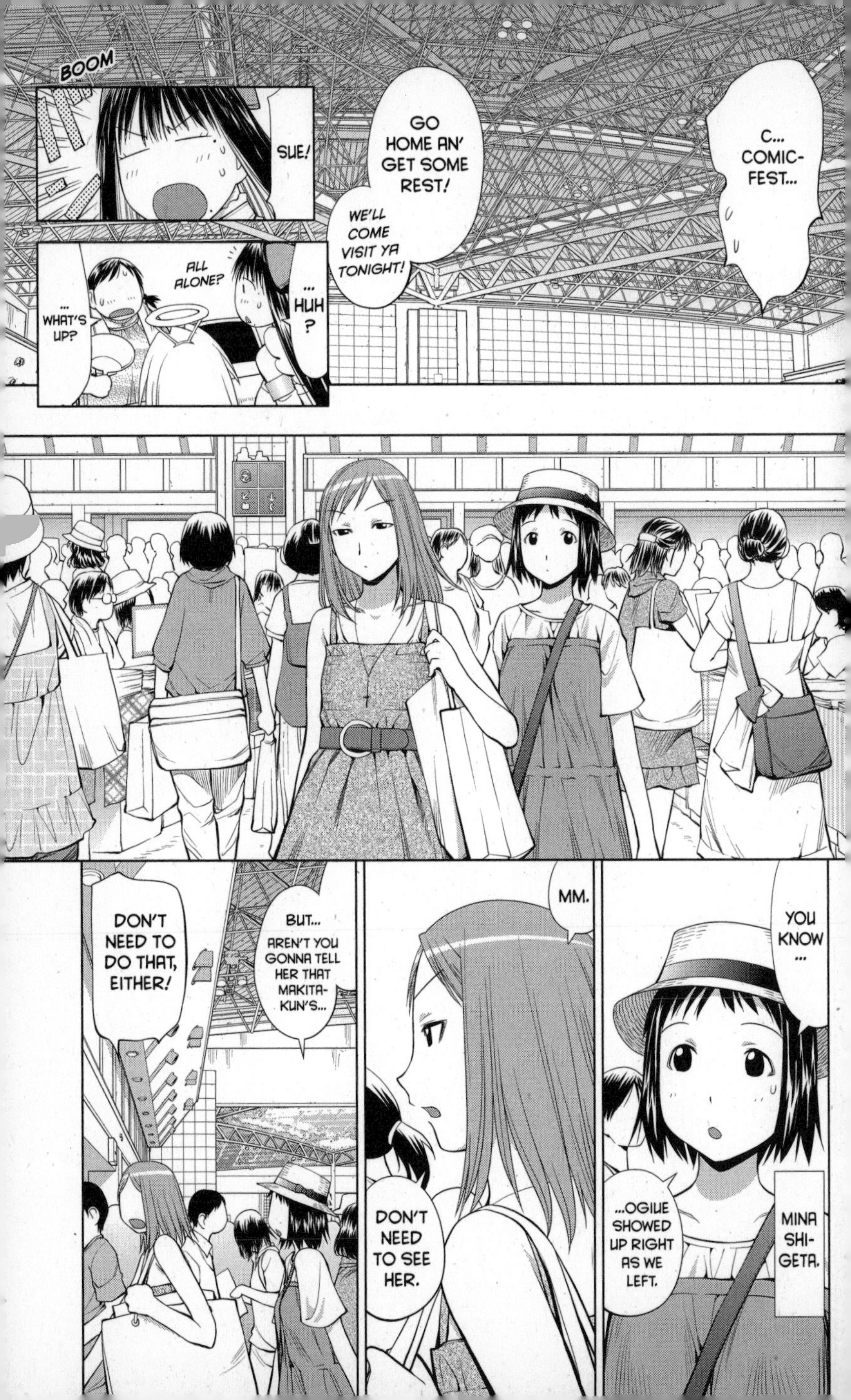
C... COMIC-FEST...
GO HOME AN' GET SOME REST!
WE'LL COME VISIT YA TONIGHT!
BOOM
SUE!
...HUH?
ALL ALONE?
...WHAT'S UP?
YOU KNOW...
MINA SHIGETA.
...OGIUE SHOWED UP RIGHT AS WE LEFT.
MM.
DON'T NEED TO SEE HER.
BUT... AREN'T YOU GONNA TELL HER THAT MAKITA-KUN'S...
DON'T NEED TO DO THAT, EITHER!

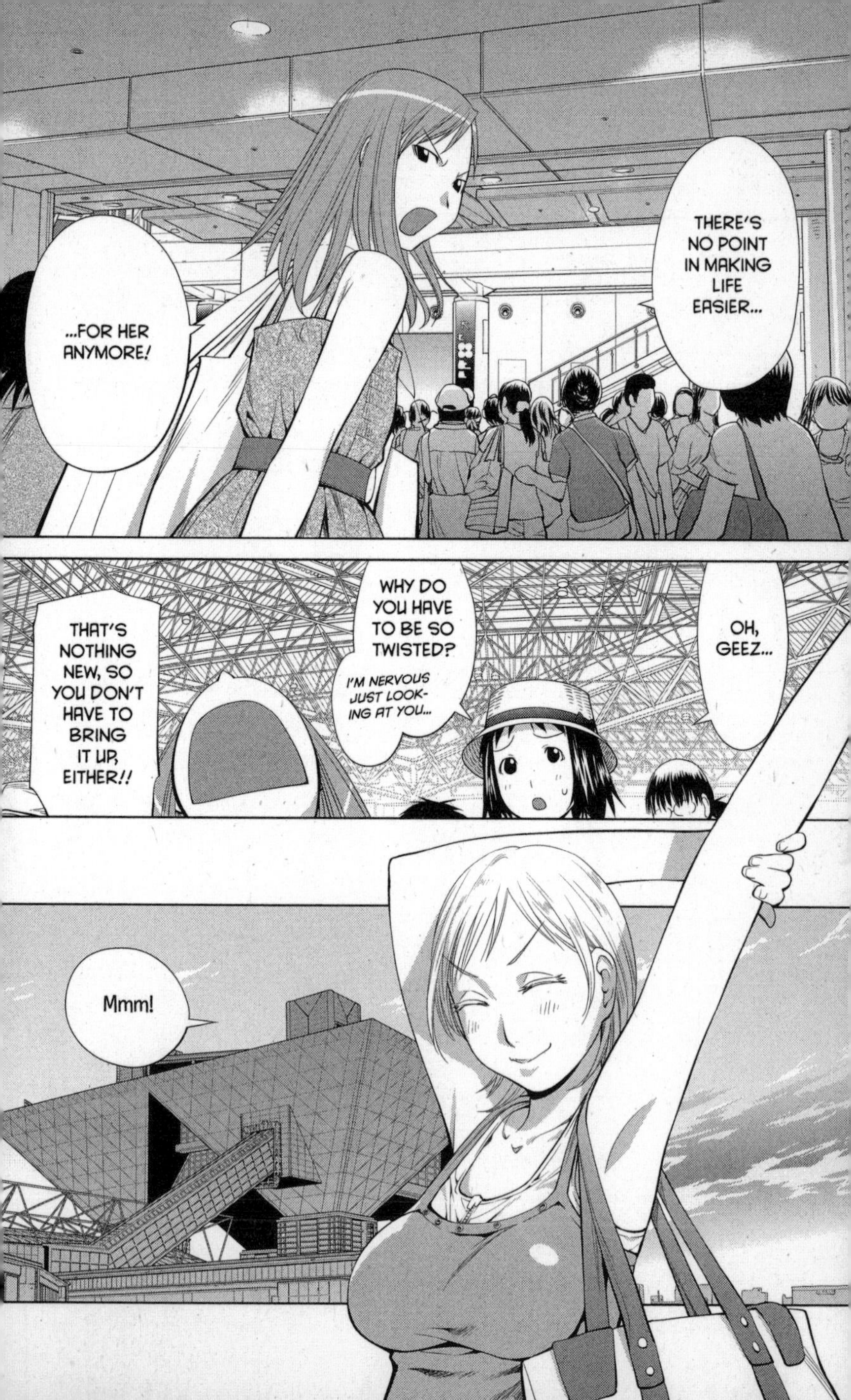
THERE'S NO POINT IN MAKING LIFE EASIER...
...FOR HER ANYMORE!
OH, GEEZ...
WHY DO YOU HAVE TO BE SO TWISTED?
I'M NERVOUS JUST LOOKING AT YOU...
THAT'S NOTHING NEW, SO YOU DON'T HAVE TO BRING IT UP, EITHER!!
Mmm!

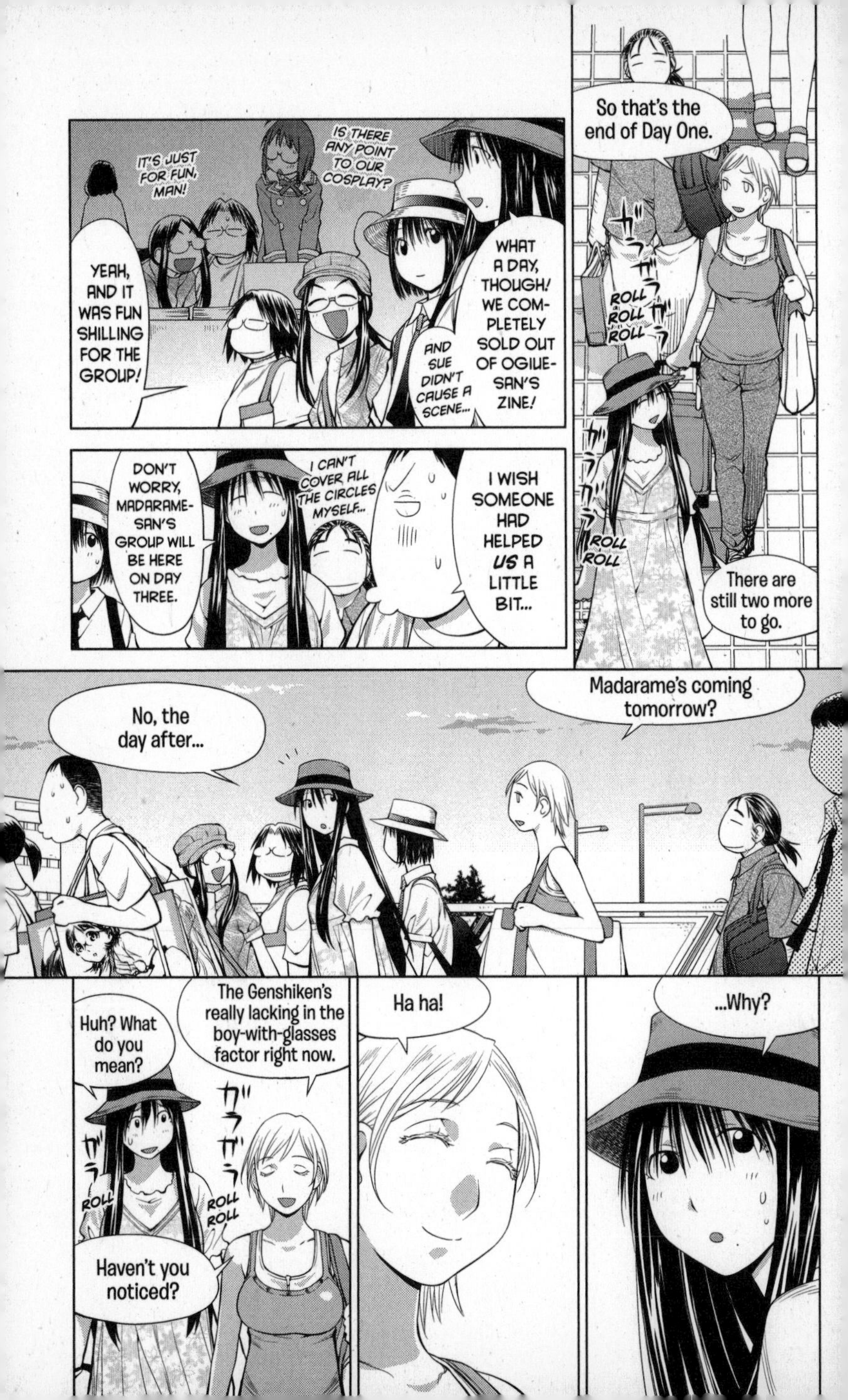

So that's the end of Day One.
ROLL ROLL ROLL
ROLL ROLL
There are still two more to go.
WHAT A DAY, THOUGH! WE COMPLETELY SOLD OUT OF OGIUE-SAN'S ZINE!
AND SUE DIDN'T CAUSE A SCENE...
IS THERE ANY POINT TO OUR COSPLAY?
IT'S JUST FOR FUN, MAN!
YEAH, AND IT WAS FUN SHILLING FOR THE GROUP!
I WISH SOMEONE HAD HELPED US A LITTLE BIT...
I CAN'T COVER ALL THE CIRCLES MYSELF...
DON'T WORRY, MADARAME-SAN'S GROUP WILL BE HERE ON DAY THREE.
Madarame's coming tomorrow?
No, the day after...
...Why?
Ha ha!
The Genshiken's really lacking in the boy-with-glasses factor right now.
Huh? What do you mean?
ROLL ROLL
ROLL
Haven't you noticed?

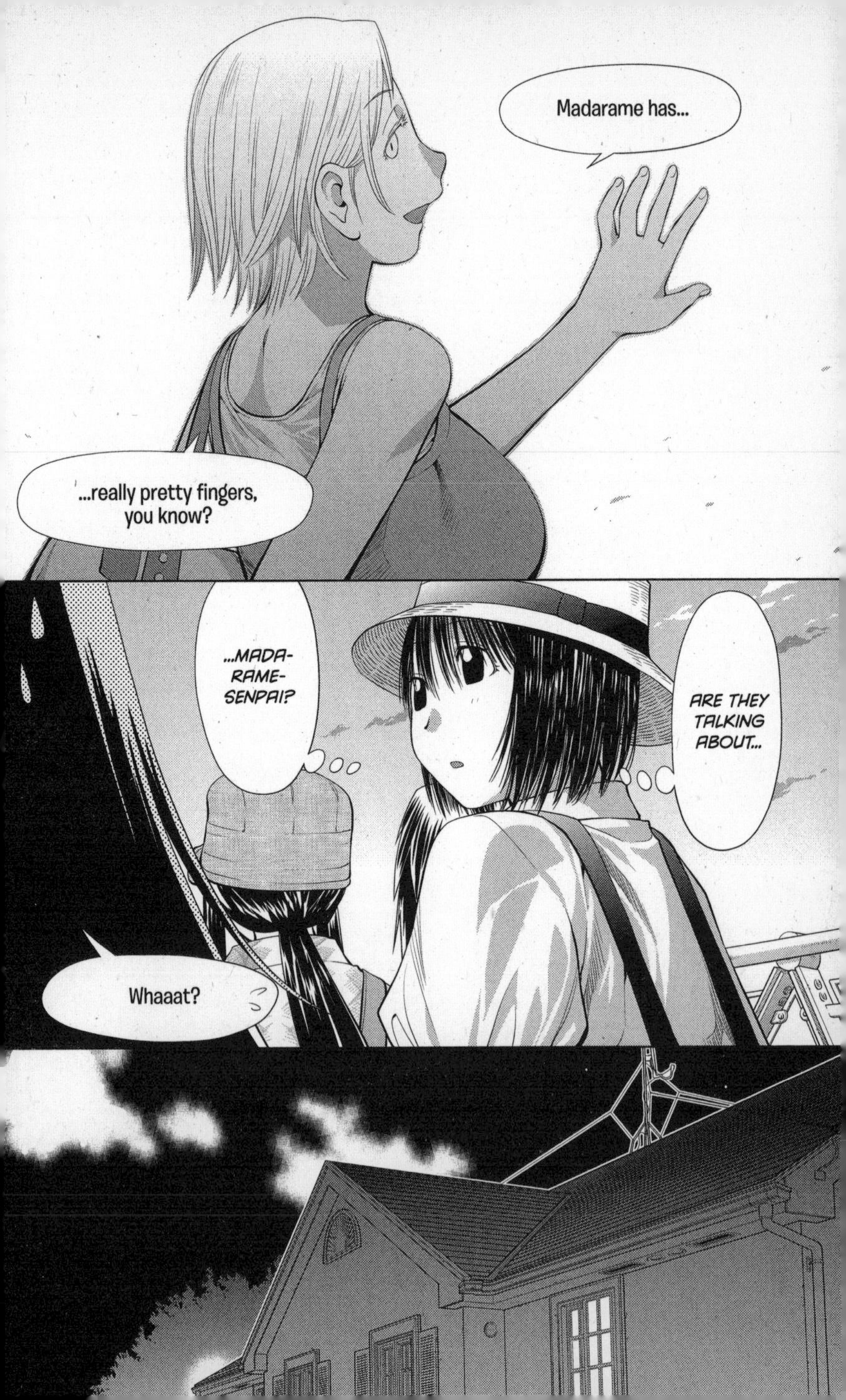
Madarame has...
...really pretty fingers, you know?
ARE THEY TALKING ABOUT...
...MADA-RAME-SENPAI?
Whaaat?

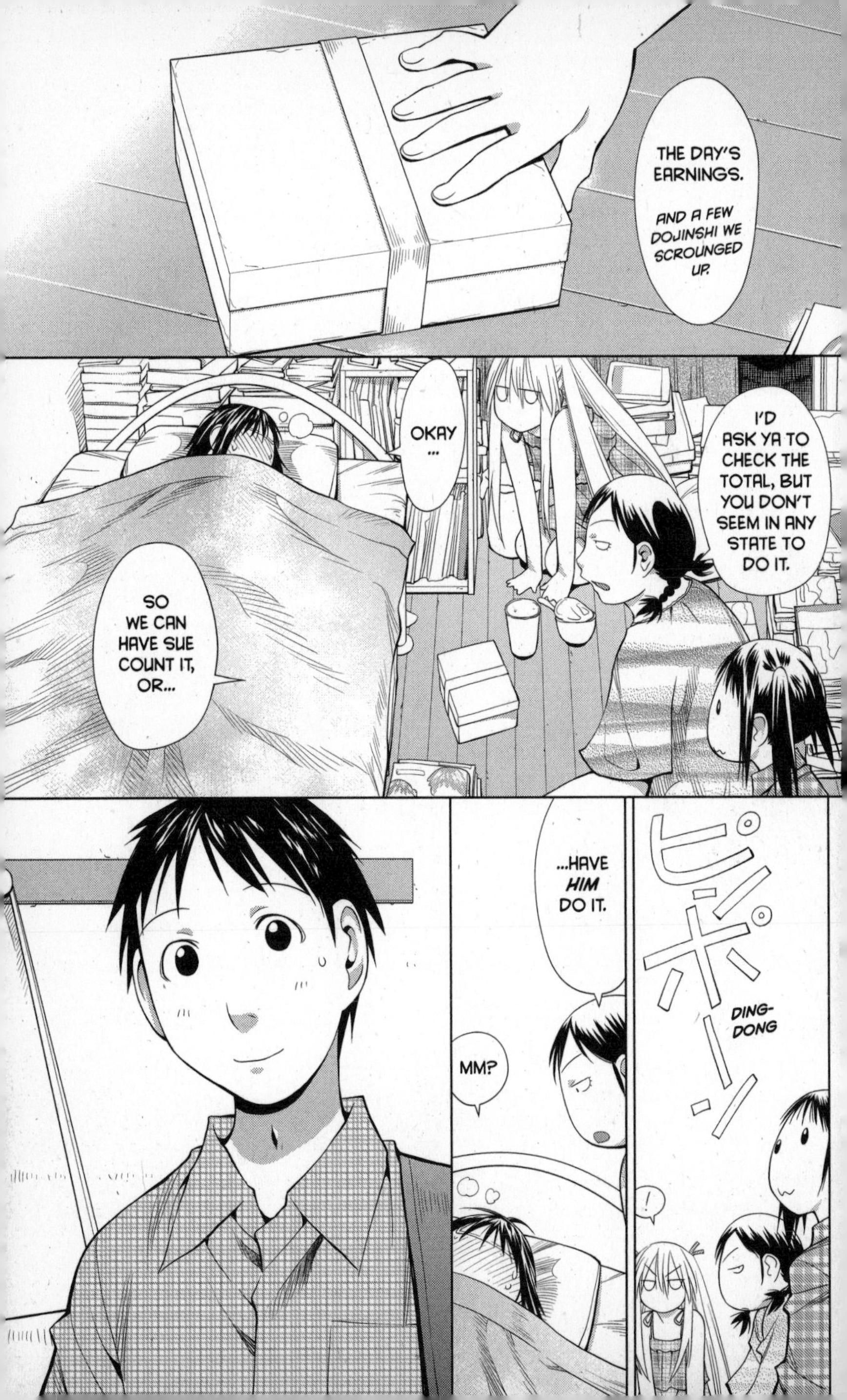
THE DAY'S EARNINGS.
AND A FEW DOJINSHI WE SCROUNGED UP.
I'D ASK YA TO CHECK THE TOTAL, BUT YOU DON'T SEEM IN ANY STATE TO DO IT.
OKAY...
SO WE CAN HAVE SUE COUNT IT, OR...
ピンポーン
DING-DONG
!
...HAVE *HIM* DO IT.
MM?

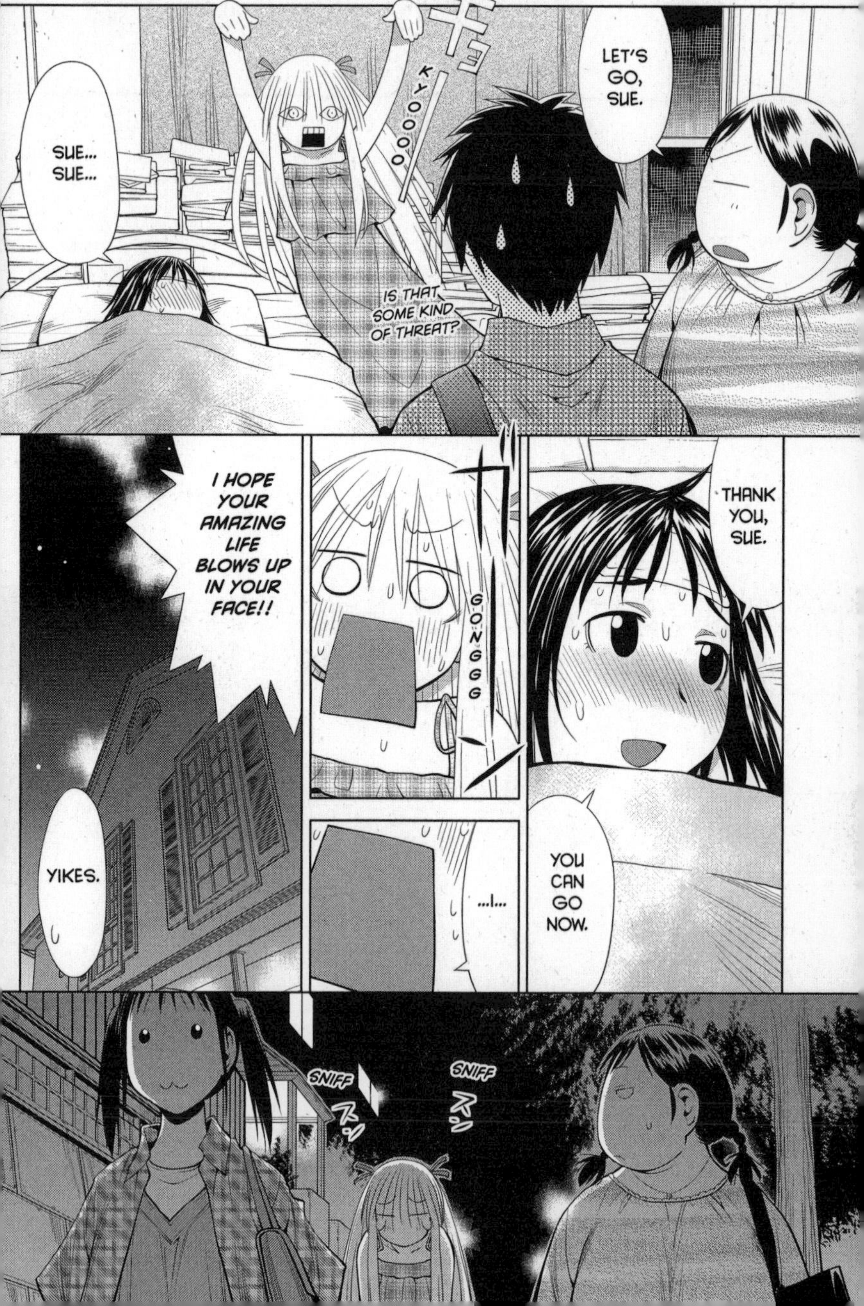
LET'S GO, SUE.
KYOOOOO
SUE... SUE...
IS THAT SOME KIND OF THREAT?
THANK YOU, SUE.
YOU CAN GO NOW.
GONGGG
...I...
I HOPE YOUR AMAZING LIFE BLOWS UP IN YOUR FACE!!
YIKES.
SNIFF
SNIFF

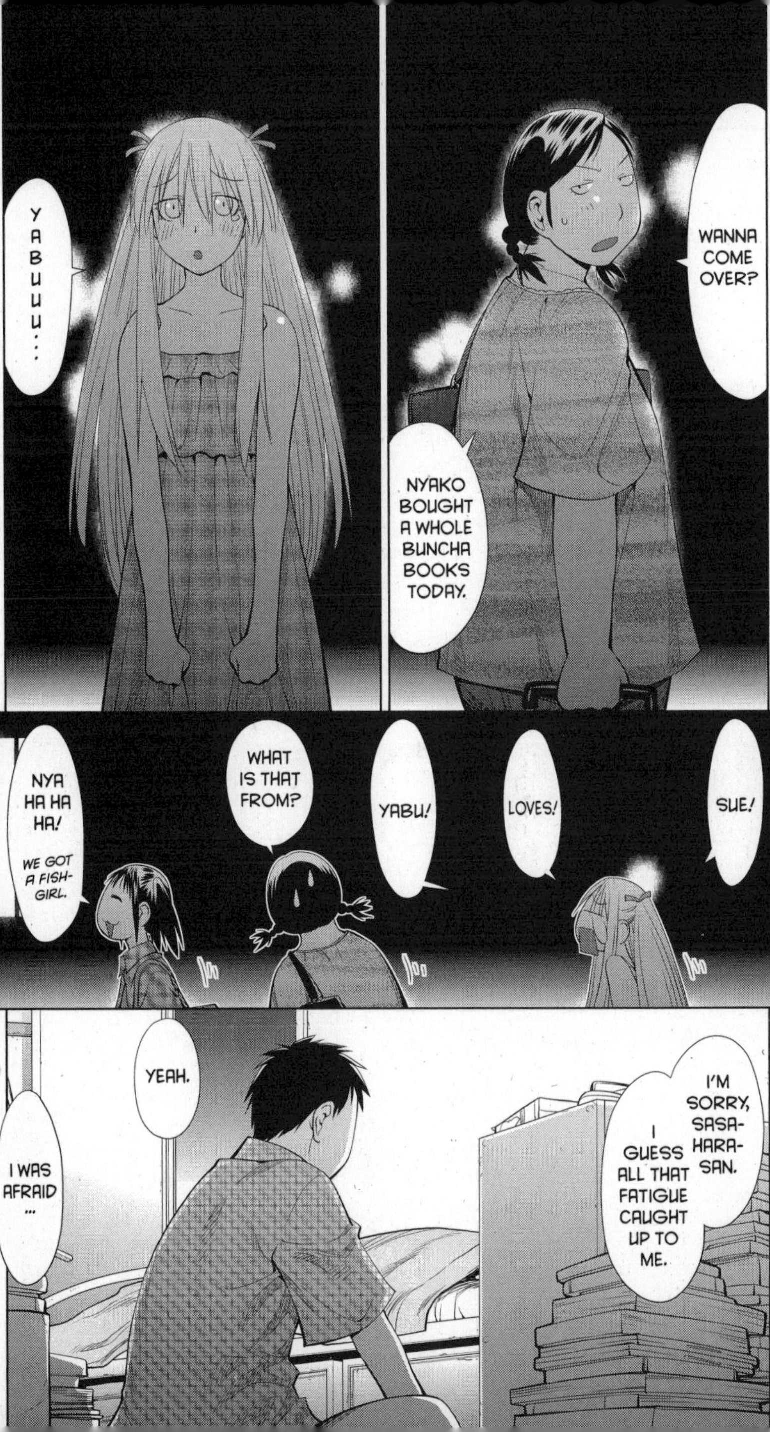
WANNA COME OVER?
NYAKO BOUGHT A WHOLE BUNCHA BOOKS TODAY.
YABUUU...
SUE!
LOVES!
YABU!
WHAT IS THAT FROM?
NYA HA HA HA!
WE GOT A FISH-GIRL.
I'M SORRY, SASA-HARA-SAN.
I GUESS ALL THAT FATIGUE CAUGHT UP TO ME.
YEAH.
I WAS AFRAID...

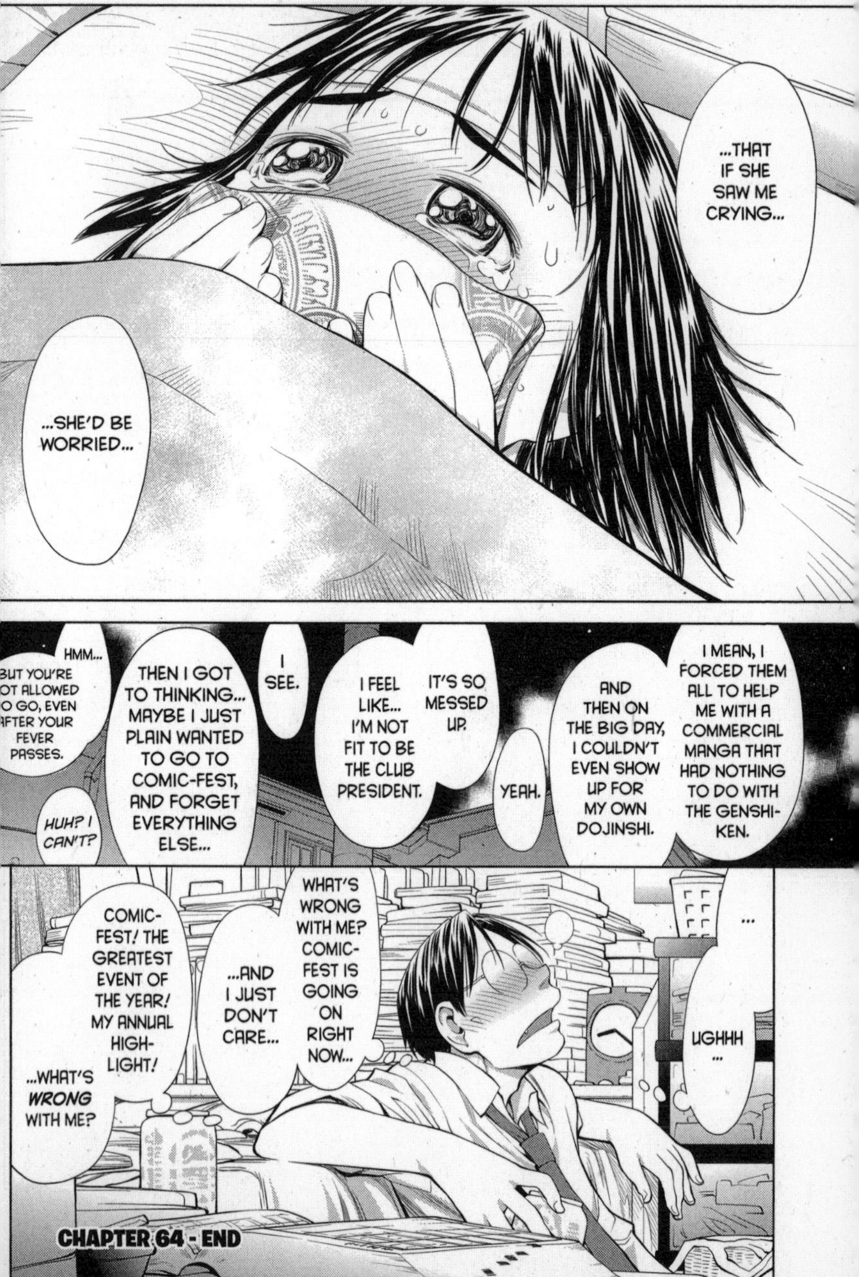
...THAT IF SHE SAW ME CRYING...
...SHE'D BE WORRIED...
I MEAN, I FORCED THEM ALL TO HELP ME WITH A COMMERCIAL MANGA THAT HAD NOTHING TO DO WITH THE GENSHI-KEN.
AND THEN ON THE BIG DAY, I COULDN'T EVEN SHOW UP FOR MY OWN DOJINSHI.
YEAH.
IT'S SO MESSED UP.
I FEEL LIKE... I'M NOT FIT TO BE THE CLUB PRESIDENT.
I SEE.
THEN I GOT TO THINKING... MAYBE I JUST PLAIN WANTED TO GO TO COMIC-FEST, AND FORGET EVERYTHING ELSE...
HMM...
BUT YOU'RE OT ALLOWED O GO, EVEN FTER YOUR FEVER PASSES.
HUH? I CAN'T?
...
UGHHH ...
WHAT'S WRONG WITH ME? COMIC-FEST IS GOING ON RIGHT NOW...
...AND I JUST DON'T CARE...
COMIC-FEST! THE GREATEST EVENT OF THE YEAR! MY ANNUAL HIGH-LIGHT!
...WHAT'S *WRONG* WITH ME?
CHAPTER 64 - END

CHAPTER 64 - MOMENTS LATE

KEEPING ABREAST ADD-ON

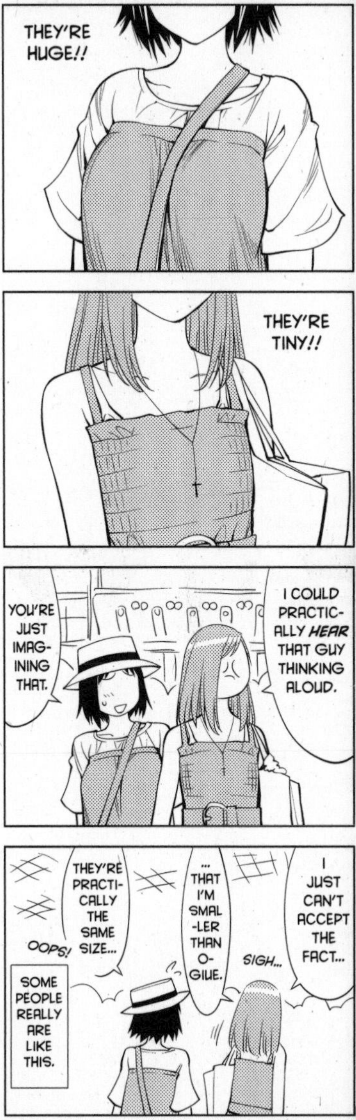
THEY'RE HUGE!!
THEY'RE TINY!!
I COULD PRACTICALLY *HEAR* THAT GUY THINKING ALOUD.
YOU'RE JUST IMAGINING THAT.
I JUST CAN'T ACCEPT THE FACT...
SIGH...
...THAT I'M SMALLER THAN OGIUE.
THEY'RE PRACTICALLY THE SAME SIZE...
OOPS!
SOME PEOPLE REALLY ARE LIKE THIS.

IN YABU'S ROOM

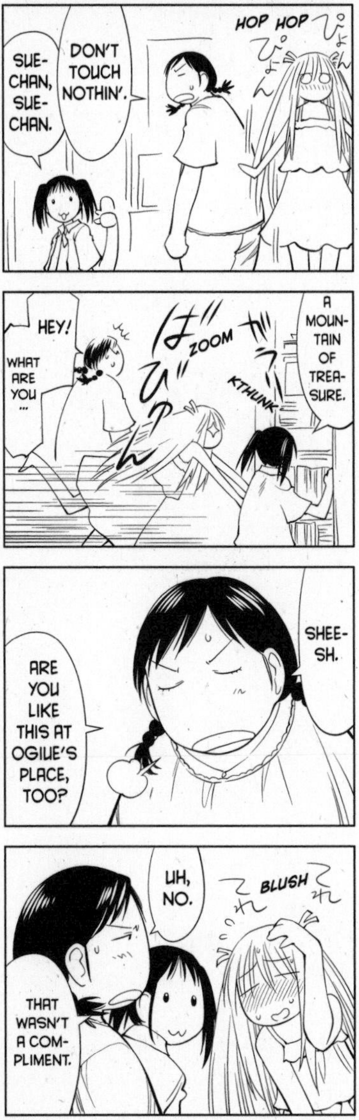
ぴょん ぴょん
HOP HOP
DON'T TOUCH NOTHIN'.
SUE-CHAN, SUE-CHAN.
A MOUNTAIN OF TREASURE.
ガッ
KTHUNK
ばひゅん
ZOOM
HEY!
WHAT ARE YOU ...
SHEE-SH.
ARE YOU LIKE THIS AT OGIUE'S PLACE, TOO?
てれ てれ
BLUSH
UH, NO.
THAT WASN'T A COMPLIMENT.

RHAPSODY IN BANGS

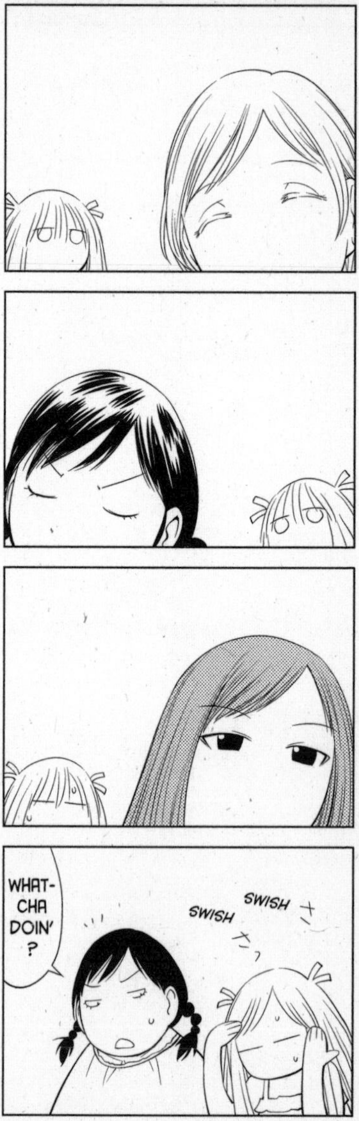
WHATCHA DOIN'?
SWISH
SWISH

RESISTANCE IS FUTILE

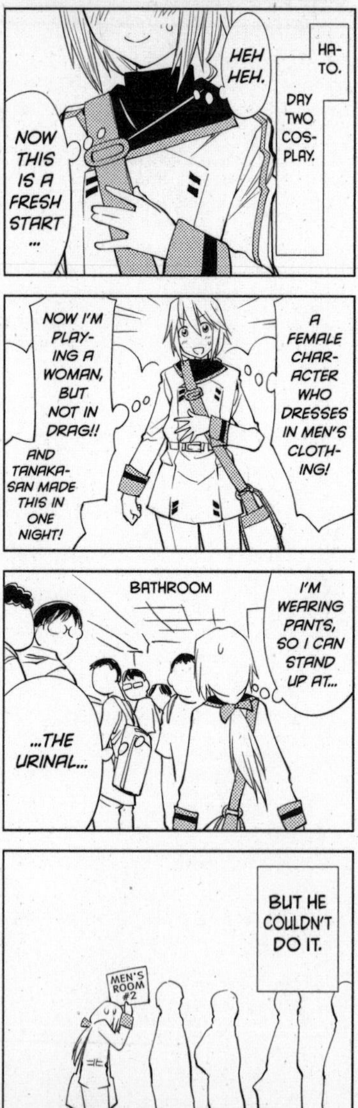
HATO. DAY TWO COSPLAY.
HEH HEH.
NOW THIS IS A FRESH START...
A FEMALE CHARACTER WHO DRESSES IN MEN'S CLOTHING!
NOW I'M PLAYING A WOMAN, BUT NOT IN DRAG!!
AND TANAKA-SAN MADE THIS IN ONE NIGHT!
I'M WEARING PANTS, SO I CAN STAND UP AT...
BATHROOM
...THE URINAL...
BUT HE COULDN'T DO IT.
MEN'S ROOM #2

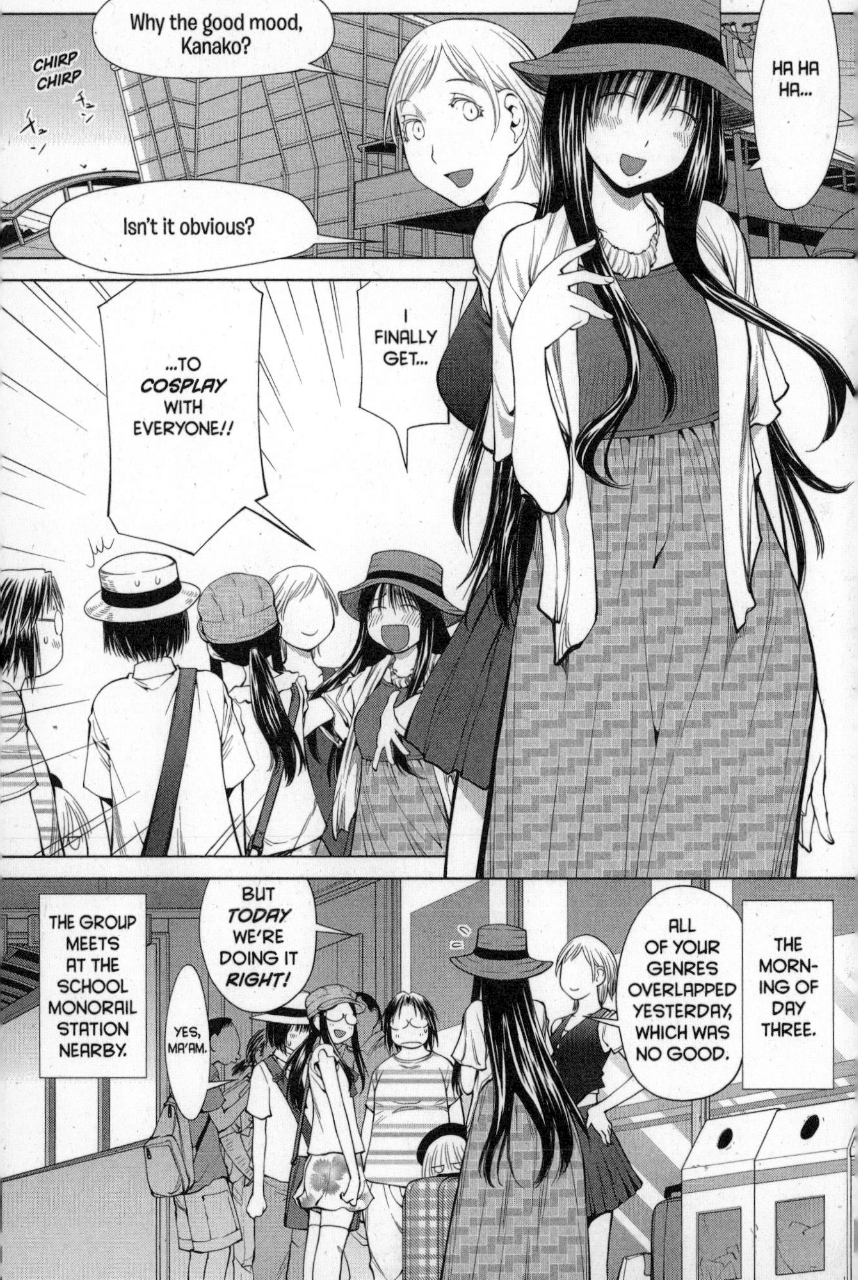
HA HA HA...
Why the good mood, Kanako?
CHIRP CHIRP
Isn't it obvious?
I FINALLY GET...
...TO *COSPLAY* WITH EVERYONE!!
THE MORNING OF DAY THREE.
ALL OF YOUR GENRES OVERLAPPED YESTERDAY, WHICH WAS NO GOOD.
BUT *TODAY* WE'RE DOING IT *RIGHT!*
YES, MA'AM.
THE GROUP MEETS AT THE SCHOOL MONORAIL STATION NEARBY.

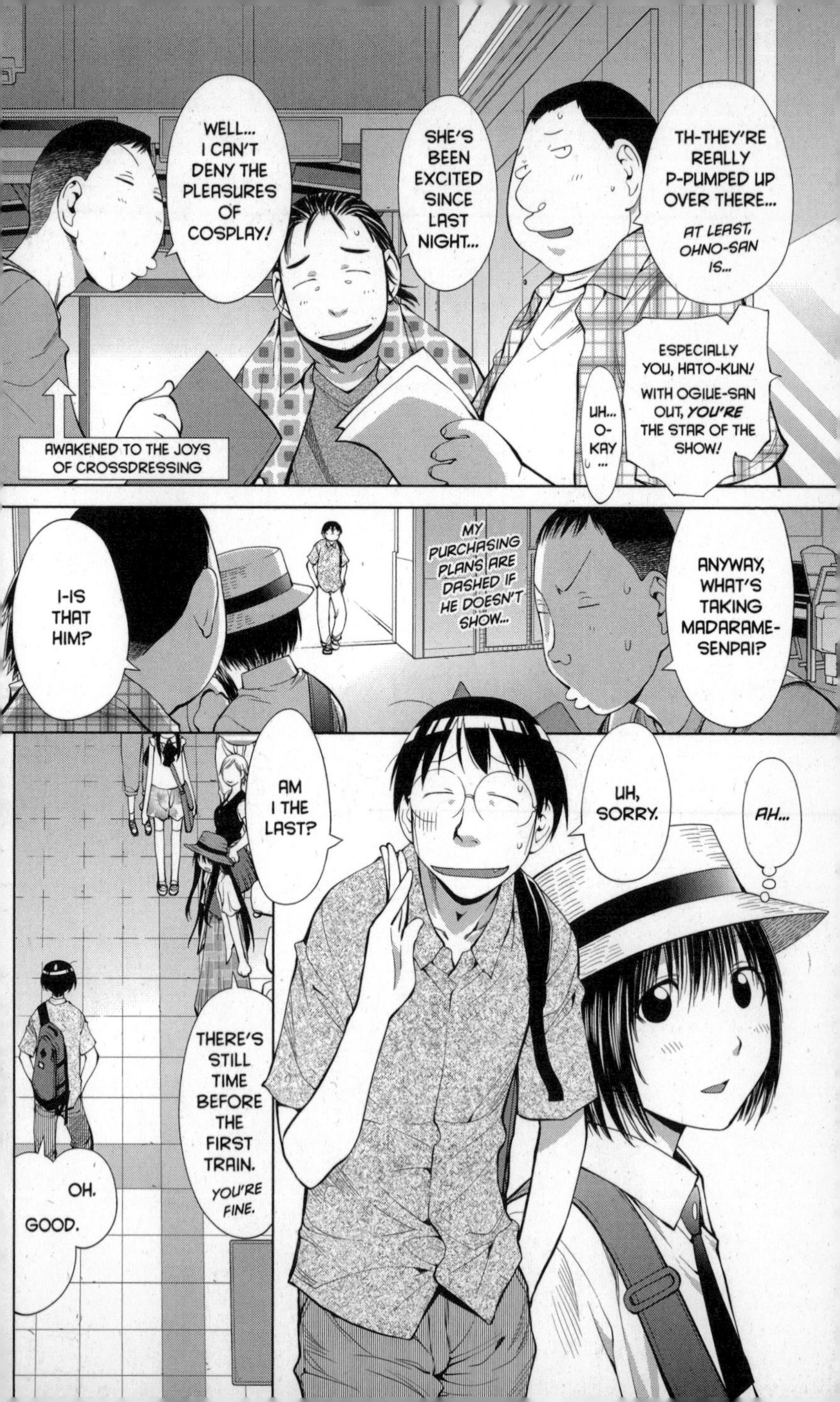
TH-THEY'RE REALLY P-PUMPED UP OVER THERE... AT LEAST, OHNO-SAN IS...
SHE'S BEEN EXCITED SINCE LAST NIGHT...
WELL... I CAN'T DENY THE PLEASURES OF COSPLAY!
ESPECIALLY YOU, HATO-KUN! WITH OGIUE-SAN OUT, YOU'RE THE STAR OF THE SHOW!
UH... O-KAY...
AWAKENED TO THE JOYS OF CROSSDRESSING
ANYWAY, WHAT'S TAKING MADARAME-SENPAI?
MY PURCHASING PLANS ARE DASHED IF HE DOESN'T SHOW...
I-IS THAT HIM?
AH...
UH, SORRY.
AM I THE LAST?
THERE'S STILL TIME BEFORE THE FIRST TRAIN. YOU'RE FINE.
OH. GOOD.

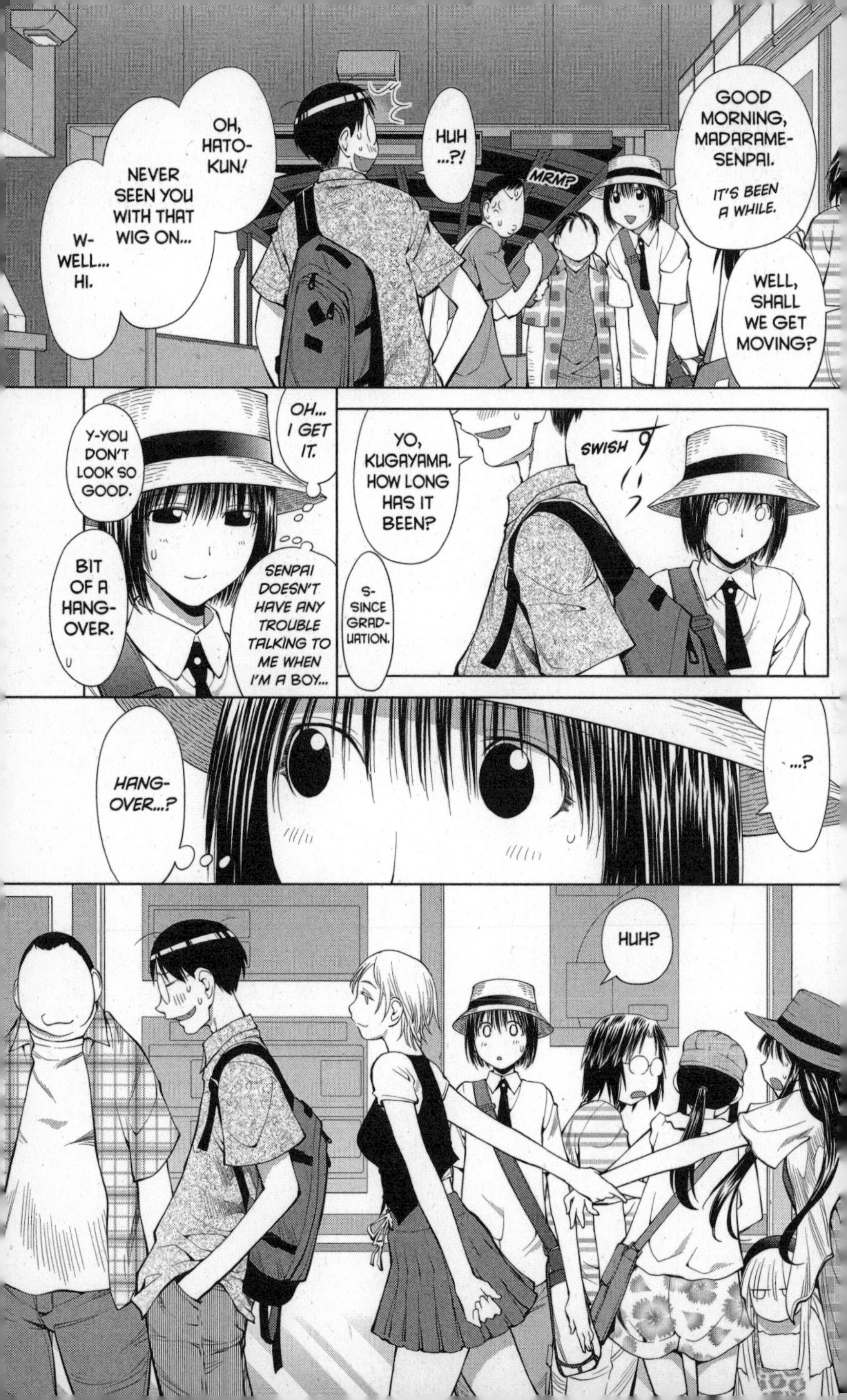
GOOD MORNING, MADARAME-SENPAI.
IT'S BEEN A WHILE.
WELL, SHALL WE GET MOVING?
MRM?
HUH ...?!
OH, HATO-KUN!
NEVER SEEN YOU WITH THAT WIG ON...
W-WELL... HI.
SWISH
YO, KUGAYAMA. HOW LONG HAS IT BEEN?
S-SINCE GRADUATION.
Y-YOU DON'T LOOK SO GOOD.
BIT OF A HANGOVER.
OH... I GET IT.
SENPAI DOESN'T HAVE ANY TROUBLE TALKING TO ME WHEN I'M A BOY...
...?
HANGOVER...?
HUH?

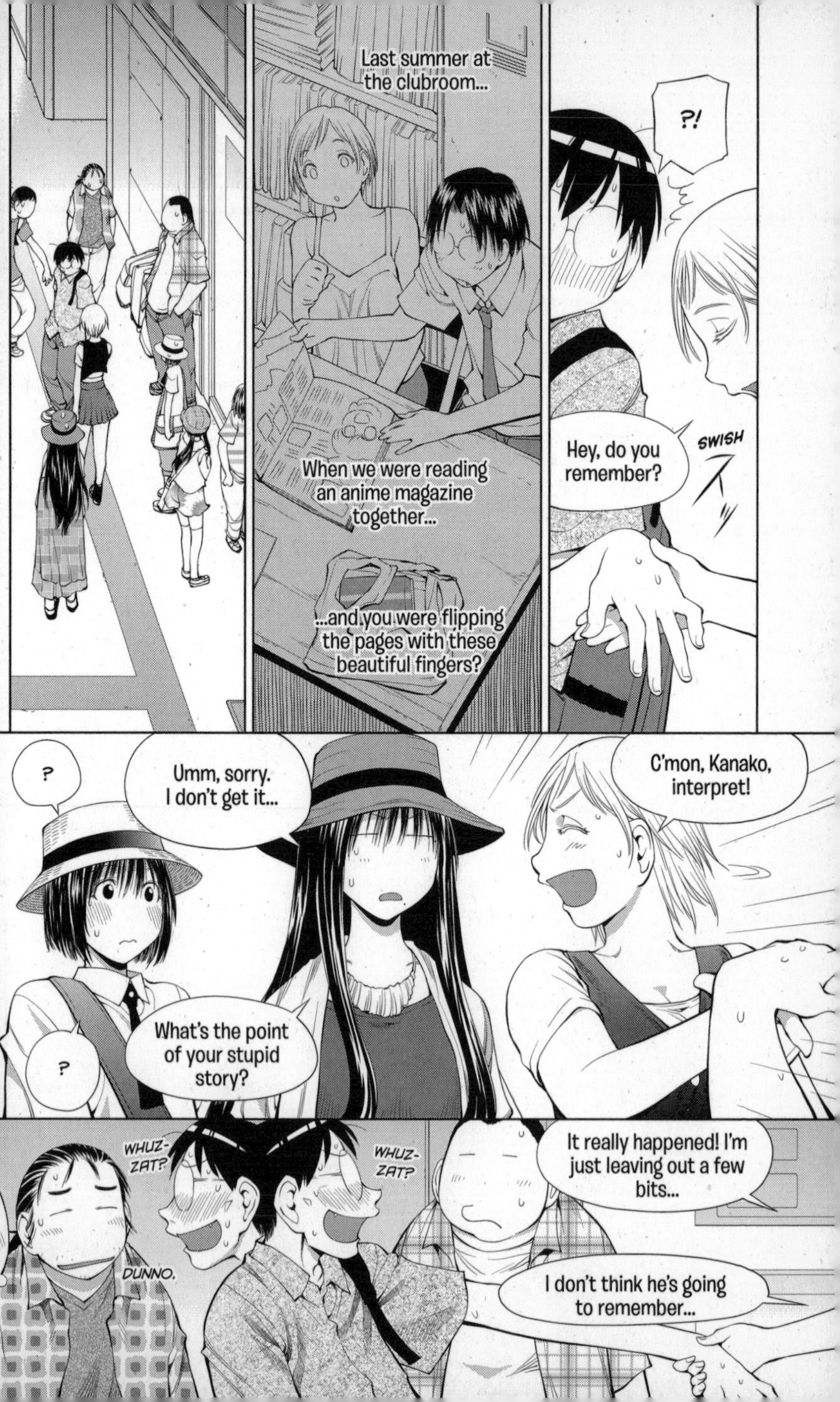

?!
Hey, do you remember?
SWISH
Last summer at the clubroom...
When we were reading an anime magazine together...
...and you were flipping the pages with these beautiful fingers?
C'mon, Kanako, interpret!
Umm, sorry. I don't get it...
?
What's the point of your stupid story?
?
It really happened! I'm just leaving out a few bits...
WHUZ-ZAT?
WHUZ-ZAT?
I don't think he's going to remember...
DUNNO.

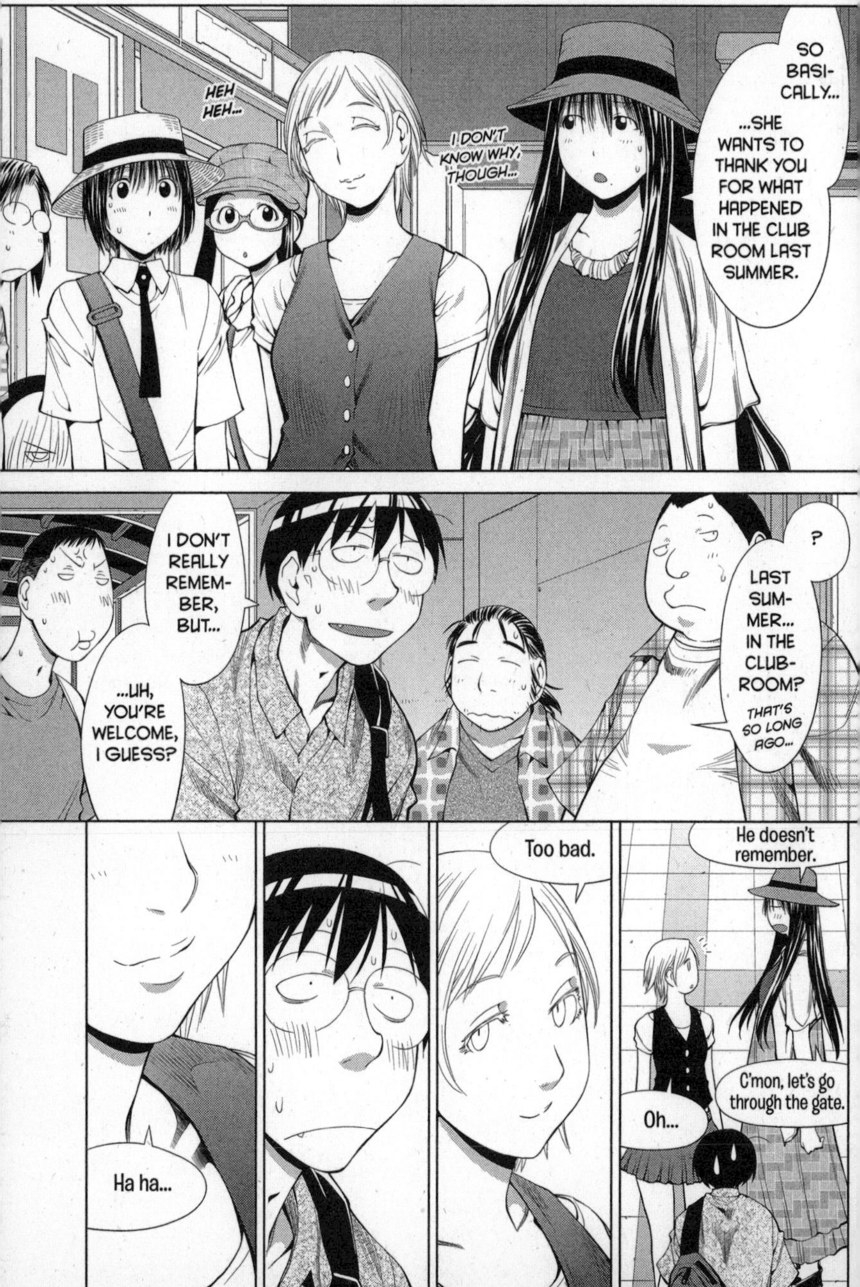
SO BASI-CALLY...
...SHE WANTS TO THANK YOU FOR WHAT HAPPENED IN THE CLUB ROOM LAST SUMMER.
I DON'T KNOW WHY, THOUGH...
HEH HEH...
?
LAST SUM-MER... IN THE CLUB-ROOM?
THAT'S SO LONG AGO...
I DON'T REALLY REMEM-BER, BUT...
...UH, YOU'RE WELCOME, I GUESS?
He doesn't remember.
C'mon, let's go through the gate.
Oh...
Too bad.
Ha ha...

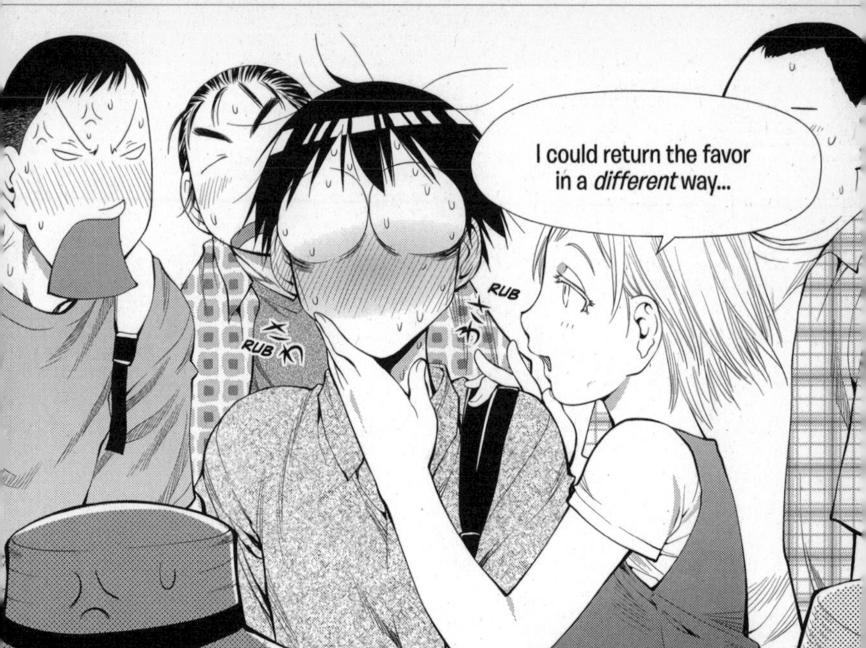
I could return the favor in a *different* way...
RUB
RUB
Stop that.

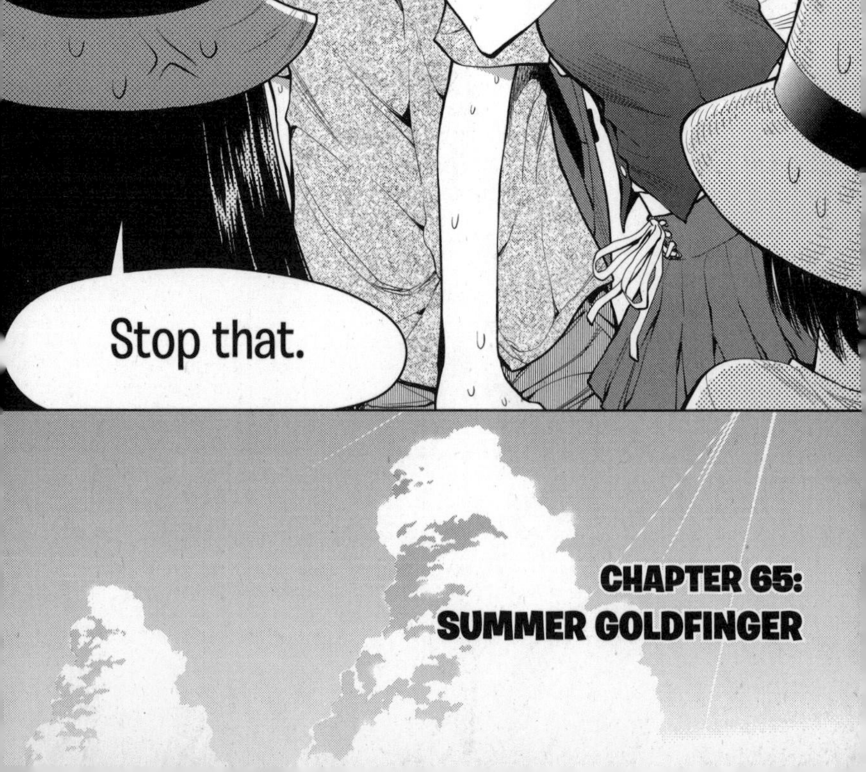
CHAPTER 65:
SUMMER GOLDFINGER

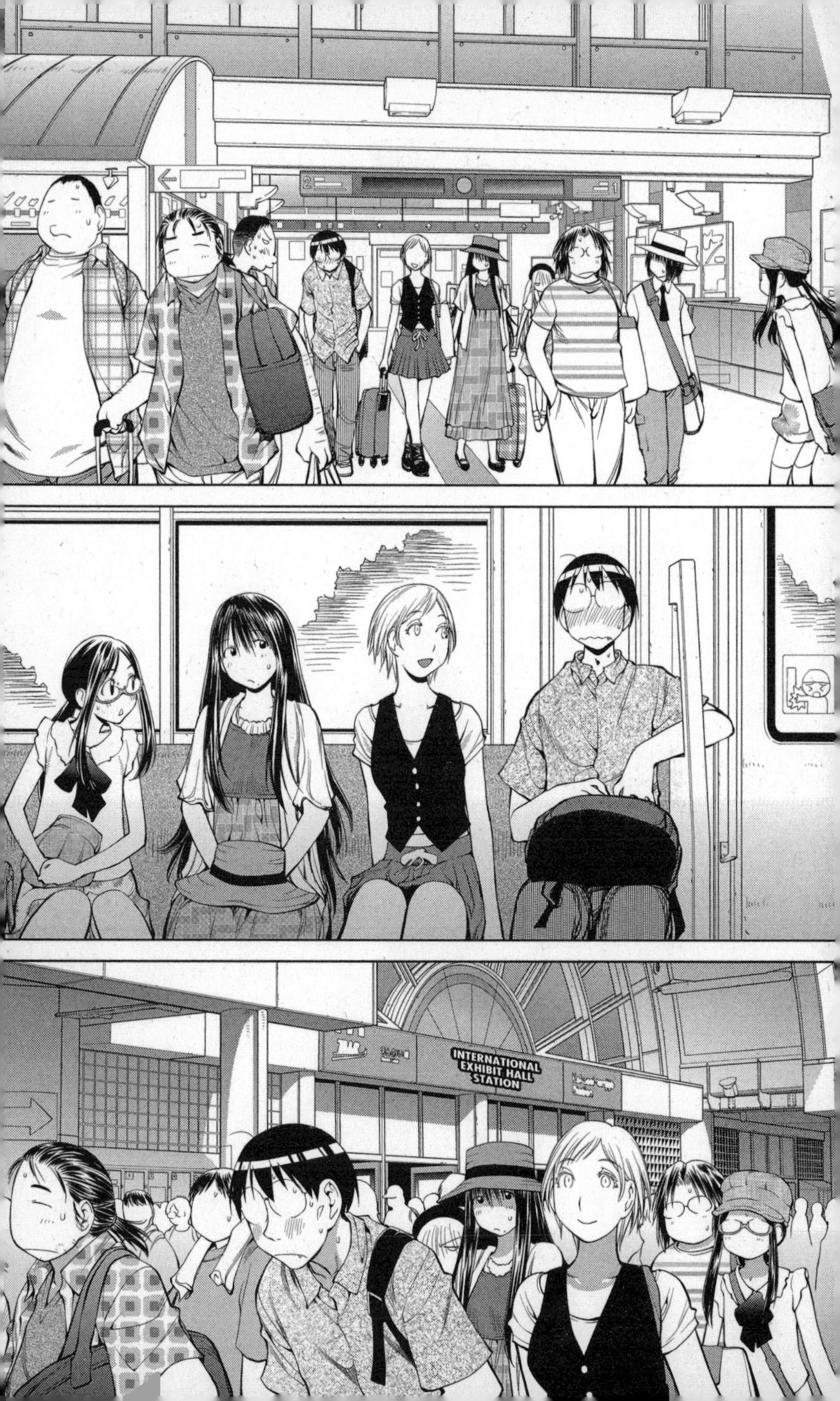
INTERNATIONAL EXHIBIT HALL STATION

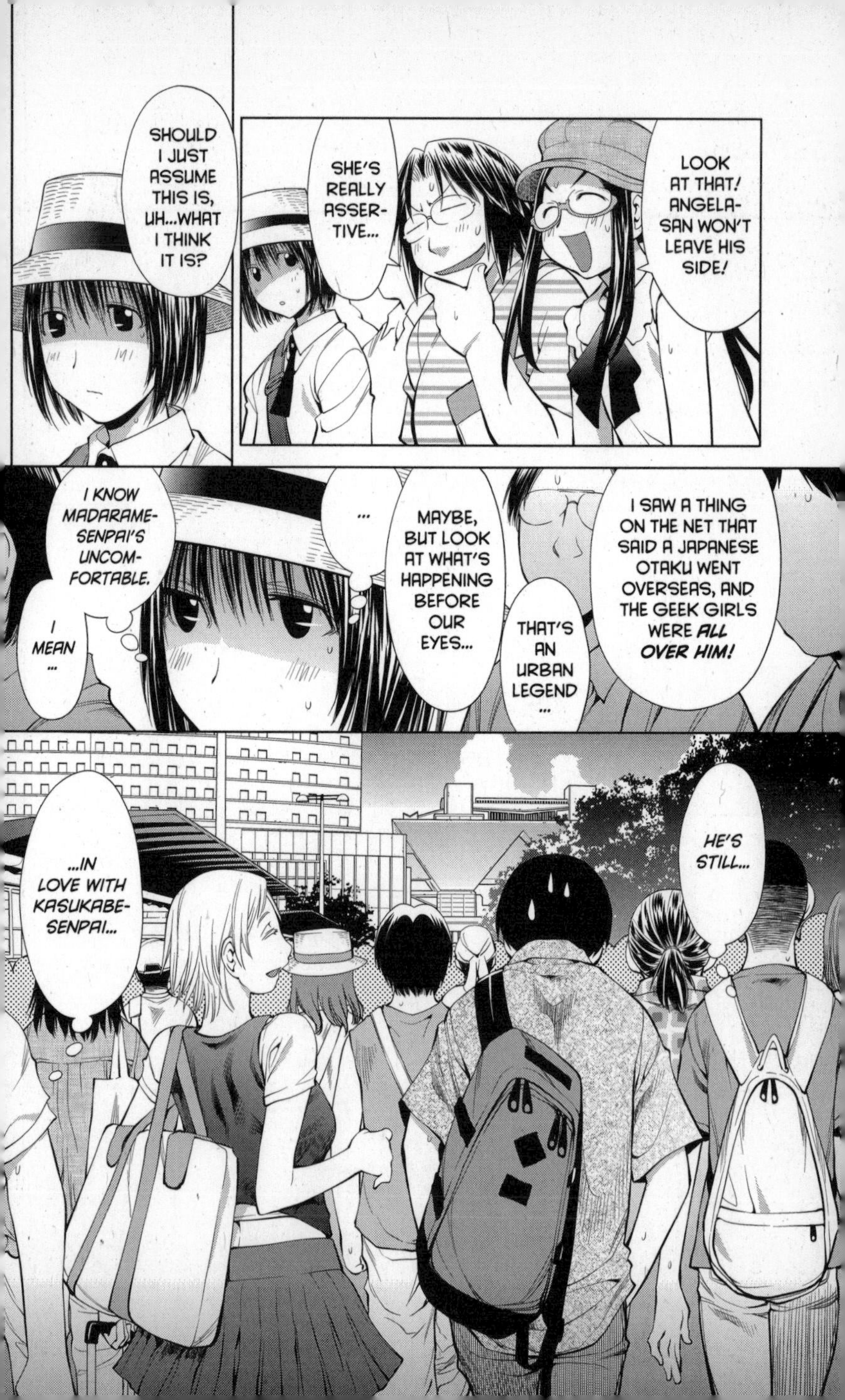
LOOK AT THAT! ANGELA-SAN WON'T LEAVE HIS SIDE!
SHE'S REALLY ASSERTIVE...
SHOULD I JUST ASSUME THIS IS, UH...WHAT I THINK IT IS?
I SAW A THING ON THE NET THAT SAID A JAPANESE OTAKU WENT OVERSEAS, AND THE GEEK GIRLS WERE **ALL OVER HIM!**
THAT'S AN URBAN LEGEND...
MAYBE, BUT LOOK AT WHAT'S HAPPENING BEFORE OUR EYES...
...
I KNOW MADARAME-SENPAI'S UNCOMFORTABLE.
I MEAN...
HE'S STILL...
...IN LOVE WITH KASUKABE-SENPAI...

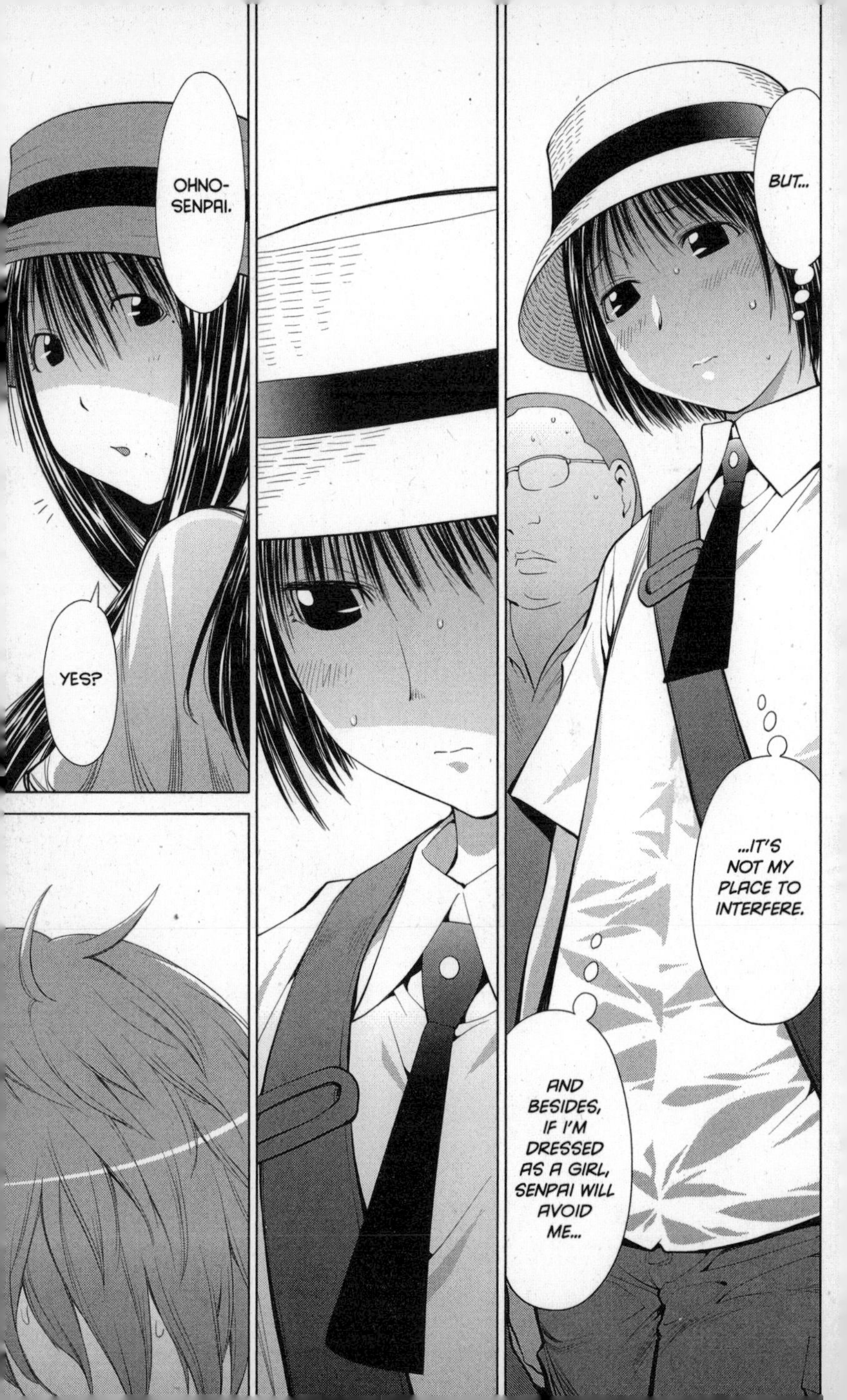
BUT...
...IT'S NOT MY PLACE TO INTERFERE.
AND BESIDES, IF I'M DRESSED AS A GIRL, SENPAI WILL AVOID ME...
OHNO-SENPAI.
YES?

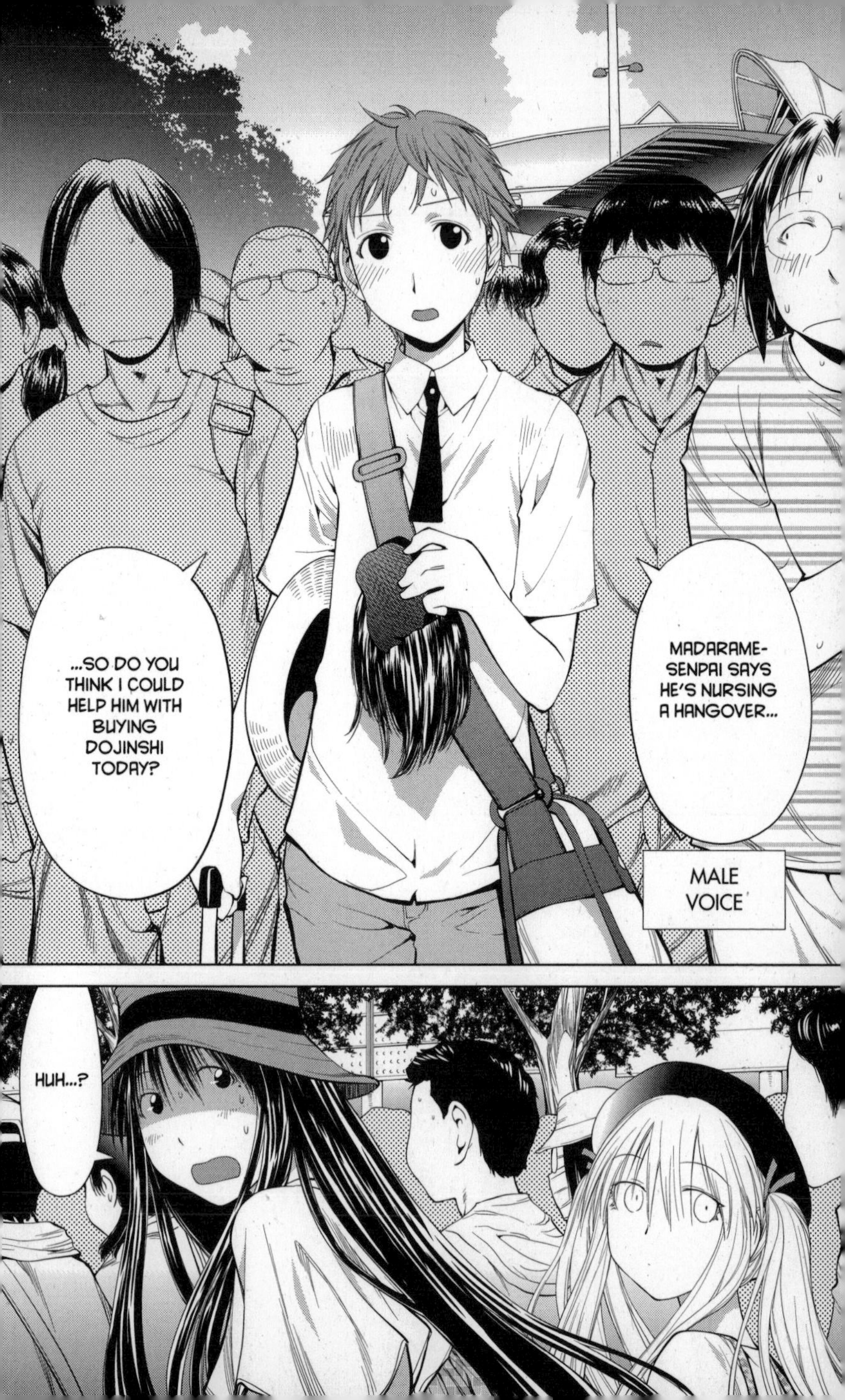
MADARAME-SENPAI SAYS HE'S NURSING A HANGOVER...
MALE VOICE
...SO DO YOU THINK I COULD HELP HIM WITH BUYING DOJINSHI TODAY?
HUH...?

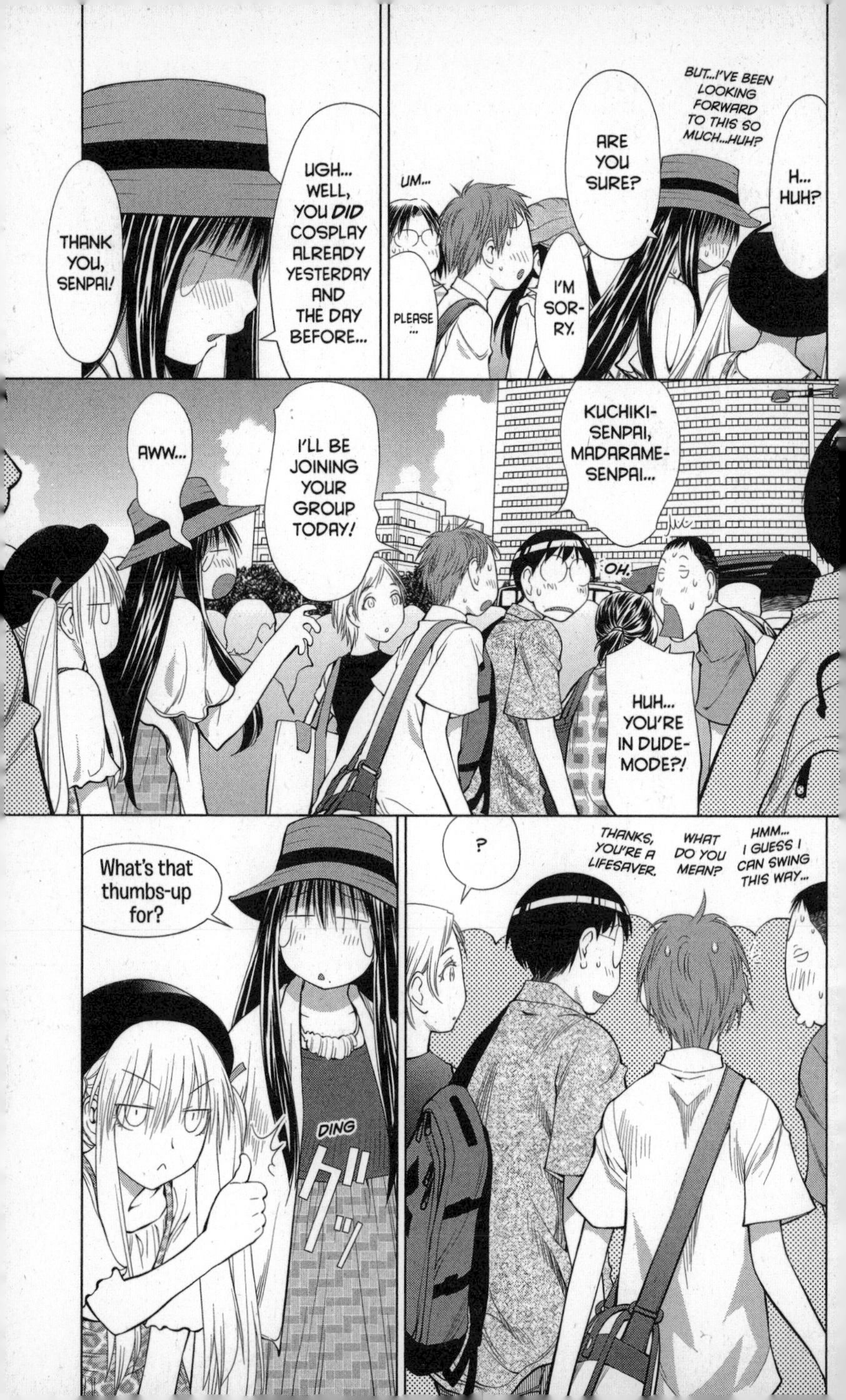
BUT...I'VE BEEN LOOKING FORWARD TO THIS SO MUCH...HUH?
H... HUH?
ARE YOU SURE?
I'M SORRY.
UM...
PLEASE...
UGH... WELL, YOU *DID* COSPLAY ALREADY YESTERDAY AND THE DAY BEFORE...
THANK YOU, SENPAI!
KUCHIKI-SENPAI, MADARAME-SENPAI...
OH.
HUH... YOU'RE IN DUDE-MODE?!
I'LL BE JOINING YOUR GROUP TODAY!
AWW...
HMM... I GUESS I CAN SWING THIS WAY...
WHAT DO YOU MEAN?
THANKS, YOU'RE A LIFESAVER.
?
What's that thumbs-up for?
DING

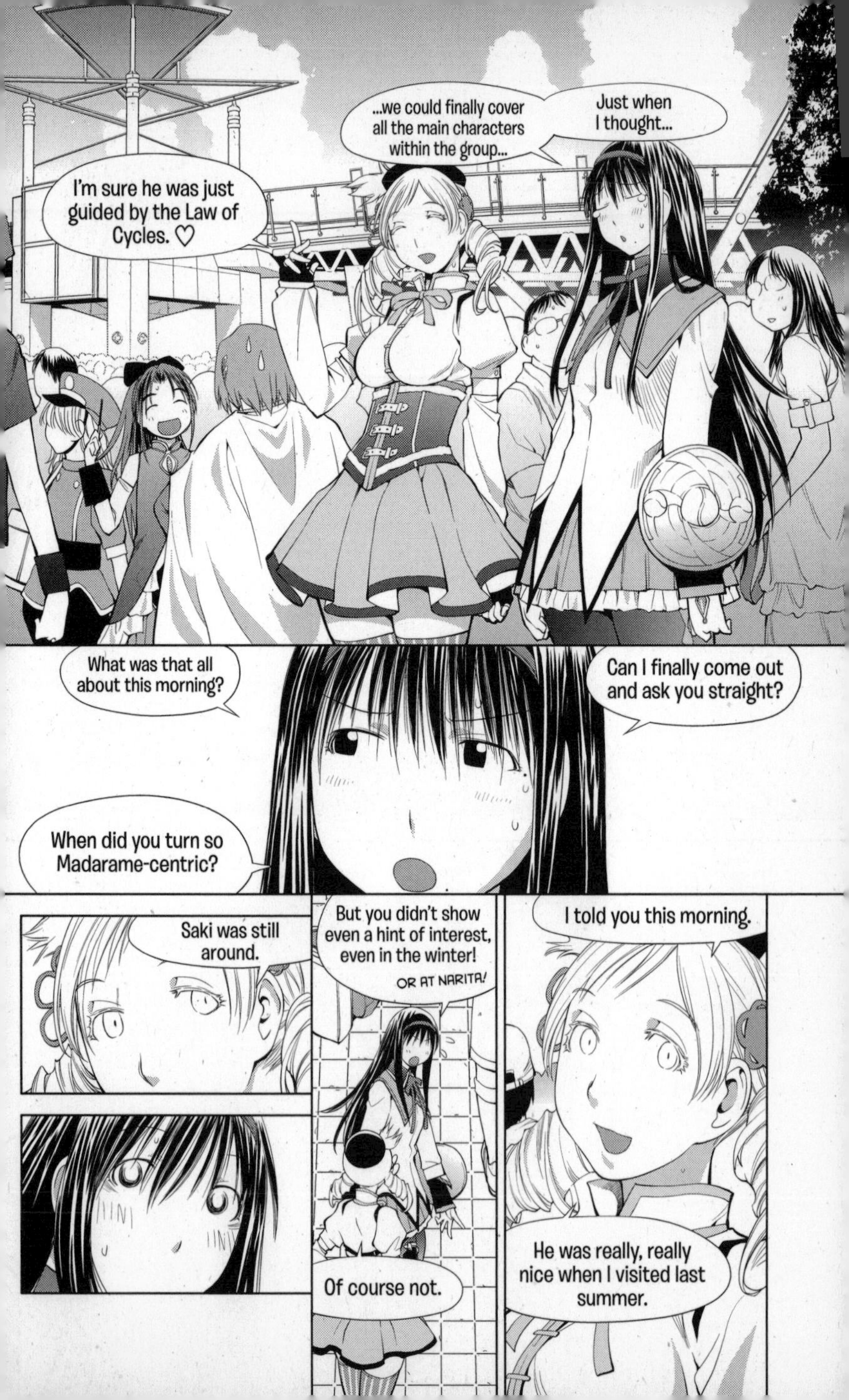
Just when I thought...
...we could finally cover all the main characters within the group...
I'm sure he was just guided by the Law of Cycles. ♡
Can I finally come out and ask you straight?
What was that all about this morning?
When did you turn so Madarame-centric?
I told you this morning.
He was really, really nice when I visited last summer.
But you didn't show even a hint of interest, even in the winter!
OR AT NARITA!
Of course not.
Saki was still around.

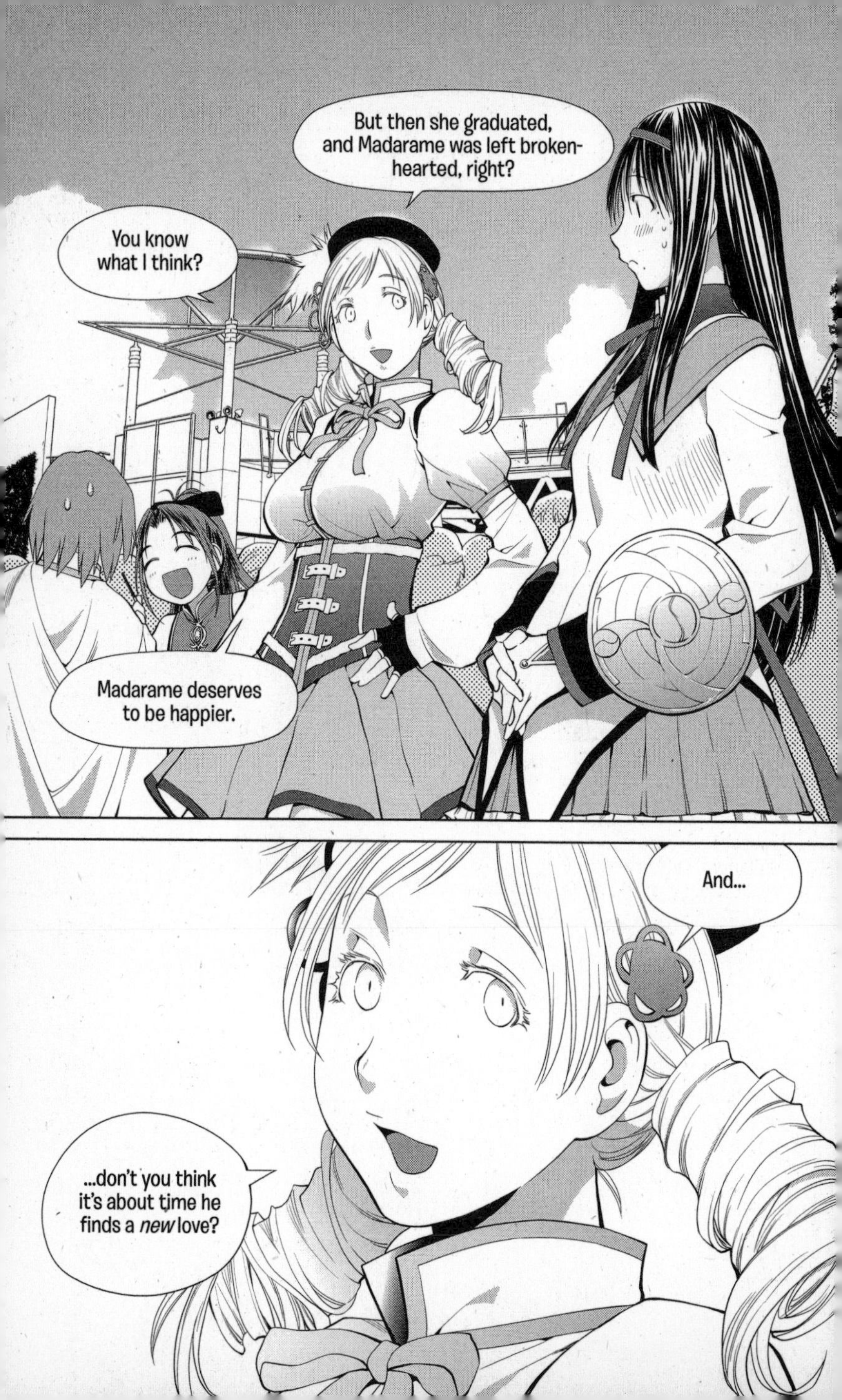
But then she graduated, and Madarame was left broken-hearted, right?
You know what I think?
Madarame deserves to be happier.
And...
...don't you think it's about time he finds a *new* love?

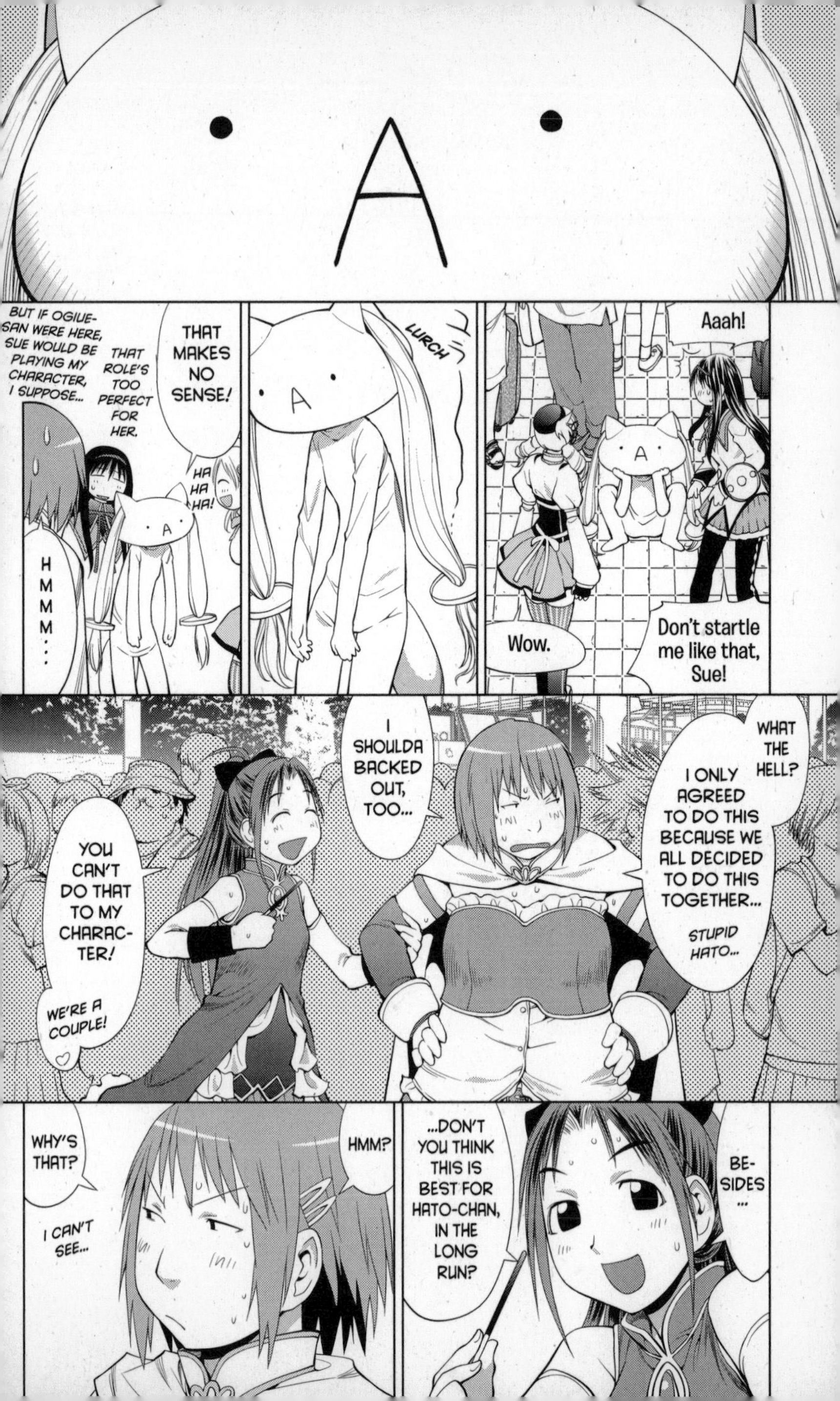

Aaah!
Don't startle me like that, Sue!
Wow.
LURCH
THAT MAKES NO SENSE!
HA HA HA!
THAT ROLE'S TOO PERFECT FOR HER.
BUT IF OGIUE-SAN WERE HERE, SUE WOULD BE PLAYING MY CHARACTER, I SUPPOSE...
HMMM...
WHAT THE HELL?
I ONLY AGREED TO DO THIS BECAUSE WE ALL DECIDED TO DO THIS TOGETHER...
STUPID HATO...
I SHOULDA BACKED OUT, TOO...
YOU CAN'T DO THAT TO MY CHARAC-TER!
WE'RE A COUPLE!
BE-SIDES...
...DON'T YOU THINK THIS IS BEST FOR HATO-CHAN, IN THE LONG RUN?
HMM?
WHY'S THAT?
I CAN'T SEE...

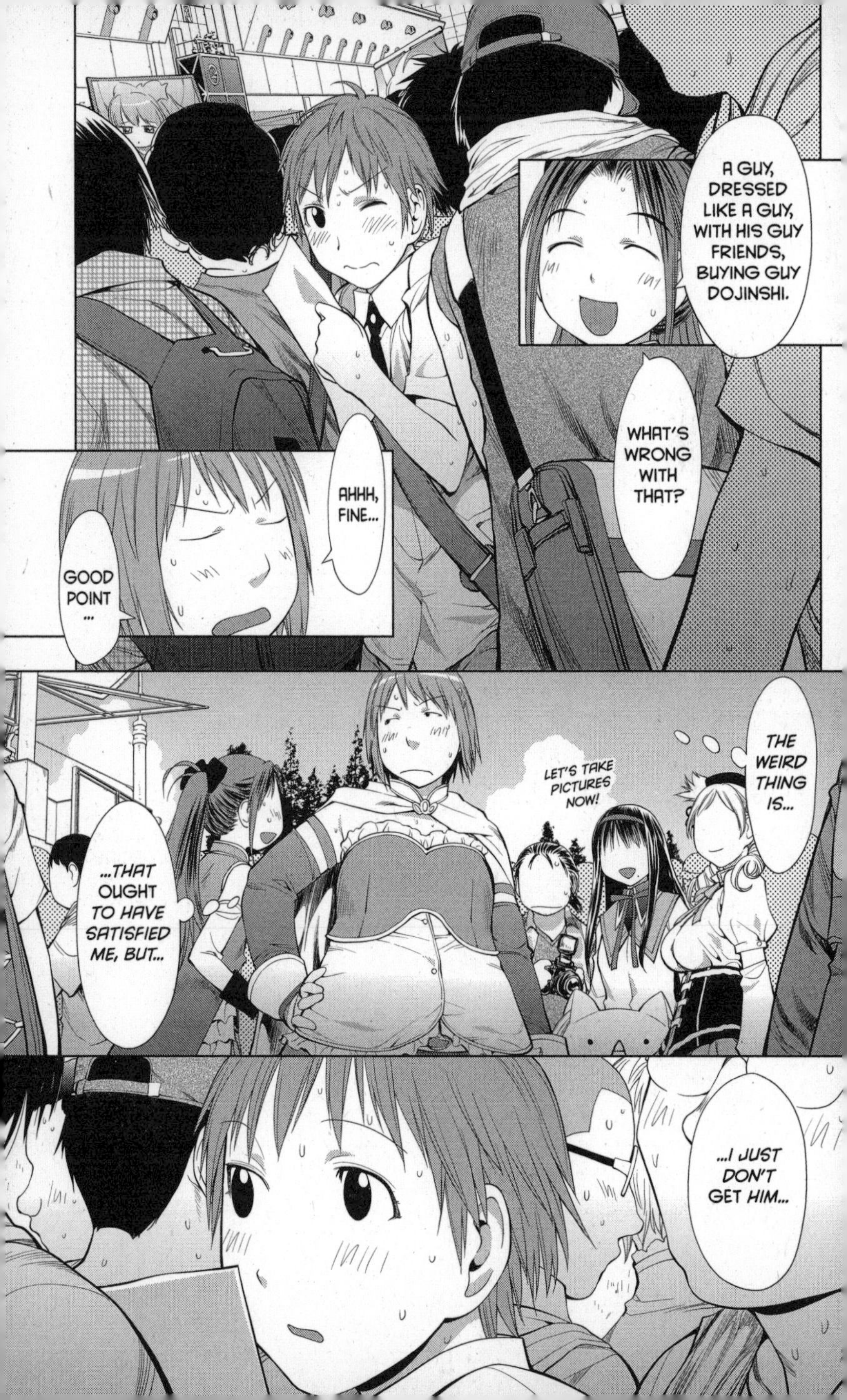
A GUY, DRESSED LIKE A GUY, WITH HIS GUY FRIENDS, BUYING GUY DOJINSHI.
WHAT'S WRONG WITH THAT?
AHHH, FINE...
GOOD POINT ...
THE WEIRD THING IS...
LET'S TAKE PICTURES NOW!
...THAT OUGHT TO HAVE SATISFIED ME, BUT...
...I JUST DON'T GET HIM...

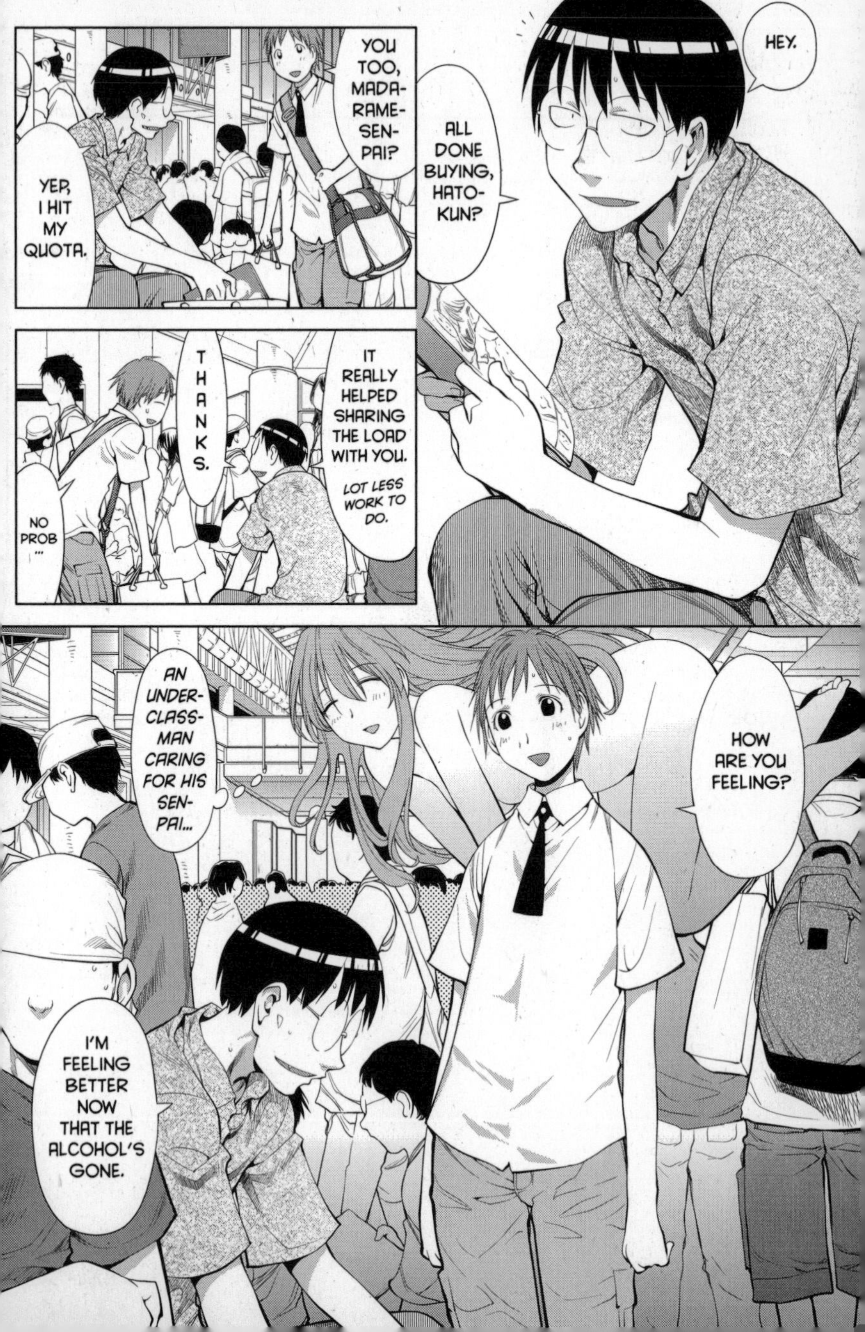
HEY.
ALL DONE BUYING, HATO-KUN?
YOU TOO, MADARAME-SENPAI?
YEP, I HIT MY QUOTA.
IT REALLY HELPED SHARING THE LOAD WITH YOU.
LOT LESS WORK TO DO.
THANKS.
NO PROB...
HOW ARE YOU FEELING?
AN UNDERCLASSMAN CARING FOR HIS SENPAI...
I'M FEELING BETTER NOW THAT THE ALCOHOL'S GONE.

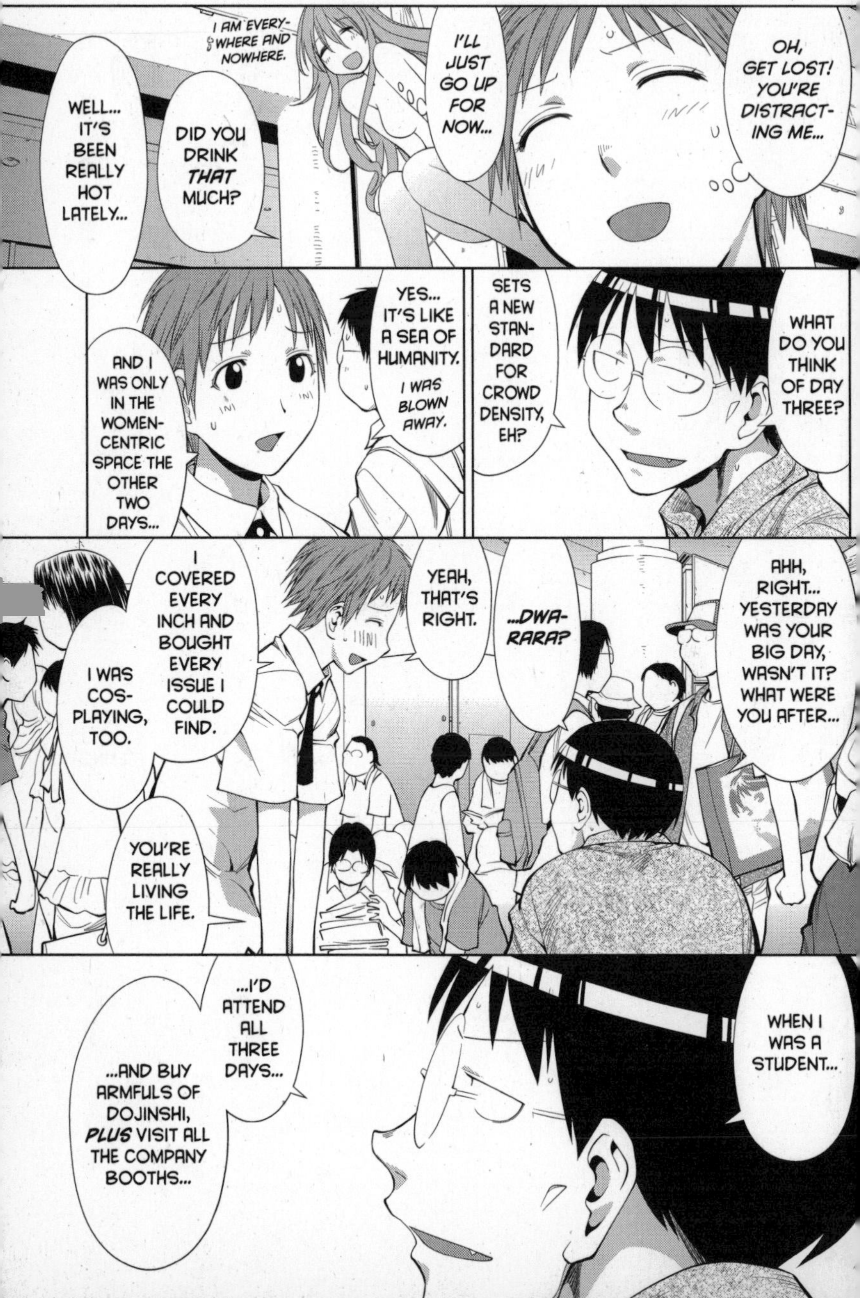
OH, GET LOST! YOU'RE DISTRACTING ME...
I'LL JUST GO UP FOR NOW...
I AM EVERYWHERE AND NOWHERE.
DID YOU DRINK THAT MUCH?
WELL... IT'S BEEN REALLY HOT LATELY...
WHAT DO YOU THINK OF DAY THREE?
SETS A NEW STANDARD FOR CROWD DENSITY, EH?
YES... IT'S LIKE A SEA OF HUMANITY.
I WAS BLOWN AWAY.
AND I WAS ONLY IN THE WOMEN-CENTRIC SPACE THE OTHER TWO DAYS...
AHH, RIGHT... YESTERDAY WAS YOUR BIG DAY, WASN'T IT? WHAT WERE YOU AFTER...
...DWARARA?
YEAH, THAT'S RIGHT.
I COVERED EVERY INCH AND BOUGHT EVERY ISSUE I COULD FIND.
I WAS COSPLAYING, TOO.
YOU'RE REALLY LIVING THE LIFE.
WHEN I WAS A STUDENT...
...I'D ATTEND ALL THREE DAYS...
...AND BUY ARMFULS OF DOJINSHI, PLUS VISIT ALL THE COMPANY BOOTHS...

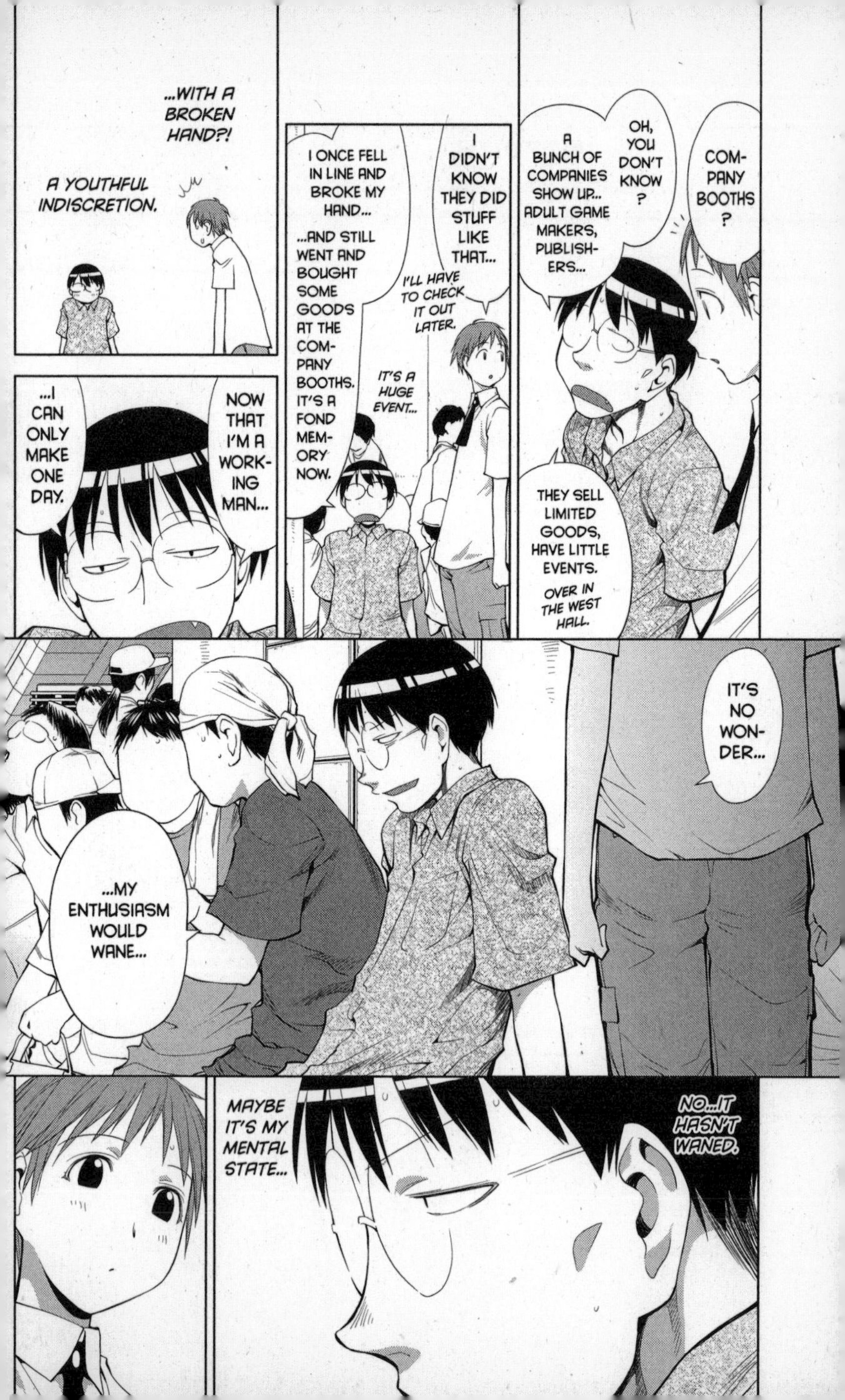
COMPANY BOOTHS?
OH, YOU DON'T KNOW?
A BUNCH OF COMPANIES SHOW UP... ADULT GAME MAKERS, PUBLISHERS...
THEY SELL LIMITED GOODS, HAVE LITTLE EVENTS.
OVER IN THE WEST HALL.
I DIDN'T KNOW THEY DID STUFF LIKE THAT...
I'LL HAVE TO CHECK IT OUT LATER.
IT'S A HUGE EVENT...
I ONCE FELL IN LINE AND BROKE MY HAND...
...AND STILL WENT AND BOUGHT SOME GOODS AT THE COMPANY BOOTHS. IT'S A FOND MEMORY NOW.
...WITH A BROKEN HAND?!
A YOUTHFUL INDISCRETION.
NOW THAT I'M A WORKING MAN...
...I CAN ONLY MAKE ONE DAY.
IT'S NO WONDER...
...MY ENTHUSIASM WOULD WANE...
NO...IT HASN'T WANED.
MAYBE IT'S MY MENTAL STATE...

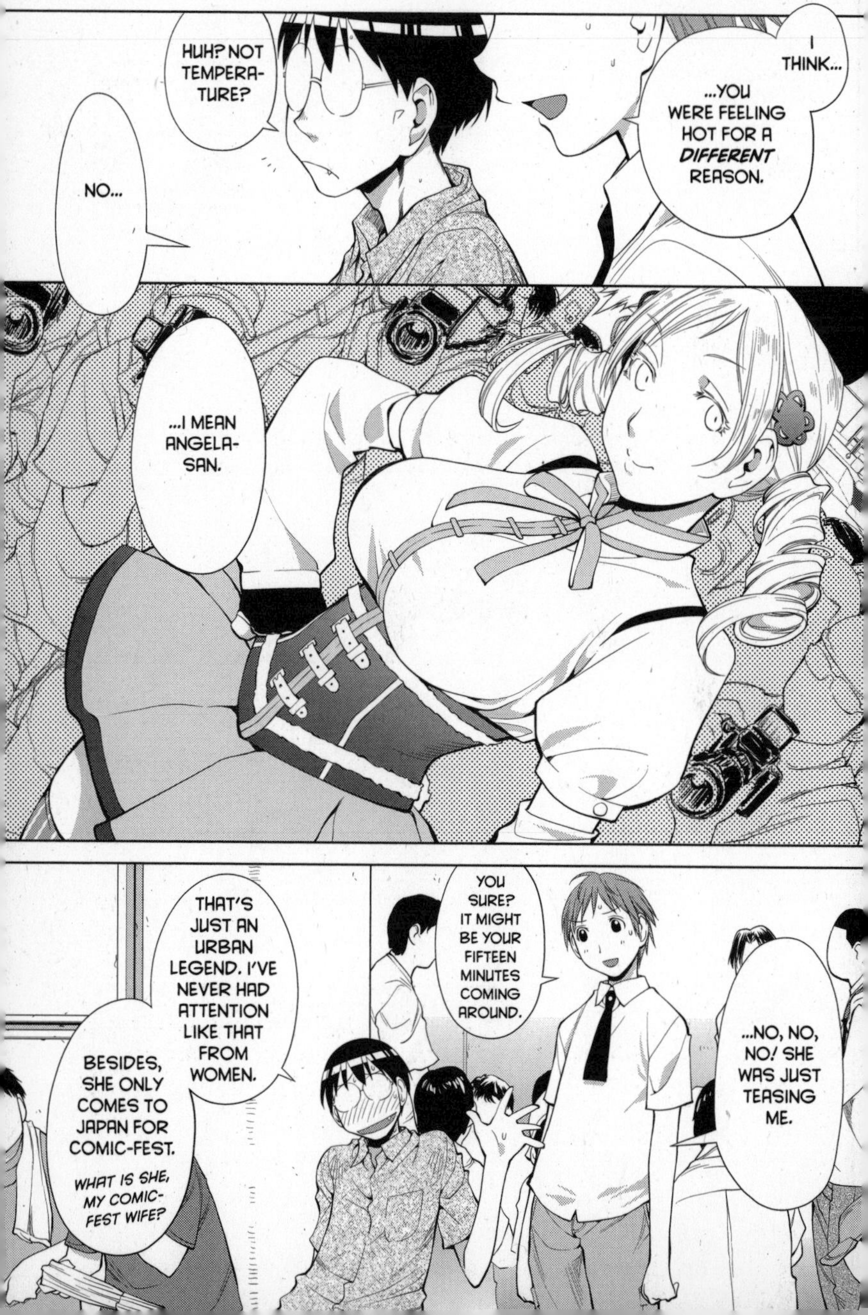
I THINK... ...YOU WERE FEELING HOT FOR A *DIFFERENT* REASON.
HUH? NOT TEMPERA-TURE?
NO...
...I MEAN ANGELA-SAN.
...NO, NO, NO! SHE WAS JUST TEASING ME.
YOU SURE? IT MIGHT BE YOUR FIFTEEN MINUTES COMING AROUND.
THAT'S JUST AN URBAN LEGEND. I'VE NEVER HAD ATTENTION LIKE THAT FROM WOMEN.
BESIDES, SHE ONLY COMES TO JAPAN FOR COMIC-FEST. *WHAT IS SHE, MY COMIC-FEST WIFE?*

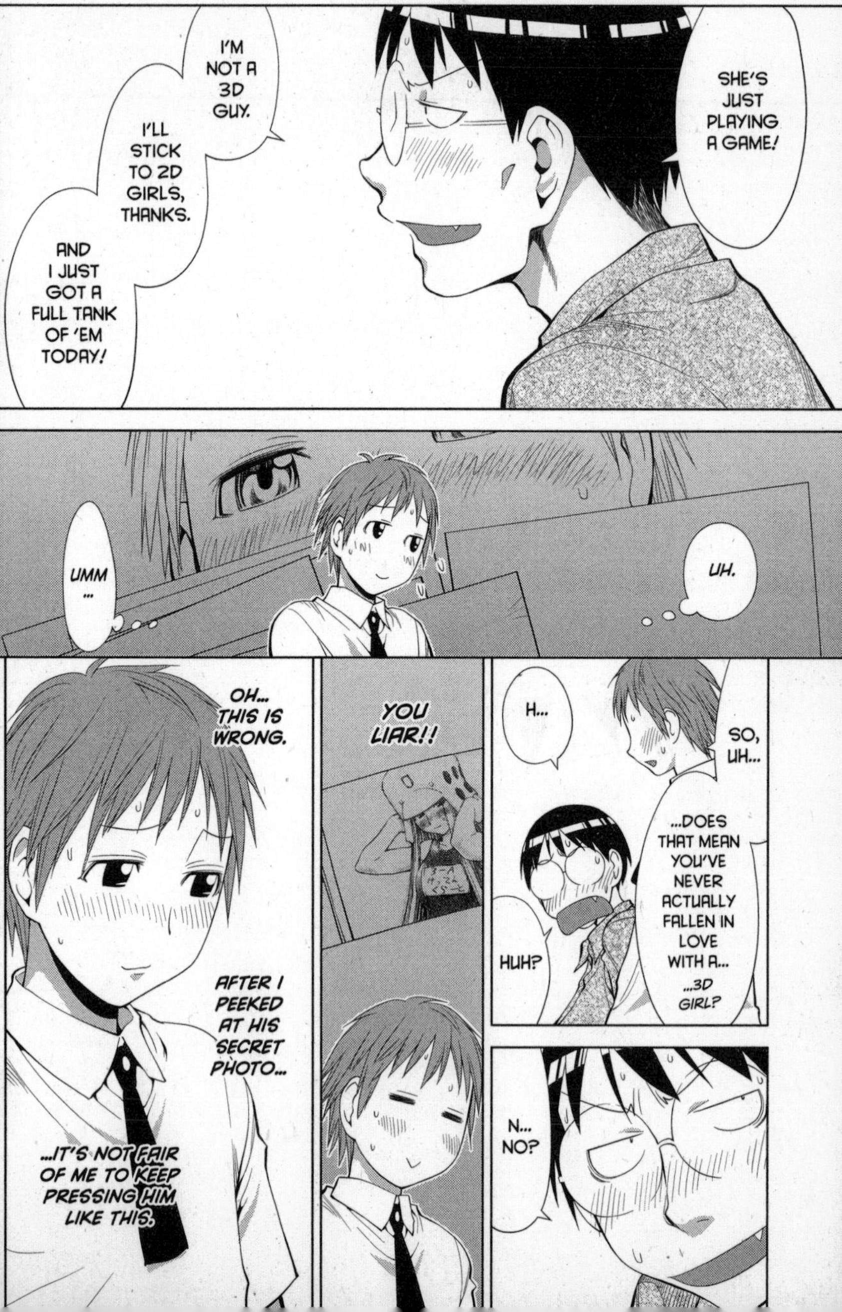
SHE'S JUST PLAYING A GAME!
I'M NOT A 3D GUY.
I'LL STICK TO 2D GIRLS, THANKS.
AND I JUST GOT A FULL TANK OF 'EM TODAY!
UH.
UMM ...
SO, UH...
H...
...DOES THAT MEAN YOU'VE NEVER ACTUALLY FALLEN IN LOVE WITH A... ...3D GIRL?
HUH?
N... NO?
YOU LIAR!!
OH... THIS IS WRONG.
AFTER I PEEKED AT HIS SECRET PHOTO...
...IT'S NOT FAIR OF ME TO KEEP PRESSING HIM LIKE THIS.

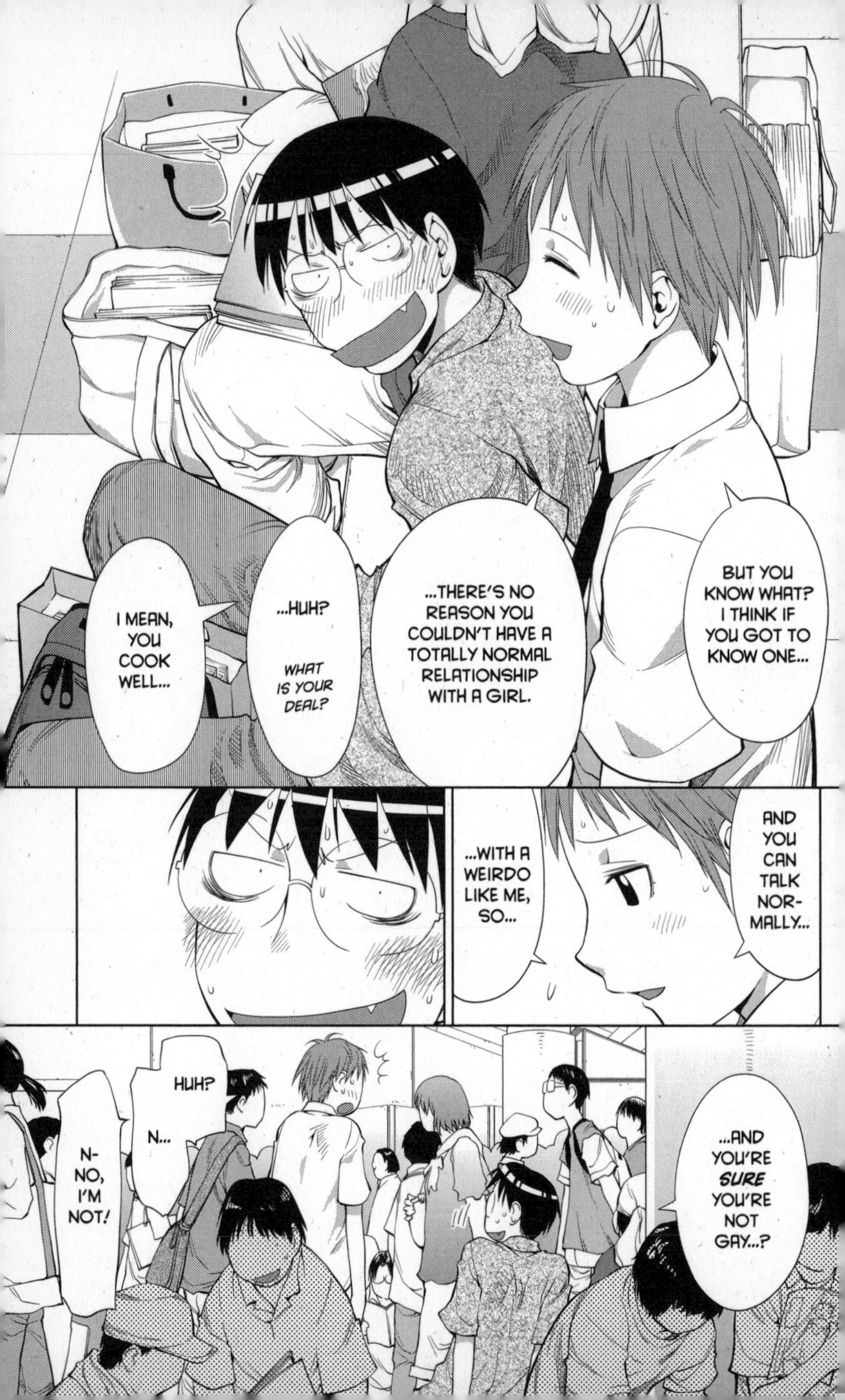
BUT YOU KNOW WHAT? I THINK IF YOU GOT TO KNOW ONE...
...THERE'S NO REASON YOU COULDN'T HAVE A TOTALLY NORMAL RELATIONSHIP WITH A GIRL.
...HUH?
WHAT IS YOUR DEAL?
I MEAN, YOU COOK WELL...
AND YOU CAN TALK NOR-MALLY...
...WITH A WEIRDO LIKE ME, SO...
...AND YOU'RE *SURE* YOU'RE NOT GAY...?
HUH?
N...
N-NO, I'M NOT!

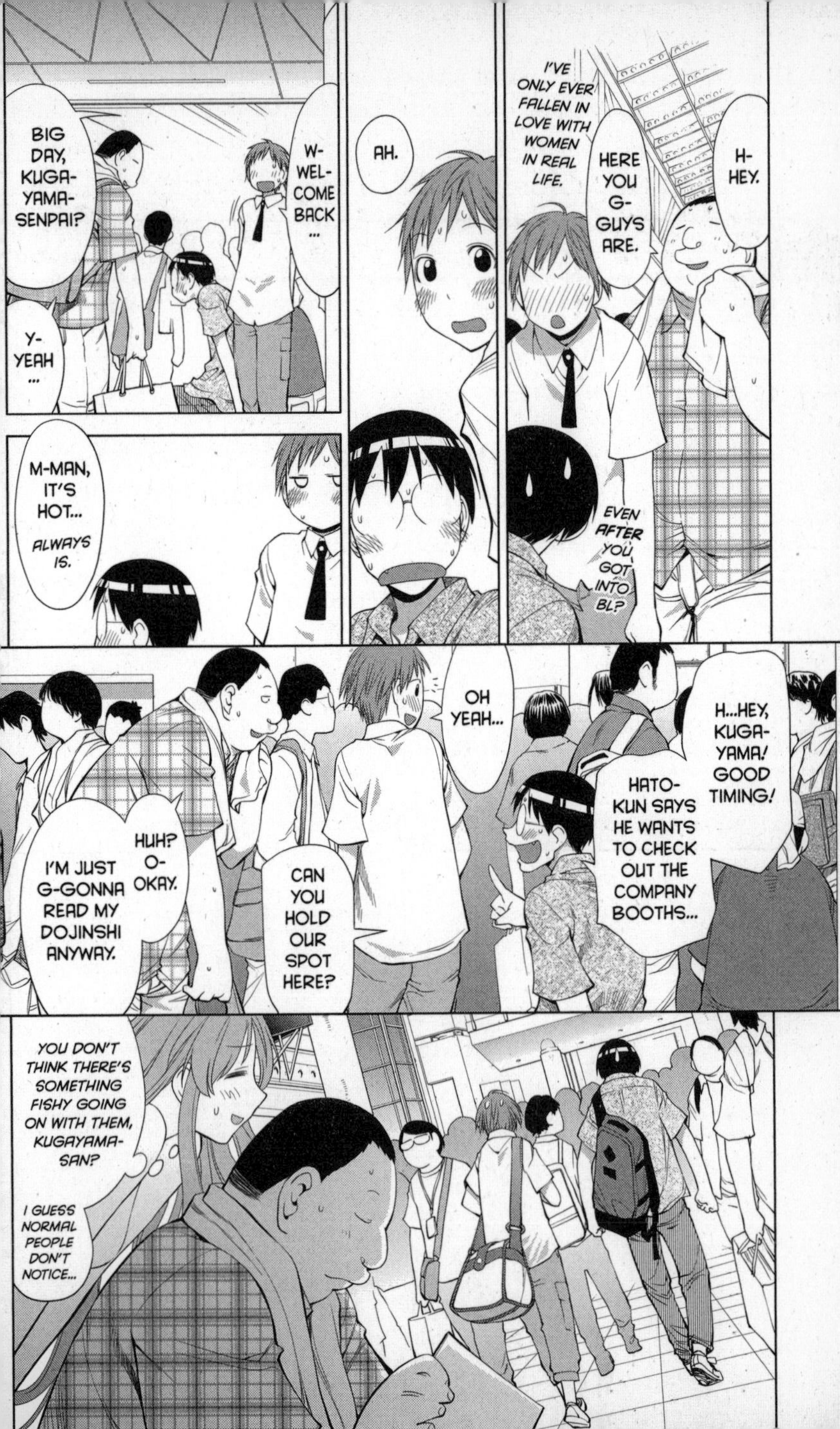
H-HEY.
HERE YOU G-GUYS ARE.
I'VE ONLY EVER FALLEN IN LOVE WITH WOMEN IN REAL LIFE.
EVEN AFTER YOU GOT INTO BL?
AH.
W-WELCOME BACK...
BIG DAY, KUGAYAMA-SENPAI?
Y-YEAH...
M-MAN, IT'S HOT...
ALWAYS IS.
H...HEY, KUGAYAMA! GOOD TIMING!
HATO-KUN SAYS HE WANTS TO CHECK OUT THE COMPANY BOOTHS...
OH YEAH...
CAN YOU HOLD OUR SPOT HERE?
HUH? O-OKAY.
I'M JUST G-GONNA READ MY DOJINSHI ANYWAY.
YOU DON'T THINK THERE'S SOMETHING FISHY GOING ON WITH THEM, KUGAYAMA-SAN?
I GUESS NORMAL PEOPLE DON'T NOTICE...

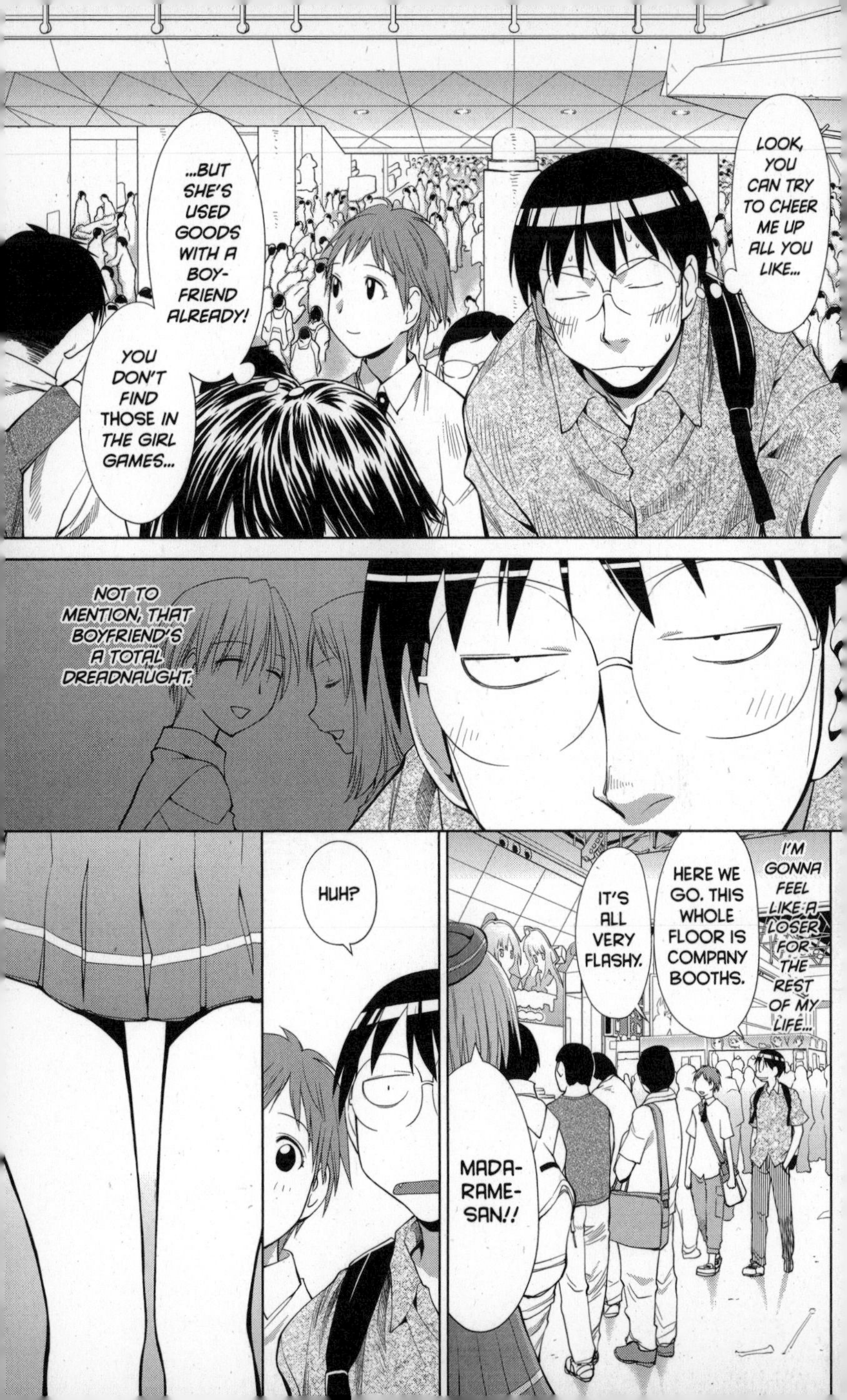
LOOK, YOU CAN TRY TO CHEER ME UP ALL YOU LIKE...
...BUT SHE'S USED GOODS WITH A BOY-FRIEND ALREADY!
YOU DON'T FIND THOSE IN THE GIRL GAMES...
NOT TO MENTION, THAT BOYFRIEND'S A TOTAL DREADNAUGHT.
I'M GONNA FEEL LIKE A LOSER FOR THE REST OF MY LIFE...
HERE WE GO. THIS WHOLE FLOOR IS COMPANY BOOTHS.
IT'S ALL VERY FLASHY.
MADA-RAME-SAN!!
HUH?

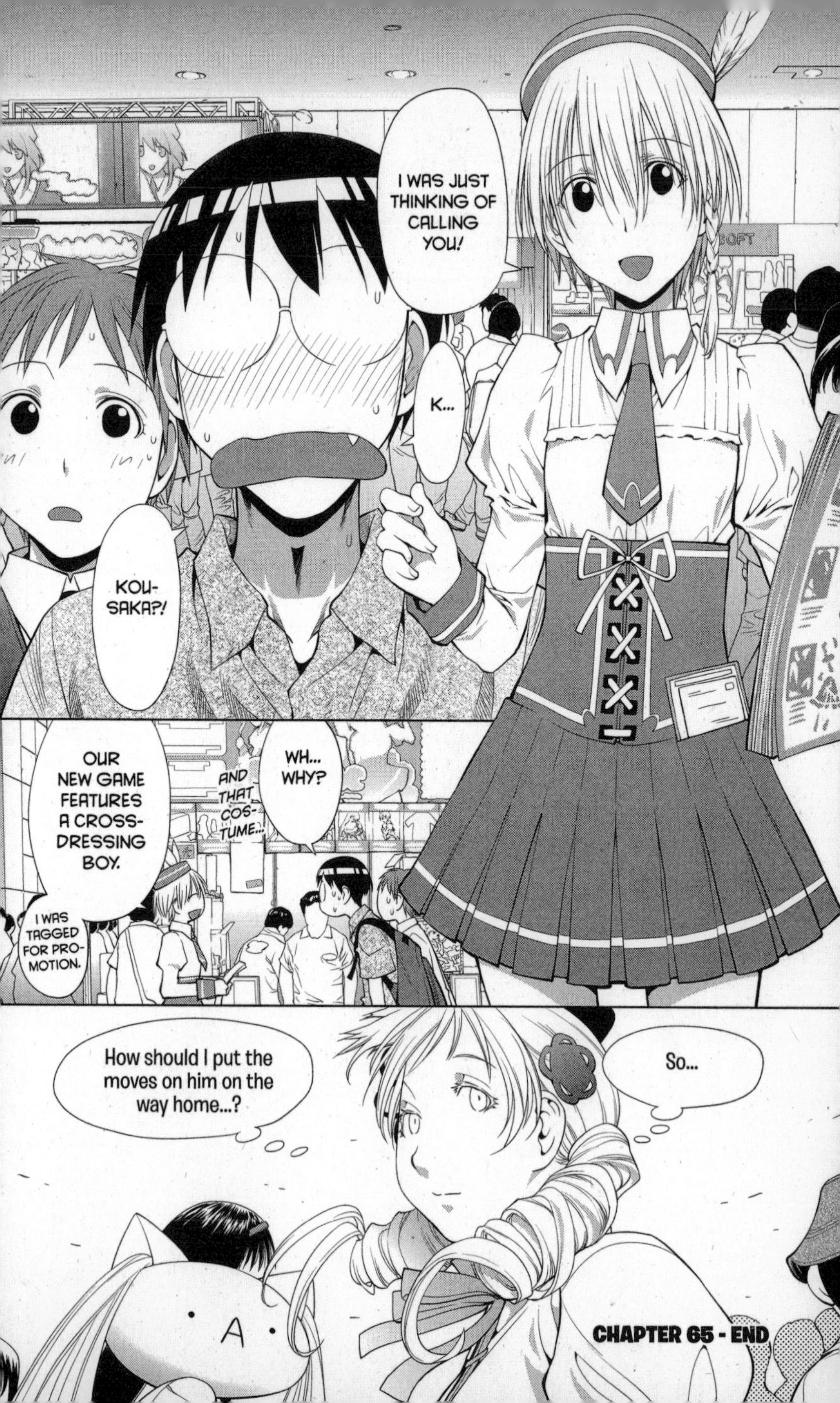
I WAS JUST THINKING OF CALLING YOU!
K...
KOU-SAKA?!
WH... WHY?
AND THAT COS-TUME...
OUR NEW GAME FEATURES A CROSS-DRESSING BOY.
I WAS TAGGED FOR PRO-MOTION.
So...
How should I put the moves on him on the way home...?
CHAPTER 65 - END

BETTER

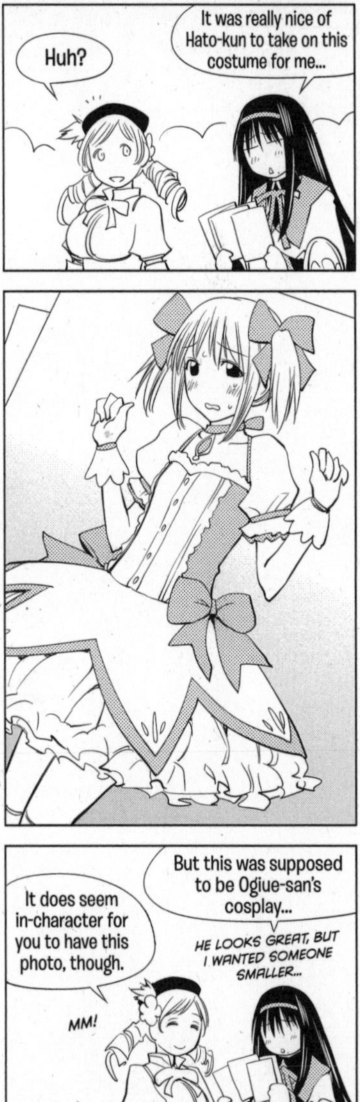
It was really nice of Hato-kun to take on this costume for me...
Huh?
But this was supposed to be Ogiue-san's cosplay...
HE LOOKS GREAT, BUT I WANTED SOMEONE SMALLER...
It does seem in-character for you to have this photo, though.
MM!

BEST

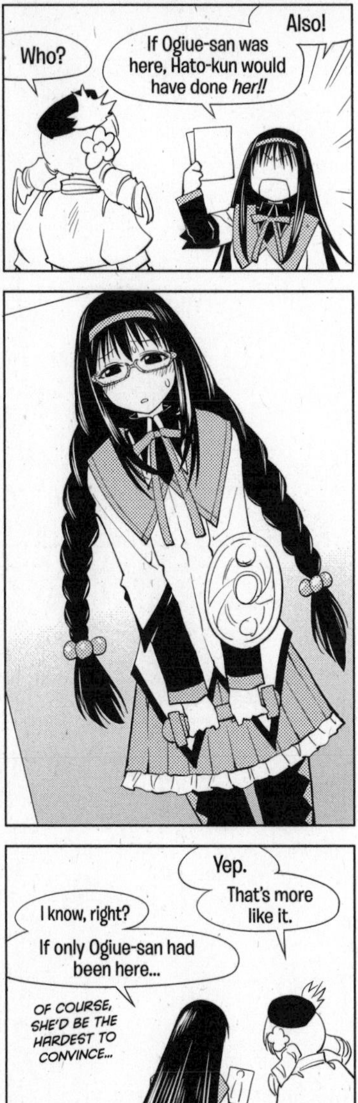
Also!
If Ogiue-san was here, Hato-kun would have done *her!!*
Who?
Yep.
That's more like it.
I know, right?
If only Ogiue-san had been here...
OF COURSE, SHE'D BE THE HARDEST TO CONVINCE...

THIS DOESN'T MAKE ANY SENSE

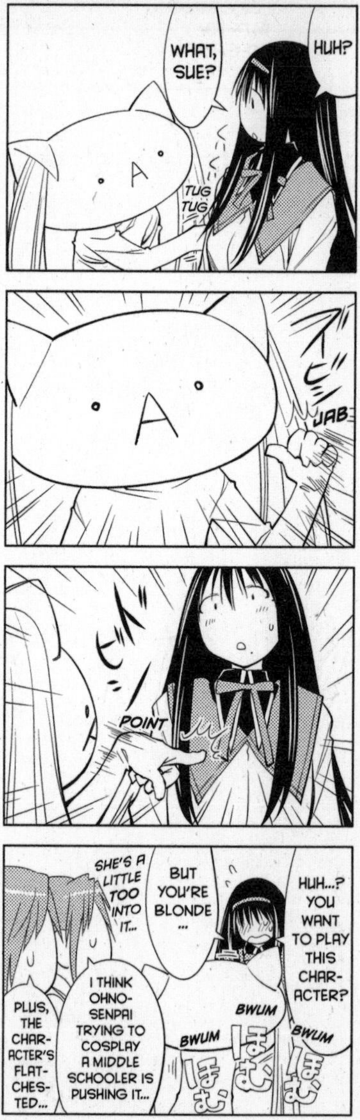
HUH?
WHAT, SUE?
TUG TUG
JAB
POINT
HUH...? YOU WANT TO PLAY THIS CHAR-ACTER?
BUT YOU'RE BLONDE ...
SHE'S A LITTLE TOO INTO IT...
BWUM
BWUM
BWUM
ほむ
ほむ
ほむ
I THINK OHNO-SENPAI TRYING TO COSPLAY A MIDDLE SCHOOLER IS PUSHING IT...
PLUS, THE CHAR-ACTER'S FLAT-CHES-TED...

MISSION IMPOSSIBLE

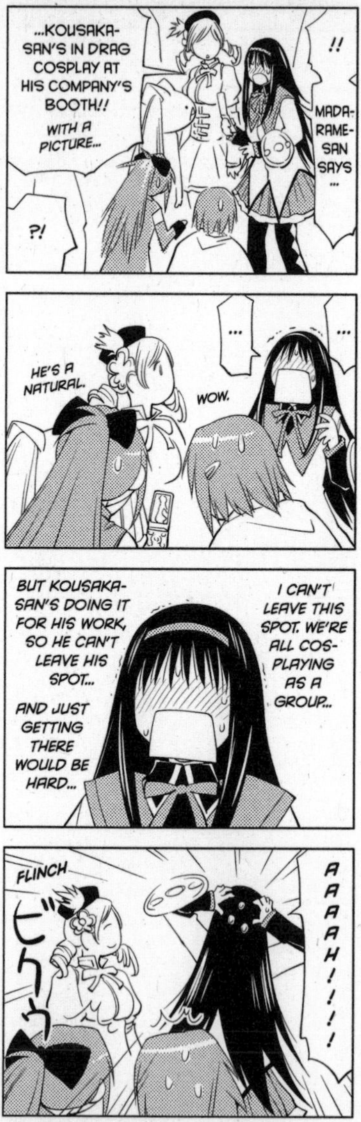
!!
MADA-RAME-SAN SAYS ...
...KOUSAKA-SAN'S IN DRAG COSPLAY AT HIS COMPANY'S BOOTH!!
WITH A PICTURE...
?!
...
...
HE'S A NATURAL.
WOW.
I CAN'T LEAVE THIS SPOT. WE'RE ALL COS-PLAYING AS A GROUP...
BUT KOUSAKA-SAN'S DOING IT FOR HIS WORK, SO HE CAN'T LEAVE HIS SPOT...
AND JUST GETTING THERE WOULD BE HARD...
AAAAAH!!!!
FLINCH
ビクゥ

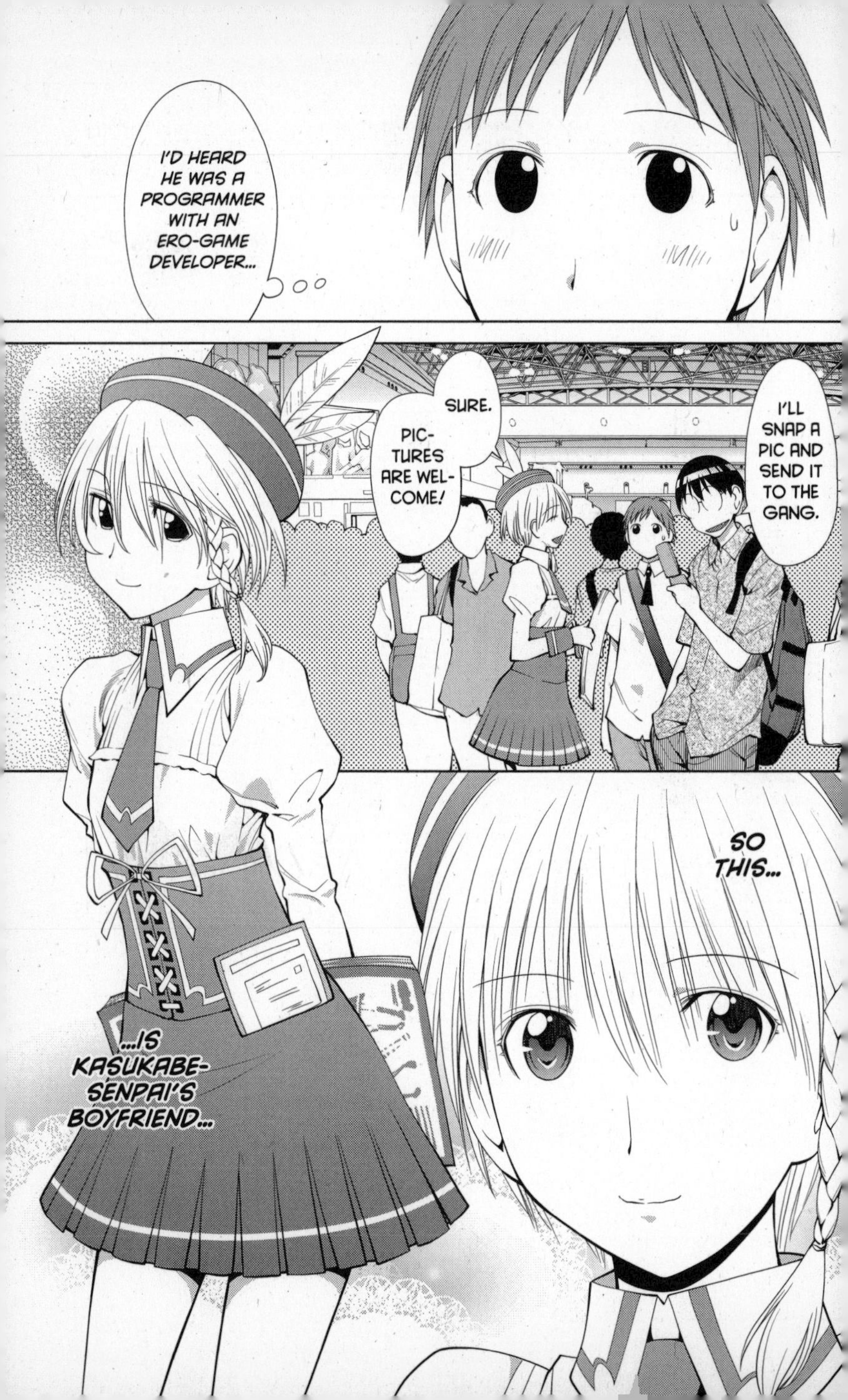
I'D HEARD HE WAS A PROGRAMMER WITH AN ERO-GAME DEVELOPER...
I'LL SNAP A PIC AND SEND IT TO THE GANG.
SURE.
PIC-TURES ARE WEL-COME!
SO THIS...
...IS KASUKABE-SENPAI'S BOYFRIEND...

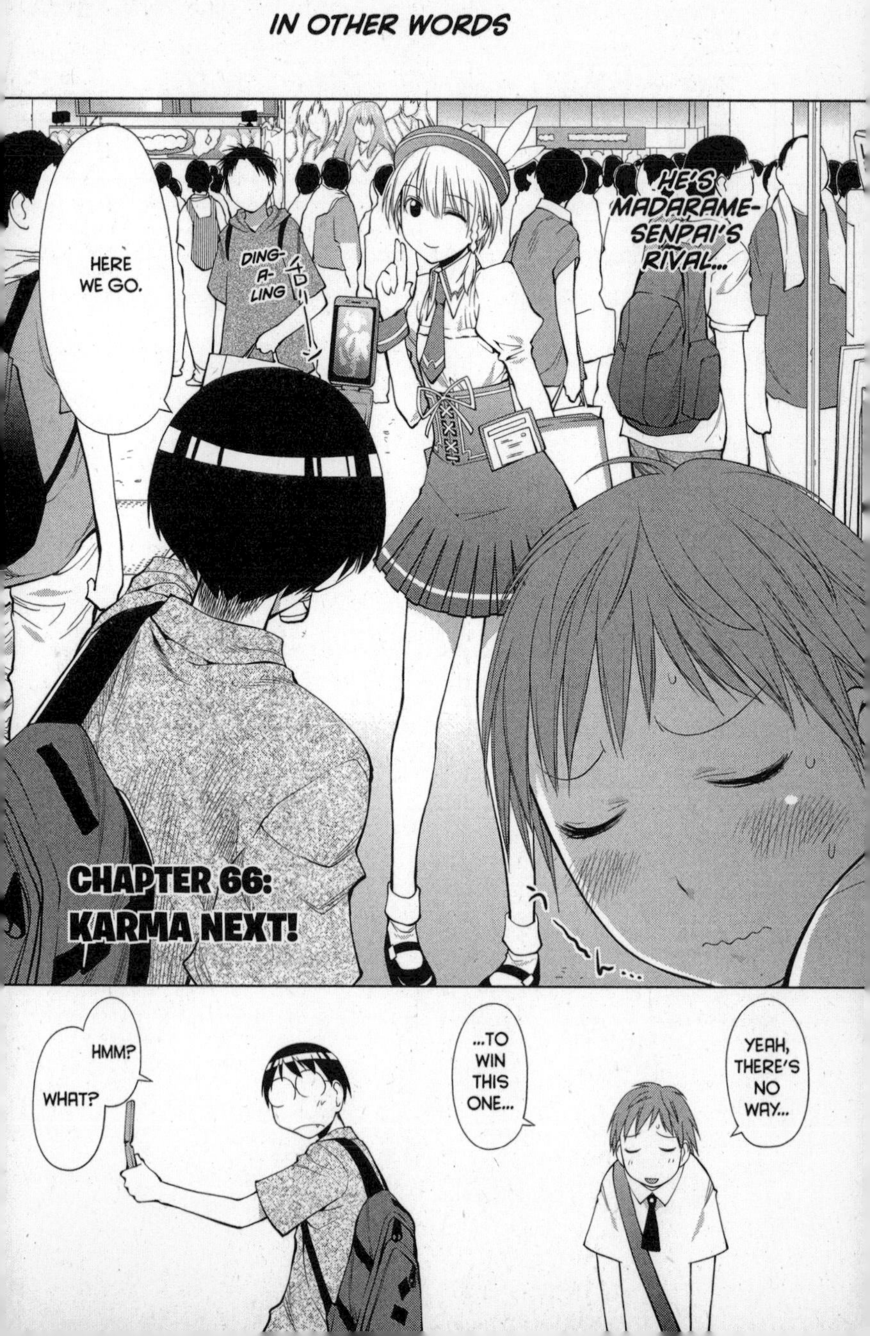
IN OTHER WORDS
HE'S MADARAME-SENPAI'S RIVAL...
DING-A-LING
HERE WE GO.
CHAPTER 66: KARMA NEXT!
YEAH, THERE'S NO WAY...
...TO WIN THIS ONE...
HMM? WHAT?

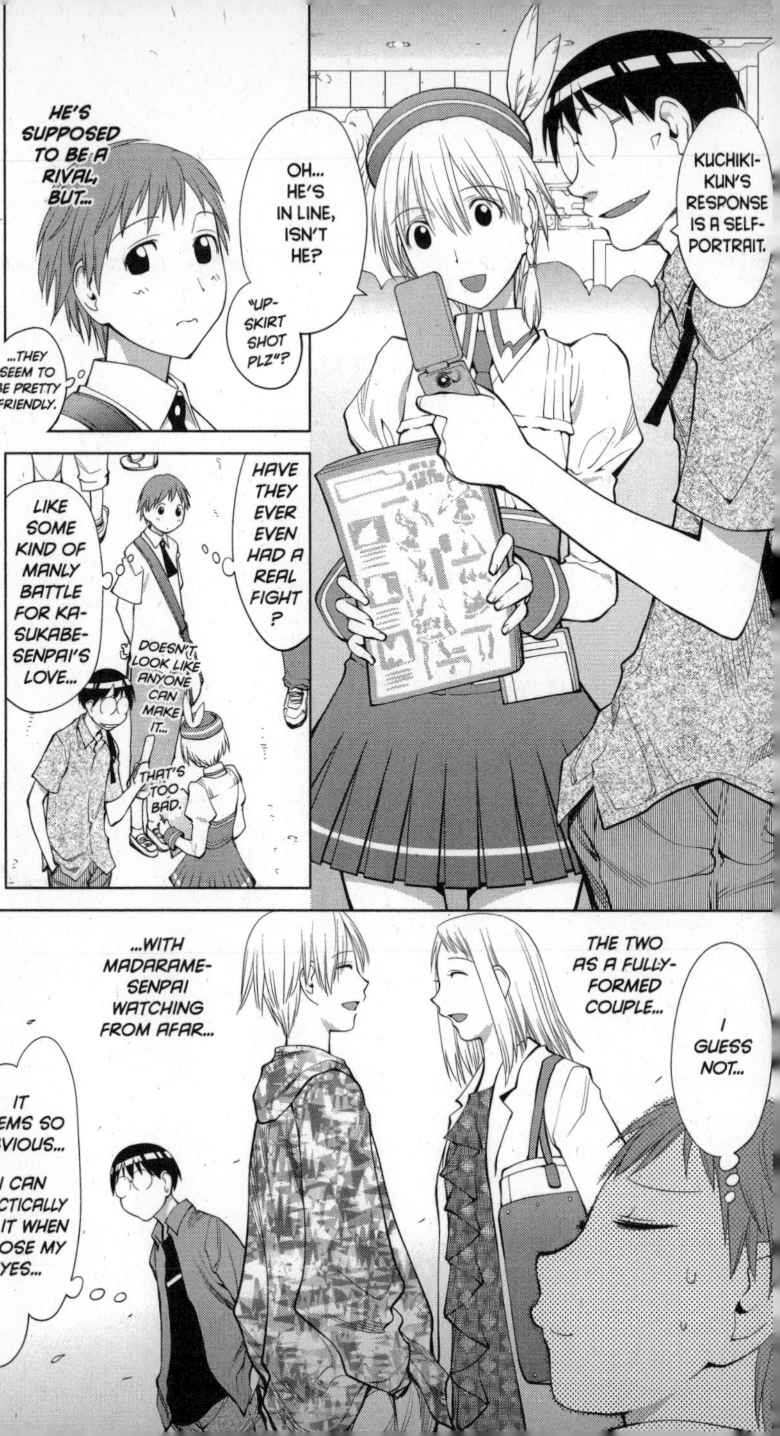
KUCHIKI-KUN'S RESPONSE IS A SELF-PORTRAIT.
OH... HE'S IN LINE, ISN'T HE?
"UP-SKIRT SHOT PLZ"?
HE'S SUPPOSED TO BE A RIVAL, BUT...
...THEY SEEM TO BE PRETTY FRIENDLY.
HAVE THEY EVER EVEN HAD A REAL FIGHT?
LIKE SOME KIND OF MANLY BATTLE FOR KA-SUKABE-SENPAI'S LOVE...
DOESN'T LOOK LIKE ANYONE CAN MAKE IT...
THAT'S TOO BAD.
THE TWO AS A FULLY-FORMED COUPLE...
...WITH MADARAME-SENPAI WATCHING FROM AFAR...
IT SEEMS SO OBVIOUS...
...I CAN PRACTICALLY SEE IT WHEN I CLOSE MY EYES...
I GUESS NOT...

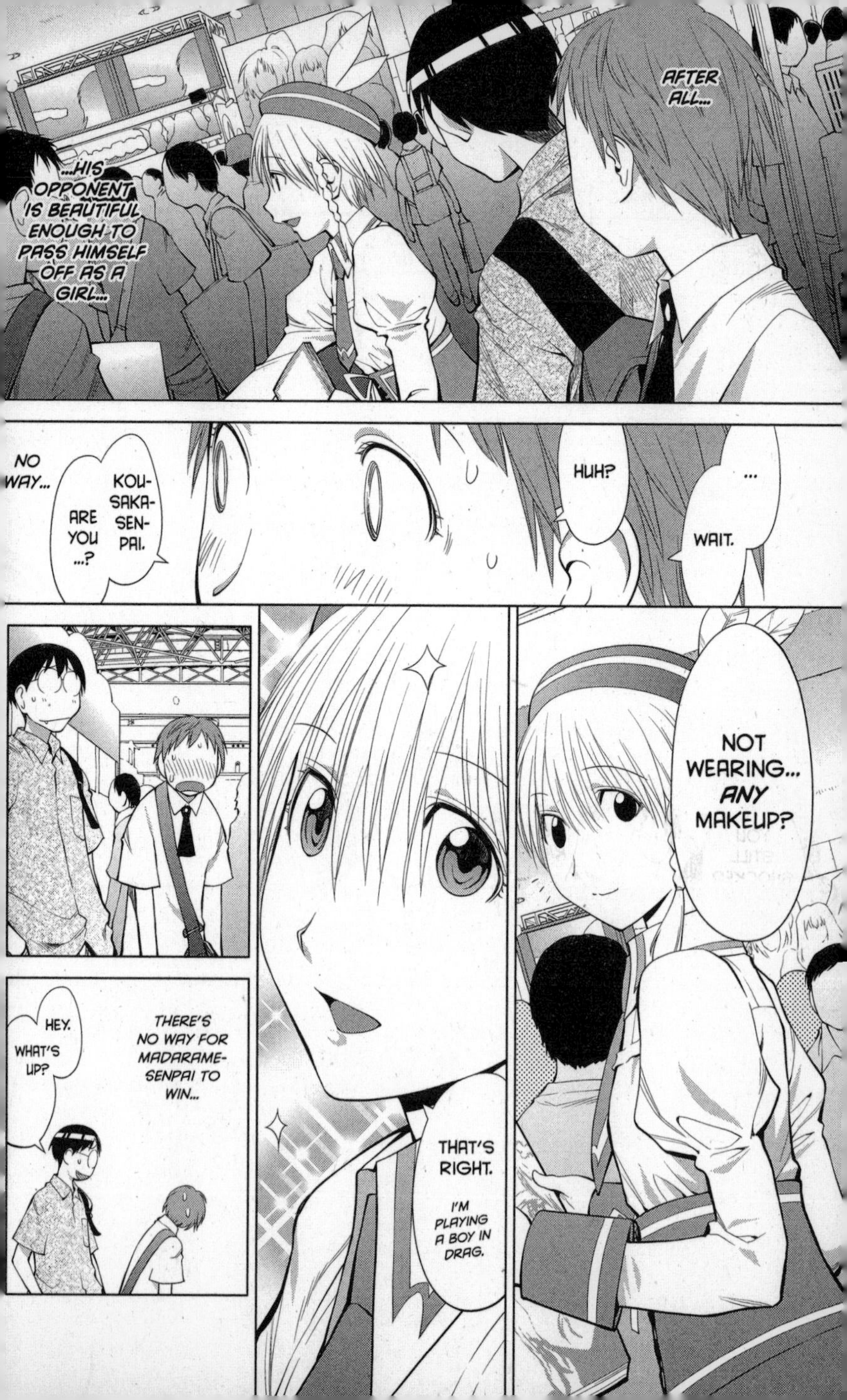
AFTER ALL...
...HIS OPPONENT IS BEAUTIFUL ENOUGH TO PASS HIMSELF OFF AS A GIRL...
...
WAIT.
HUH?
KOU-SAKA-SEN-PAI.
ARE YOU ...?
NO WAY...
NOT WEARING... *ANY* MAKEUP?
THAT'S RIGHT.
I'M PLAYING A BOY IN DRAG.
THERE'S NO WAY FOR MADARAME-SENPAI TO WIN...
HEY.
WHAT'S UP?

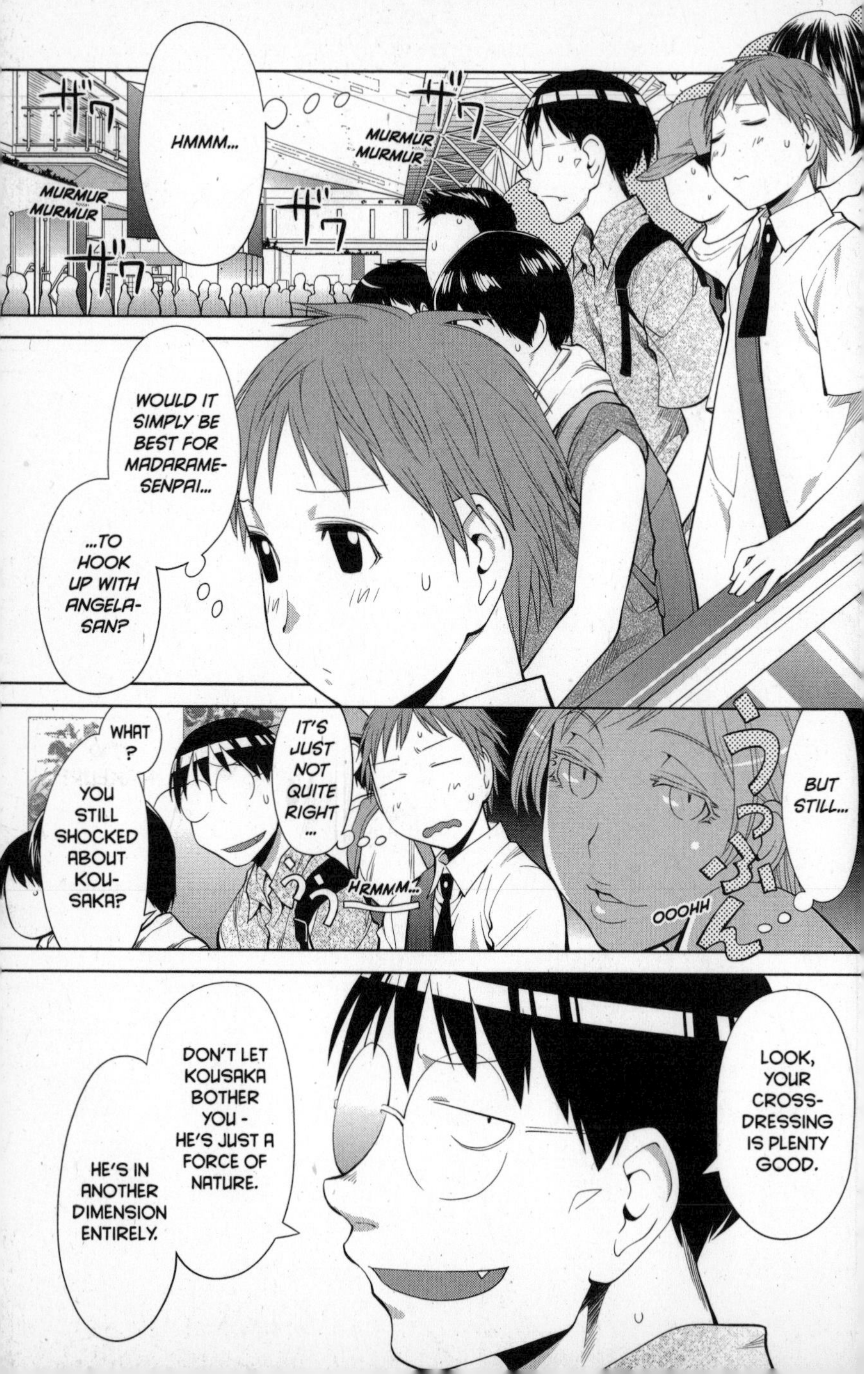
MURMUR MURMUR
HMMM...
MURMUR MURMUR
WOULD IT SIMPLY BE BEST FOR MADARAME-SENPAI...
...TO HOOK UP WITH ANGELA-SAN?
BUT STILL...
OOOHH
IT'S JUST NOT QUITE RIGHT...
HRMMM...
WHAT?
YOU STILL SHOCKED ABOUT KOU-SAKA?
LOOK, YOUR CROSS-DRESSING IS PLENTY GOOD.
DON'T LET KOUSAKA BOTHER YOU - HE'S JUST A FORCE OF NATURE.
HE'S IN ANOTHER DIMENSION ENTIRELY.

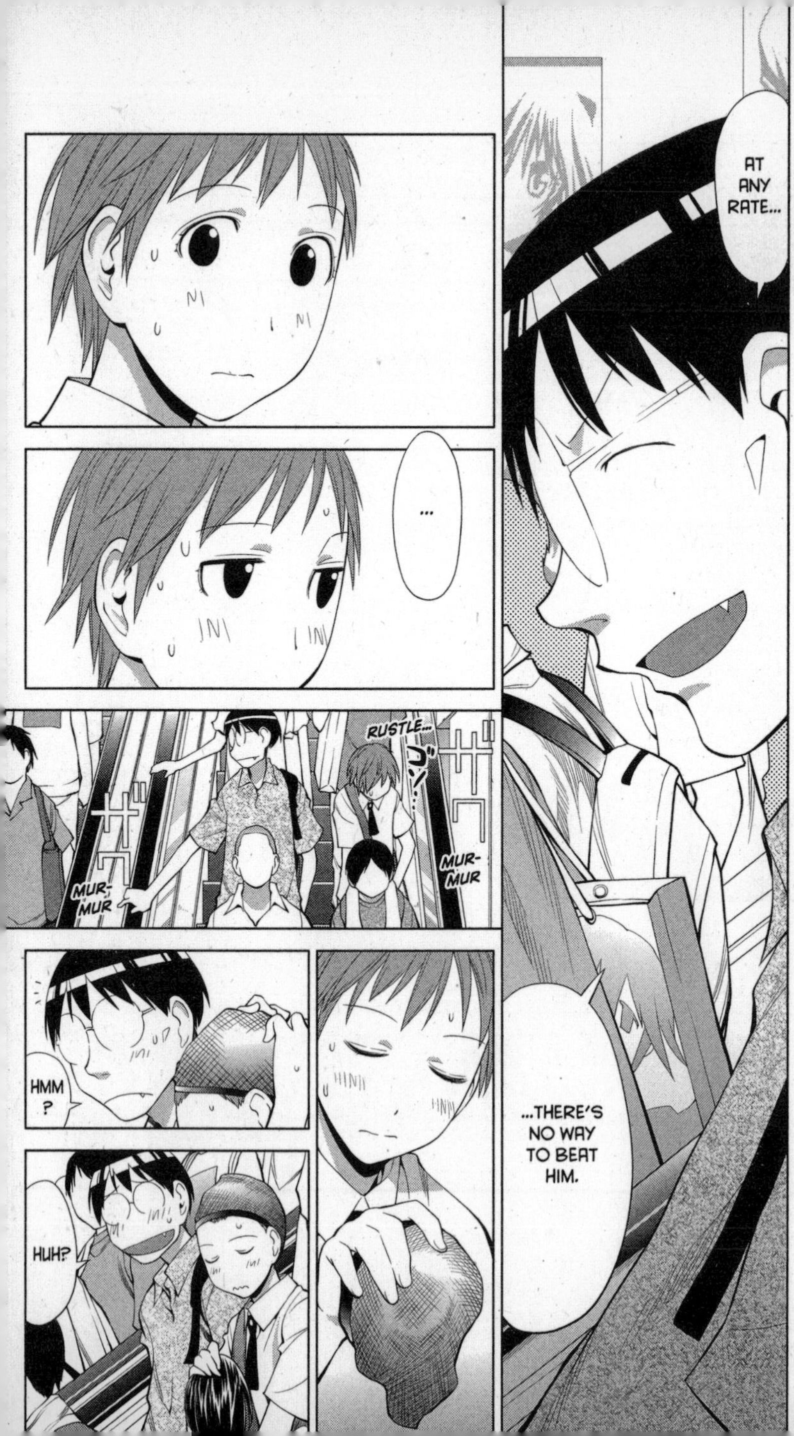
AT ANY RATE...
...THERE'S NO WAY TO BEAT HIM.
...
RUSTLE...
MUR-MUR
MUR-MUR
HMM?
HUH?

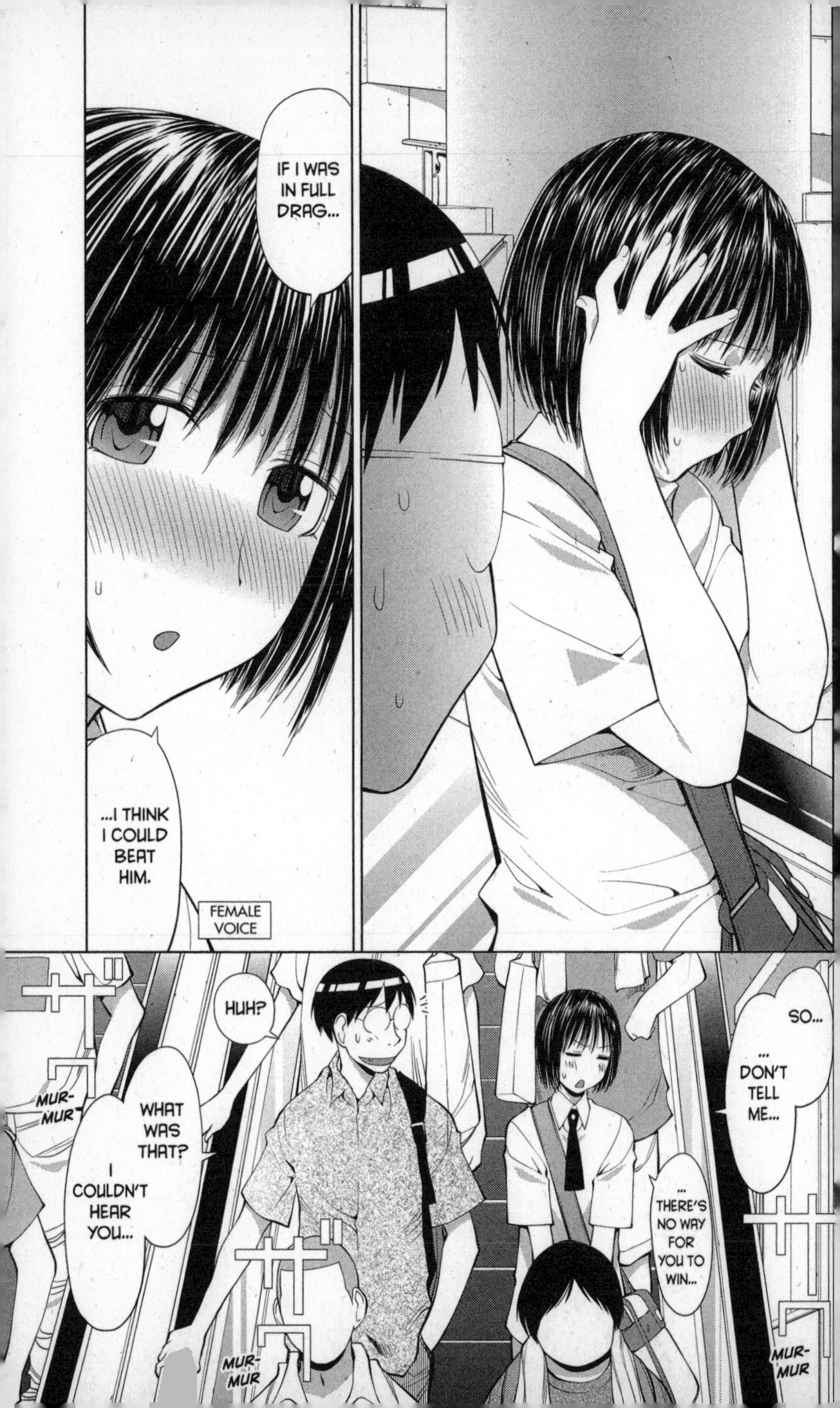
IF I WAS IN FULL DRAG...
...I THINK I COULD BEAT HIM.
FEMALE VOICE
SO...
... DON'T TELL ME...
... THERE'S NO WAY FOR YOU TO WIN...
MUR-MUR
HUH?
WHAT WAS THAT?
I COULDN'T HEAR YOU...
MUR-MUR
MUR-MUR

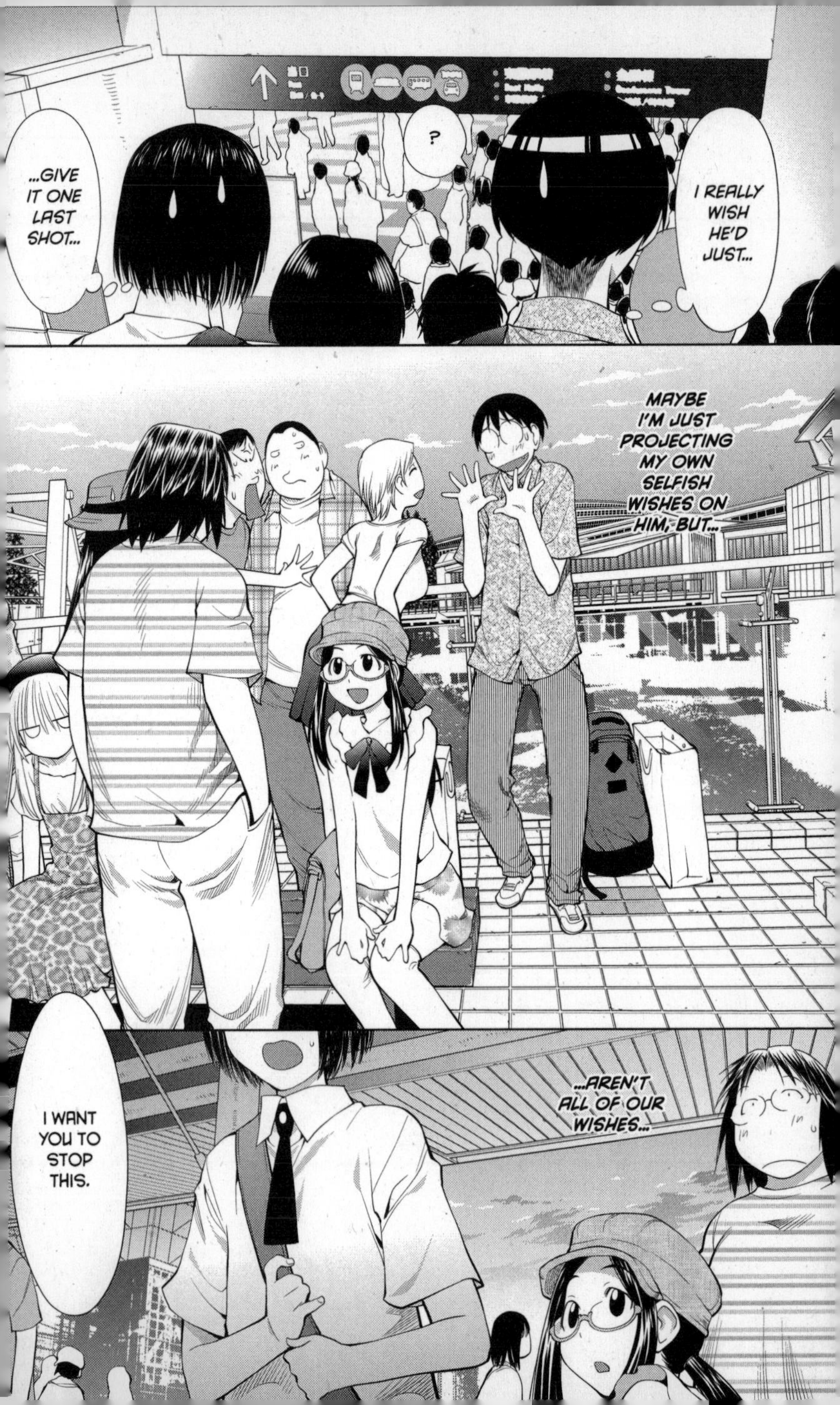
I REALLY WISH HE'D JUST...
?
...GIVE IT ONE LAST SHOT...
MAYBE I'M JUST PROJECTING MY OWN SELFISH WISHES ON HIM, BUT...
...AREN'T ALL OF OUR WISHES...
I WANT YOU TO STOP THIS.

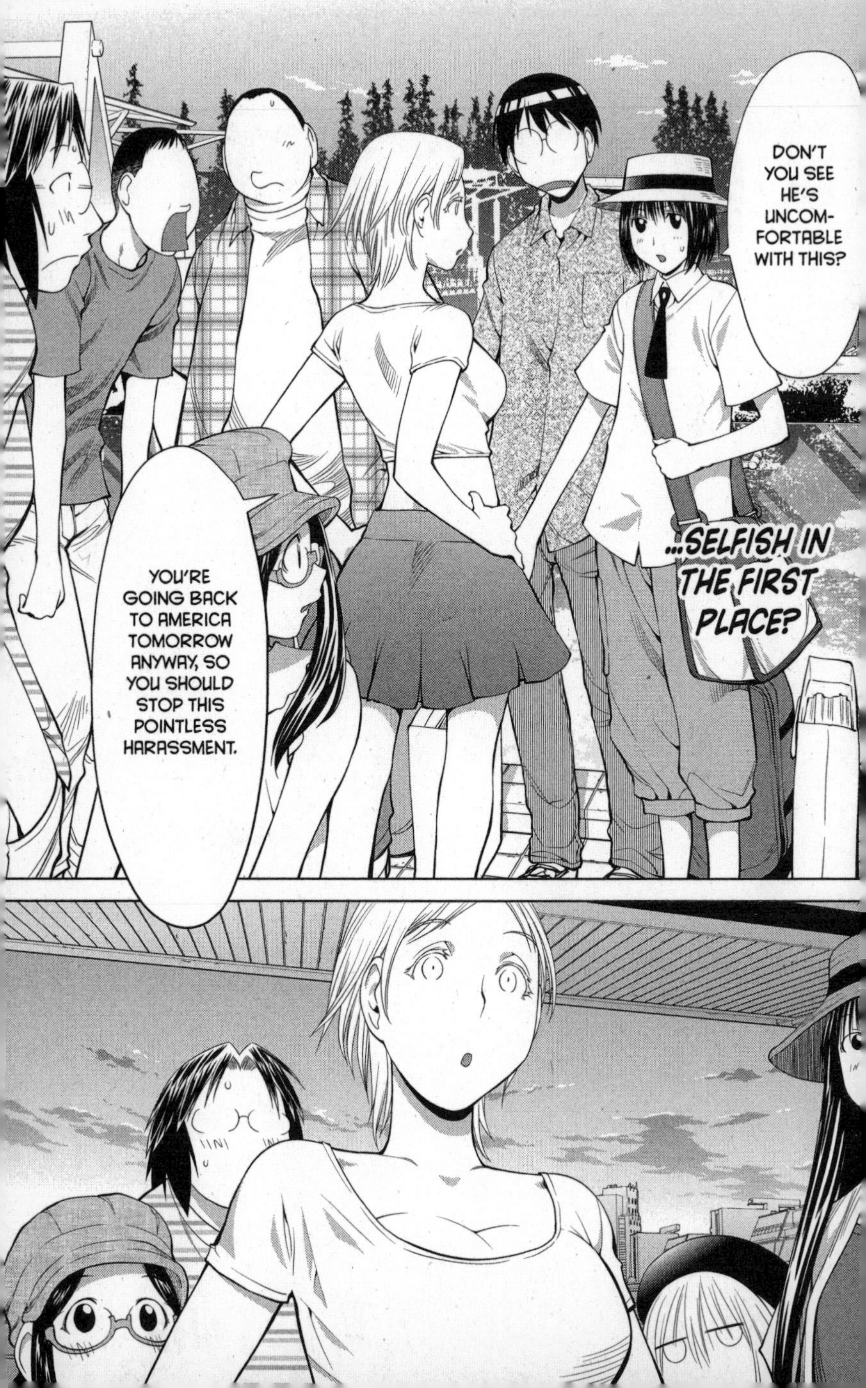
DON'T YOU SEE HE'S UNCOM-FORTABLE WITH THIS?
...SELFISH IN THE FIRST PLACE?
YOU'RE GOING BACK TO AMERICA TOMORROW ANYWAY, SO YOU SHOULD STOP THIS POINTLESS HARASSMENT.

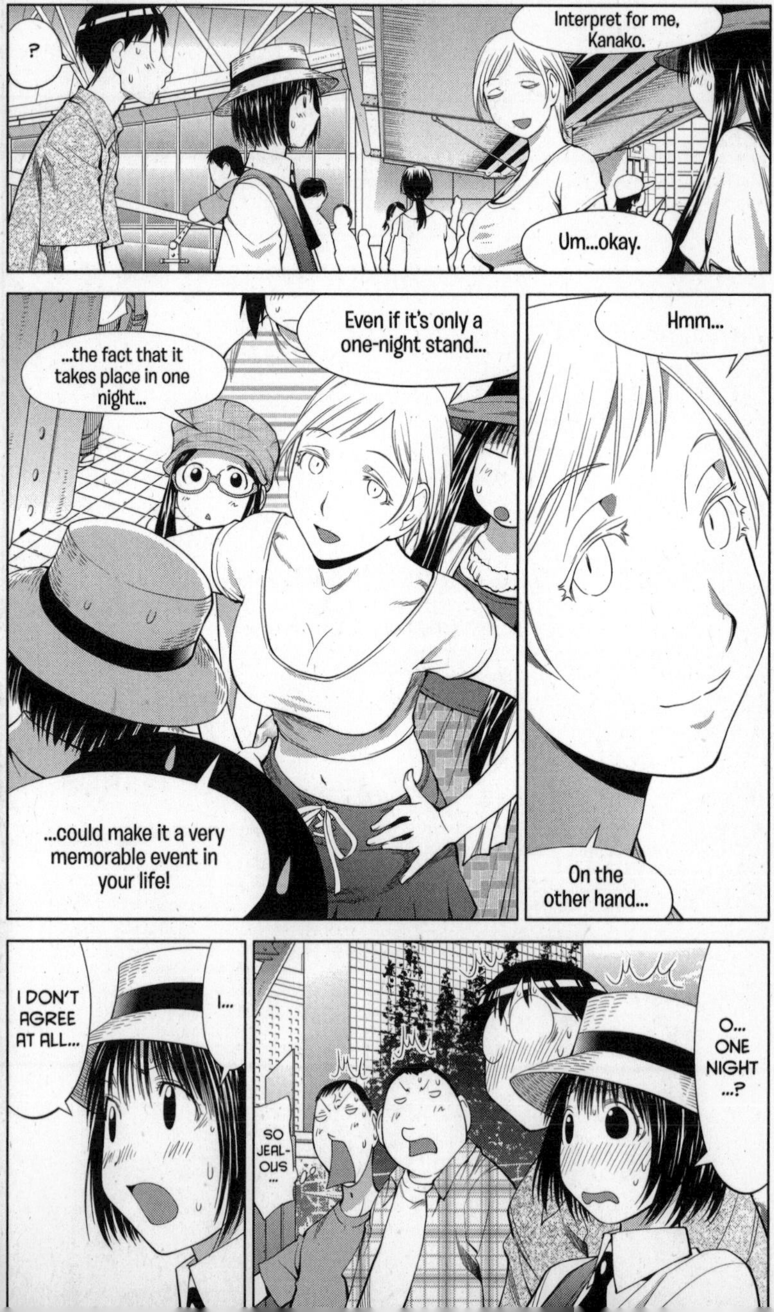

Interpret for me, Kanako.
Um...okay.
?
Hmm...
On the other hand...
Even if it's only a one-night stand...
...the fact that it takes place in one night...
...could make it a very memorable event in your life!
O... ONE NIGHT ...?
SO JEAL-OUS ...
I...
I DON'T AGREE AT ALL...

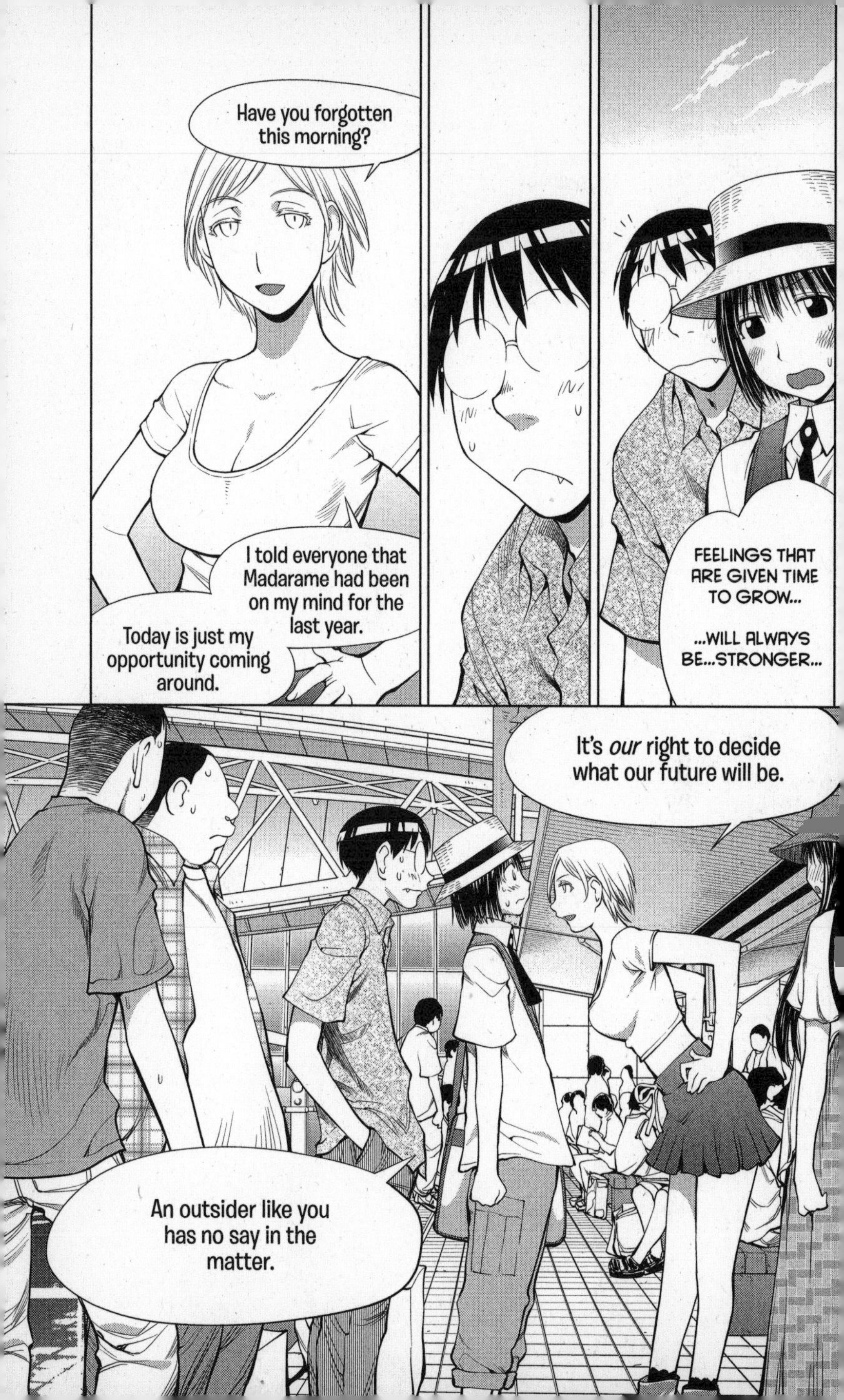
FEELINGS THAT ARE GIVEN TIME TO GROW...
...WILL ALWAYS BE...STRONGER...
Have you forgotten this morning?
I told everyone that Madarame had been on my mind for the last year.
Today is just my opportunity coming around.
It's *our* right to decide what our future will be.
An outsider like you has no say in the matter.

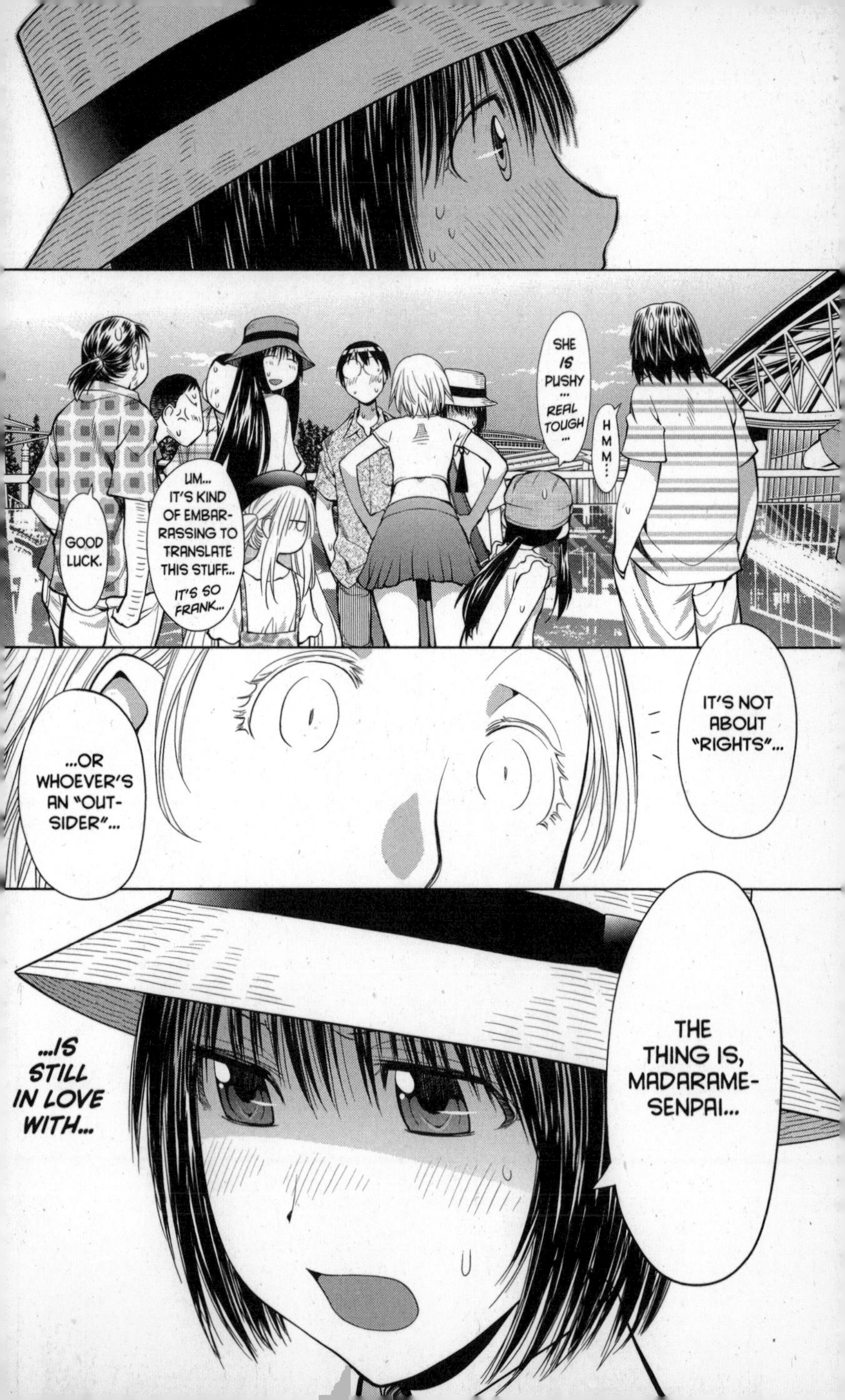
SHE *IS* PUSHY... REAL TOUGH...
HMM...
UM... IT'S KIND OF EMBARRASSING TO TRANSLATE THIS STUFF... IT'S SO FRANK...
GOOD LUCK.
IT'S NOT ABOUT "RIGHTS"...
...OR WHOEVER'S AN "OUTSIDER"...
THE THING IS, MADARAME-SENPAI...
...IS STILL IN LOVE WITH...

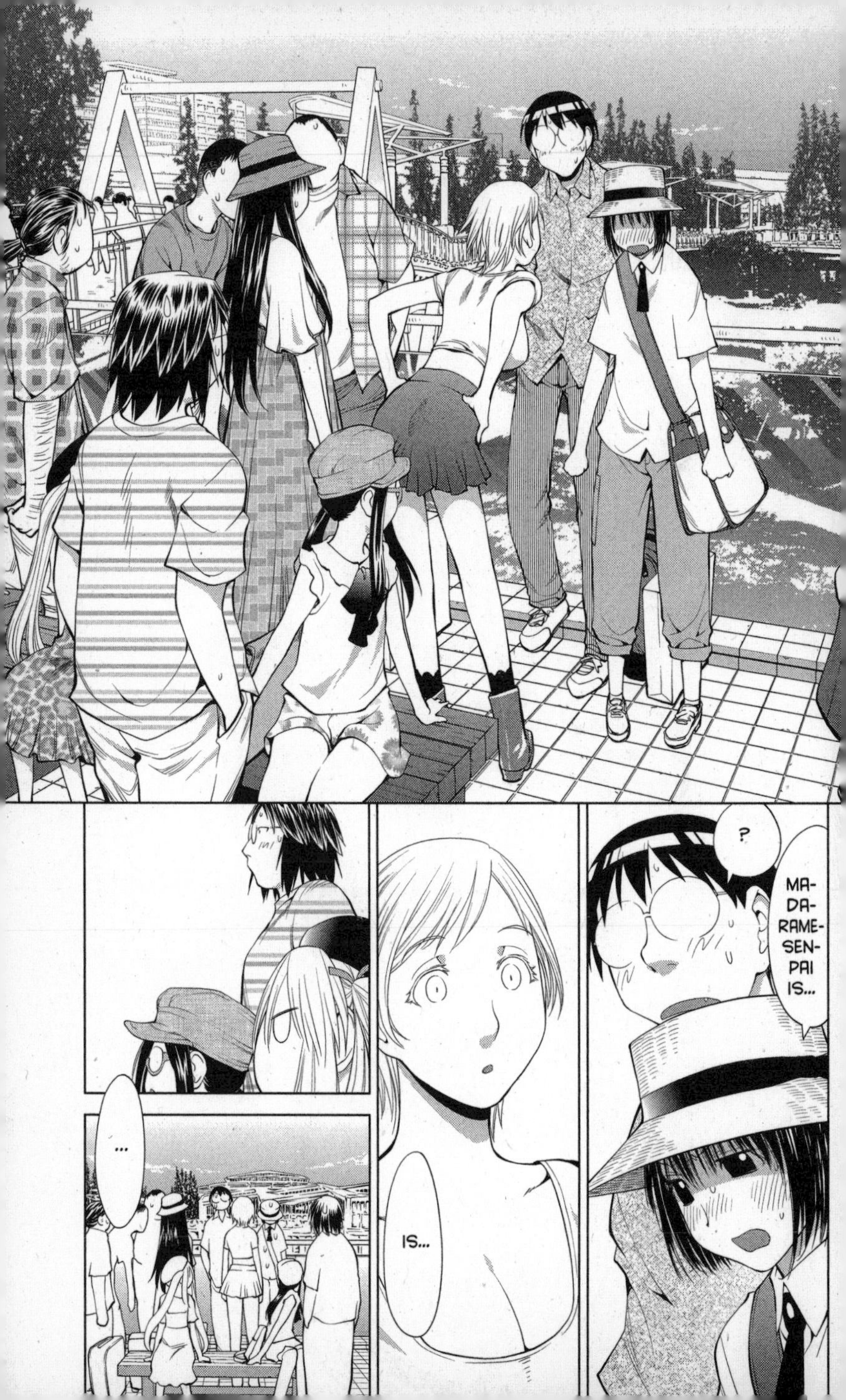
?
MA-DA-RAME-SEN-PAI IS...
IS...
...

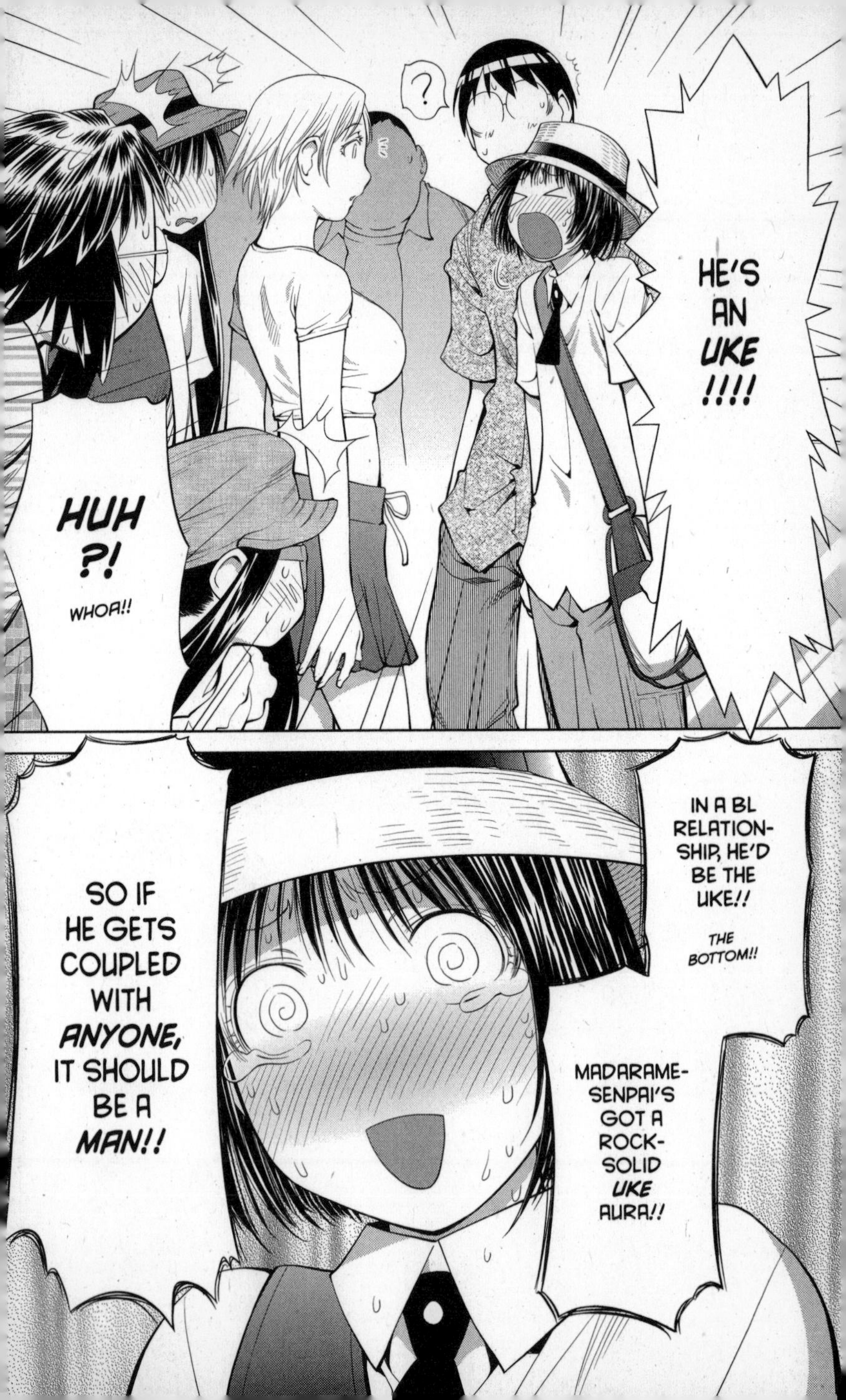

HE'S AN UKE !!!!
?
HUH ?!
WHOA!!
IN A BL RELATIONSHIP, HE'D BE THE UKE!!
THE BOTTOM!!
MADARAME-SENPAI'S GOT A ROCK-SOLID UKE AURA!!
SO IF HE GETS COUPLED WITH ANYONE, IT SHOULD BE A MAN!!

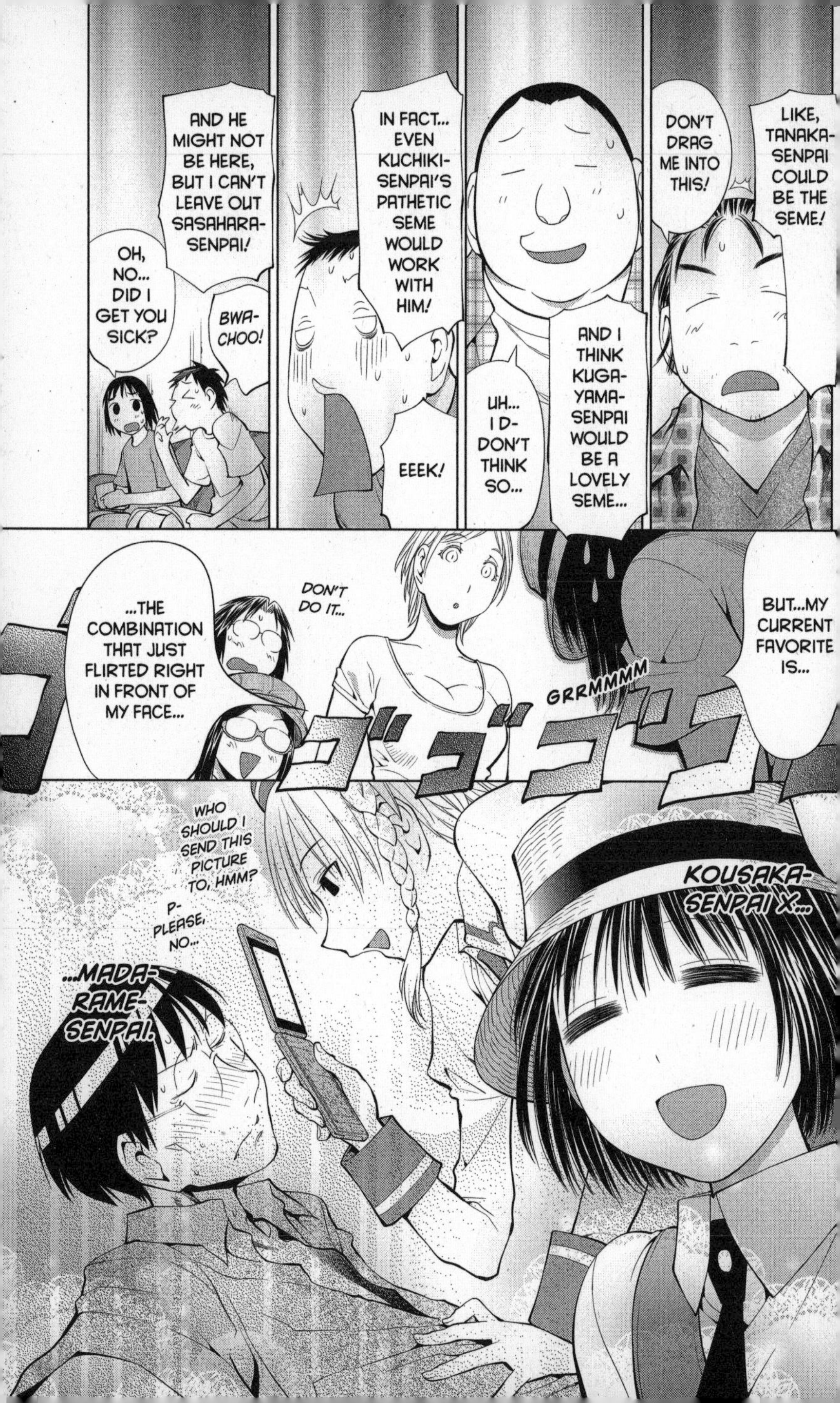
LIKE, TANAKA-SENPAI COULD BE THE SEME!
DON'T DRAG ME INTO THIS!
AND I THINK KUGA-YAMA-SENPAI WOULD BE A LOVELY SEME...
UH... I D-DON'T THINK SO...
IN FACT... EVEN KUCHIKI-SENPAI'S PATHETIC SEME WOULD WORK WITH HIM!
EEEK!
AND HE MIGHT NOT BE HERE, BUT I CAN'T LEAVE OUT SASAHARA-SENPAI!
BWA-CHOO!
OH, NO... DID I GET YOU SICK?
BUT...MY CURRENT FAVORITE IS...
GRRMMMM
DON'T DO IT...
...THE COMBINATION THAT JUST FLIRTED RIGHT IN FRONT OF MY FACE...
KOUSAKA-SENPAI X...
WHO SHOULD I SEND THIS PICTURE TO, HMM?
P-PLEASE, NO...
...MADA-RAME-SENPAI.

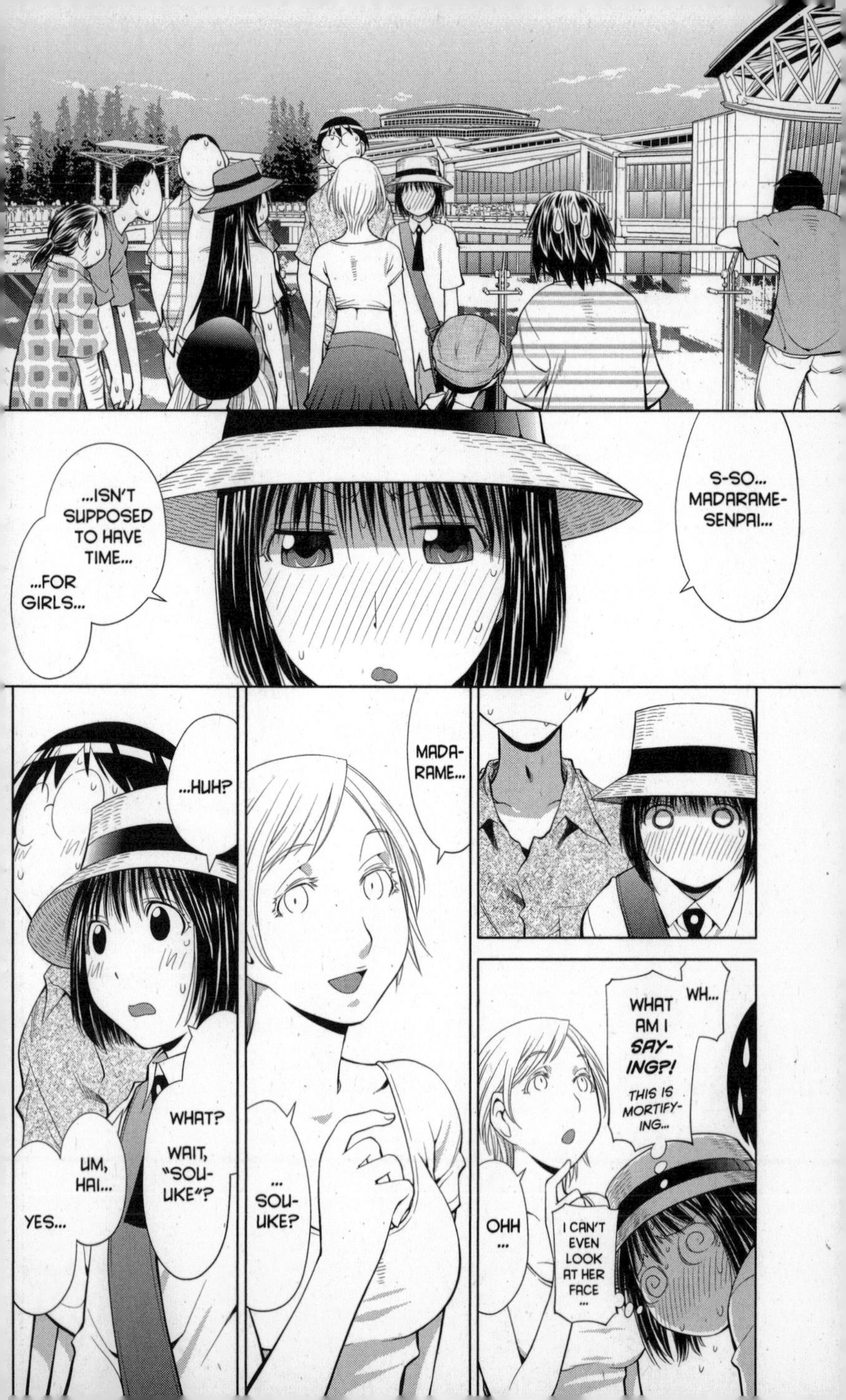
S-SO... MADARAME-SENPAI...
...ISN'T SUPPOSED TO HAVE TIME... ...FOR GIRLS...
WH...
WHAT AM I SAYING?!
THIS IS MORTIFYING...
I CAN'T EVEN LOOK AT HER FACE...
OHH...
MADARAME...
...SOU-UKE?
...HUH?
WHAT? WAIT, "SOU-UKE"?
UM, HAI... YES...

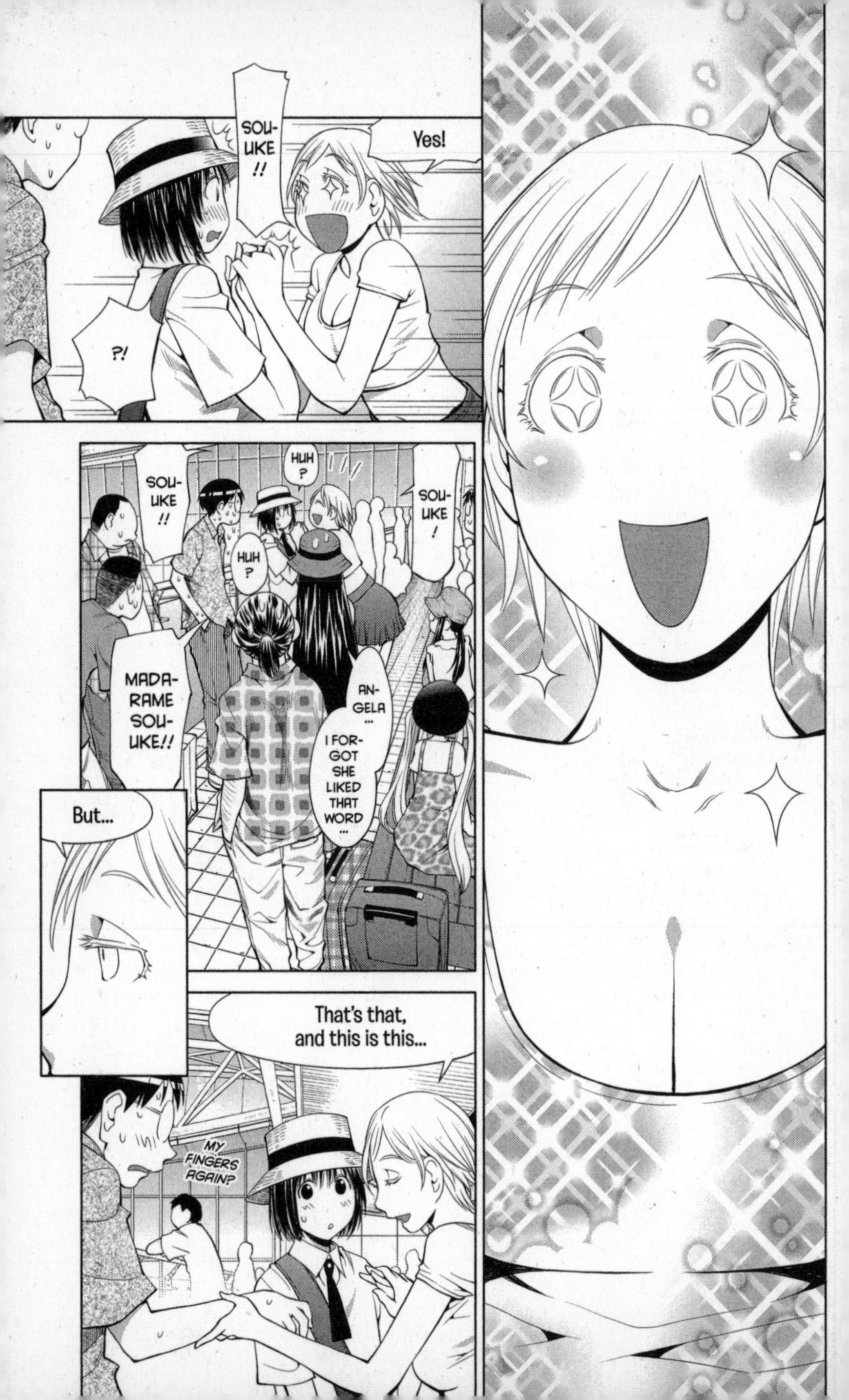
Yes!
SOU-UKE!!
?!
SOU-UKE!
HUH?
SOU-UKE!!
HUH?
MADA-RAME SOU-UKE!!
AN-GELA... I FOR-GOT SHE LIKED THAT WORD...
But...
That's that, and this is this...
MY FINGERS AGAIN?

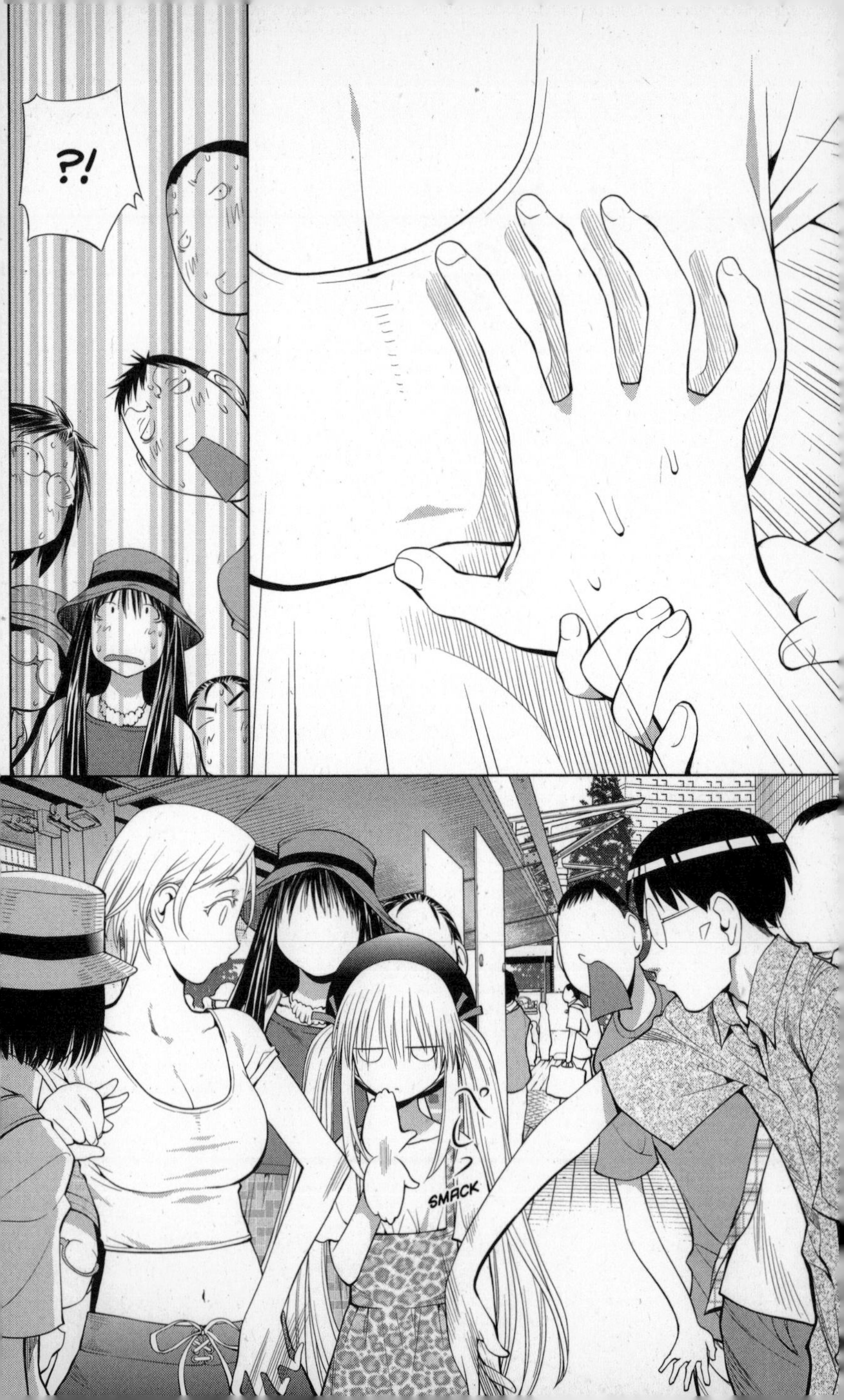
?!
SMACK

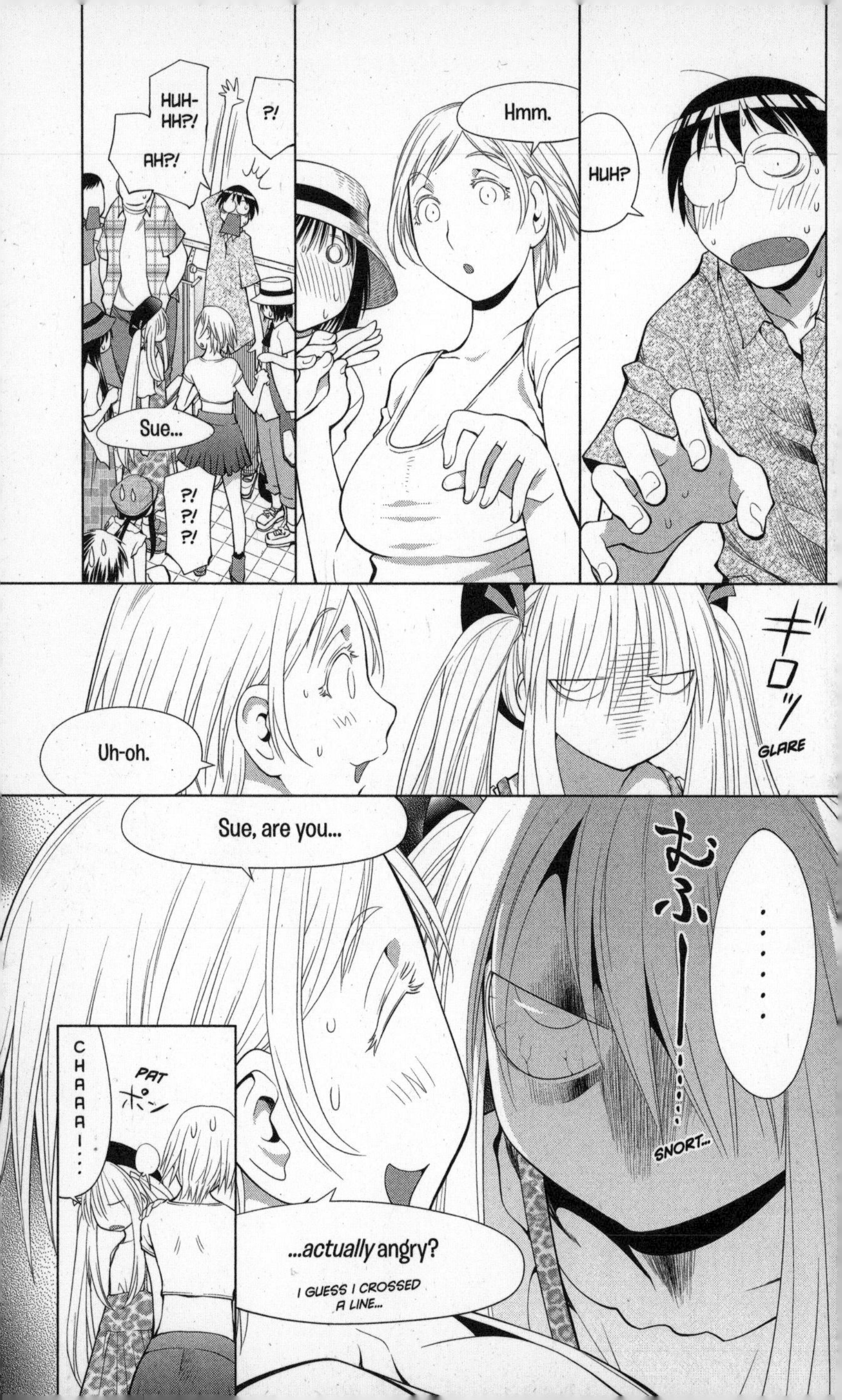
HUH?
Hmm.
?!
HUH-HH?!
AH?!
Sue...
?! ?! ?!
ギロッ
GLARE
Uh-oh.
Sue, are you...
むふー
......
SNORT...
...actually angry?
I GUESS I CROSSED A LINE...
CHAAAI...
PAT
ポン

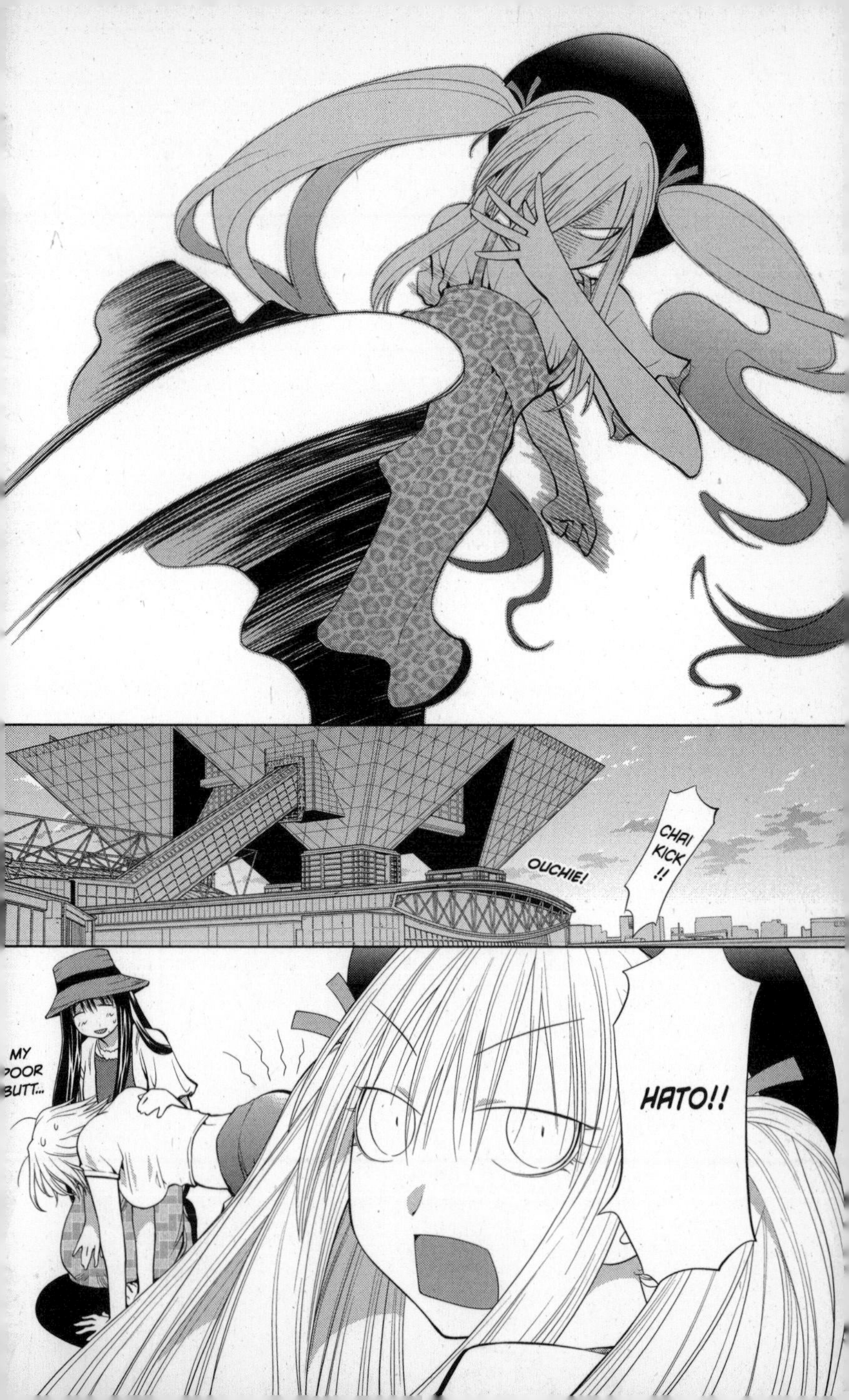

CHAI KICK !!
OUCHIE!
HATO!!
MY POOR BUTT...

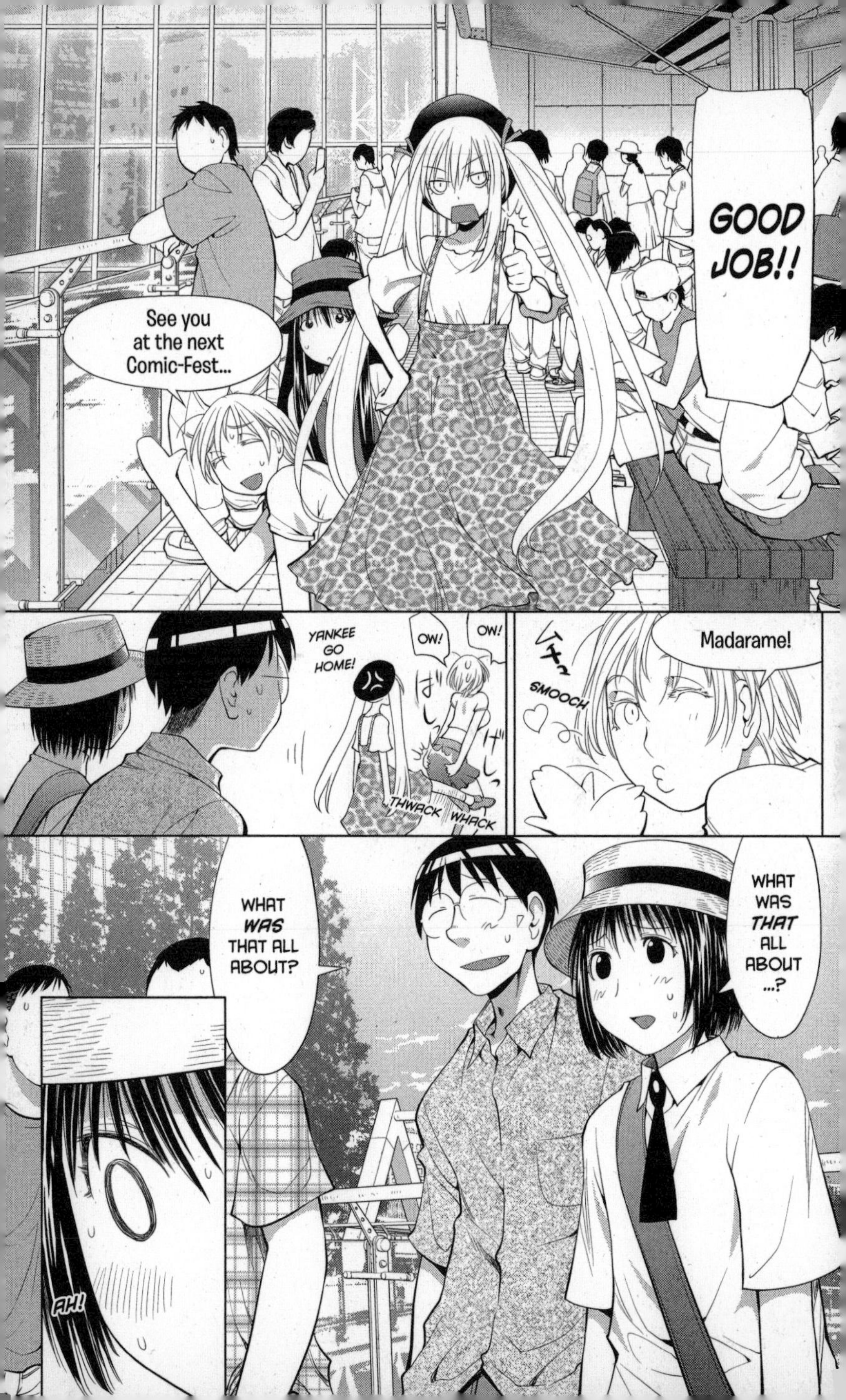
GOOD JOB!!
See you at the next Comic-Fest...
Madarame!
SMOOCH
OW!
OW!
YANKEE GO HOME!
THWACK
WHACK
WHAT WAS THAT ALL ABOUT ...?
WHAT WAS THAT ALL ABOUT?
AH!

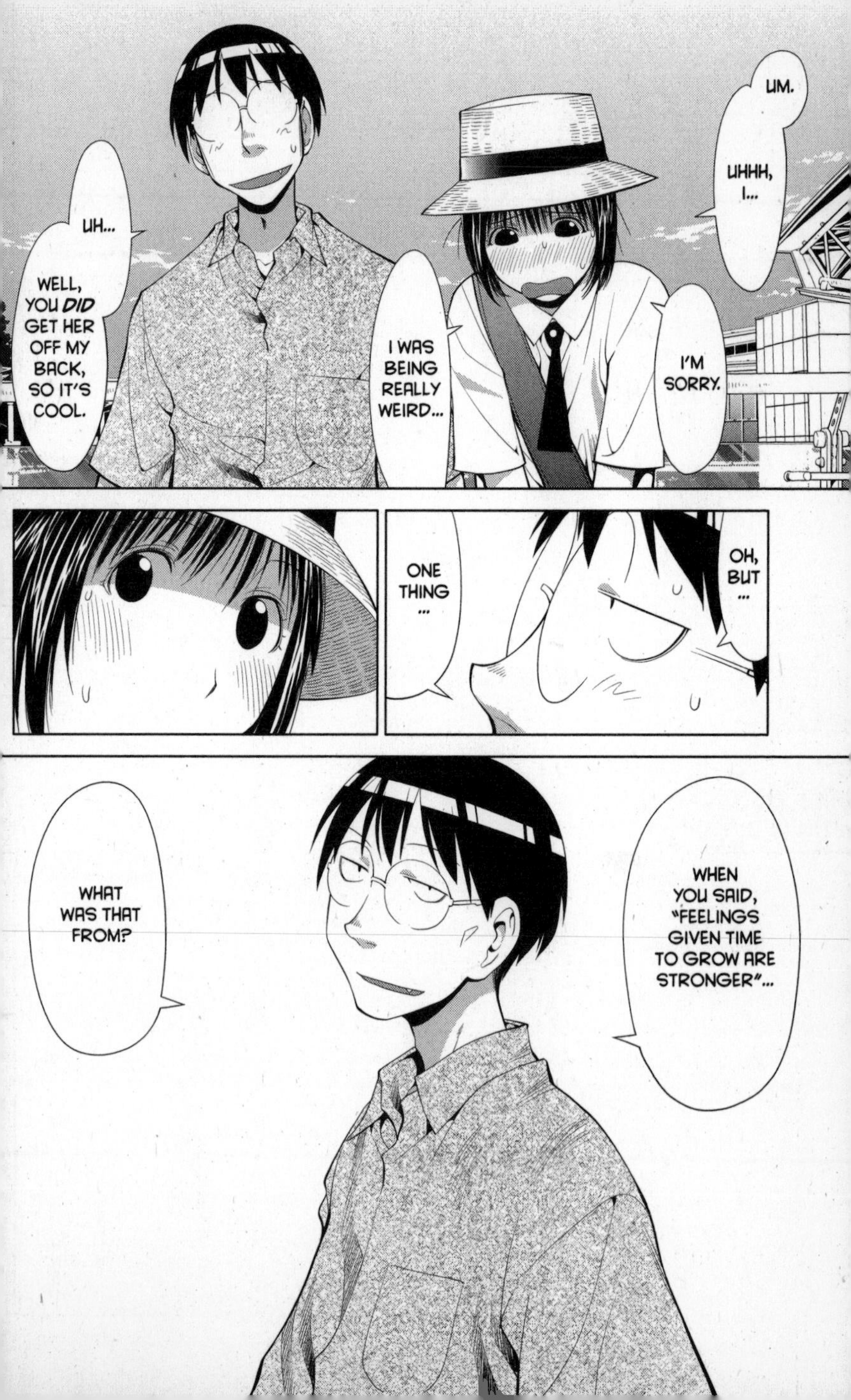
UM.
UHHH, I...
I'M SORRY.
I WAS BEING REALLY WEIRD...
UH...
WELL, YOU *DID* GET HER OFF MY BACK, SO IT'S COOL.
OH, BUT ...
ONE THING ...
WHEN YOU SAID, "FEELINGS GIVEN TIME TO GROW ARE STRONGER"...
WHAT WAS THAT FROM?

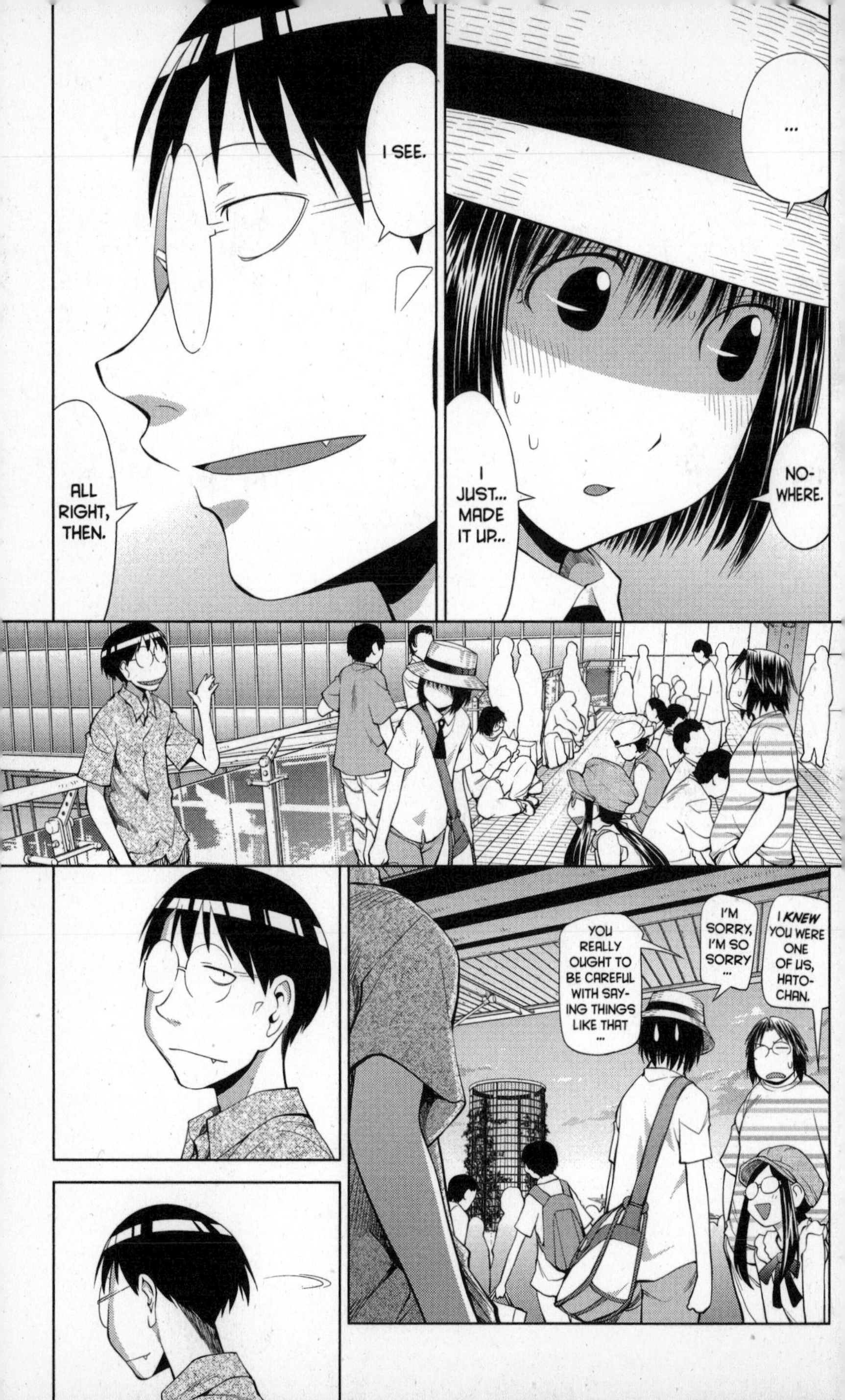
...
NO-WHERE.
I JUST... MADE IT UP...
I SEE.
ALL RIGHT, THEN.
I *KNEW* YOU WERE ONE OF US, HATO-CHAN.
I'M SORRY, I'M SO SORRY...
YOU REALLY OUGHT TO BE CAREFUL WITH SAYING THINGS LIKE THAT...

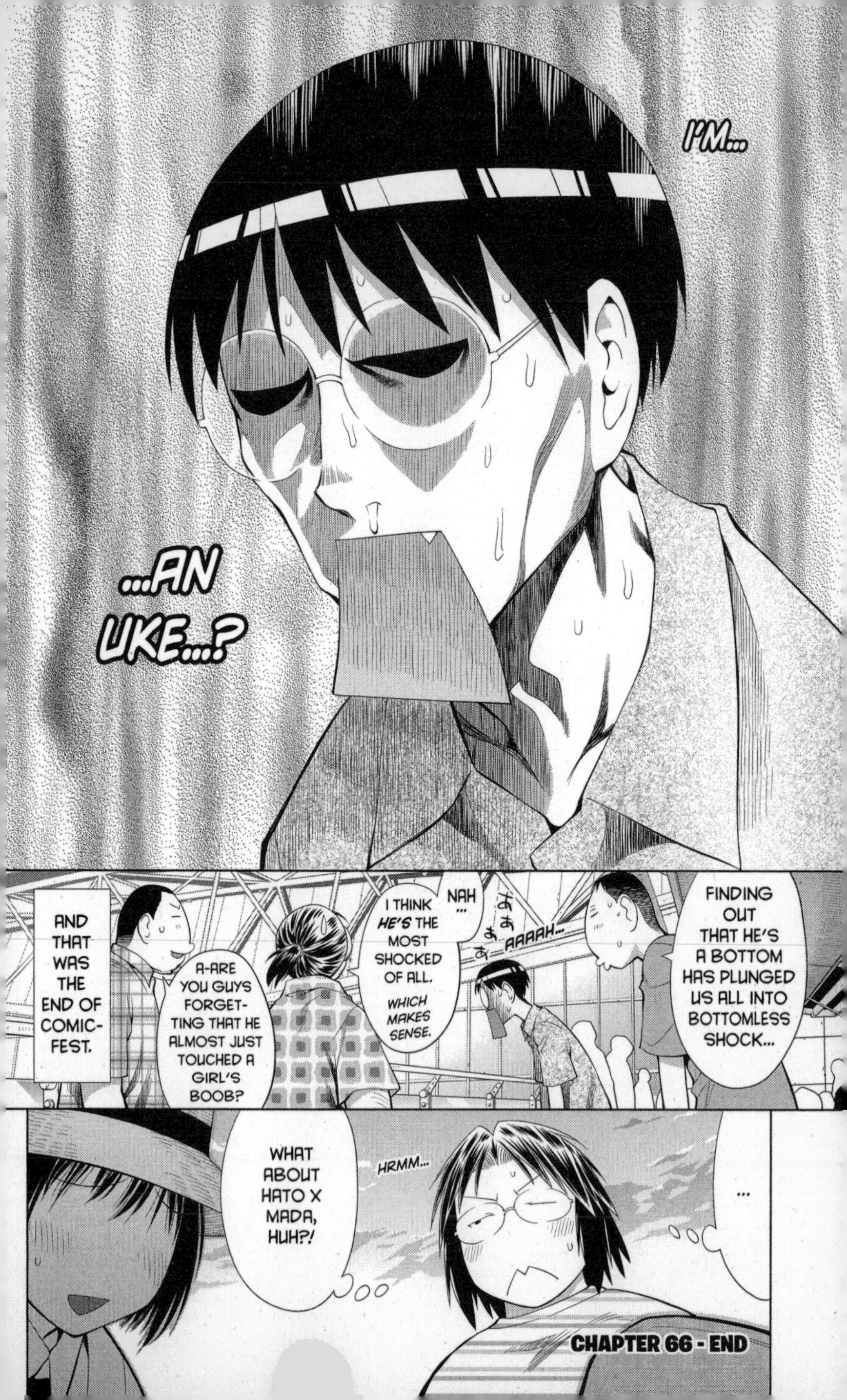
I'M...
...AN UKE...?
FINDING OUT THAT HE'S A BOTTOM HAS PLUNGED US ALL INTO BOTTOMLESS SHOCK...
AAAAAH...
ああああ
NAH ...
I THINK HE'S THE MOST SHOCKED OF ALL.
WHICH MAKES SENSE.
A-ARE YOU GUYS FORGETTING THAT HE ALMOST JUST TOUCHED A GIRL'S BOOB?
AND THAT WAS THE END OF COMIC-FEST.
...
HRMM...
WHAT ABOUT HATO X MADA, HUH?!
CHAPTER 66 - END

HATO-CHAN NEAR THE WEST HALL ROOF

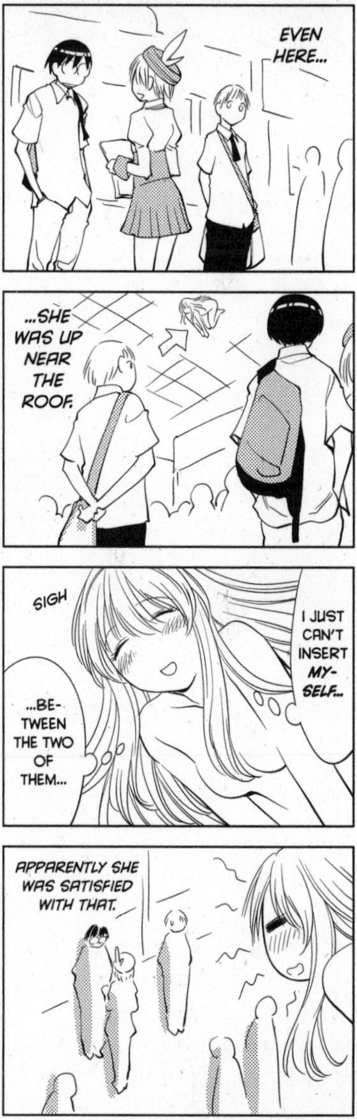
EVEN HERE...
...SHE WAS UP NEAR THE ROOF.
I JUST CAN'T INSERT *MY*SELF...
SIGH
...BETWEEN THE TWO OF THEM...
APPARENTLY SHE WAS SATISFIED WITH THAT.

THIS SUCKS...BUT...

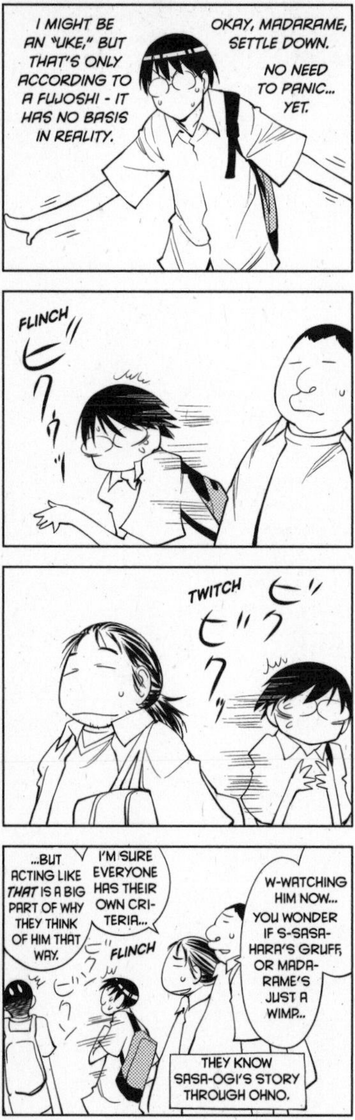
OKAY, MADARAME, SETTLE DOWN.
NO NEED TO PANIC... YET.
I MIGHT BE AN "UKE," BUT THAT'S ONLY ACCORDING TO A FUJOSHI - IT HAS NO BASIS IN REALITY.
FLINCH
TWITCH
W-WATCHING HIM NOW... YOU WONDER IF S-SASAHARA'S GRUFF, OR MADARAME'S JUST A WIMP...
I'M SURE EVERYONE HAS THEIR OWN CRITERIA...
...BUT ACTING LIKE *THAT* IS A BIG PART OF WHY THEY THINK OF HIM THAT WAY.
FLINCH
THEY KNOW SASA-OGI'S STORY THROUGH OHNO.

LONG-TERM PROJECT

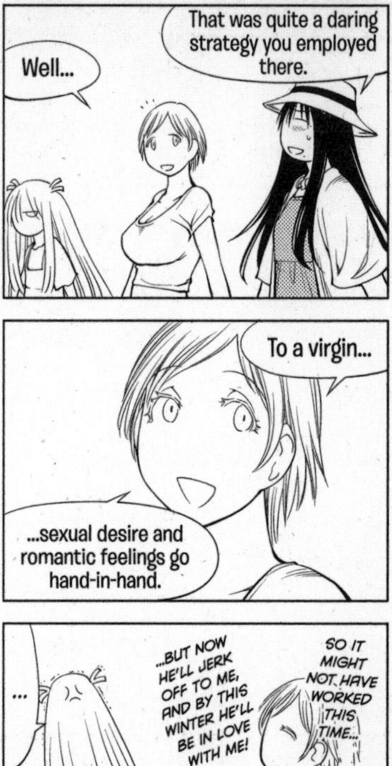
That was quite a daring strategy you employed there.
Well...
To a virgin...
...sexual desire and romantic feelings go hand-in-hand.
SO IT MIGHT NOT HAVE WORKED THIS TIME...
...BUT NOW HE'LL JERK OFF TO ME, AND BY THIS WINTER HE'LL BE IN LOVE WITH ME!
...
AH... AHHH...
HUH ?!
FOOT SQUASH
SMACK

MY NEW JOKE

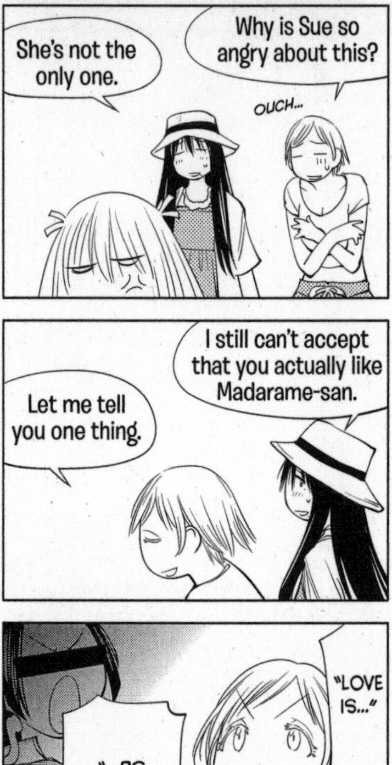
Why is Sue so angry about this?
She's not the only one.
OUCH...
I still can't accept that you actually like Madarame-san.
Let me tell you one thing.
"LOVE IS..."
"...AS STRONG AS A HURRI"
CA-- NGFH!!
NOW YOU'RE JUST A COMIC DUO...
HERE ?
KTHUDD

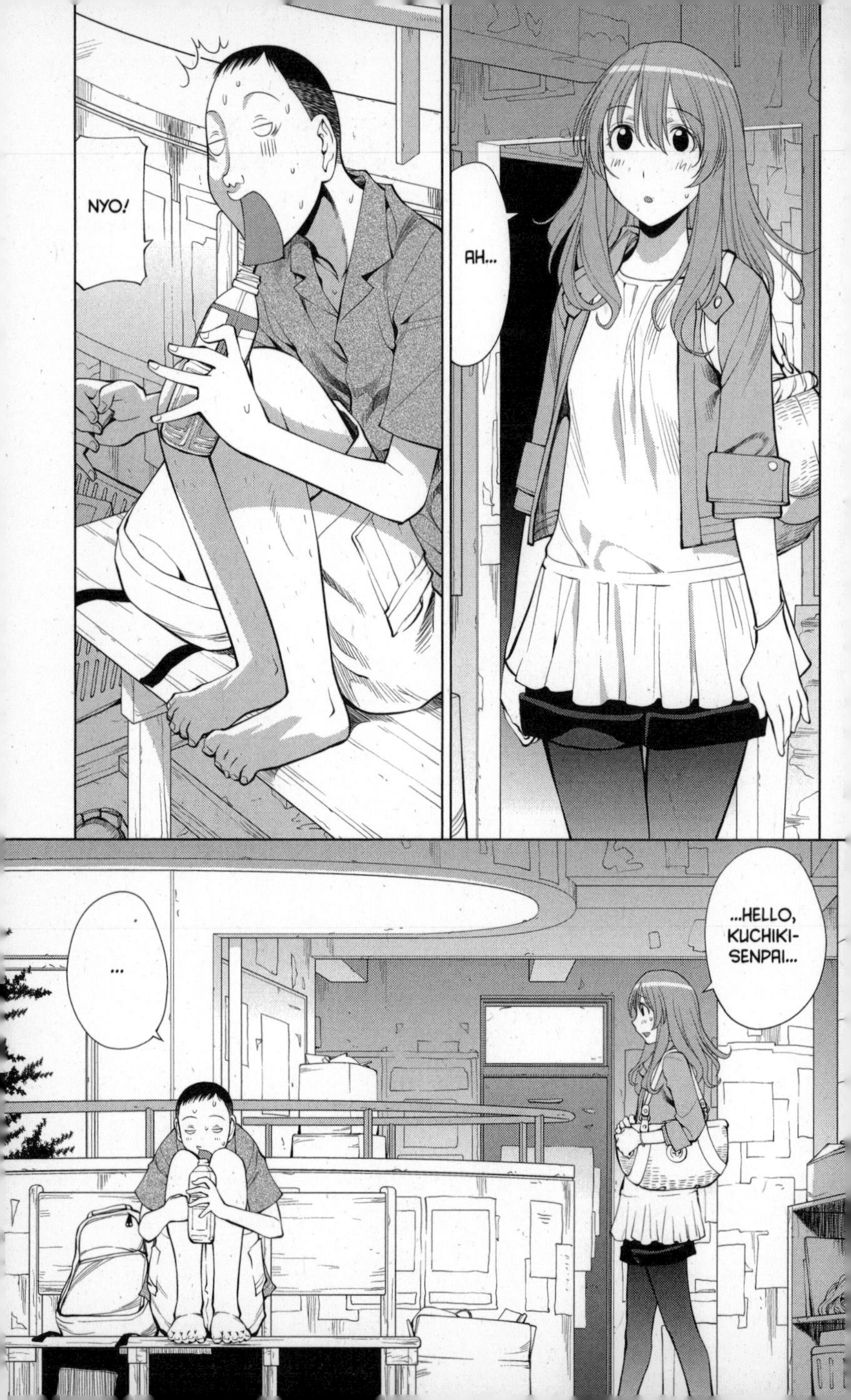
AH...
NYO!
...HELLO, KUCHIKI-SENPAI...
...

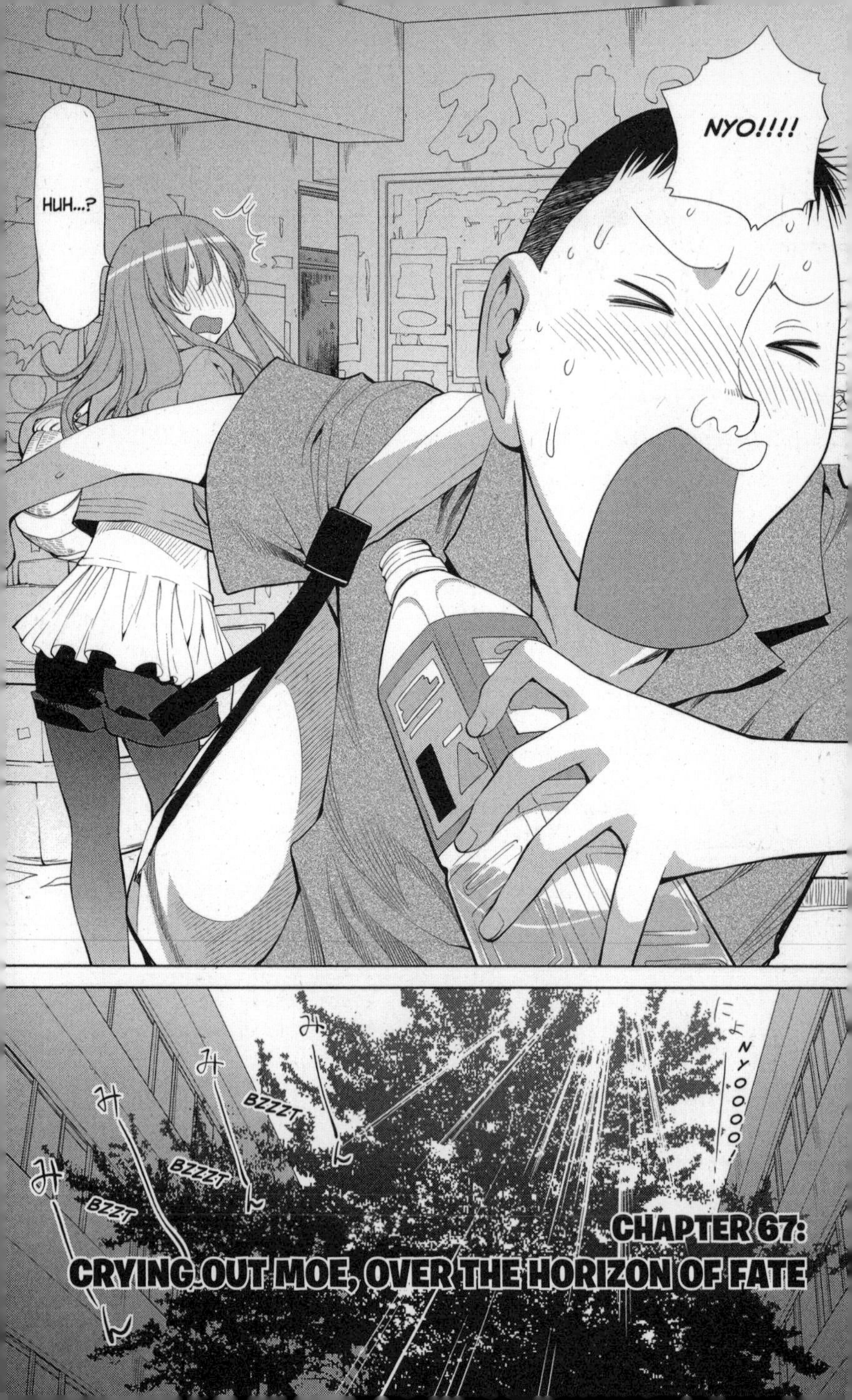
NYO!!!!
HUH...?
にょ
NYOOOOO...!
みーん
BZZZT
みーん
BZZZT
みーん
BZZT
みーん

CHAPTER 67:
CRYING OUT MOE, OVER THE HORIZON OF FATE

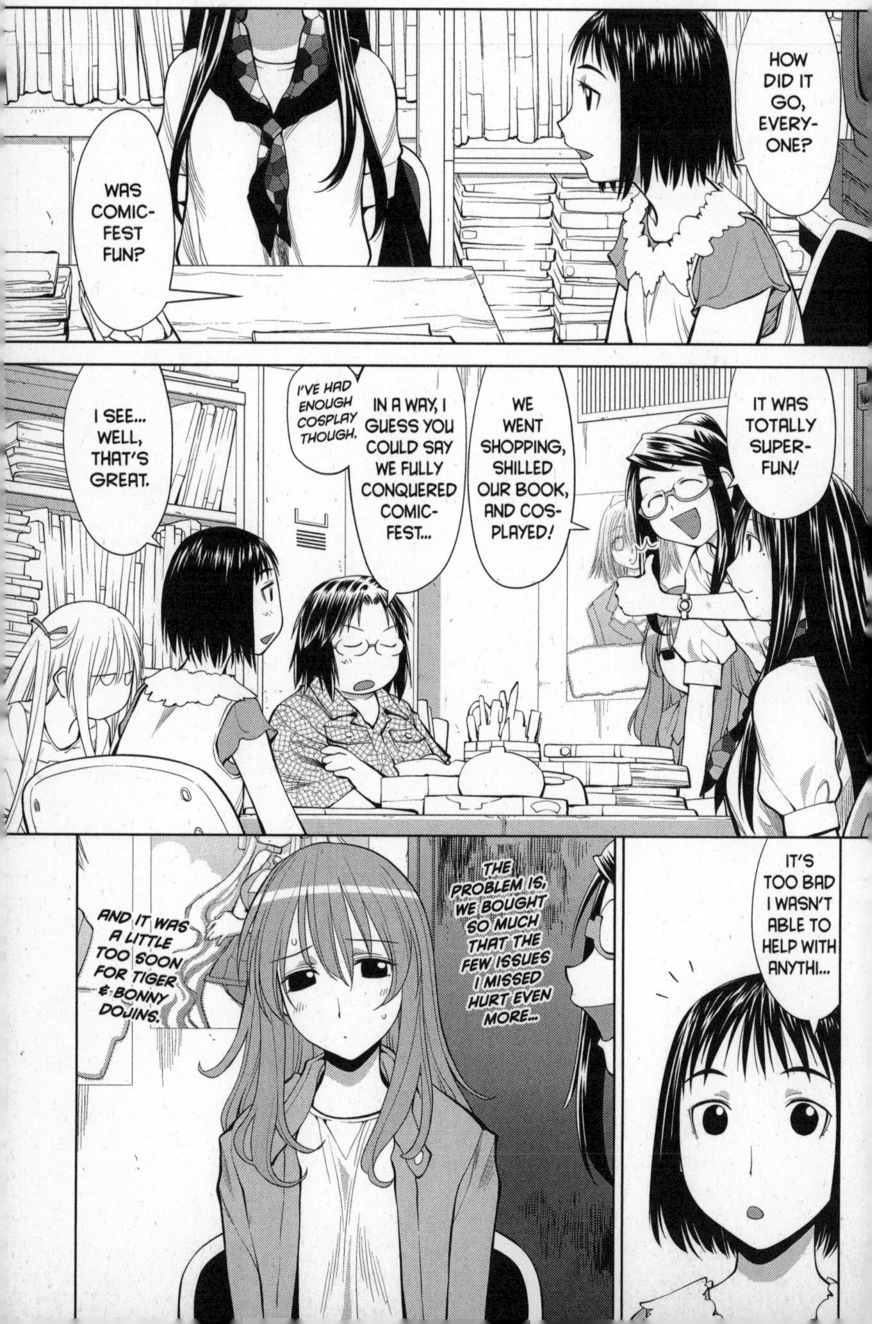
HOW DID IT GO, EVERY-ONE?
WAS COMIC-FEST FUN?
IT WAS TOTALLY SUPER-FUN!
WE WENT SHOPPING, SHILLED OUR BOOK, AND COS-PLAYED!
IN A WAY, I GUESS YOU COULD SAY WE FULLY CONQUERED COMIC-FEST...
I'VE HAD ENOUGH COSPLAY THOUGH.
I SEE... WELL, THAT'S GREAT.
IT'S TOO BAD I WASN'T ABLE TO HELP WITH ANYTHI...
THE PROBLEM IS, WE BOUGHT SO MUCH THAT THE FEW ISSUES I MISSED HURT EVEN MORE...
AND IT WAS A LITTLE TOO SOON FOR TIGER & BONNY DOJINS.

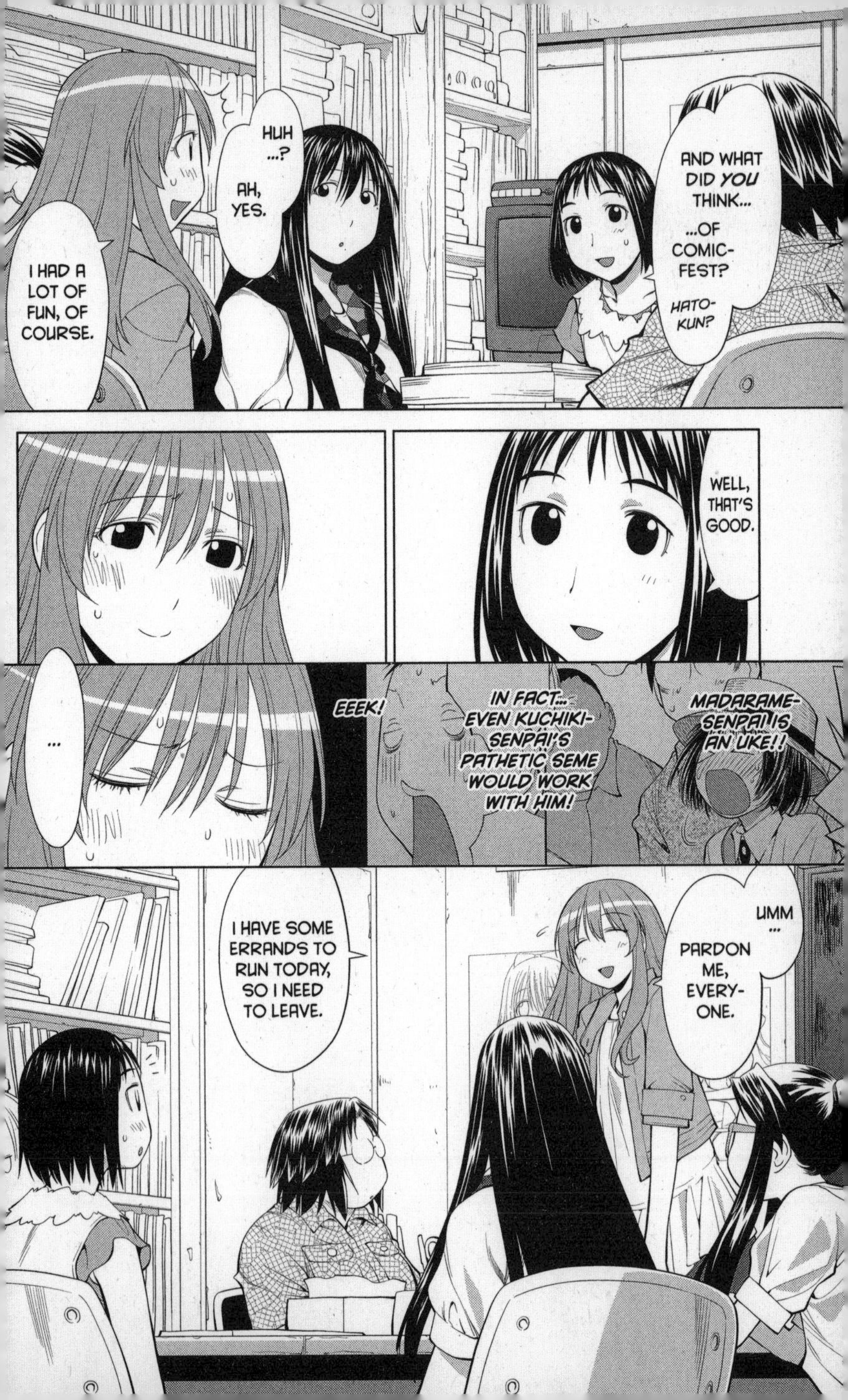
AND WHAT DID *YOU* THINK... ...OF COMIC-FEST?
HATO-KUN?
HUH ...?
AH, YES.
I HAD A LOT OF FUN, OF COURSE.
WELL, THAT'S GOOD.
MADARAME-SENPAI IS AN UKE!!
IN FACT... EVEN KUCHIKI-SENPAI'S PATHETIC SEME WOULD WORK WITH HIM!
EEEK!
...
UMM ...
PARDON ME, EVERY-ONE.
I HAVE SOME ERRANDS TO RUN TODAY, SO I NEED TO LEAVE.

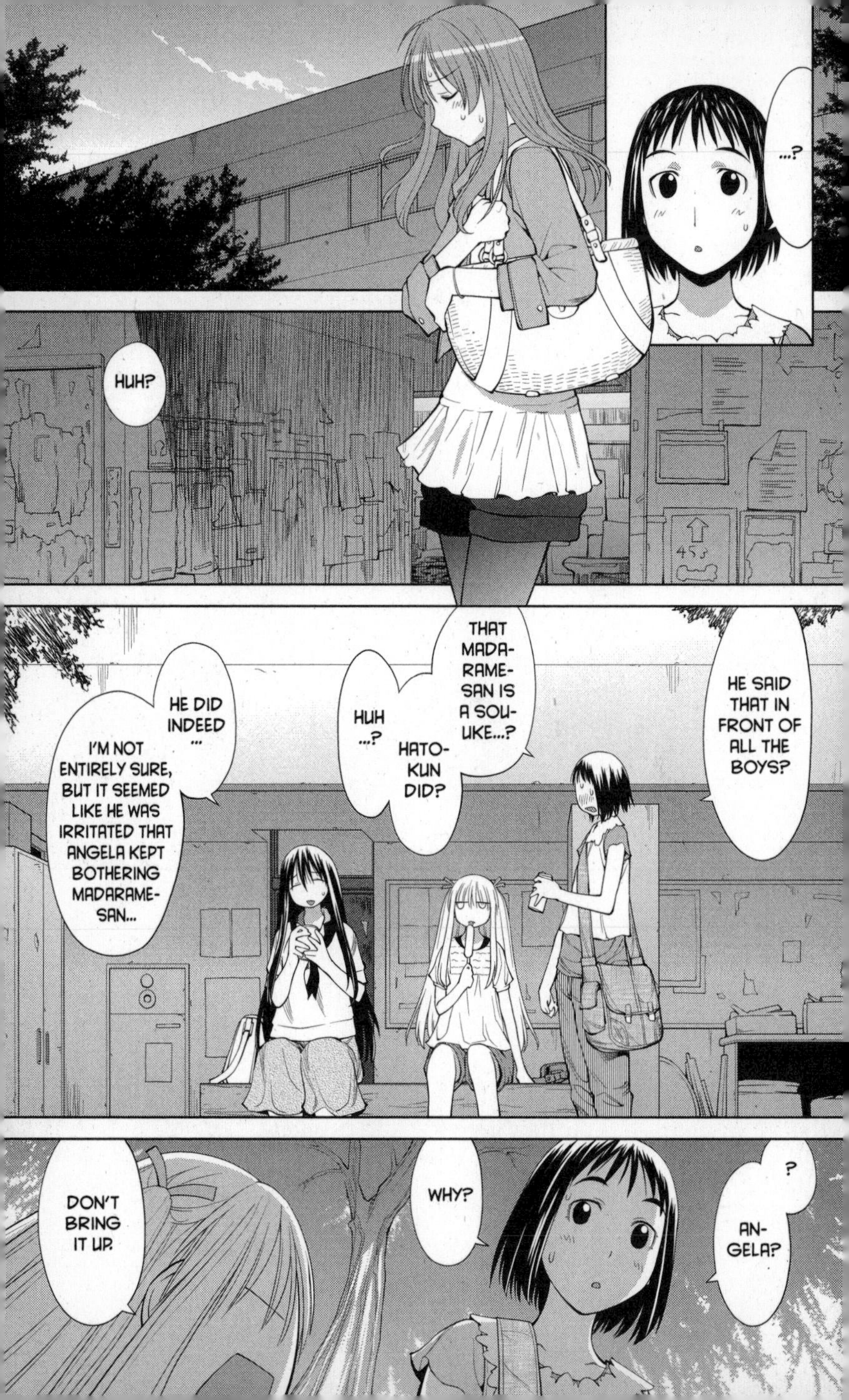
...?
HUH?
HE SAID THAT IN FRONT OF ALL THE BOYS?
THAT MADARAME-SAN IS A SOU-UKE...?
HATO-KUN DID?
HUH ...?
HE DID INDEED ...
I'M NOT ENTIRELY SURE, BUT IT SEEMED LIKE HE WAS IRRITATED THAT ANGELA KEPT BOTHERING MADARAME-SAN...
?
AN-GELA?
WHY?
DON'T BRING IT UP.

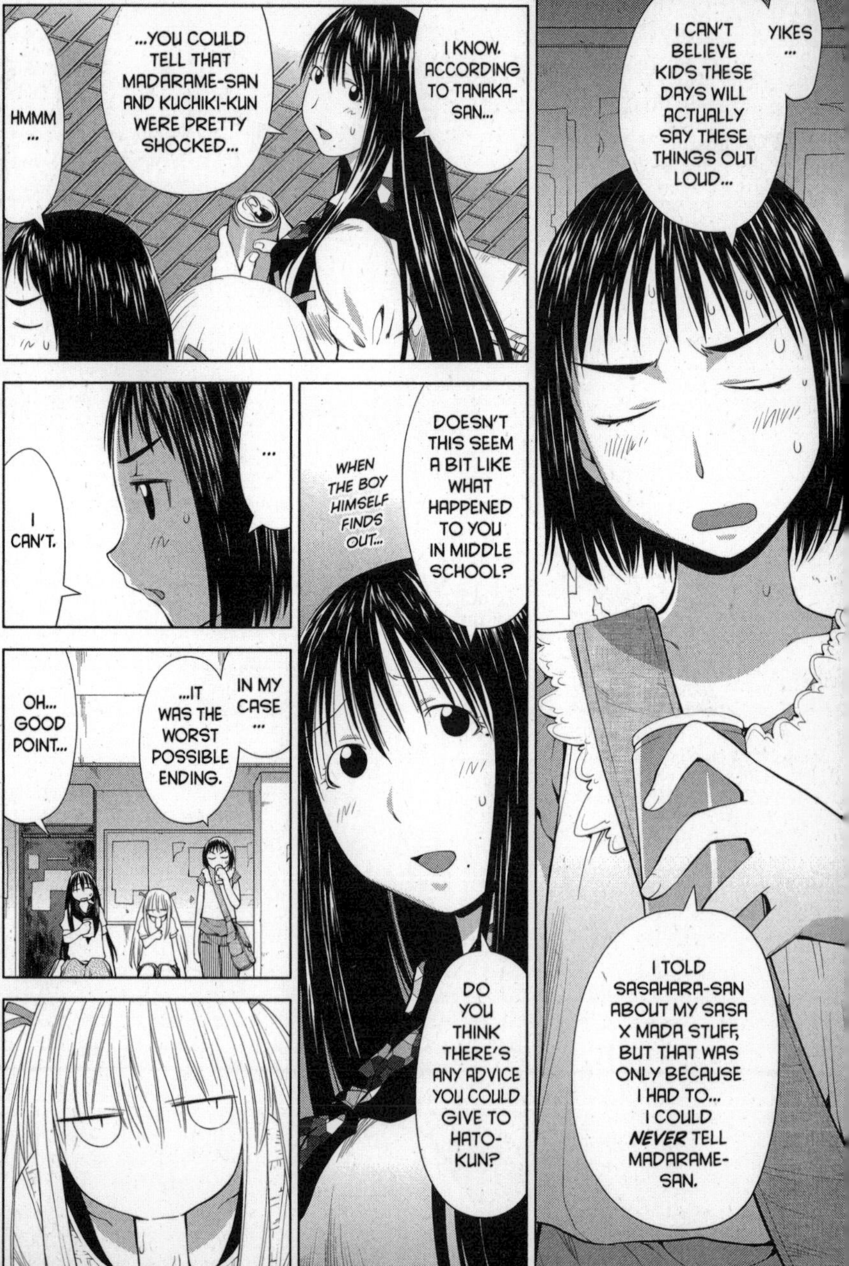
YIKES...
I CAN'T BELIEVE KIDS THESE DAYS WILL ACTUALLY SAY THESE THINGS OUT LOUD...
I TOLD SASAHARA-SAN ABOUT MY SASA X MADA STUFF, BUT THAT WAS ONLY BECAUSE I HAD TO... I COULD ***NEVER*** TELL MADARAME-SAN.
I KNOW. ACCORDING TO TANAKA-SAN...
...YOU COULD TELL THAT MADARAME-SAN AND KUCHIKI-KUN WERE PRETTY SHOCKED...
HMMM...
DOESN'T THIS SEEM A BIT LIKE WHAT HAPPENED TO YOU IN MIDDLE SCHOOL?
WHEN THE BOY HIMSELF FINDS OUT...
DO YOU THINK THERE'S ANY ADVICE YOU COULD GIVE TO HATO-KUN?
...
I CAN'T.
IN MY CASE...
...IT WAS THE WORST POSSIBLE ENDING.
OH... GOOD POINT...

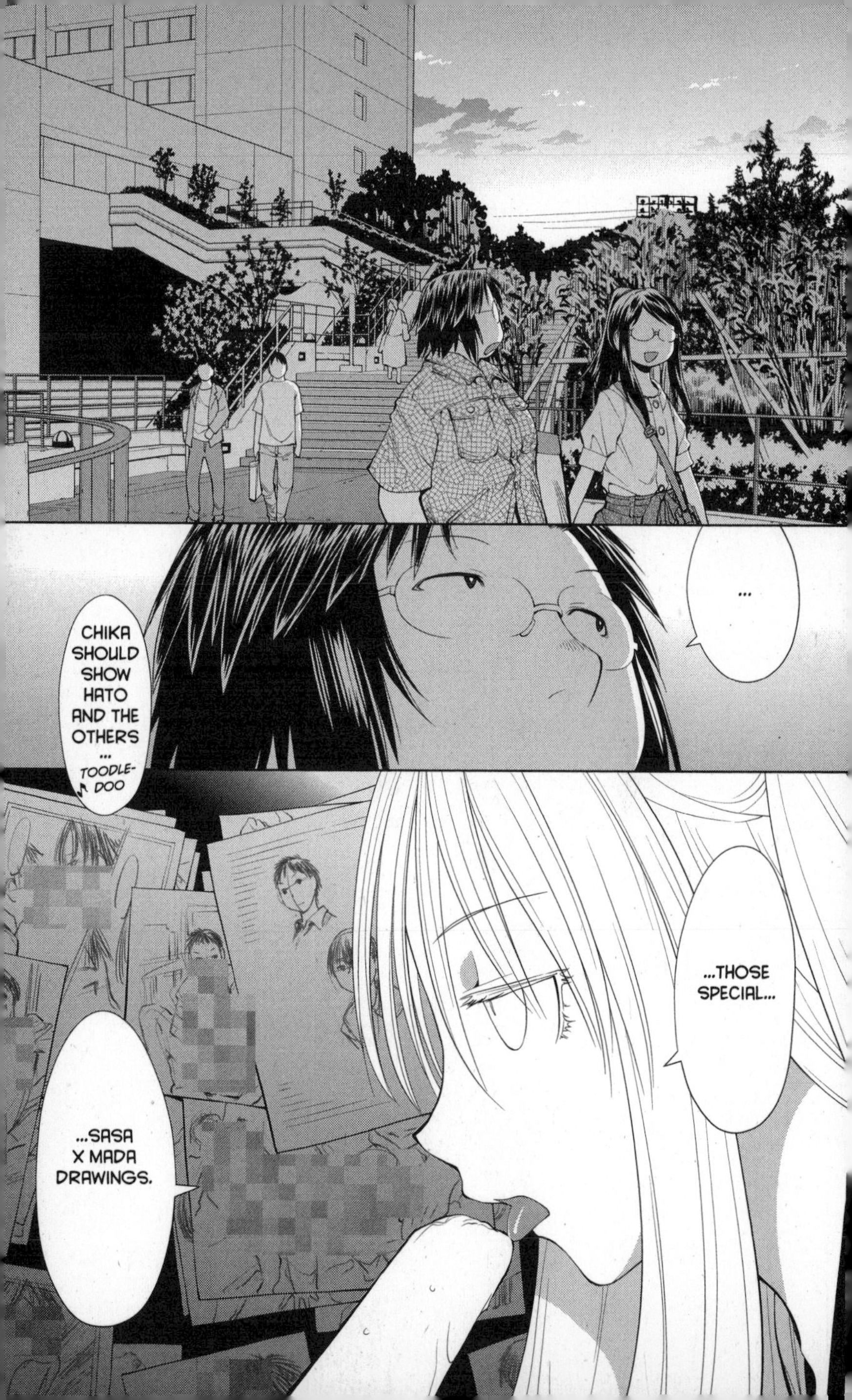
...
CHIKA SHOULD SHOW HATO AND THE OTHERS ...
TOODLE-DOO
...THOSE SPECIAL...
...SASA X MADA DRAWINGS.

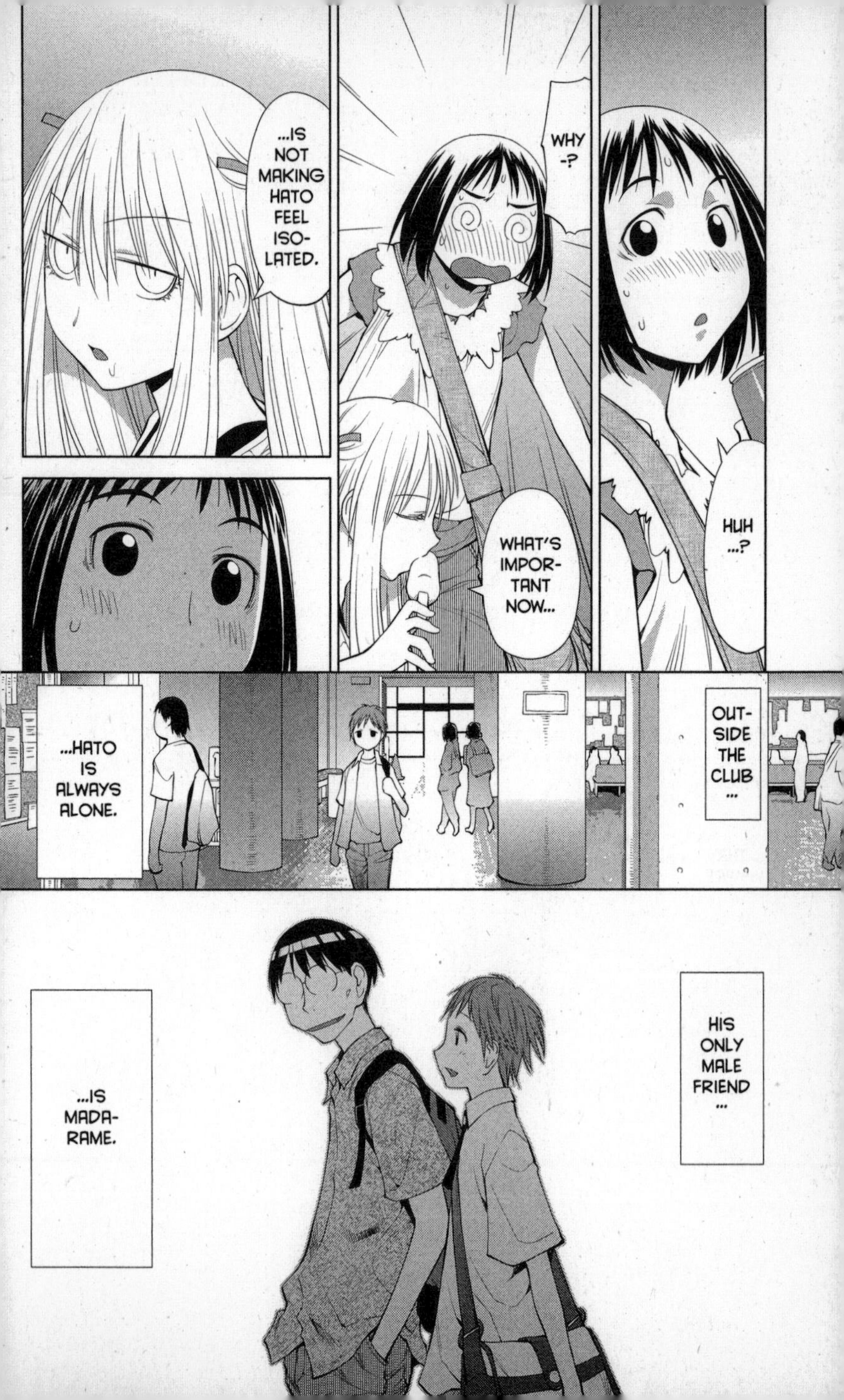
HUH ...?
WHY -?
WHAT'S IMPORTANT NOW...
...IS NOT MAKING HATO FEEL ISOLATED.
OUTSIDE THE CLUB ...
...HATO IS ALWAYS ALONE.
HIS ONLY MALE FRIEND ...
...IS MADARAME.

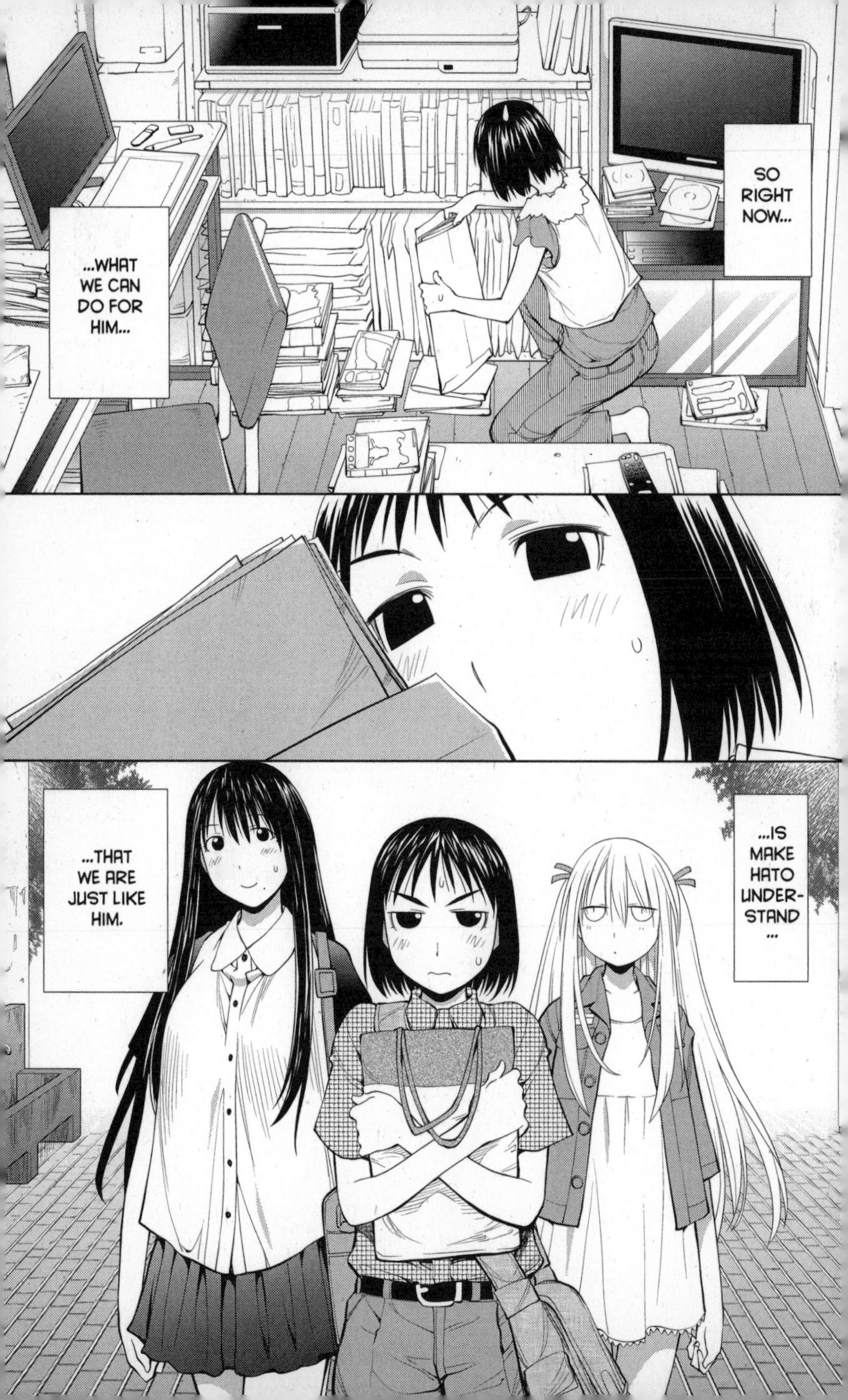
SO RIGHT NOW...
...WHAT WE CAN DO FOR HIM...
...IS MAKE HATO UNDER-STAND ...
...THAT WE ARE JUST LIKE HIM.

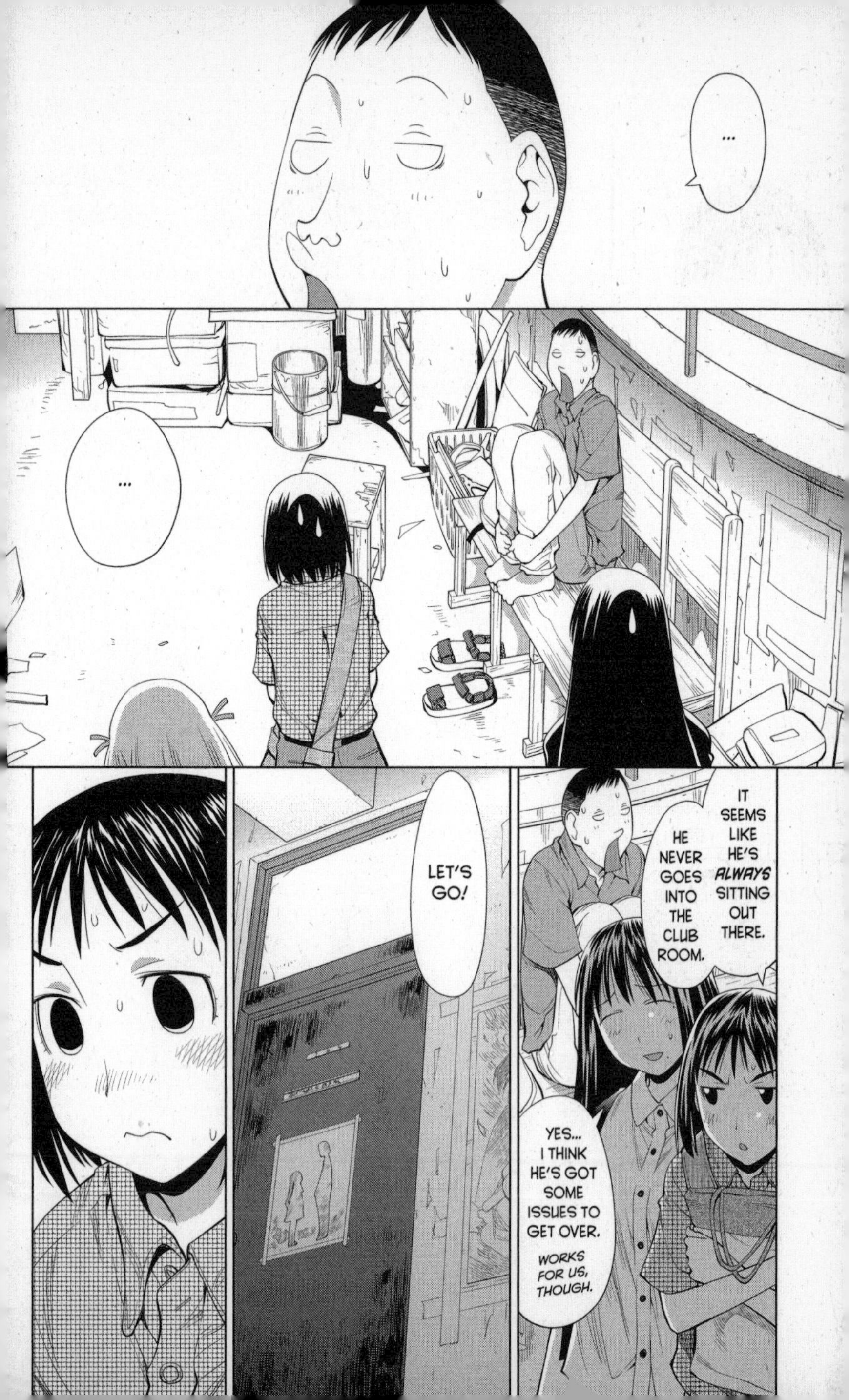
...
...
IT SEEMS LIKE HE'S *ALWAYS* SITTING OUT THERE.
HE NEVER GOES INTO THE CLUB ROOM.
YES... I THINK HE'S GOT SOME ISSUES TO GET OVER.
WORKS FOR US, THOUGH.
LET'S GO!

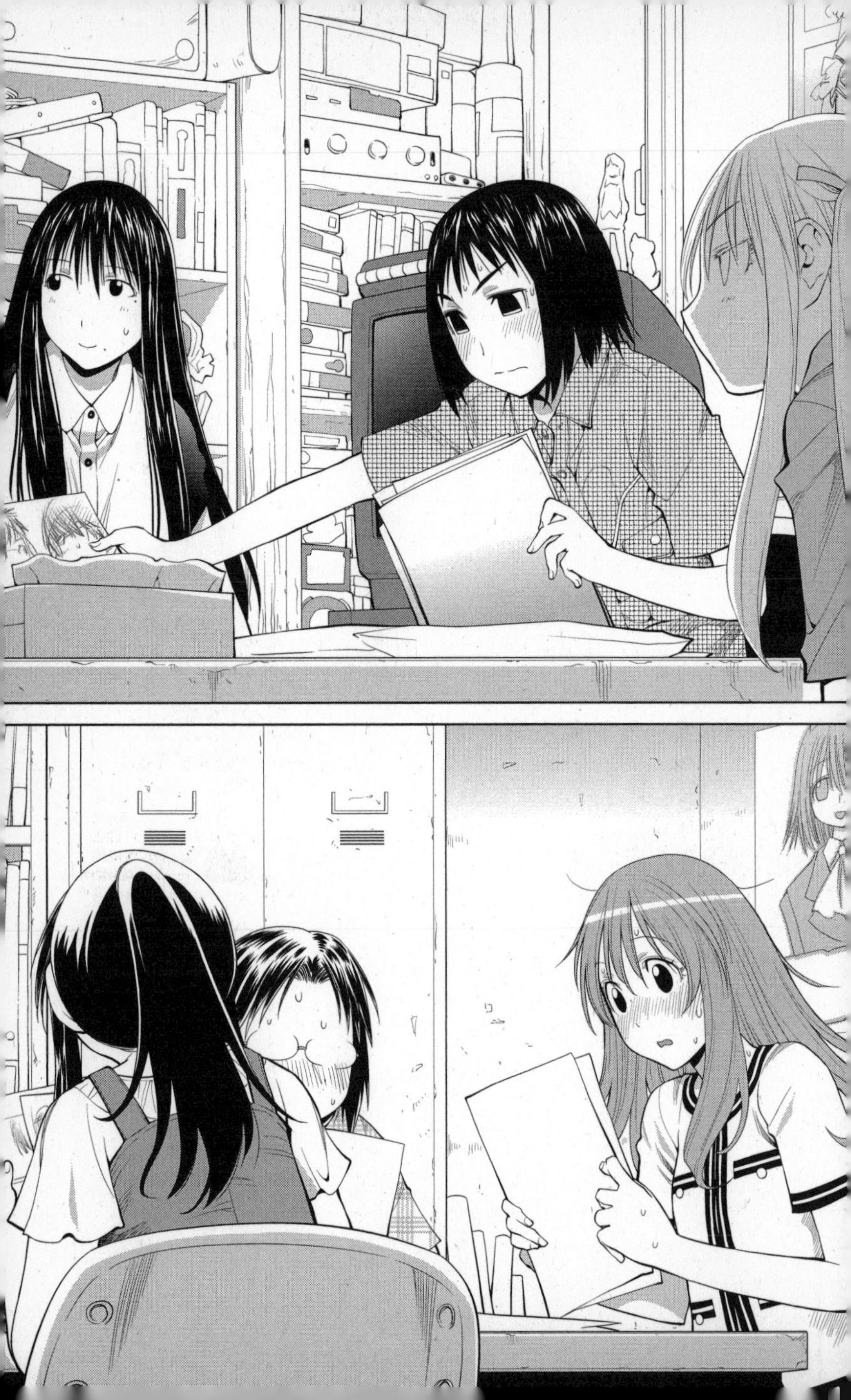

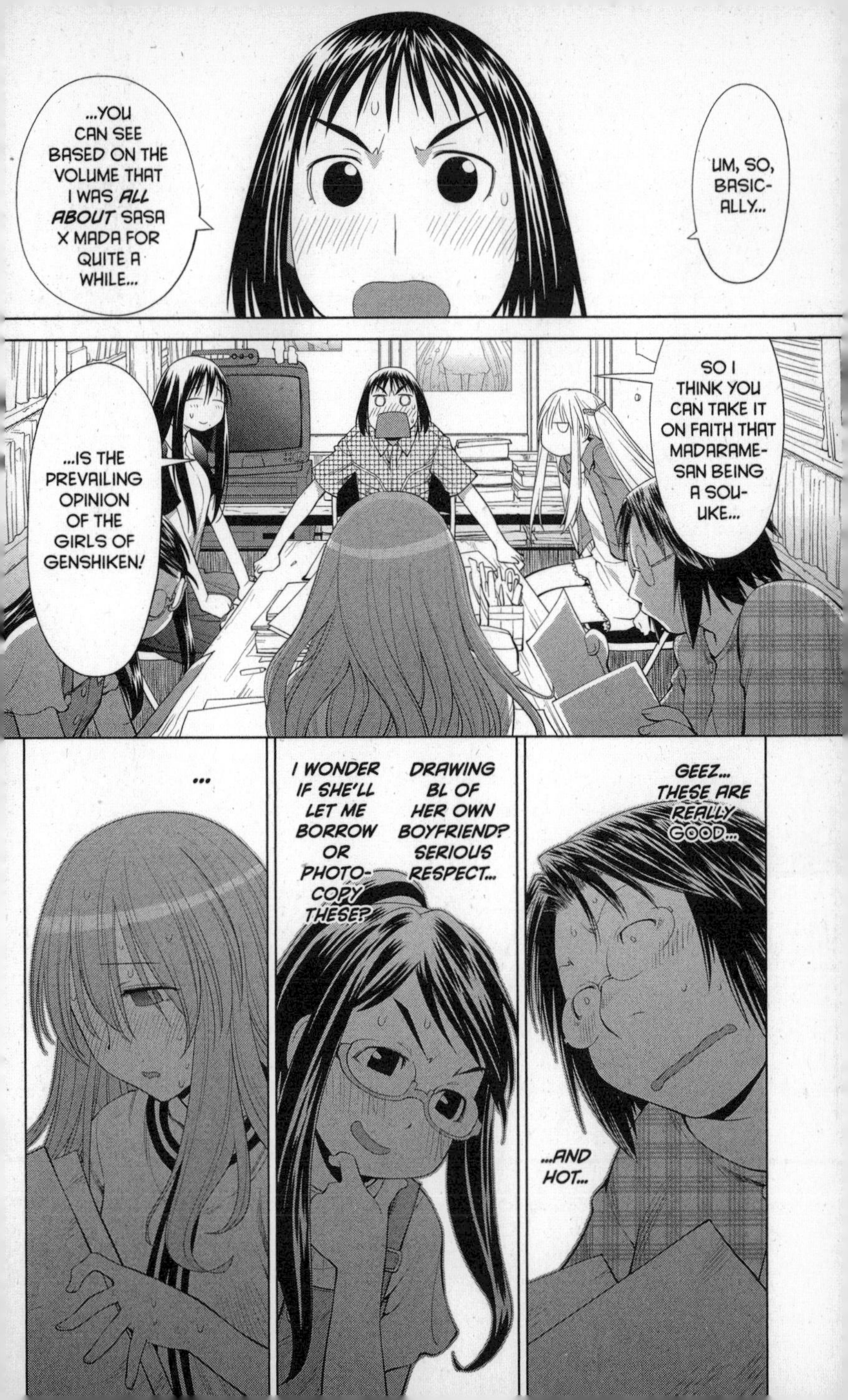
UM, SO, BASICALLY...
...YOU CAN SEE BASED ON THE VOLUME THAT I WAS ALL ABOUT SASA X MADA FOR QUITE A WHILE...
SO I THINK YOU CAN TAKE IT ON FAITH THAT MADARAME-SAN BEING A SOU-UKE...
...IS THE PREVAILING OPINION OF THE GIRLS OF GENSHIKEN!
GEEZ... THESE ARE REALLY GOOD...
...AND HOT...
DRAWING BL OF HER OWN BOYFRIEND? SERIOUS RESPECT...
I WONDER IF SHE'LL LET ME BORROW OR PHOTOCOPY THESE?
...

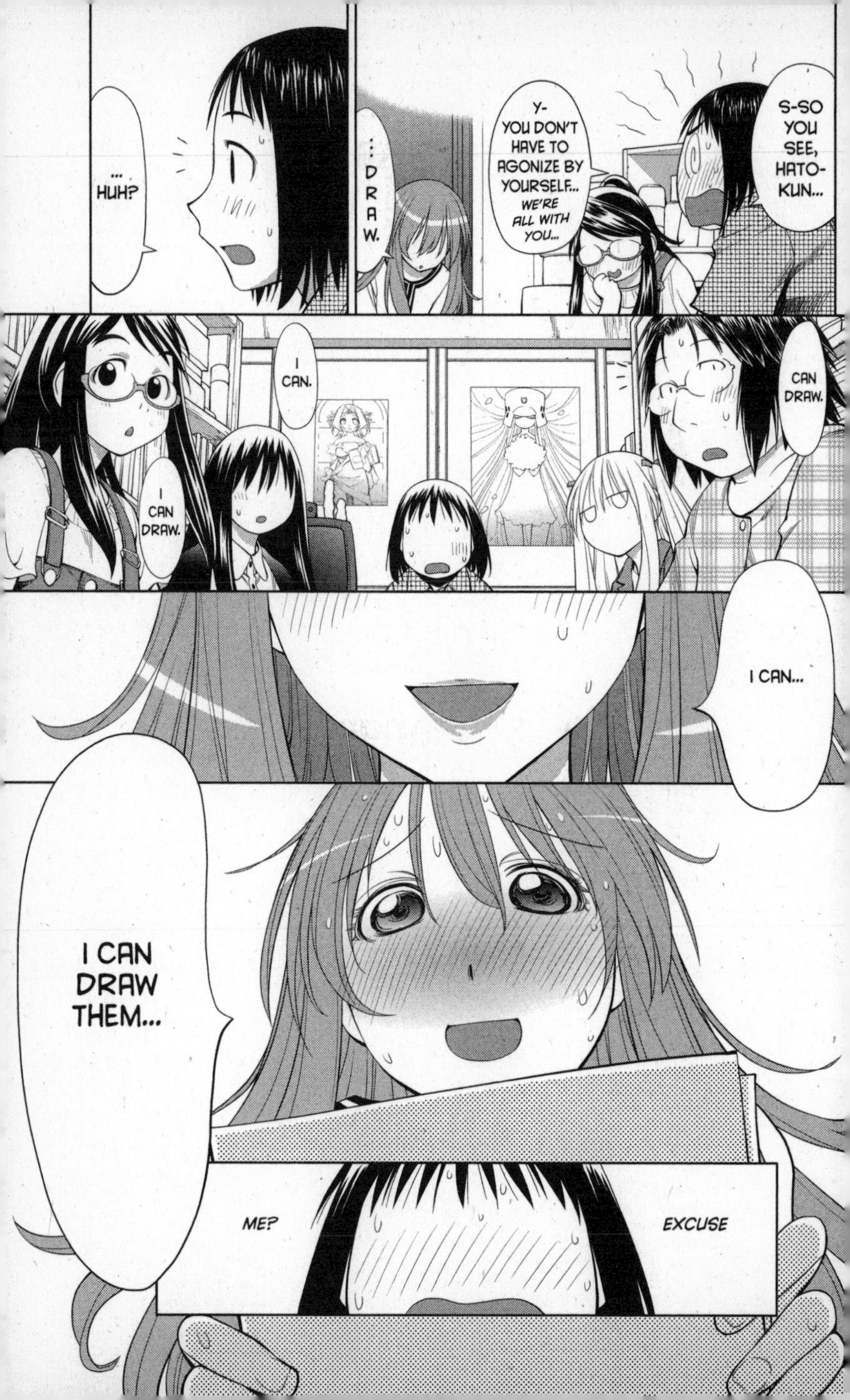
S-SO YOU SEE, HATO-KUN...
Y- YOU DON'T HAVE TO AGONIZE BY YOURSELF... WE'RE ALL WITH YOU...
...DRAW.
... HUH?
CAN DRAW.
I CAN.
I CAN DRAW.
I CAN...
I CAN DRAW THEM...
EXCUSE
ME?

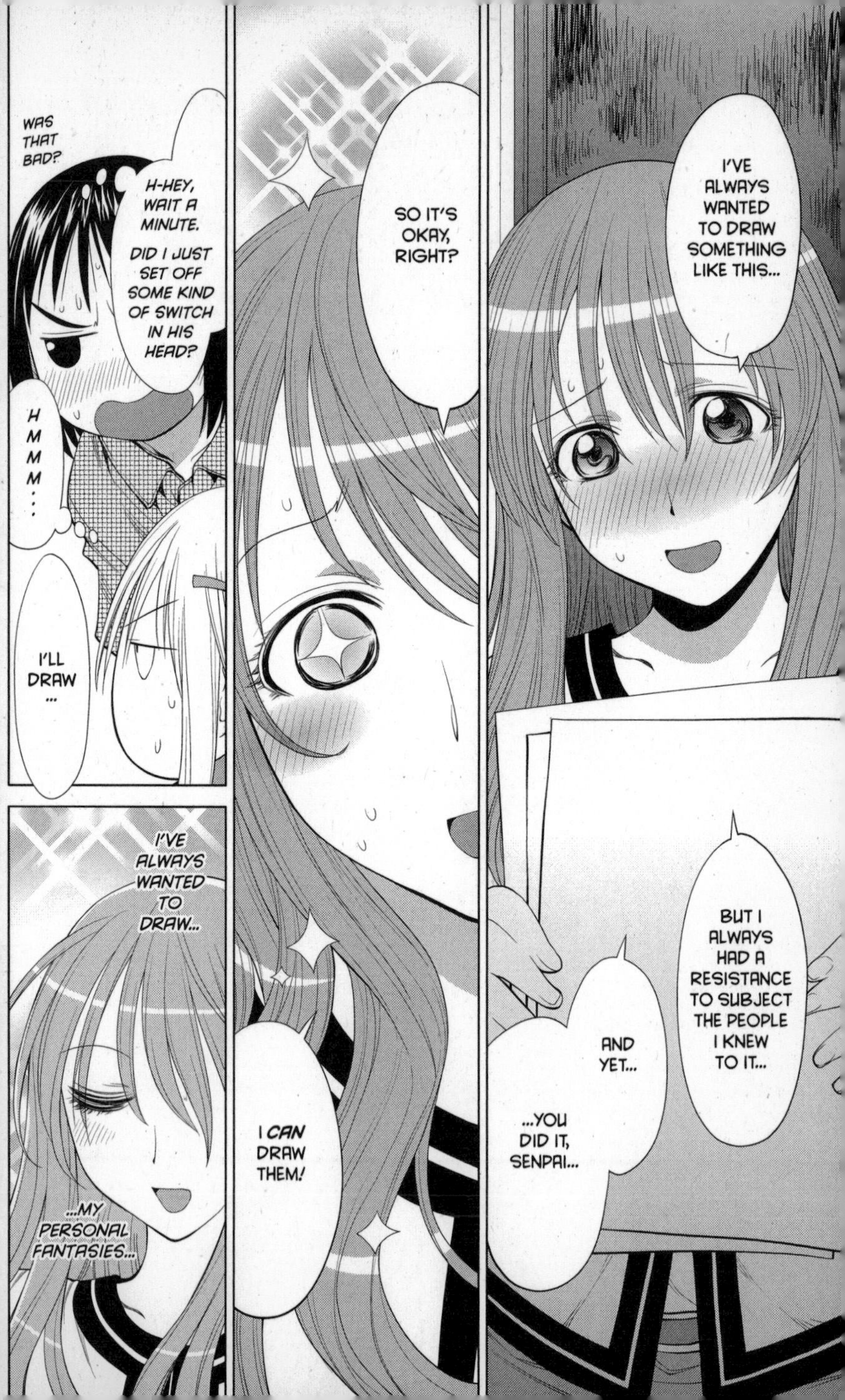
I'VE ALWAYS WANTED TO DRAW SOMETHING LIKE THIS...
BUT I ALWAYS HAD A RESISTANCE TO SUBJECT THE PEOPLE I KNEW TO IT...
AND YET...
...YOU DID IT, SENPAI...
SO IT'S OKAY, RIGHT?
I *CAN* DRAW THEM!
H-HEY, WAIT A MINUTE.
DID I JUST SET OFF SOME KIND OF SWITCH IN HIS HEAD?
WAS THAT BAD?
HMMM...
I'LL DRAW...
I'VE ALWAYS WANTED TO DRAW...
...MY PERSONAL FANTASIES...

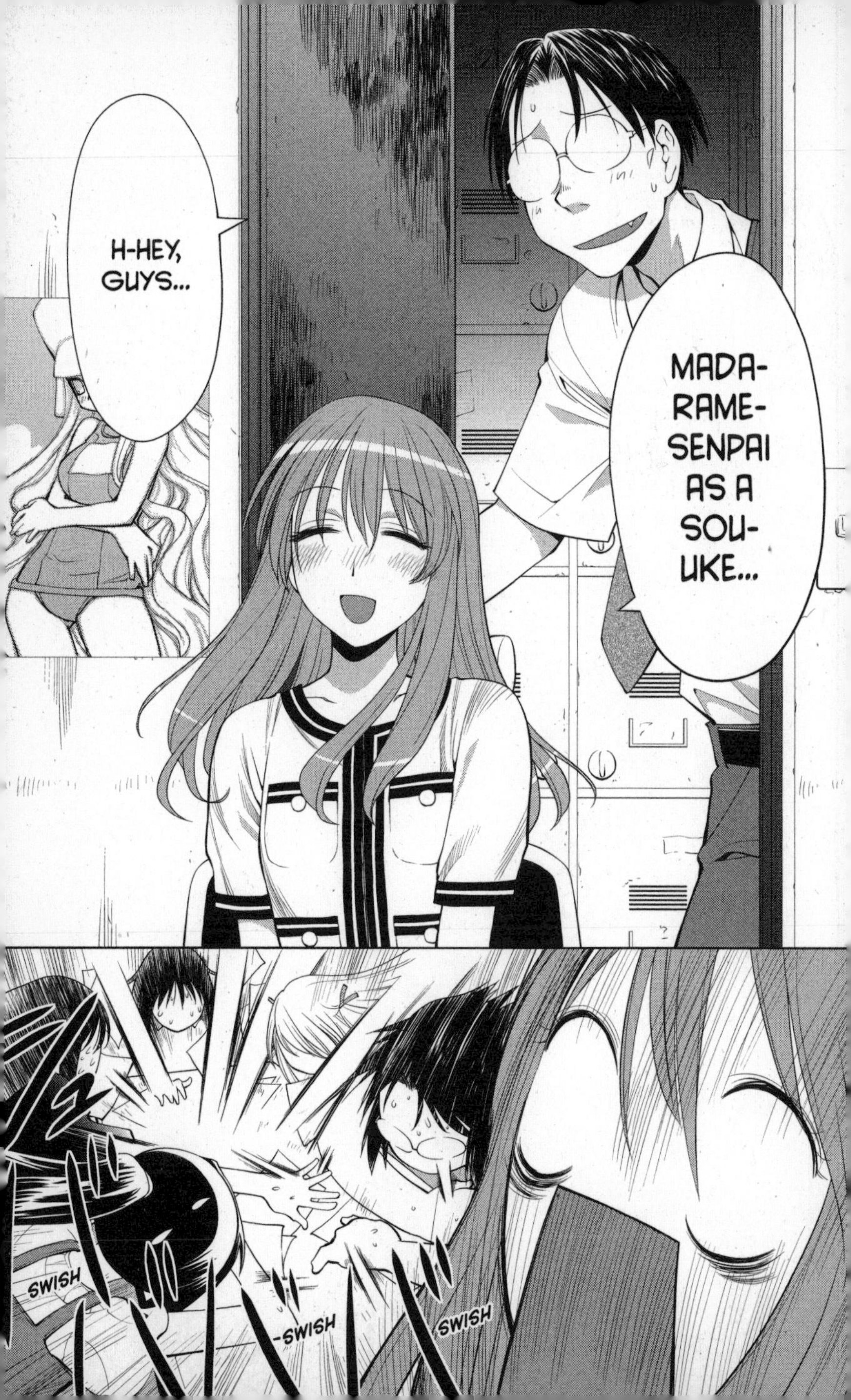
MADARAME-SENPAI AS A SOU-UKE...
H-HEY, GUYS...
SWISH
-SWISH
SWISH

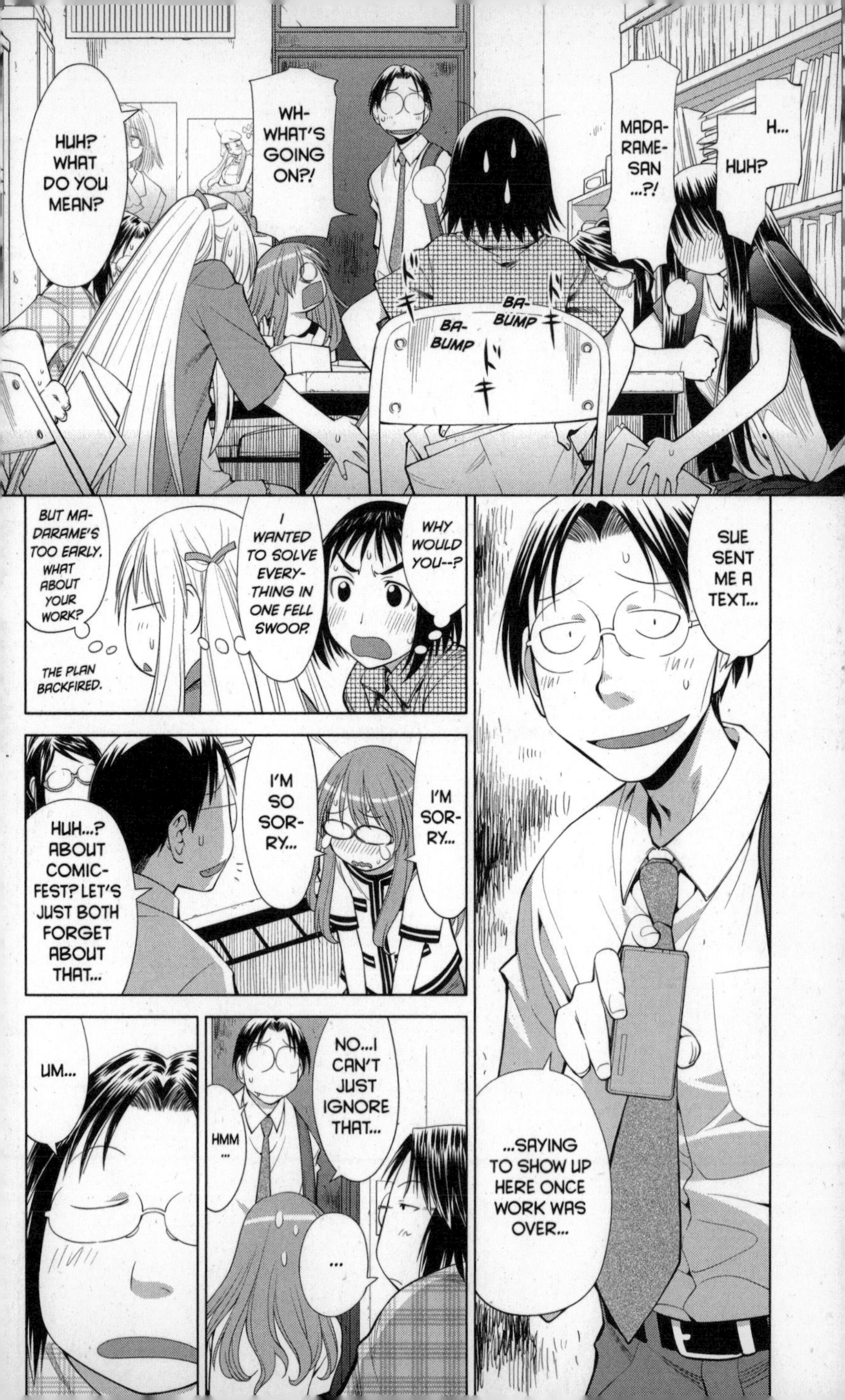
H... HUH?
MADA-RAME-SAN ...?!
WH-WHAT'S GOING ON?!
HUH? WHAT DO YOU MEAN?
ドキ
BA-BUMP
ドキ
BA-BUMP
SUE SENT ME A TEXT...
...SAYING TO SHOW UP HERE ONCE WORK WAS OVER...
WHY WOULD YOU--?
I WANTED TO SOLVE EVERY-THING IN ONE FELL SWOOP.
BUT MA-DARAME'S TOO EARLY. WHAT ABOUT YOUR WORK?
THE PLAN BACKFIRED.
I'M SOR-RY...
I'M SO SOR-RY...
HUH...? ABOUT COMIC-FEST? LET'S JUST BOTH FORGET ABOUT THAT...
NO...I CAN'T JUST IGNORE THAT...
HMM ...
...
UM...

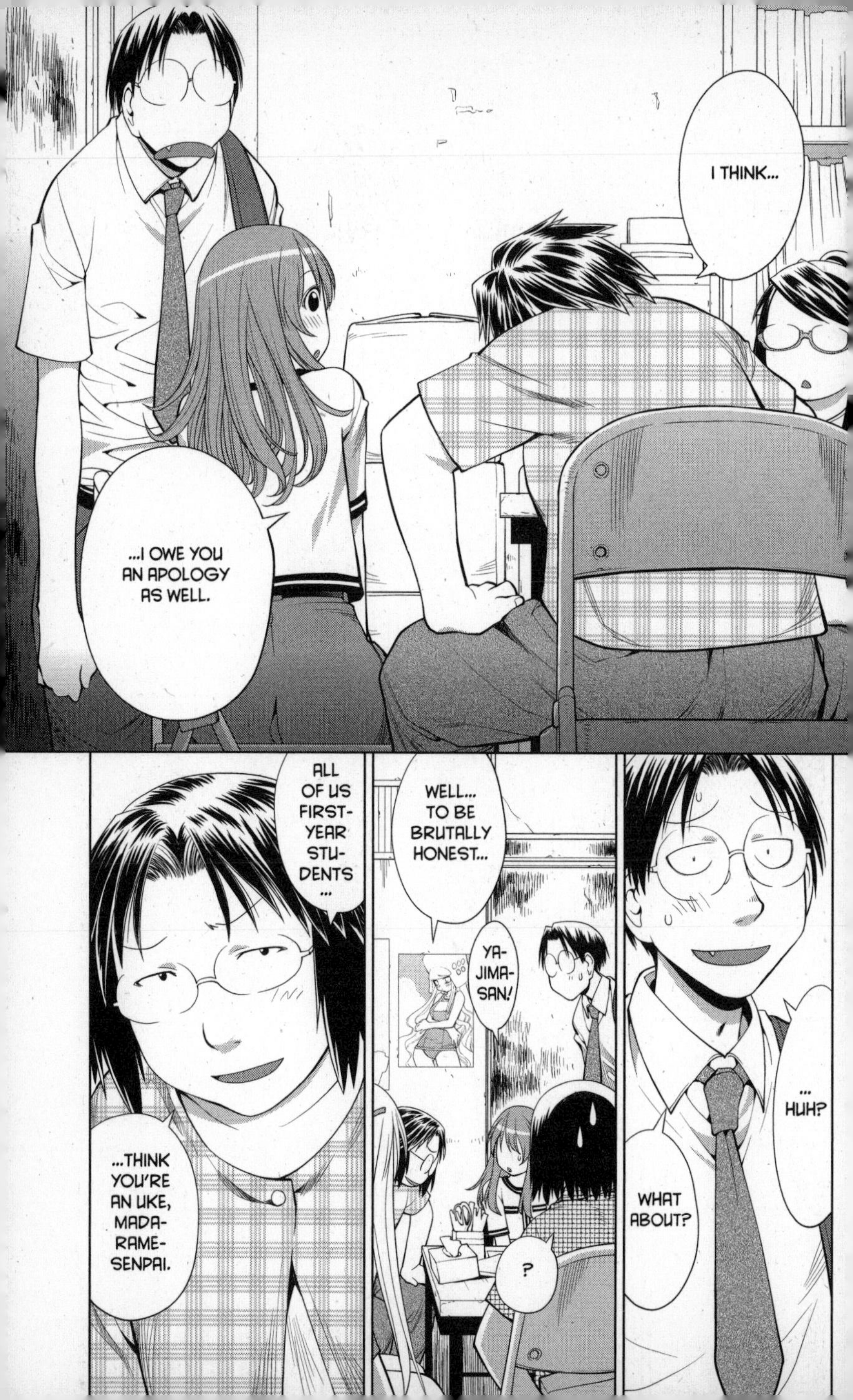
I THINK...
...I OWE YOU AN APOLOGY AS WELL.
... HUH?
WHAT ABOUT?
WELL... TO BE BRUTALLY HONEST...
YA-JIMA-SAN!
?
ALL OF US FIRST-YEAR STU-DENTS...
...THINK YOU'RE AN UKE, MADA-RAME-SENPAI.

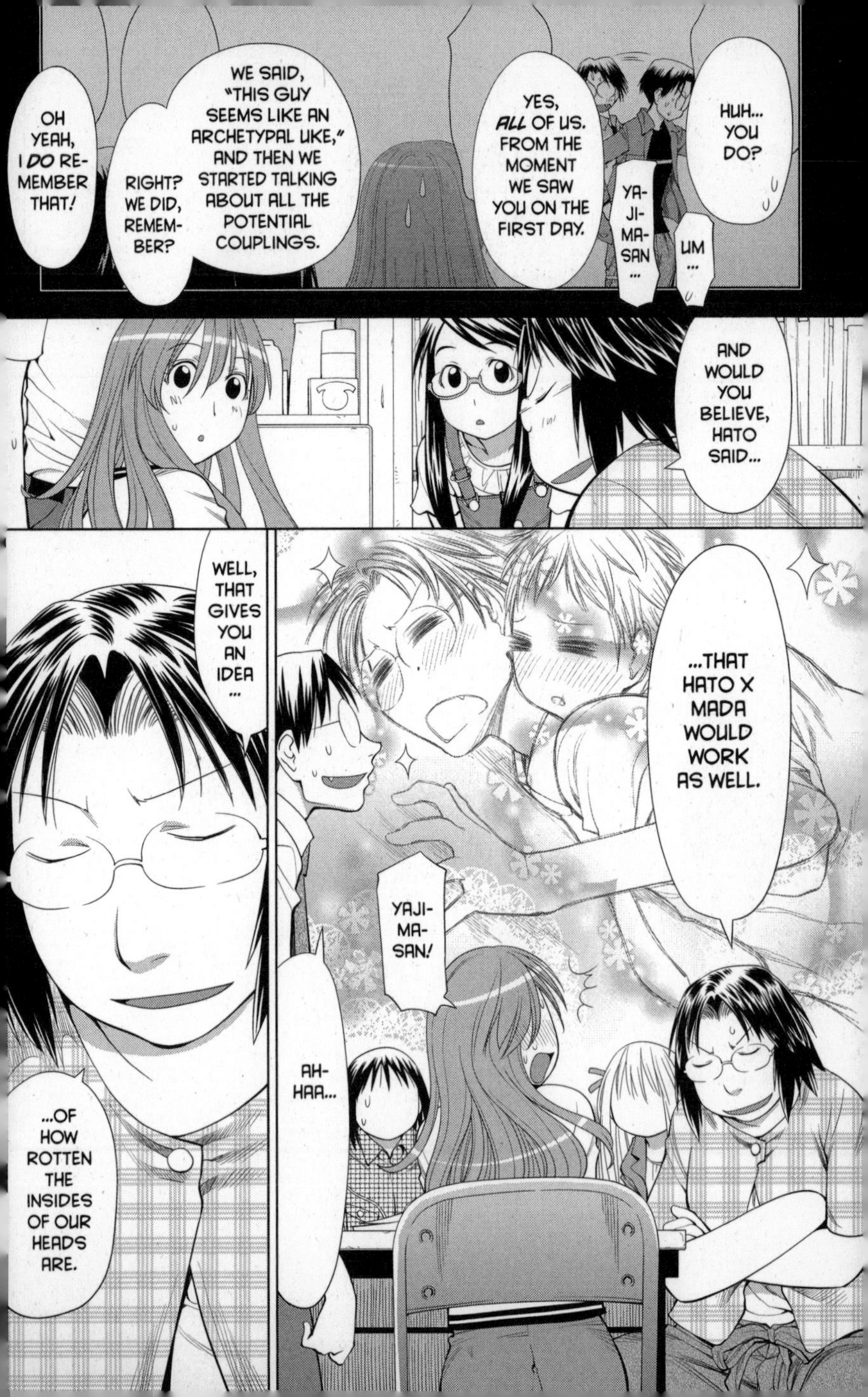
HUH... YOU DO?
UM...
YA-JI-MA-SAN...
YES, *ALL* OF US. FROM THE MOMENT WE SAW YOU ON THE FIRST DAY.
WE SAID, "THIS GUY SEEMS LIKE AN ARCHETYPAL UKE," AND THEN WE STARTED TALKING ABOUT ALL THE POTENTIAL COUPLINGS.
RIGHT? WE DID, REMEMBER?
OH YEAH, I *DO* REMEMBER THAT!
AND WOULD YOU BELIEVE, HATO SAID...
...THAT HATO X MADA WOULD WORK AS WELL.
YAJI-MA-SAN!
AH-HAA...
WELL, THAT GIVES YOU AN IDEA...
...OF HOW ROTTEN THE INSIDES OF OUR HEADS ARE.

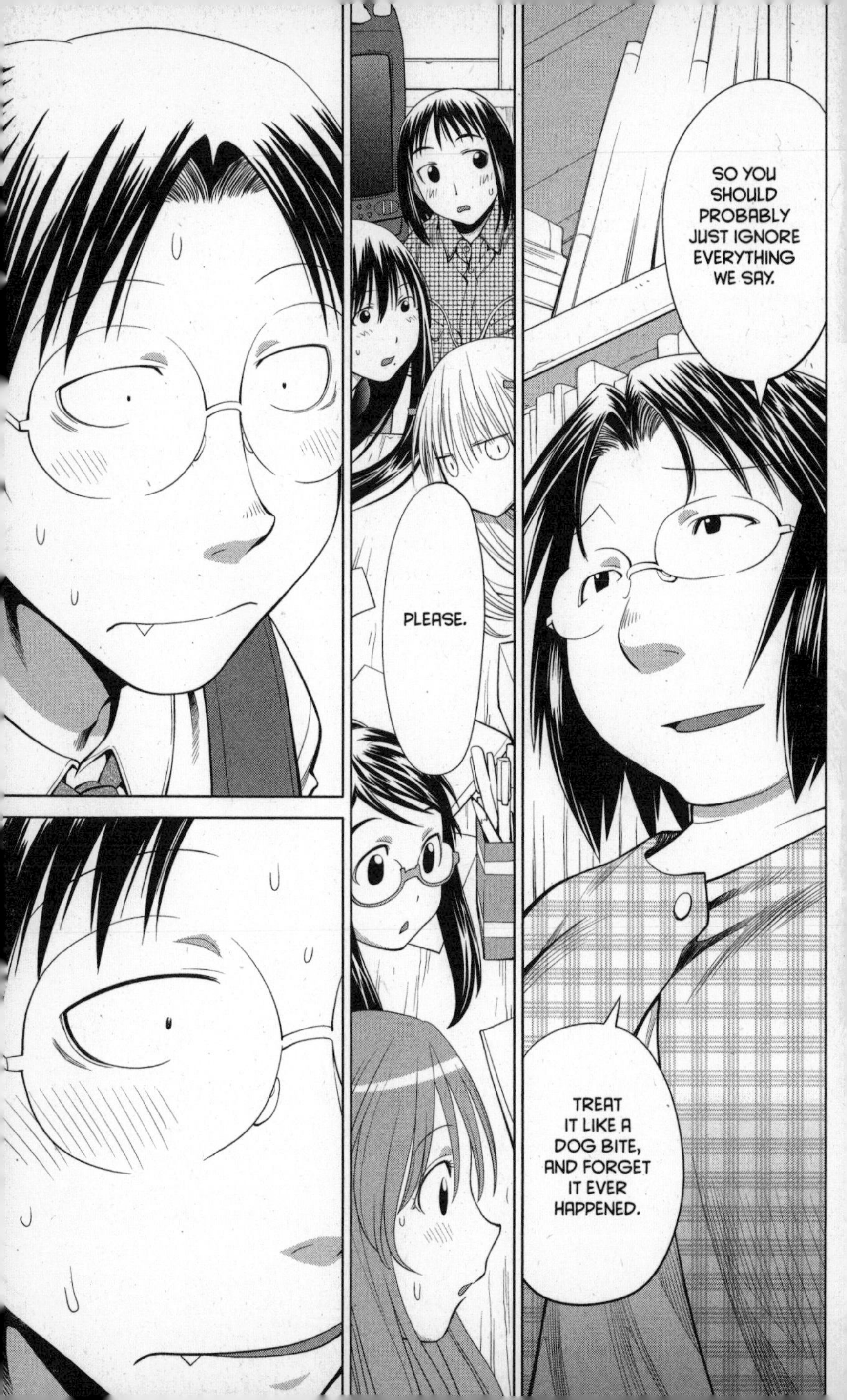
SO YOU SHOULD PROBABLY JUST IGNORE EVERYTHING WE SAY.
TREAT IT LIKE A DOG BITE, AND FORGET IT EVER HAPPENED.
PLEASE.

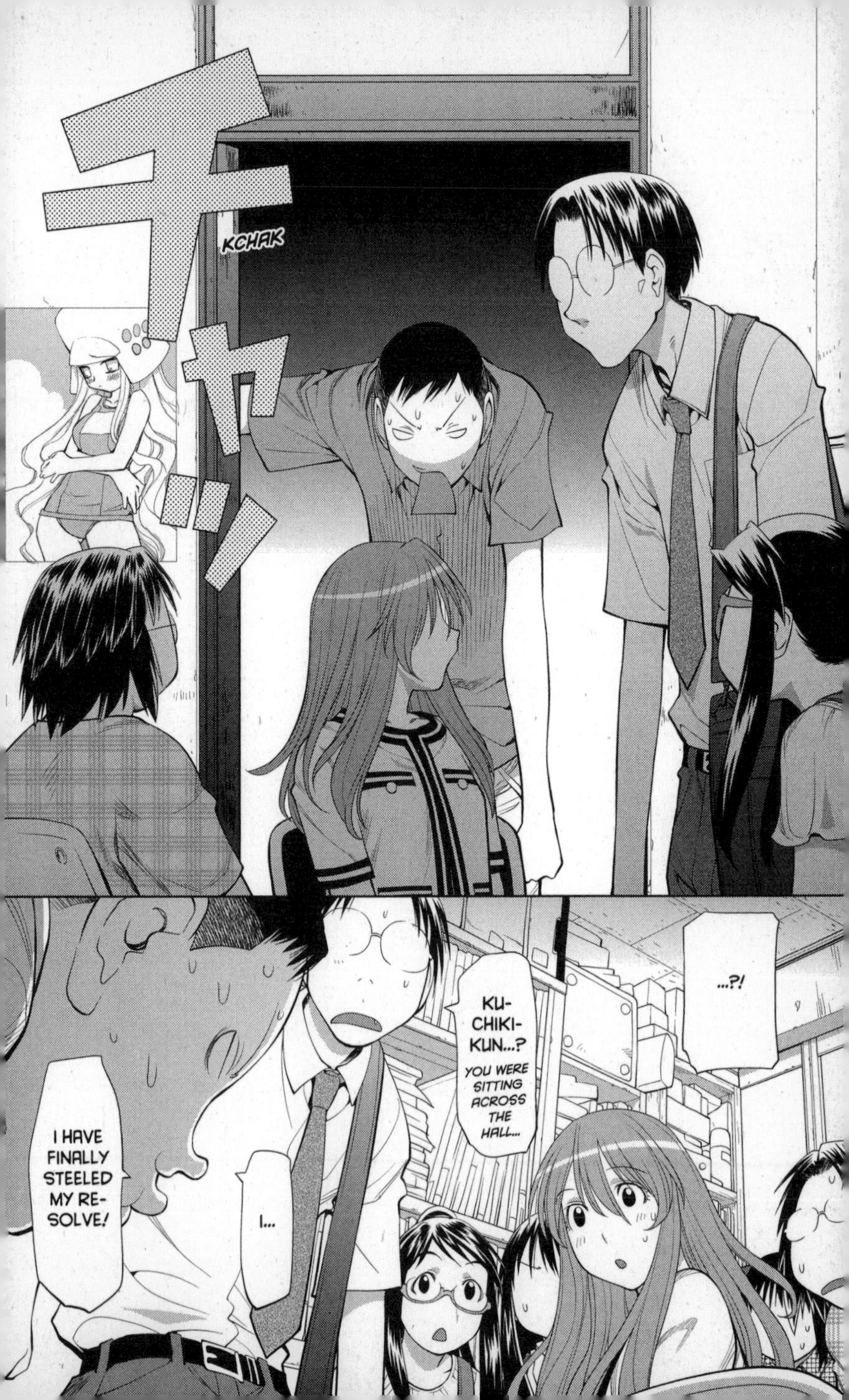
KCHAK
...?!
KU-CHIKI-KUN...? YOU WERE SITTING ACROSS THE HALL...
I...
I HAVE FINALLY STEELED MY RE-SOLVE!

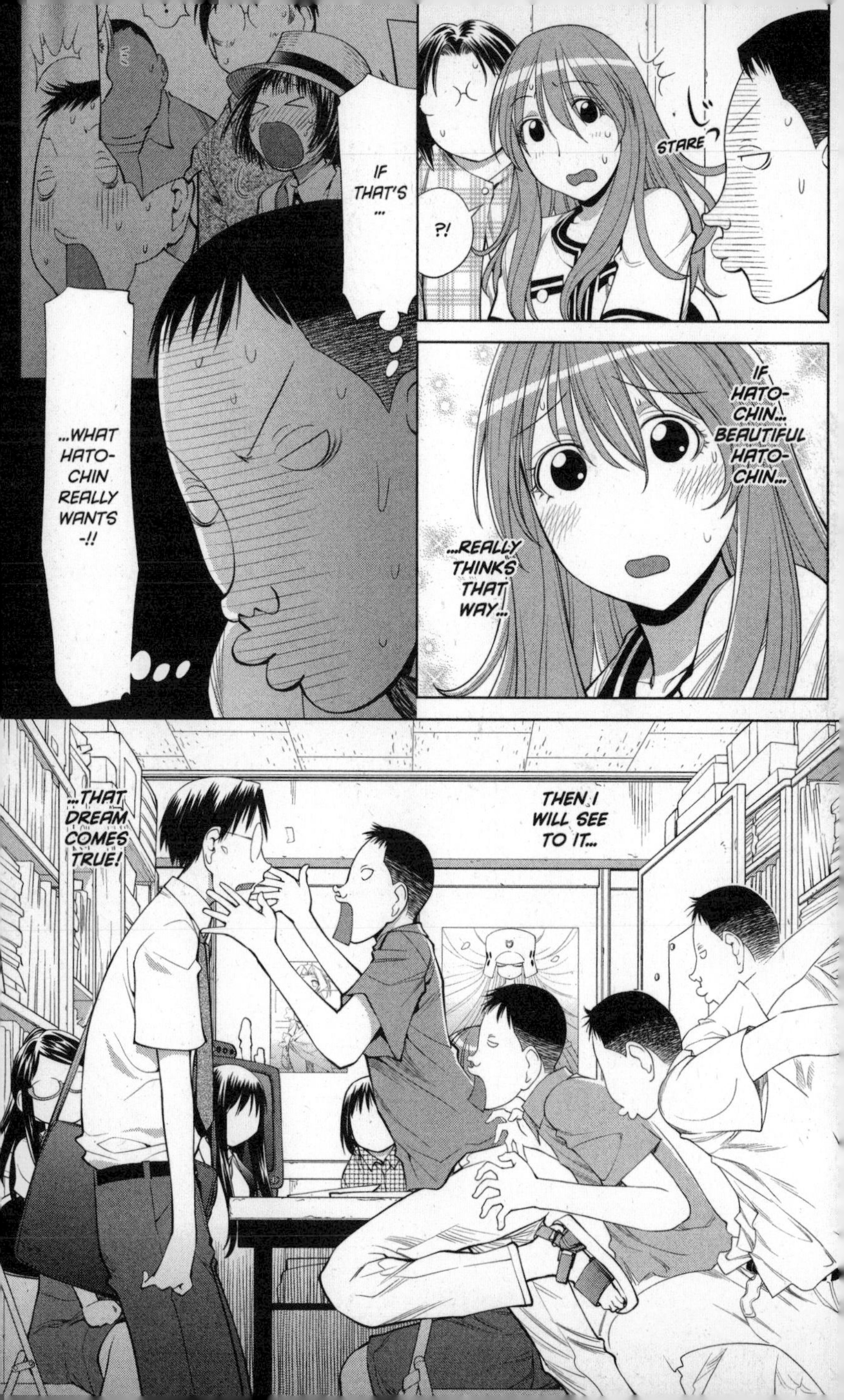

じーっ
STARE
?!
IF HATO-CHIN... BEAUTIFUL HATO-CHIN...
...REALLY THINKS THAT WAY...
IF THAT'S ...
...WHAT HATO-CHIN REALLY WANTS-!!
...
THEN I WILL SEE TO IT...
...THAT DREAM COMES TRUE!

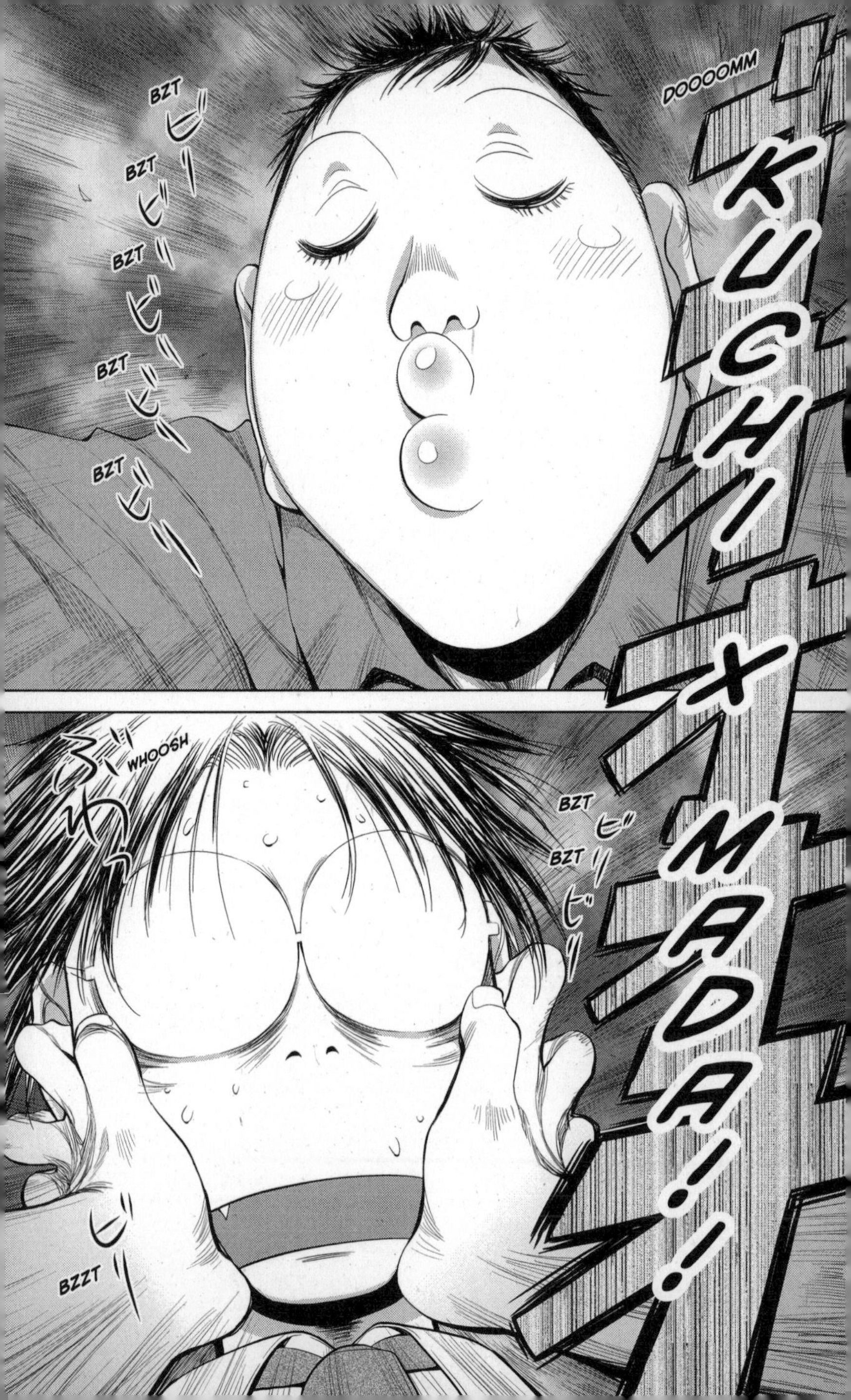
DOOOOMM
KUCHI X MADA!!
BZT
BZT
BZT
BZT
BZT
WHOOSH
ふわっ
BZT
BZT
BZZT

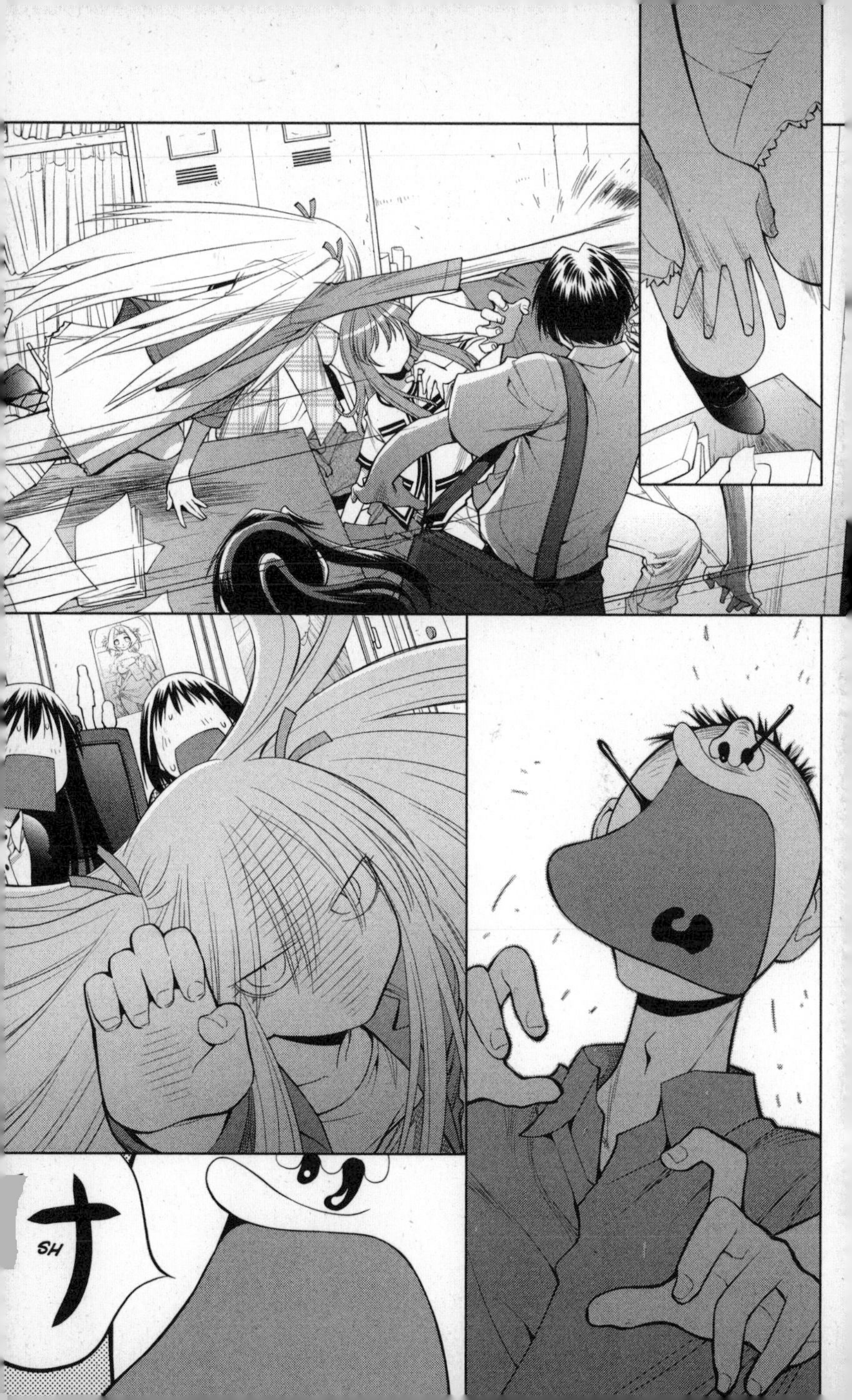
ナ
SH

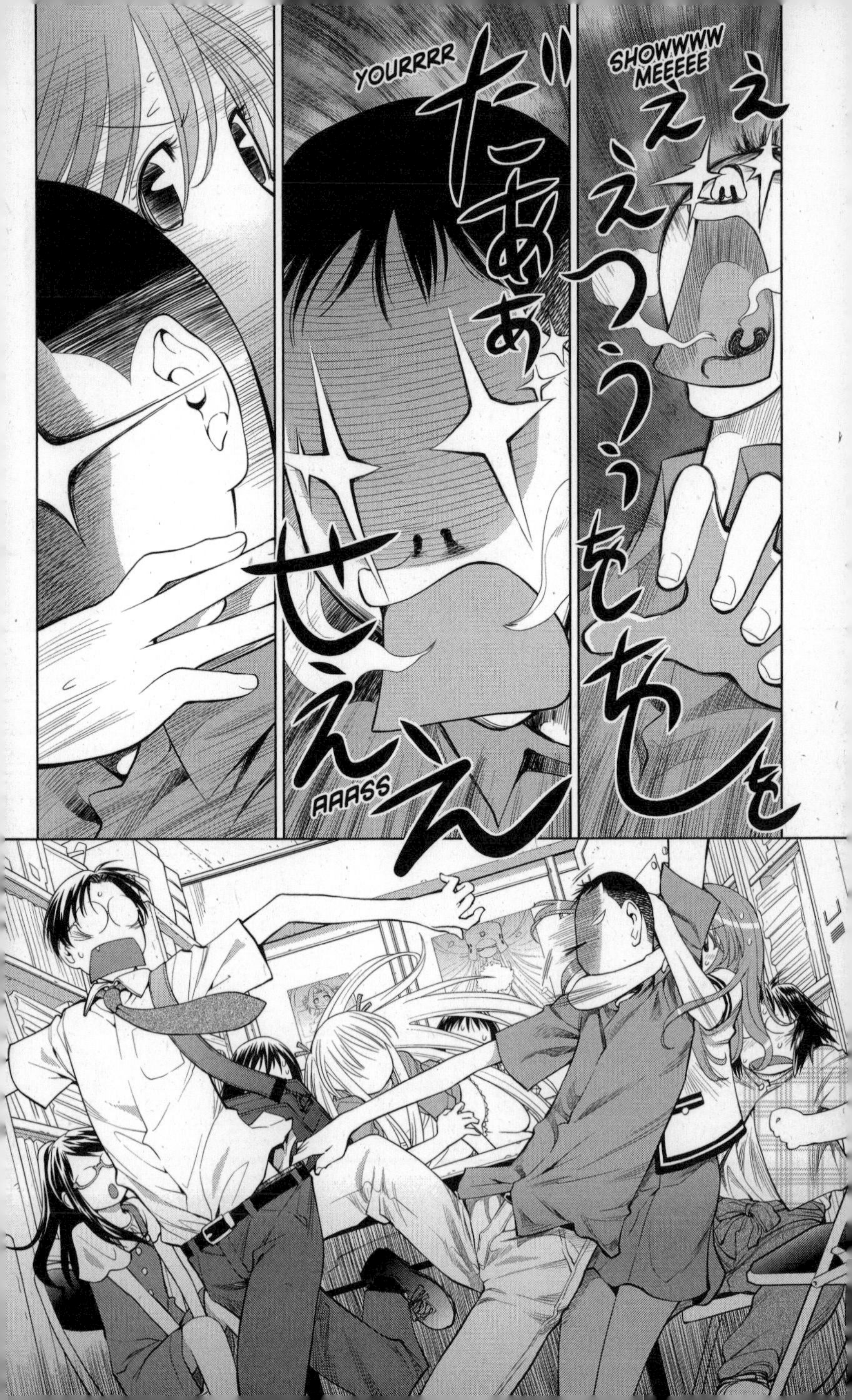
SHOWWWW MEEEEE
YOURRRR
AAASS

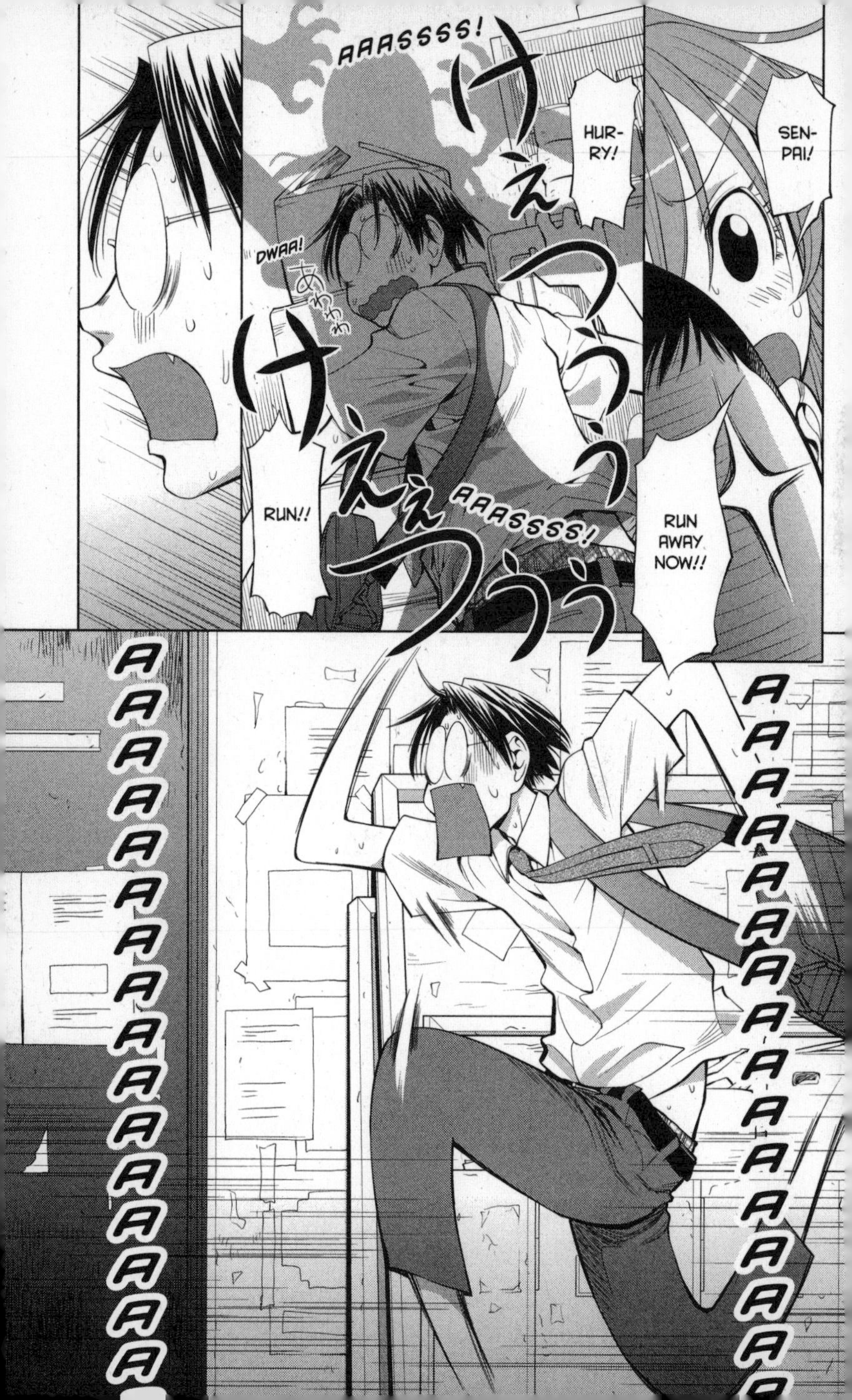
SEN-PAI!
RUN AWAY NOW!!
HURRY!
AAASSSS!
けえつううう
DWAA!
あわわわ
けえつううう
AAASSSSS!
RUN!!
AAAAAAAAAAAAAAAAA
AAAAAAAAAAAAAAAAAA

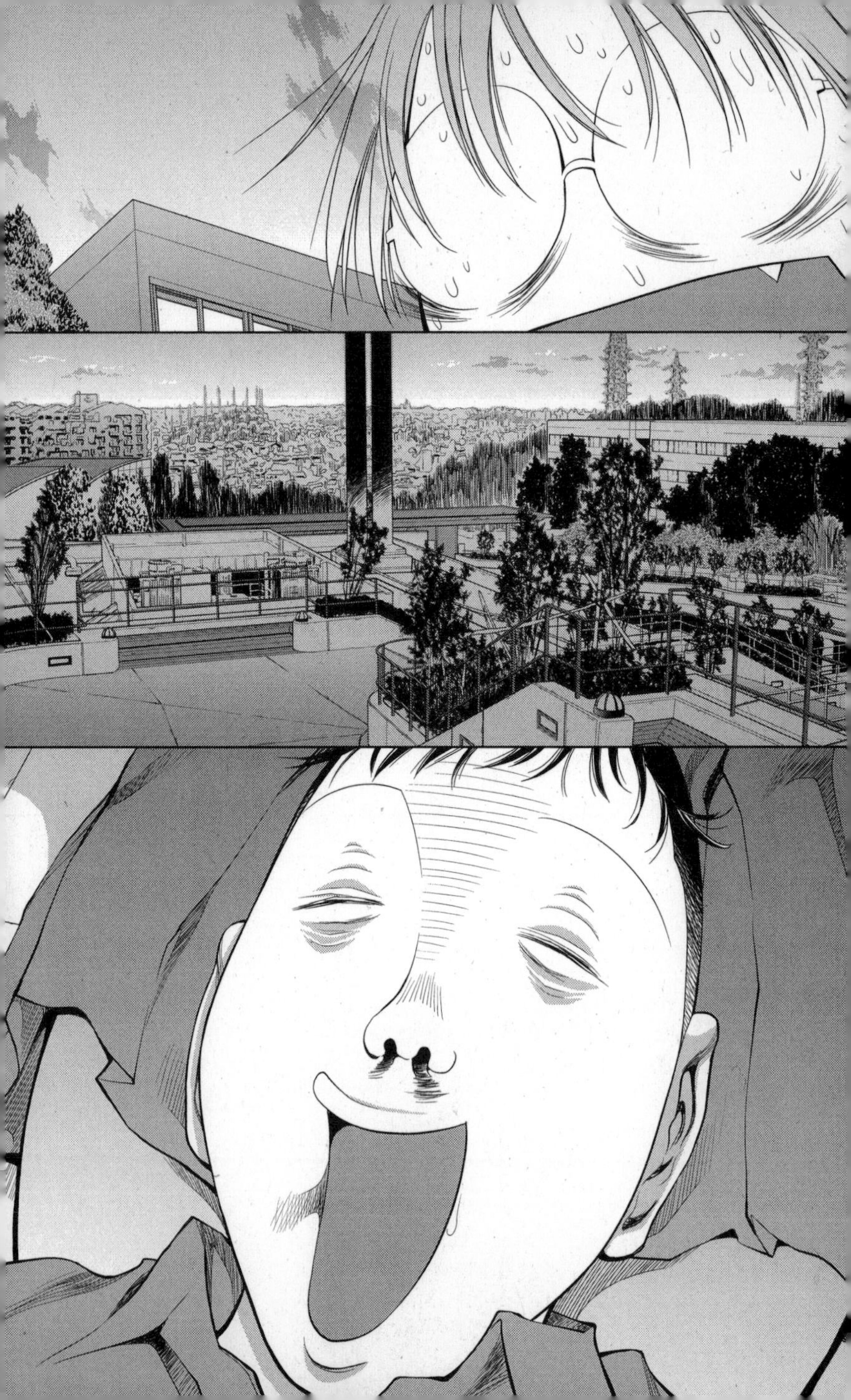

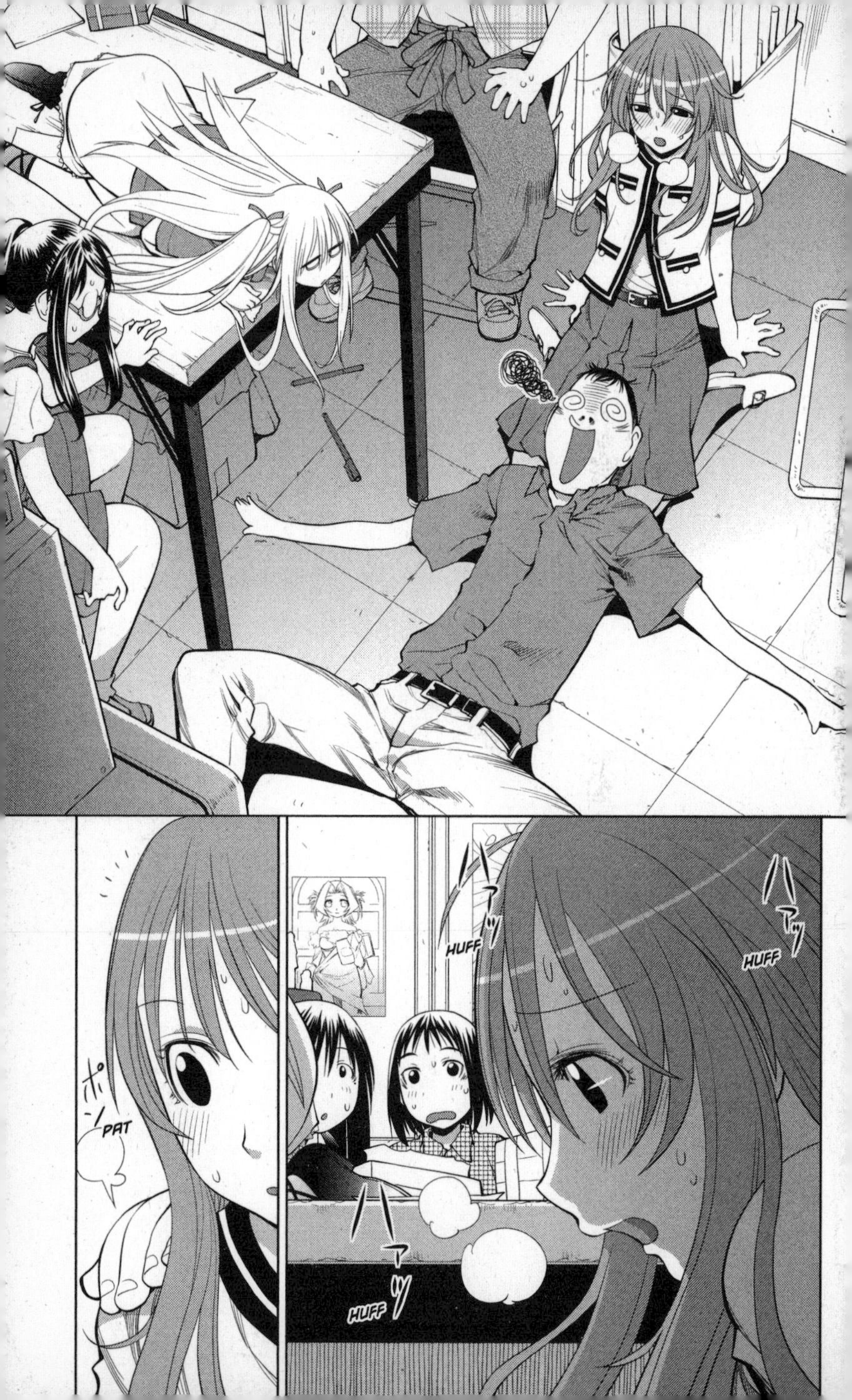
ハァッ
HUFF
ハァッ
HUFF
ハァッ
HUFF
ポン
PAT

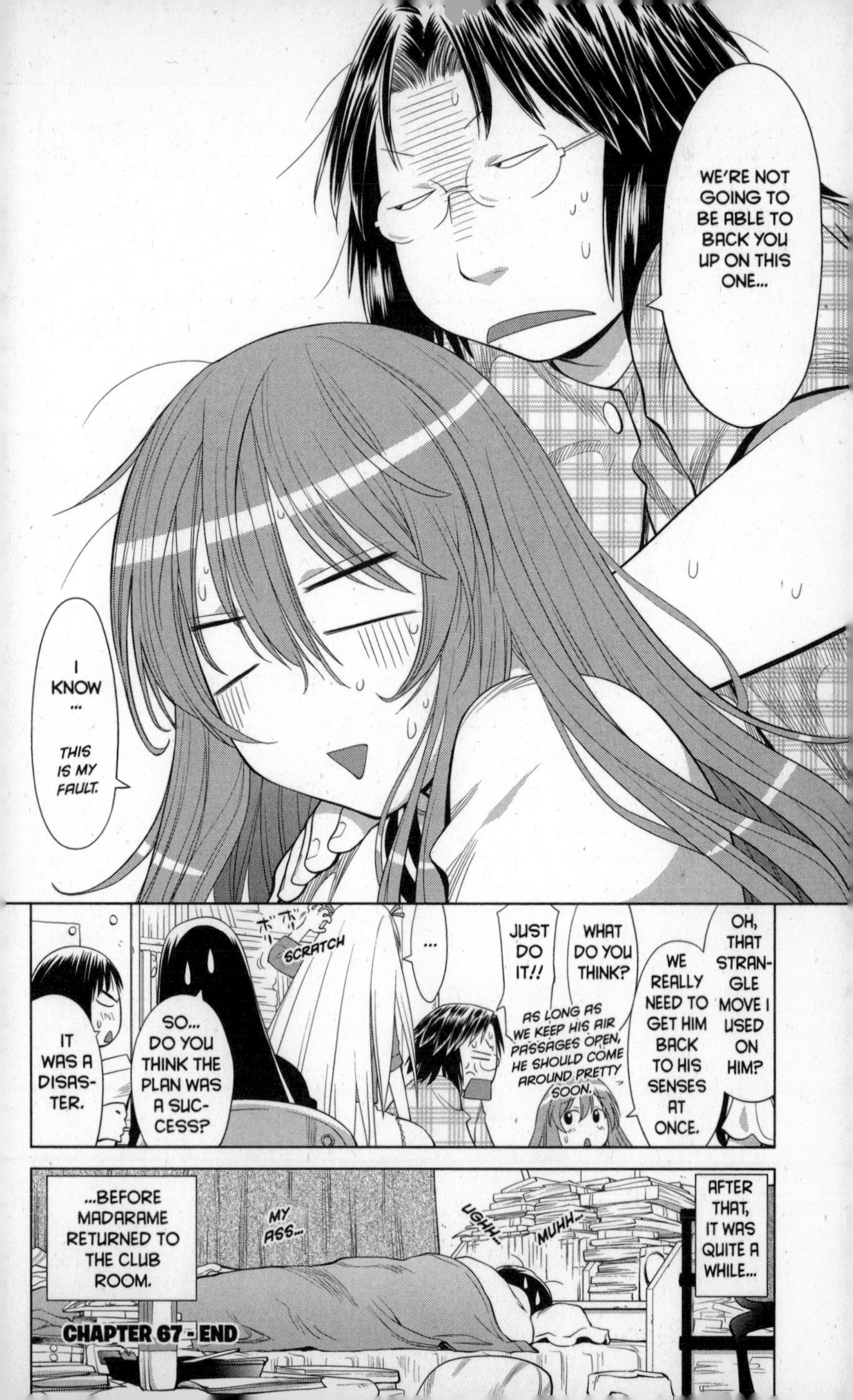
WE'RE NOT GOING TO BE ABLE TO BACK YOU UP ON THIS ONE...
I KNOW... THIS IS MY FAULT.
OH, THAT STRANGLE MOVE I USED ON HIM?
WE REALLY NEED TO GET HIM BACK TO HIS SENSES AT ONCE.
WHAT DO YOU THINK?
JUST DO IT!!
AS LONG AS WE KEEP HIS AIR PASSAGES OPEN, HE SHOULD COME AROUND PRETTY SOON.
...
SCRATCH
SO... DO YOU THINK THE PLAN WAS A SUCCESS?
IT WAS A DISASTER.
AFTER THAT, IT WAS QUITE A WHILE...
MUHH...
UGHH...
MY ASS...
...BEFORE MADARAME RETURNED TO THE CLUB ROOM.
CHAPTER 67 - END

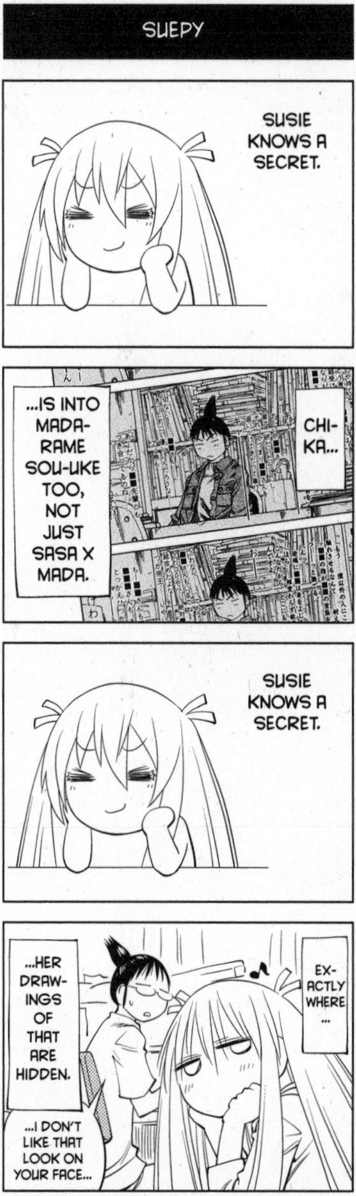
SUEPY
SUSIE KNOWS A SECRET.
CHI-KA...
...IS INTO MADA-RAME SOU-UKE TOO, NOT JUST SASA X MADA.
SUSIE KNOWS A SECRET.
EX-ACTLY WHERE...
...HER DRAW-INGS OF THAT ARE HIDDEN.
...I DON'T LIKE THAT LOOK ON YOUR FACE...

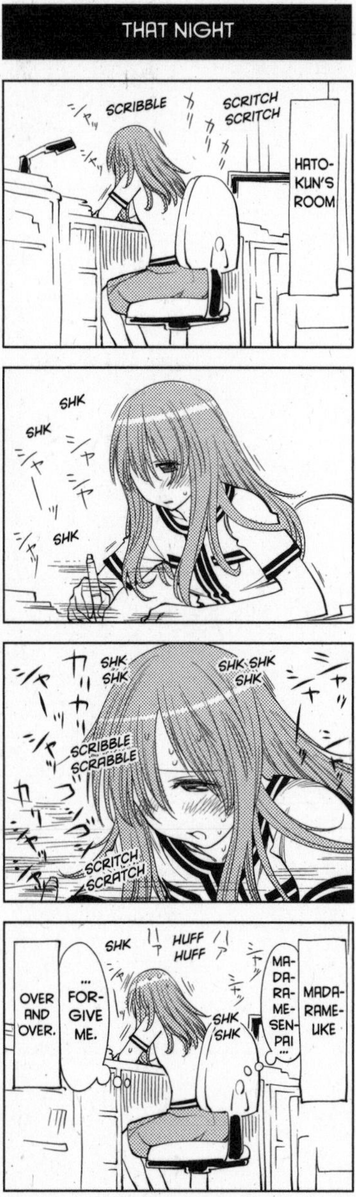
THAT NIGHT
HATO-KUN'S ROOM
SCRITCH SCRITCH
SCRIBBLE
SHK
SHK
SHK
SHK SHK SHK
SHK SHK
SCRIBBLE SCRABBLE
SCRITCH SCRATCH
MADA-RAME-UKE
MA-DA-RA-ME-SEN-PAI...
HUFF HUFF
SHK SHK
SHK
...FOR-GIVE ME.
OVER AND OVER.

CHAPTER 67 - MOMENTS LATER

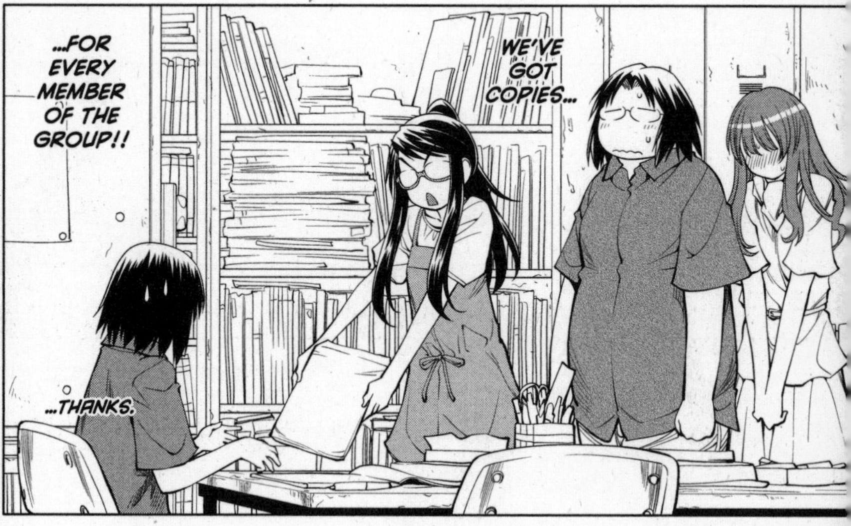
WE'VE GOT COPIES...
...FOR EVERY MEMBER OF THE GROUP!!
...THANKS.

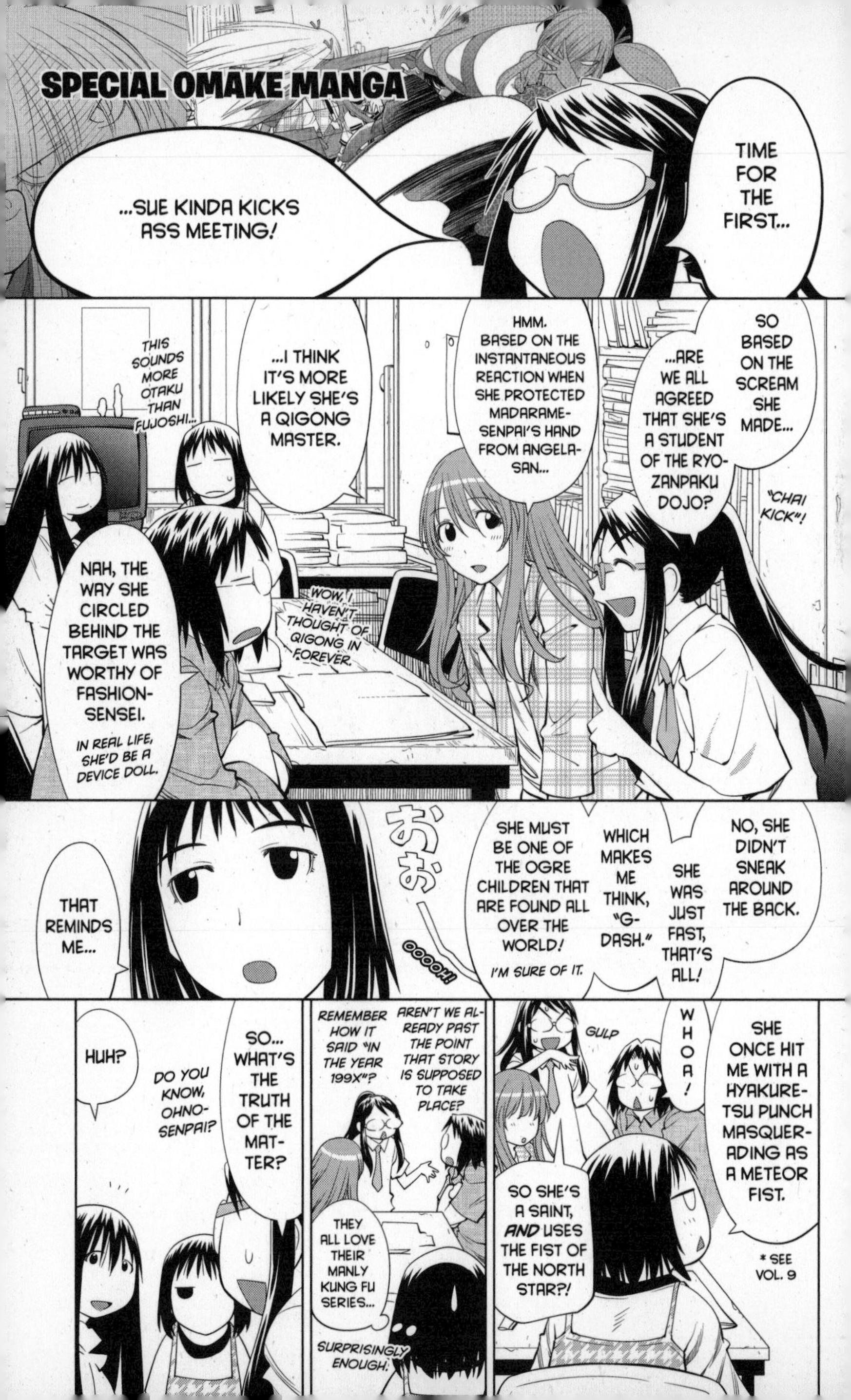
SPECIAL OMAKE MANGA
TIME FOR THE FIRST...
...SUE KINDA KICKS ASS MEETING!
SO BASED ON THE SCREAM SHE MADE...
...ARE WE ALL AGREED THAT SHE'S A STUDENT OF THE RYO-ZANPAKU DOJO?
"CHAI KICK"!
HMM. BASED ON THE INSTANTANEOUS REACTION WHEN SHE PROTECTED MADARAME-SENPAI'S HAND FROM ANGELA-SAN...
...I THINK IT'S MORE LIKELY SHE'S A QIGONG MASTER.
THIS SOUNDS MORE OTAKU THAN FUJOSHI...
WOW, I HAVEN'T THOUGHT OF QIGONG IN FOREVER.
NAH, THE WAY SHE CIRCLED BEHIND THE TARGET WAS WORTHY OF FASHION-SENSEI.
IN REAL LIFE, SHE'D BE A DEVICE DOLL.
NO, SHE DIDN'T SNEAK AROUND THE BACK.
SHE WAS JUST FAST, THAT'S ALL!
WHICH MAKES ME THINK, "G-DASH."
SHE MUST BE ONE OF THE OGRE CHILDREN THAT ARE FOUND ALL OVER THE WORLD!
I'M SURE OF IT.
おおー
OOOOH!
THAT REMINDS ME...
SHE ONCE HIT ME WITH A HYAKURE-TSU PUNCH MASQUER-ADING AS A METEOR FIST.
WHOA!
GULP
SO SHE'S A SAINT, AND USES THE FIST OF THE NORTH STAR?!
* SEE VOL. 9
AREN'T WE ALREADY PAST THE POINT THAT STORY IS SUPPOSED TO TAKE PLACE?
REMEMBER HOW IT SAID "IN THE YEAR 199X"?
THEY ALL LOVE THEIR MANLY KUNG FU SERIES...
SURPRISINGLY ENOUGH.
SO... WHAT'S THE TRUTH OF THE MATTER?
DO YOU KNOW, OHNO-SENPAI?
HUH?

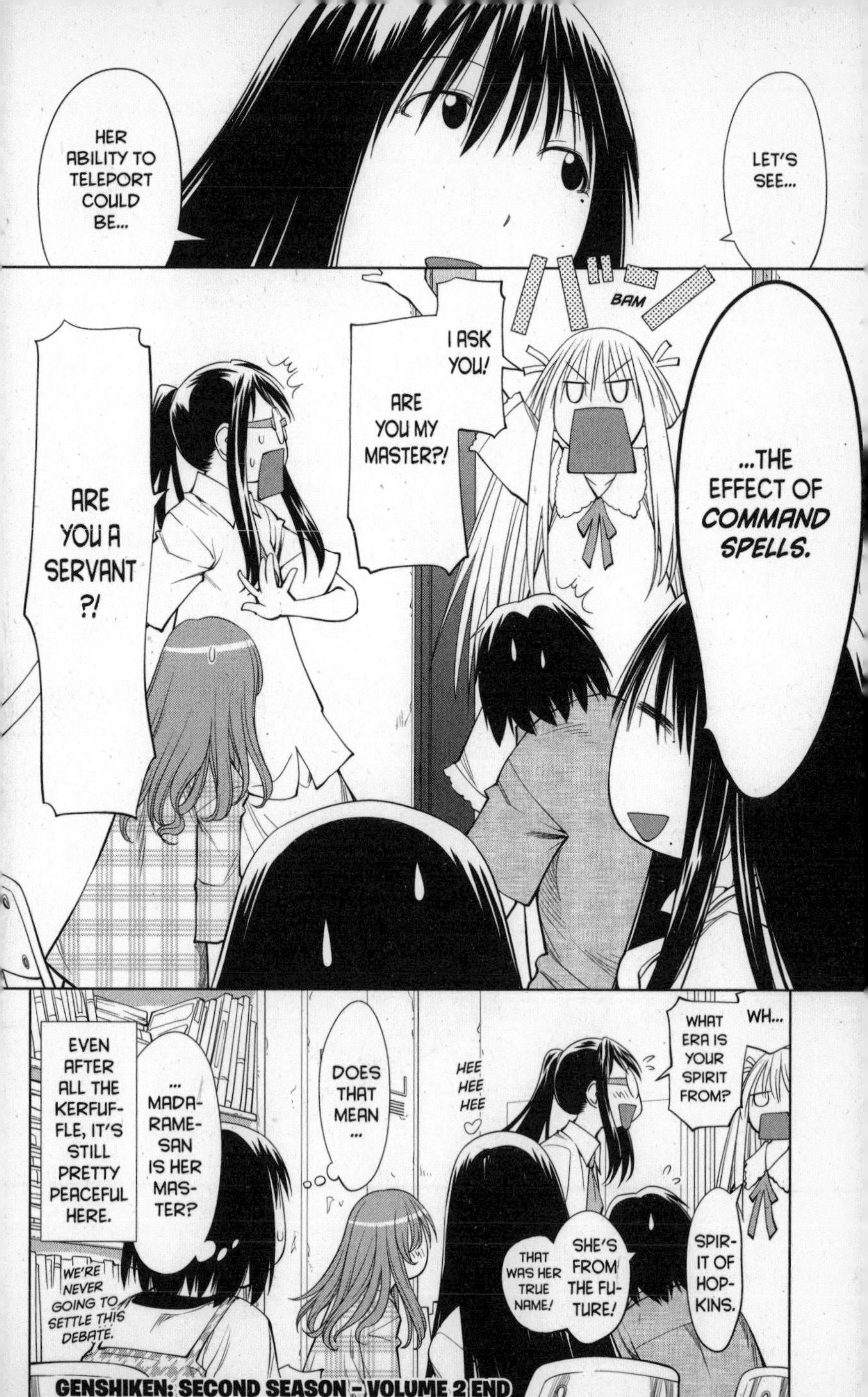
LET'S SEE...
HER ABILITY TO TELEPORT COULD BE...
...THE EFFECT OF COMMAND SPELLS.
BAM
I ASK YOU!
ARE YOU MY MASTER?!
ARE YOU A SERVANT?!
WH...
WHAT ERA IS YOUR SPIRIT FROM?
SPIRIT OF HOPKINS.
SHE'S FROM THE FUTURE!
THAT WAS HER TRUE NAME!
HEE HEE HEE
DOES THAT MEAN...
...MADARAME-SAN IS HER MASTER?
EVEN AFTER ALL THE KERFUFFLE, IT'S STILL PRETTY PEACEFUL HERE.
WE'RE NEVER GOING TO SETTLE THIS DEBATE.
GENSHIKEN: SECOND SEASON - VOLUME 2 END

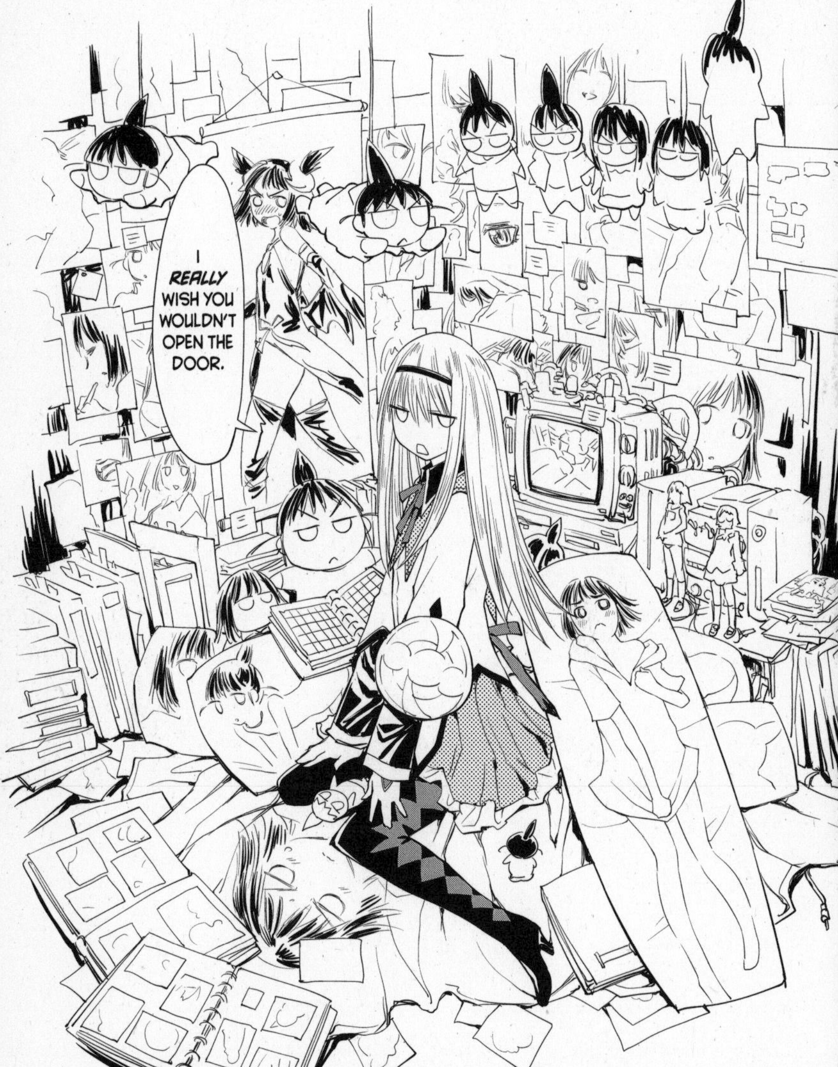
I *REALLY* WISH YOU WOULDN'T OPEN THE DOOR.

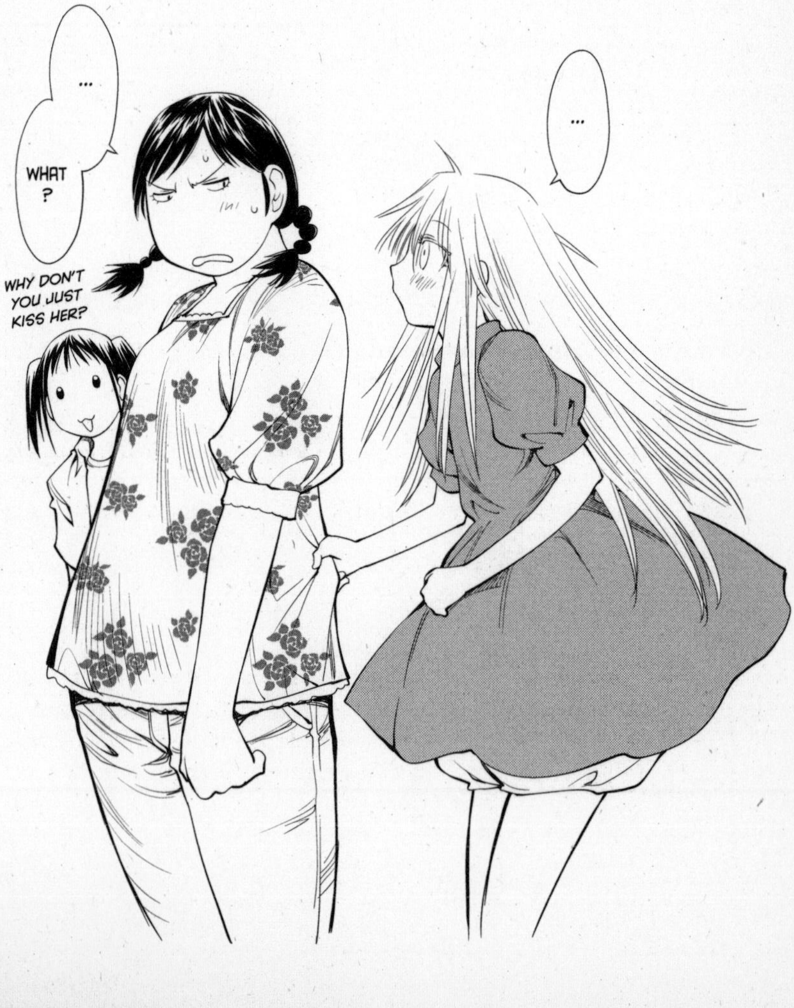
...
...
WHAT ?
WHY DON'T YOU JUST KISS HER?

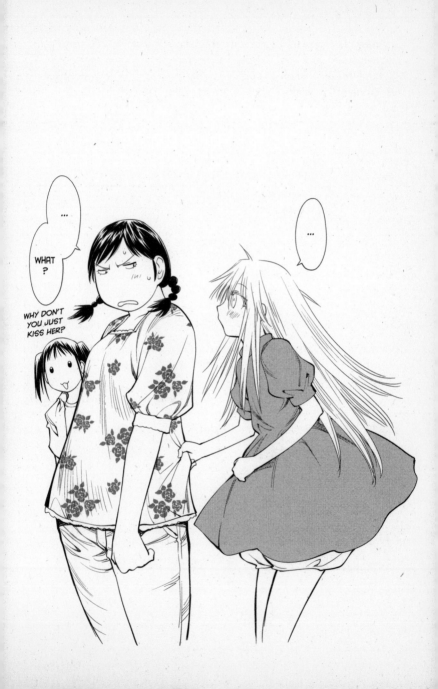

Translation Notes

Japanese is a tricky language for most Westerners, and translation is often more art than science. For your edification and reading pleasure, here are notes on some of the places where we could have gone in a different direction with our translation of the work, or where a Japanese cultural reference is used.

Nice boat, page 7

An internet meme arising after the finale of the anime series *School Days*, which was originally delayed at the last minute. A teenage girl murdered her father the day before the airing of the final episode, and in an attempt to avoid broadcasting poorly-timed violent material, the TV network canceled *School Days* and replaced it with a slideshow of relaxing images to classical music. One picture was of a Norwegian cruise ship sailing through fjords, which spawned an Internet meme of the picture captioned with "Nice Boat."

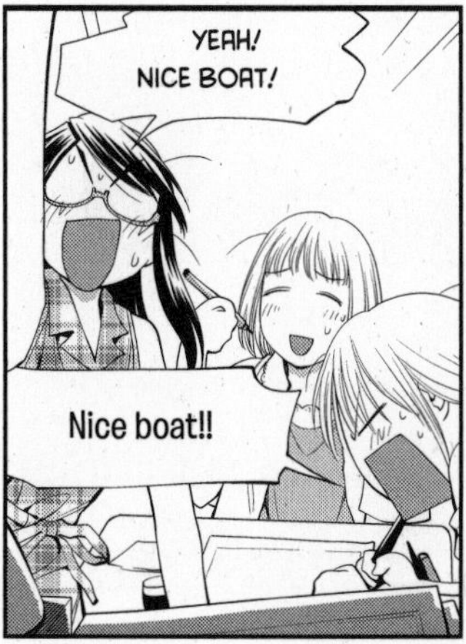
YEAH! NICE BOAT!
Nice boat!!

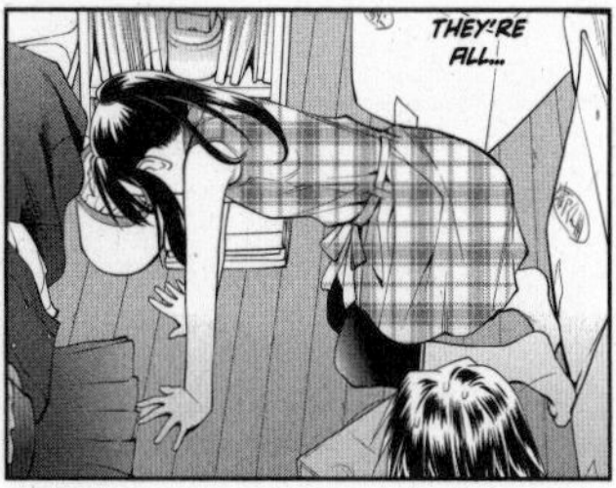
THEY'RE ALL...

orz, page 16

An Internet emoticon of Asian origin, meant to represent a person on hands and knees, face down to the ground, indicating despair (see Rika Yoshitake's posture).

Sue's cosplay, page 27

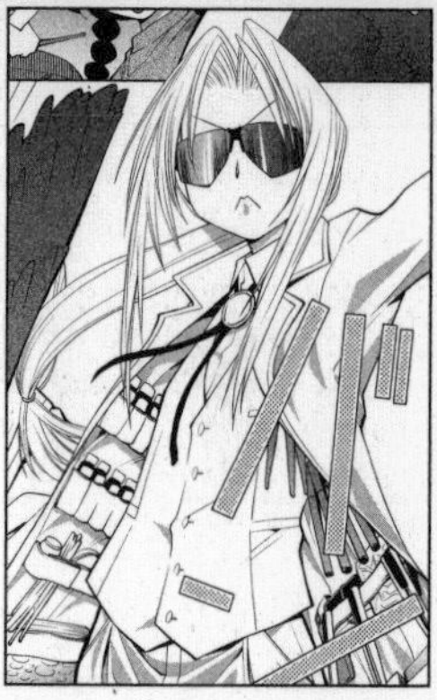

Sue's character here is the protagonist of *Comic Master J,* a manga series about a superhero artist who helps out struggling manga artists facing an imminent deadline with his superhuman speed and skill (but for an exorbitant price).

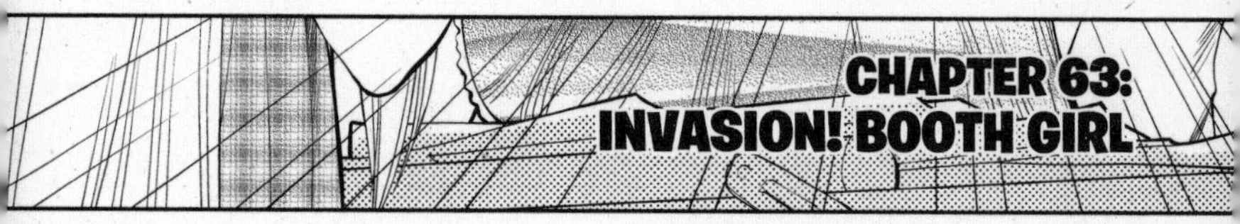
CHAPTER 63:
INVASION! BOOTH GIRL

Invasion! Booth Girl, page 36

A parody of the anime/manga series *Invasion! Squid Girl,* a comedy about a human personification of squid who comes to land to wreak vengeance on humankind for polluting the ocean.

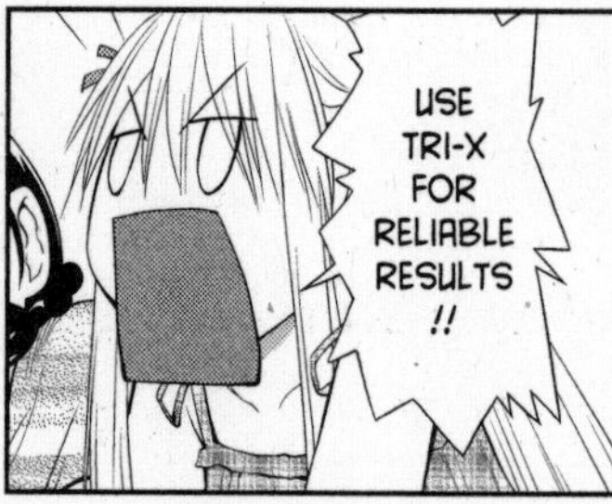
USE TRI-X FOR RELIABLE RESULTS !!

Tri-X, page 55

A reference from the 1980s series *Kyukyoku Chojin R* (Ultimate Superhuman R), a comedy about a teenage robot who attempts to live a normal life. At school he joins the photography club, which is dominated by the aggressive and haughty Tosaka-senpai, whom Sue is quoting lecturing on photography film.

Il Palazzo, page 86

A character from the comedy manga/anime series *Excel Saga,* Il Palazzo is the leader of the shadowy organization ACROSS and the boss of cheery protagonist Excel. He is a fiery orator (if a bit absentminded) and the members of the organization must salute him with, "Hail Il Palazzo!"

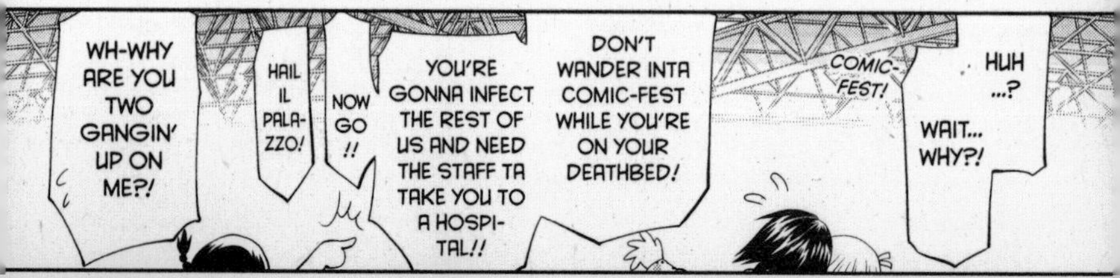
HUH ...?
WAIT... WHY?!
COMIC-FEST!
DON'T WANDER INTA COMIC-FEST WHILE YOU'RE ON YOUR DEATHBED!
YOU'RE GONNA INFECT THE REST OF US AND NEED THE STAFF TA TAKE YOU TO A HOSPI-TAL!!
NOW GO !!
HAIL IL PALA-ZZO!
WH-WHY ARE YOU TWO GANGIN' UP ON ME?!

Sue loves Yabu, page 93
A parody of the iconic line delivered by Ponyo in the Ghibli film *Ponyo,* when the goldfish girl Ponyo says, "Ponyo! Loves! Sosuke!"

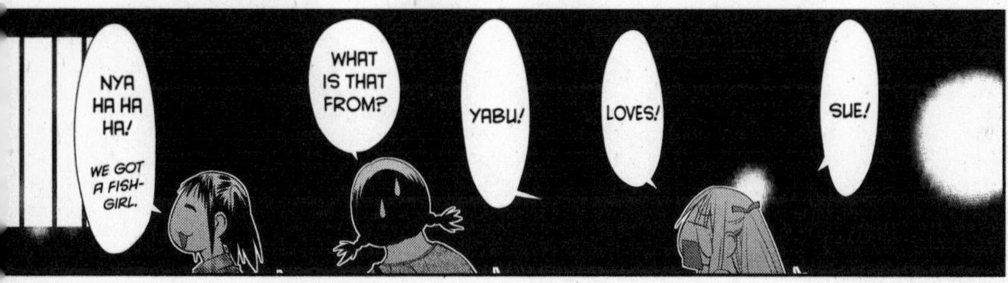
SUE!
LOVES!
YABU!
WHAT IS THAT FROM?
NYA HA HA HA!
WE GOT A FISH-GIRL.

***Madoka Magica,* page 108**
The Genshiken group cosplay is themed around the cast of "magical girl" anime series *Madoka Magica.* Kanako is playing cold and distant Homura, Angela is playing friendly and selfless Mami, Yajima is playing tomboy Sayaka, Rika is playing selfish Kyoko, and Sue is playing the mascot animal Kyubey. Hato (as seen in the post-chapter material) was supposed to cosplay the main character Madoka.

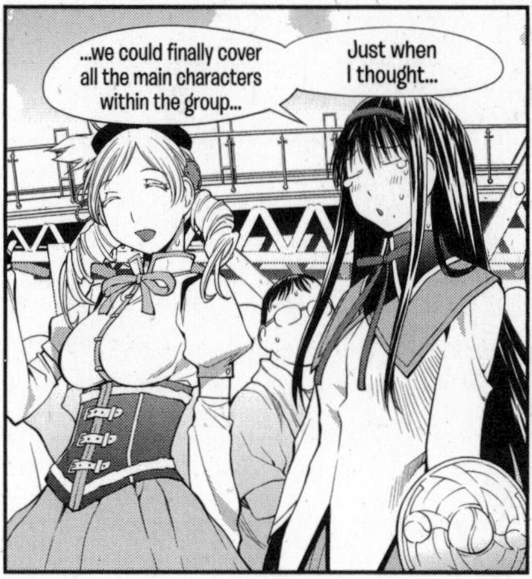
Just when I thought...
...we could finally cover all the main characters within the group...

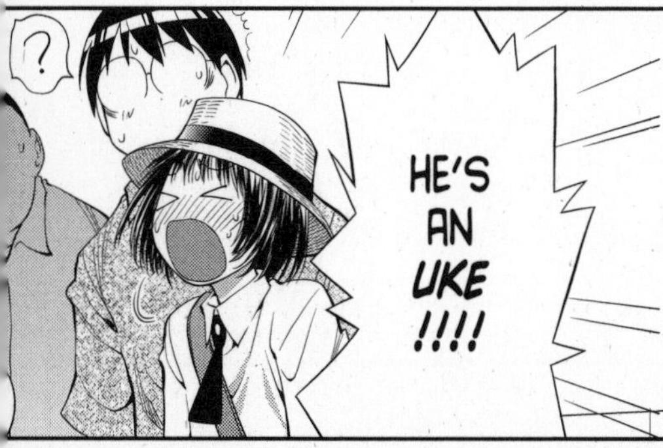
?
HE'S AN *UKE* !!!!

Sou-uke, page 136
In BL (boy's love) terminology, a *sou-uke* ("all-receiving") character is one whose passive and submissive nature means that no matter who he is paired with, he will be the *uke,* or "bottom," in the relationship.

Chai Kick, page 142

A move from the Muay Thai fighter Apachai from the martial arts manga/ anime series *Kenichi: The Mightiest Disciple*. The story covers the journey of teenage Kenichi, who leaves his normal life to train in martial arts at the mysterious Ryozanpaku dojo.

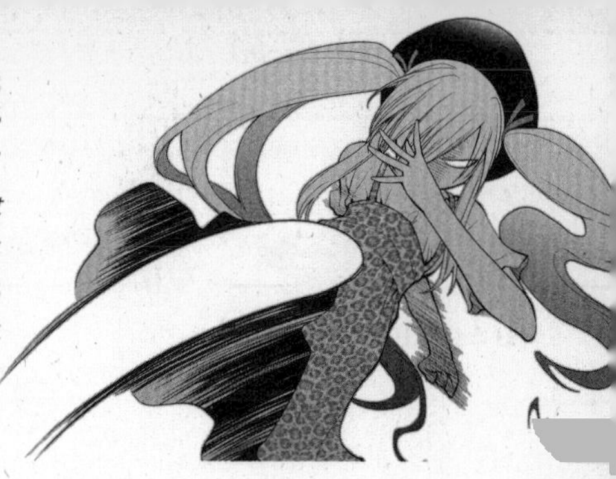

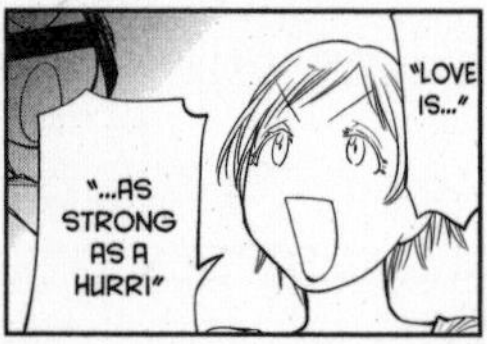
"LOVE IS..."
"...AS STRONG AS A HURRI"

"Love is a hurricane," page 148

A quote from *One Piece* character Boa Hancock, the "most beautiful woman in the world."

Tiger & Bonny, page 151

A parody of superhero anime series *Tiger & Bunny*. The reference to it being "too early" indicates (as often happens) that the series was announced so recently that all Comic-Fest participating artists were already locked into their current issues and couldn't produce a fresh dojinshi in time for the event.

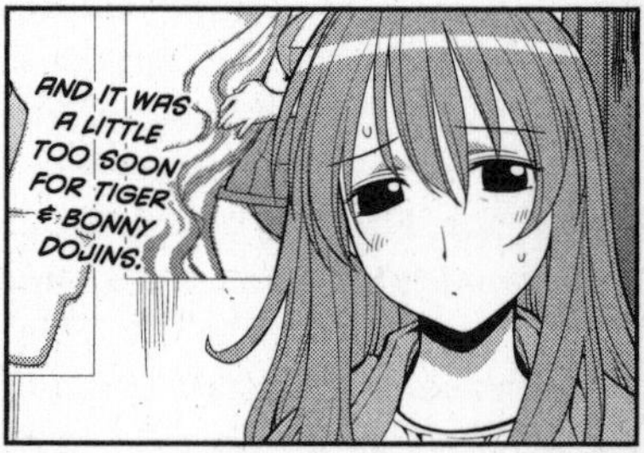
AND IT WAS A LITTLE TOO SOON FOR TIGER & BONNY DOJINS.

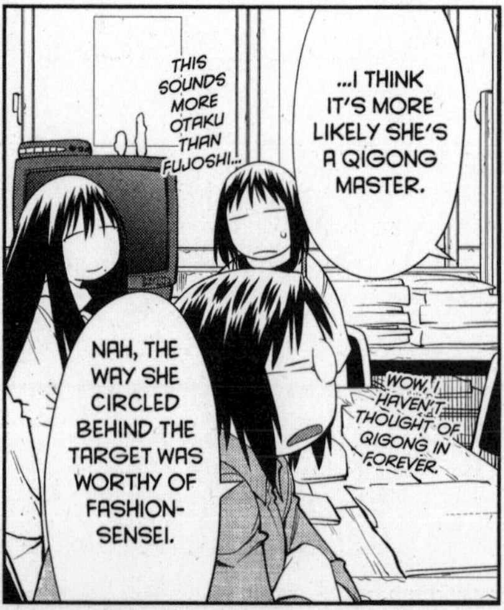
...I THINK IT'S MORE LIKELY SHE'S A QIGONG MASTER.
THIS SOUNDS MORE OTAKU THAN FUJOSHI...
WOW, I HAVEN'T THOUGHT OF QIGONG IN FOREVER.
NAH, THE WAY SHE CIRCLED BEHIND THE TARGET WAS WORTHY OF FASHION-SENSEI.

Qigong, page 179

A Chinese form of exercise or meditation that is designed to help qi (or chi, or ki) flow throughout the body in a healthy way. Though in reality, qigong is a light series of exercises, in extreme circumstances it's depicted as a type of martial arts, and thus in many manga/ anime series, qigong is almost always shown as a mystical fighting style.

Fashion-sensei, page 179

A nickname for Tite Kubo, the author of *Bleach*, who is infamous for his personal sense of style.

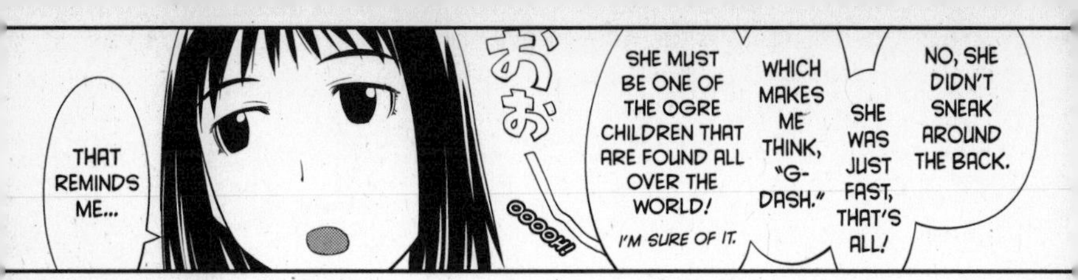
NO, SHE DIDN'T SNEAK AROUND THE BACK.
SHE WAS JUST FAST, THAT'S ALL!
WHICH MAKES ME THINK, "G-DASH."
SHE MUST BE ONE OF THE OGRE CHILDREN THAT ARE FOUND ALL OVER THE WORLD!
I'M SURE OF IT.
おお
OOOOH!!
THAT REMINDS ME...

Ogre child, page 179

A reference to *Baki the Grappler,* the macho martial arts series following the exploits of Baki Hanma, who wants to be the greatest warrior in the world and defeat his father. Following *Baki the Grappler* was the sequel series *New Grappler Baki,* and the third series is *Baki: Son of Ogre,* referring to Baki's incredibly powerful father.

Saint Seiya and *Fist of the North Star,* page 179

Two classic *Shonen Jump* series from the 1980s. *Saint Seiya* features warriors with the powers of various constellations of the Zodiac, and main character Pegasus Seiya's signature move is the "Meteor Fist," which is a rain of fists that resemble meteors. *Fist of the North Star* was a post-apocalyptic kung fu series detailing the exploits of Kenshiro, who uses an overpowering form of martial arts that hits pressure points in the human body. His trademark "Hyakuretsu Punch" is a flurry of punches that destroys all internal organs and causes instant death.

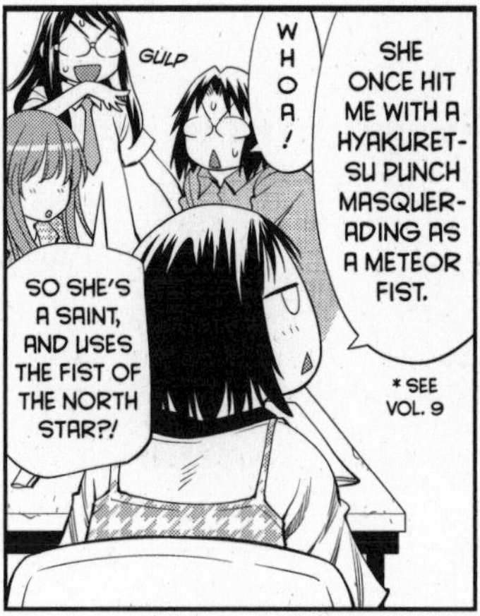
SHE ONCE HIT ME WITH A HYAKURET-SU PUNCH MASQUER-ADING AS A METEOR FIST.
WHOA!
GULP
* SEE VOL. 9
SO SHE'S A SAINT, AND USES THE FIST OF THE NORTH STAR?!

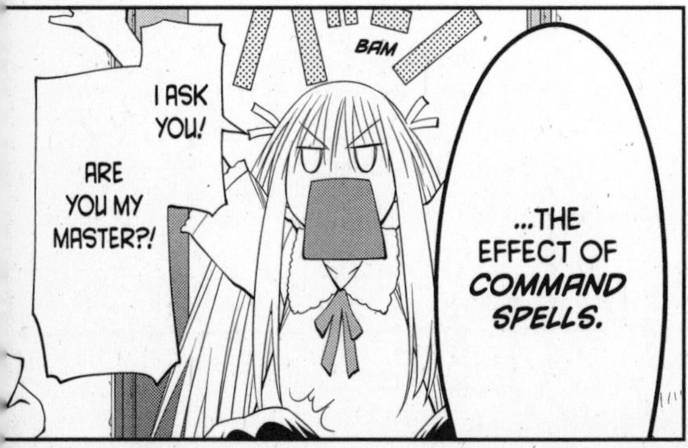
...THE EFFECT OF COMMAND SPELLS.
BAM
I ASK YOU!
ARE YOU MY MASTER?!

Command spells, page 180

A reference to the anime/game series *Fate/stay night,* in which Servants, magical reincarnations of famous heroes throughout human history, fight battles for their Masters in a massive Holy Grail War.

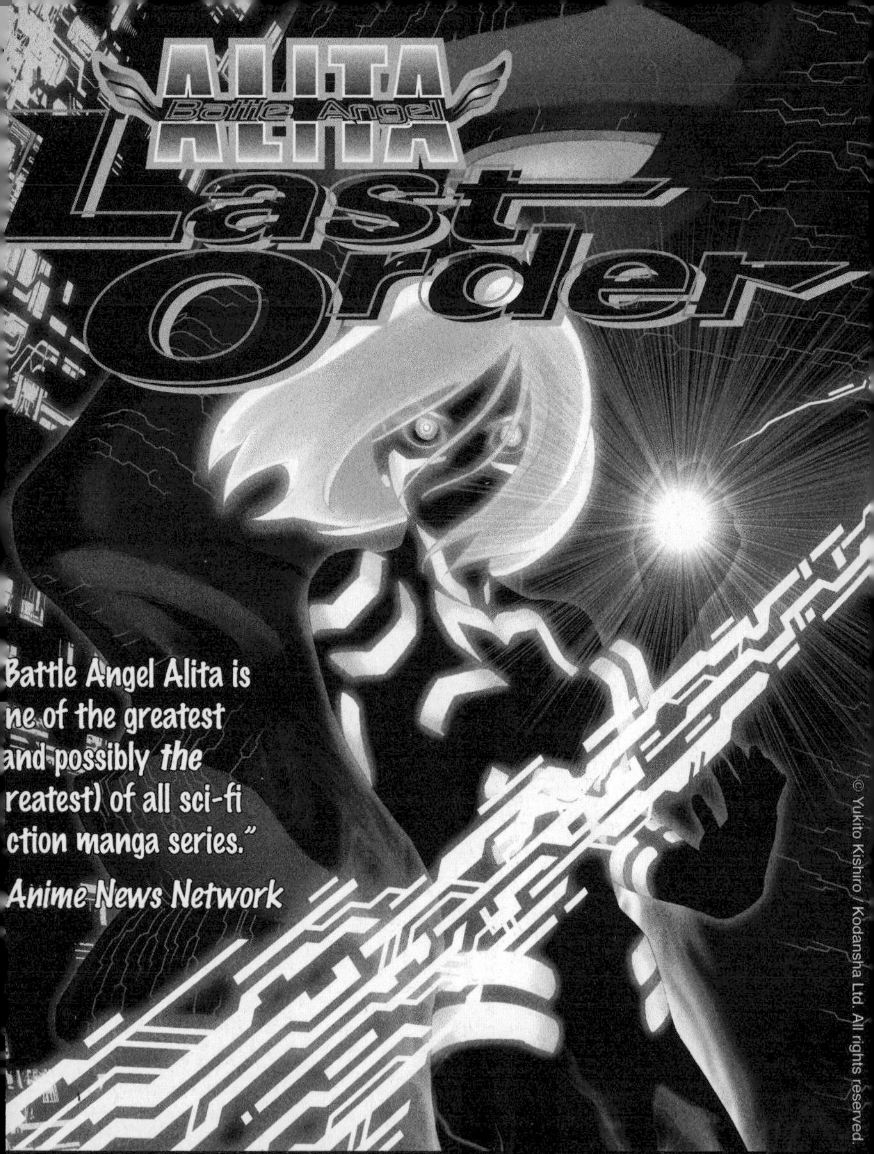

ALITA
Battle Angel
Last Order

"Battle Angel Alita is
one of the greatest
(and possibly *the*
greatest) of all sci-fi
action manga series."

Anime News Network

The Cyberpunk Legend is Back!

In deluxe omnibus editions of 600+ pages,
including ALL-NEW original stories by
Alita creator Yukito Kishiro!
Vol. 1 Coming March 2013

KC
KODANSHA COMICS

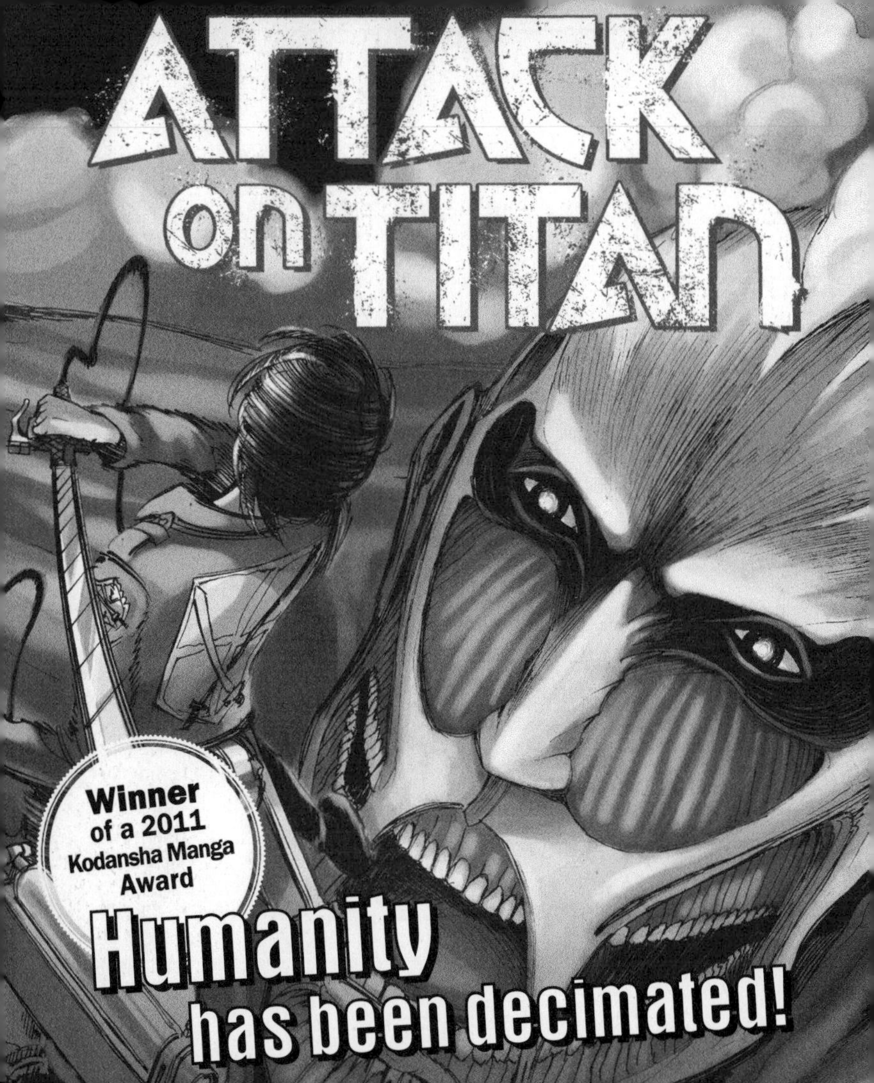

ATTACK on TITAN

Humanity
has been decimated!

A century ago, the bizarre creatures known as
Titans devoured most of the world's population,
driving the remainder into a walled stronghold.
Now, the appearance of an immense new Titan
threatens the few humans left, and one restless
boy decides to seize the chance to fight for his
freedom, and the survival of his species!

KC
KODANS
COMIC

ANIMAL LAND

MAKOTO RAIKU

WELCOME TO THE JUNGLE

In a world of animals
where the strong eat the weak,
Monoko the tanuki stumbles
across a strange creature
the like of which has never
been seen before -
a human baby!

While the newborn has no
claws or teeth to protect itself,
it does have the rare ability
to speak to and understand
all the different animal.

ANIMAL LAND 1
MAKOTO RAIKU

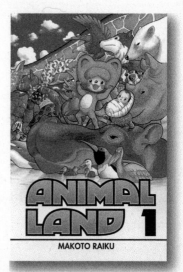

Special extras in each volume! Read them all!

RATING OT AGES 10+

VISIT WWW.KODANSHACOMICS.COM TO:

- View release date calendars for upcoming volumes
- Find out the latest about new Kodansha Comics series

KC KODANSHA COMICS

Genshiken: Second Season volume 2 is a work of fiction. Names, characters, places, and incidents are the products of the author's imagination or are used fictitiously. Any resemblance to actual events, locales, or persons, living or dead, is entirely coincidental.

A Kodansha Comics Trade Paperback Original.

Published in the United States by Kodansha Comics, an imprint of Kodansha USA Publishing, LLC, New York.

Publication rights for this English edition arranged through Kodansha Ltd., Tokyo.

First published in Japan in 2011 by Kodansha Ltd., Tokyo, as *Genshiken Nidaime no ni 11*.

ISBN 978-1-61262-242-2

Printed in the United States of America.

www.kodanshacomics.com

9 8 7 6 5 4 3 2 1

Translator: Stephen Paul
Lettering: Aaron Alexovich

TOMARE! STOP

You're going the wrong way!

Manga is a completely different type of reading experience.

To start at the beginning, Go to the end!

That's right! Authentic manga is read the traditional Japanese way—from right to left, exactly the opposite of how American books are read. It's easy to follow: Just go to the other end of the book and read each page—and each panel—from right side to left side, starting at the top right. Now you're experiencing manga as it was meant to be!